STATISTICAL TESTING

OF

BUSINESS-CYCLE THEORIES

STATISTICAL TESTING

OF

BUSINESS-CYCLE THEORIES

BY

J. TINBERGEN

I. A Method and Its Application to Investment Activity

II. Business Cycles in the United States of America 1919–1932

NEW YORK

AGATHON PRESS, INC.

1968

Reprinted, with permission of the United Nations, by

AGATHON PRESS, INC.
150 Fifth Avenue
New York, N. Y. 10011

New material ©, 1968, by Agathon Press, Inc.

Library of Congress Catalog Card Number: 68-16357

Printed in the United States of America

INTRODUCTION TO THE AGATHON EDITION

When this book was originally published, it presented its readers with some of the first attempts to apply econometric methods. More particularly, Part II offered an econometric model of the mechanism of the cyclical movements of the 1919–1932 American economy which so dramatically determined the world's economic and perhaps political fate in the thirties.

The methods used are now outmoded and much better ones have been devised. In a cooperative endeavor by some twenty outstanding American econometricians, a model has now been constructed which is far superior to the one described in this study. The Brookings Institution, which undertook to sponsor this joint research project, rightly understood that teamwork is necessary. Their work has been preceded by similar undertakings by Professors L. R. Klein and A. S. Goldberger for the United States and by many other colleagues for other countries.

There remains one feature in my 1937/8 model which, to my knowledge, has never been rejected explicitly and yet has not been taken over by any of my successors in this field. It is the role played by speculation—especially, around 1929, by stockmarket speculation. I wonder whether this reprint might give rise to an explicit analysis or critique of this feature, which—it should be admitted beforehand—no longer indeed plays such a role in cyclical movements. Moreover, these movements themselves are now so much more under control that their study has almost become a subject for economic historians rather than for policy-makers.

The idea of analyzing the possible, the probable, and the most desirable development of an economy with the aid of econometric models, somewhat doubted at the moment of the first publication of this book, has now been accepted by a large section of the profession.

This is why I am pleased that Agathon Press, Inc., took the initiative to reprint the book, which has for so long been out of print. I want to express my gratitude to them and to the United Nations, as the heirs of the League of Nations, for their permission to reproduce the text.   — J. TINBERGEN

Rotterdam, October 1967

STATISTICAL TESTING

OF

BUSINESS-CYCLE THEORIES

I

A METHOD

and its Application to

INVESTMENT ACTIVITY

BY

J. TINBERGEN

LEAGUE OF NATIONS
Economic Intelligence Service
GENEVA
1939

Series of League of Nations Publications

II. ECONOMIC AND FINANCIAL
1938. II.A. 23.

CONTENTS

3923 — S.d.N. 1.470 (F.) 1.665 (A.). 2/39. Imp. Kundig.

ANALYTICAL TABLE OF CONTENTS

CHAPTER IV. — RESIDENTIAL BUILDING

CHAPTER V. — NET INVESTMENT IN RAILWAY ROLLING-STOCK

CHAPTER VI. — APPLICATION OF RESULTS : FURTHER INVESTIGATIONS

APPENDIX A. — DETAILS OF CALCULATIONS

APPENDIX B. — STATISTICAL TABLES

PREFACE

About two years ago the League published a book of which Professor Gottfried VON HABERLER, now of Harvard University, was the author, under the title " Prosperity and Depression ". The purpose of this book was to examine existing theories concerning the nature of what is currently termed the trade cycle, with a view to ascertaining what they had in common, the points at which differences of opinion arose and, in so far as possible, the causes of those differences. Its publication constituted the completion of the first stage of an enquiry into the nature and causes of the trade cycle that had been begun some years earlier. The second stage, as explained in the preface to Professor von Haberler's book, was to consist of an attempt " to confront these various theories with the historical facts—to subject them, in so far as those facts can be quantitatively expressed, to statistical analysis ", and, in so far as they cannot be so expressed, to compare them with the recounted records of the past.

The present volume, entitled " Statistical Testing of Business-cycle Theories—A Method, and its Application to Investment Activity ", is the first instalment of a brief series of pamphlets which it is proposed to issue in execution of one of the tasks involved by the second stage of the enquiry. It has been prepared by Professor J. TINBERGEN, who has been seconded for this purpose from the Central Statistical Bureau of the Netherlands. The primary object of this volume is to explain the statistical method which—subject to any suggestions that may be received—it is proposed to employ. With a view to illustrating this method—known as multiple correlation analysis—three examples of its application to economic phenomena have been given; these examples relate to fluctuations in total investment, residential building and net investment in railway rolling-stock.

The results obtained in the elaboration of these examples will, it is believed, prove of interest to students of the business cycle; but those results are in fact only incidental to the primary objects of this publication, which are, as I have stated, to explain the system of statistical analysis employed and, it is hoped, to arouse discussion concerning it that may prove of value to those in charge of the enquiry.

The manuscript of this volume has already been sent to a number of statisticians in different countries for comment, and two meetings of economists and statisticians have been held at which the assumptions made and methods adopted have been discussed. Thanks are due to all those who have helped by their criticisms and suggestions, and especially to Professor D. H. ROBERTSON, who has ungrudgingly put his time at the disposal of the League for the purpose of consultation with Professor TINBERGEN on the economic issues involved.

This introductory volume on method will be followed shortly by the first of the proposed analytical studies, which will be devoted to post-war business cycles in the United States of America. It is hoped that, before that study is completed, further comments and suggestions concerning the method here explained may be received either through Press reviews or directly from those who are interested and competent in this primary problem of methodology.

A. LOVEDAY,

*Director of the Financial Section and
Economic Intelligence Service.*

Geneva, January 1939.

CHAPTER I

INTRODUCTION

———

§ 1. Purpose of the Study

The purpose of this series of studies is to submit to statistical test some of the theories which have been put forward regarding the character and causes of cyclical fluctuation in business activity. Many of these theories, however, do not exist in a form immediately appropriate for statistical testing while most of them take account of the same body of economic phenomena—viz., the behaviour of investment, consumption, incomes, prices, etc. Accordingly, the method of procedure here adopted is, not to test the various theories one by one (a course which would involve much repetition), but to examine in succession, in the light of the various explanations which have been offered, the relation between certain groups of economic phenomena.

The enquiry is, by its nature, restricted to the examination of measurable phenomena. Non-measurable phenomena may, of course, at times exercise an important influence on the course of events; and the results of the present analysis must be supplemented by such information about the extent of that influence as can be obtained from other sources.

§ 2. Method employed

The method of study here employed, sometimes described as " econometric business cycle research," is a synthesis of *statistical business cycle research* and *quantitative economic theory*. A little may be said about each of these two elements.

(1) In the early phases of *statistical business cycle research*, attention was paid to somewhat superficial phenomena, such as the length of cycles, the degree of simple correlation between series and the relative amplitudes of their movements, the decomposition of series into trend, seasonal components, etc. Certainly all this work had its value, especially for the *negative* evidence it afforded on the validity of certain theories. For the purpose of applying more searching tests, however, it is necessary to dig deeper. An apparently simple relation, such as that between prices and production, is often not a direct causal relation at all, but a more or less complicated chain of many such relations. It is the object of analysis to identify and to test these direct causal relations: production, for instance, may be regarded as determined by the volume of orders; the volume of orders by the income of consumers and by prices; income by employment, wage rates and so on.

The part which the statistician can play in this process of analysis must not be misunderstood. The theories which he submits to examination are handed over to him by the economist, and with the economist the responsibility for them must remain; for no statistical test can prove a theory to be correct. It can, indeed, prove that theory to be incorrect, or at least incomplete, by showing that it does not cover a particular set of facts: but, even if one theory appears to be in accordance with the facts, it is still possible that there is another theory, also in accordance with the facts, which is the " true " one, as may be shown by new facts or further theoretical investigations. Thus the sense in which the statistician can provide " verification " of a theory is a limited one.

On the other hand, the rôle of the statistician is not confined to " verification ". As the above example illustrates, the direct causal relations of which we are in search are generally relations, not between two series only—one cause and one effect—but between one dependent series and several causes. And what we want to discover is, not merely what causes are operative, but also *with what strength each of them operates*: otherwise it is impossible to find out the nature of the combined effect of causes working in opposite directions. On this problem—the problem of " measurement ", as it may be called—the statistician can throw light by the use of the method called multiple correlation analysis. The details of this method are described in non-technical language in Chapter II, and in mathematical language in Appendix A.[1]

(2) *Economic theory*, to be capable of statistical test, must be expressed in quantitative—*i.e.*, in mathematical—form. What has usually been known, however, as mathematical economics deals chiefly with the conditions of an *equilibrium* which tends to be established in the long run, but is certainly not realised in the course of cyclical fluctuations. To be useful, therefore, for business cycle research, economic theory needs to be made " dynamic ". A " dynamic " theory, in the sense which is here attached to that ambiguous word, is one which deals with the short-term reactions of one variate upon others, but without neglecting the lapse of time between cause and effect. The equations in which it is expressed thus relate to non-simultaneous events, and take a form which Swedish economists have described as " sequence analysis ".

Take, for instance, the static concept of the functional relation between price and quantity supplied.[2] To convert this into a " reaction relation " or " direct causal relation " three things must be done. First, the relation must be exhibited in terms of cause and effect. Secondly, any time difference (lag) found to exist between change in price and change in quantity supplied should be mentioned explicitly—though in some cases, if the lag is very short (*i.e.*, if adaptation is almost instantaneous), it may legitimately be ignored. Thirdly, if quantity supplied varies to an important degree through causes other than changes in price (for instance, through changes in cost or in productive capacity), the influence of these other causes must be shown, and not left concealed in a *ceteris paribus* clause; though here again minor causes — *i.e.*, those whose combined effects are small — may legitimately be

---

[1] It is only in recent years that this method, developed especially by Mr. G. Udny Yule, and long known to mathematical statisticians, has been systematically applied in economic research, though some scattered applications to economic problems were made as long ago as 1906.

[2] This instance is taken for the sake of illustration only. In the study of cyclical fluctuations other " reaction relations ", such as those determining the movements in total outlay on investment or on consumption, appear to be of greater importance.

ignored, the formulation being confined to exhibiting the influence of major causes only. The necessary additions to static theory have, as a matter of fact, sometimes been found as a result of statistical research; in that sense, the statistician may supply theoretical suggestions to the economist.

Thus we find that the correlation analysis suggested by statistical technique and the sequence analysis dictated by " dynamicised " economic theory converge and are synthesised in the method employed in this study—the method, namely, of econometric business cycle research.

§ 3. MACRO-ECONOMIC APPROACH

There is one further feature of the method here employed which calls for remark. Economic analysis may be applied to the behaviour of individual persons or firms; or to the behaviour of " industries ", defined in some more or less arbitrary manner; or, again, to the behaviour of whole groups of industries, such as those producing consumption and investment goods respectively, and of whole categories of economic persons, such as those engaged in the credit market, or the labour market, as a whole. It is this last type of economic approach (sometimes spoken of as the " macro-economic " approach) which will be employed in this study. For it is this type of approach which seems most relevant to cyclical fluctuation, and which alone makes it possible to limit the number of variates considered to a figure which permits of their being effectively handled. It goes without saying that, in this approach, the coefficients found do not give any indications of the behaviour of individual entrepreneurs, consumers, etc., but only of the average reactions of many individuals.

CHAPTER II

ELEMENTARY OUTLINE OF THE METHOD
OF CORRELATION ANALYSIS

———

§ 4. SIMPLE CORRELATION

As has been pointed out in the previous chapter, the object of correlation analysis is twofold: (1) to test whether some expected relation between two or more variates exists (verification) and, (2) if so, to find the strength of the influences exerted by each causal phenomenon (measurement). The exact meaning of these terms and the consecutive steps in the analysis will now be discussed. It seems useful to begin with simple correlation.

Simple correlation. Simple correlation is expected to exist if the fluctuations in any series Y are supposed to be caused (or chiefly caused) by the fluctuations in only one other series X. The simplest type of analysis that can be made in this case is to draw a scatter diagram. In such a

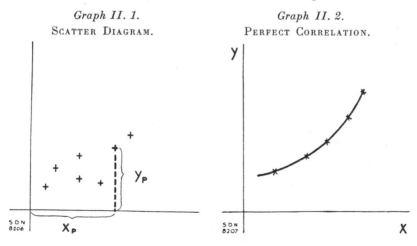

| *Graph II. 1.* | *Graph II. 2.* |
| SCATTER DIAGRAM. | PERFECT CORRELATION. |

diagram (*cf.* Graph II. 1) each point, such as P, is so situated that, with a given scale, the length of its two " co-ordinates " X_P and Y_P are equal to corresponding values of X and Y. The collection of points obtained (" the scatter ") may or may not lie approximately on one simple curve.

Perfect correlation. The extreme case of perfect correlation presents itself when all points lie exactly on one curve. (Graph II. 2). In that case, the values of Y are exactly determined by those of the corresponding X's. X and Y are said to show a " functional relationship ", and Y is a function of X, or X a function of Y. In other words, there is complete or perfect correlation between X and Y. Knowledge as to which is the cause can come only from outside.

Perfect linear correlation and perfect curvilinear correlation. The curve may or may not be a straight line. If it is, the function or correlation is said to be linear; if not, it is called curvilinear. Linear relationship between X and Y does not necessarily mean proportionality; this occurs only if the straight line passes through the " origin " of the system of co-ordinates (*i.e.*, the point with co-ordinates zero-zero). A still more special case is that of equality between X and Y: then the line has to pass not only through (0,0) but also through every other point (*a, a*) with equal co-ordinates (Graph II. 3).

Graph II. 3.

TYPES OF LINEAR CORRELATION.

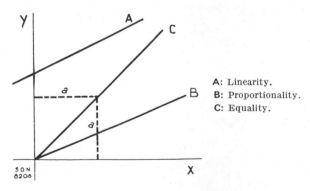

A: Linearity.
B: Proportionality.
C: Equality.

The curve through the points is called the *regression*
Regression *curve.* If it is a straight line, its slope is termed the
curves and regression slope and may be measured by a " *regression*
coefficients. *coefficient* ": this coefficient indicates the increase
in Y which corresponds to a unit increase in X. In
the table below, which indicates corresponding values for X and Y,
arranged in ascending order, a unit increase in X clearly corresponds
to an increase of 2 in Y. The regression coefficient is therefore 2.
The relation between X and Y may also be described by the
formula Y $= 10 + 2$ X.

X	Y
10	30
11	32
12	34
13	36
14	38
15	40

" Corresponding values " of X and Y will often
Lags. be values for the same period. In some cases,
however, the relation is between values of X and
later values of Y. The time difference between corresponding
values of X and Y is called the lag; Y lags behind X or X leads Y.
It will be clear that if X is cause and Y effect, then X will lead Y.
This fact may sometimes be used in order to find out which of
two series is cause, which effect.[1]

The provisional determination of lags is best done with the help
of an historical graph, showing the development in time of both
series.

An example is to be found in Graph II.4, where two series have
been drawn representing:

(A) Total volume of non-farm residential building in the United
States, 1920-1935.

---

[1] One has, however, to be careful: it may happen, *e.g.*, that X leads Y,
so that it would seem as if X were cause, Y effect. At the same time,
however, $\dot{Y}$ (the rate of increase in Y) may lead X, and therefore $\dot{Y}$ may
equally well be cause of X. Finally, it is possible that both causal connections
exist: $\dot{Y}_t$ determining X_{t+1} and X_{t+1} determining Y_{t+2}.

(B) Total stock of houses, United States, deviations from trend (inverted).[1]

Graph II. 4.

EXAMPLE OF LAG.

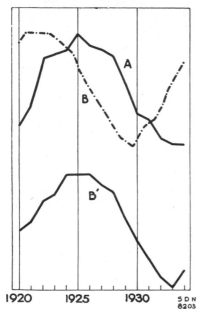

1920   1925   1930   S D N
8203

It is at once clear that there is a lag of about three years and a-half between A and B. An immediate comparison of A with B′, where any value B′ equals the value of B three years and a-half earlier, confirms the existence of this lag.

Imperfect correlation. As a rule, the scatter will not show perfect organisation.

There may, however, still be a tendency for the points to group along a curve: then *imperfect correlation* is said to exist. That curve will now no longer be exactly determined. Various choices as to its type are possible, some of which will be discussed later. Once a choice has been made, the deviations between the actual points and the curve may be measured. Here also several methods of measurement may be chosen; but, after this second choice has been made, a measure for the degree of organisation can be given.

Correlation index; correlation coefficient. The usual measure taken in the case of a general curve is the *correlation index*, which in the case of a straight line is reduced to a simpler measure called *correlation coefficient*. Both expressions have the property of being always less than or equal to unity; and they reach unity only if there is perfect correlation between the two variates (in the case of the correlation coefficient,

---

[1] The trend of a series is a series indicating its general tendency. Details as to calculation of trend will be found in Appendix A.

if there is perfect linear correlation). Conversely, if they are equal to unity, there is perfect correlation (in the case of the correlation coefficient, perfect linear correlation).

Regression curves and coefficients. The notions of regression curve and regression coefficient, introduced above for the case of perfect correlation, are also used in cases of imperfect correlation; but they now depend on certain choices.

First, the type of curve has to be chosen. Usually a straight line is first tried. Secondly, a method of measuring deviations of the points from that line has to be devised. They may be measured in the direction of the Y-axis, in the direction of the X-axis or in other ways.

Graph II. 5 illustrates the procedure. The points representing the given observations are indicated by P_1, P_2, etc. As a regression curve, the line AB has been chosen. The deviations of P_1, P_2, etc., from AB, measured in the direction of the Y-axis, are indicated by P_1Q_1, P_2Q_2, etc. Those measured in the direction of the X-axis are indicated by P_1R_1, P_2R_2, etc.

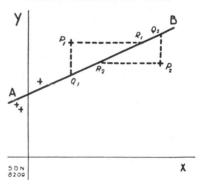

Graph II. 5.

MEASUREMENT OF DEVIATIONS FROM A REGRESSION LINE.

The third step is to adopt some method for determining the curve in such a way that the deviations just defined will be as small as possible. Usually the "method of least squares" is taken: the sum of the squares of the deviations is made a minimum. In other words, that line is chosen as a regression line which shows the minimum sum of squares.

If deviations are measured in the Y direction—*i.e.*, in the direction of the dependent variate—the line obtained is called the *firs elementary regression line*. If deviations are measured in the X direction, the *second elementary regression line* is obtained. Each of the regression lines will be characterised by a regression slope and a regression coefficient.

In the case of perfect linear correlation, these two regression lines coincide, and no trouble arises as regards the choice indicated. When the correlation is not perfect, the difference between the two regression coefficients gives an idea of the degree of organisation of the scatter.

All that has been said applies as well to series x, y, etc., indicating the deviations which X, Y, etc., show from their average value $\overline{X}$, $\overline{Y}$, etc. over the period studied.

The correlation coefficient and the regression coefficients enable the two objects of the analysis to be substantially attained. The correlation coefficient tells whether or not the assumed relation between X and Y is exact, and therefore gives an answer to the verification problem. The regression coefficients indicate about how large a change in Y corresponds to a given change in X, and therefore answer the question of measurement. A first rough test of the economic significance of the coefficients is afforded by their signs, which may or may not be such as economic theory would lead one to expect.

Example. Graph II. 6 gives the scatter diagram between X, " value added " per ton of pig-iron, and Y, pig-iron production for Germany, 1881-1911. Value added per ton, which equals price minus raw-material cost, has been taken in order to eliminate the effect of the most important changes in production cost. Production has been measured in a somewhat unusual way, in order to eliminate influences of growth in productive capacity—viz., as the percentage deviation from trend. The relation is in its essence a supply relation, in which disturbing influences of cost and capacity changes have been eliminated by one of several possible methods. The scatter is moderately organised, and the only indication of curvilinearity is in the single point to the right, corresponding to the boom year 1900. Leaving aside this point, two elementary

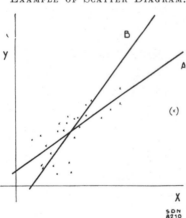

Graph II. 6.

EXAMPLE OF SCATTER DIAGRAM.

linear regressions have been calculated and the corresponding lines drawn. The first elementary regression formula runs:

$$Y - \overline{Y} = 0.71 \, (X - \overline{X})$$

in which $\overline{X}$ is the average value of all X's (except that for 1900) and $\overline{Y}$ is the average value of all Y's (except 1900). The meaning of the regression equation is that an increase of one point in X causes an increase of 0.71 points in Y. The second elementary regression would yield the figure 1.37 instead of 0.71 and shows that a rather high degree of uncertainty prevails here. The economic significance of these figures is closely connected with the elasticity of supply. In fact, it follows from the above definitions that an increase in prices by one unit, raw-material cost being supposed equal, would cause an increase in production of about 0.71% (the trend value of production being used as a basis). As the average price for the period was 59.7 Marks per ton, it may easily be deduced that the elasticity of supply was then 0.42. If the second elementary regression had been used, a figure of 0.82 would have been obtained.

A first rough test of the economic trustworthiness of this figure is to see whether it has the right sign —*i.e.*, whether positive price changes are connected with positive changes in supply.

§ 5. Multiple Correlation

Multiple correlation. As has already been said, in by far the greatest number of cases of economic importance, more than one cause is ordinarily assumed to have acted. Fluctuations in a series x_1 will have to be explained by the fluctuations in a number of other ("explanatory") series x_2, x_3, etc. To begin with, the nature of this problem may best be illustrated by an historical graph of all the series involved (*cf.* Graph II. 7). For

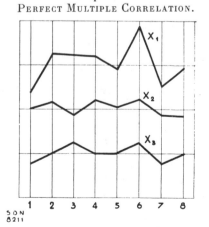

Graph II. 7.
Perfect Multiple Correlation.

the sake of simplicity, we may again start with a case of perfect linear relationship.

Perfect *linear* *multiple* *correlation.* The problem then is to find the figures b_2, b_3, etc., by which the series x_2, x_3, etc., have to be multiplied in order that the sum $b_2 x_2 + b_3 x_3 + \ldots$, calculated for each time-point, may equal the corresponding figure for x_1. In the theoretical example of Graph II. 7, these numbers are 2 and 5. In fact, $2x_2 + 5x_3$ gives exactly x_1 for each observation. The graph shows some elementary features which are important for the carrying-out of the analysis and may therefore be stated. The decline in year 5 is caused entirely by series x_2, x_3 showing no decline at all in that year. On the other hand, the rise in year 8 can only be explained by x_3, as x_2 does not rise in that year. These two examples clearly show that only a combination of x_2 and x_3 can give the right result. Moreover, it is the combination with coefficients 2 and 5 which gives the best result, as is seen very clearly in year 3, where only that combination will produce the absence of change in x_1. These elementary remarks are intended to demonstrate that considerations of this kind may be helpful in the study of actual relationships, since they may show, after a mere visual inspection of the statistical material, whether or not success is to be expected.

Regression *coefficients.* As in the case of simple correlation, the coefficients 2 and 5 in the above example are called regression coefficients. As before, the regression coefficient indicates the increase (or decrease) in x_1 caused by a unit increase of x_2 or x_3 respectively; and, as before, a first rough test can be applied to this conclusion by enquiring whether the coefficient has the sign which economic theory would lead one to expect.

Influence *of* x₂. In the expression $2x_2 + 5x_3$, the term $2x_2$ (in general $b_2 x_2$) may be called " the influence of x_2 " and $5x_3$ " the influence of x_3 ". In using these terms, one must, however, bear in mind that this expression is justified only so far as the economic theory which has prompted the calculation is accepted as valid. The special value of such a term

in year t may be called " the influence exerted in that year ";
whereas the strength of that influence in a given period may be
characterised by, *e.g.*, the standard deviation of the term—*i.e.*,
$2\sigma_{x_2}$, etc. All these expressions are independent of the units in
which x_2 or x_3, etc., is measured.

Partial
scatter
diagrams.
In multiple correlation analysis, the scatter diagram
may still be used, but with a somewhat different
function. Plotting three or more variates in a plane
is not easy; but, instead, two or more partial scatter
diagrams may be considered. The first uses as co-
ordinates x_2 and $x_1 - 5x_3$ (in general, $x_1 - b_3x_3$): *i.e.*, x_1 " minus
the influence of x_3 ", or " corrected for changes in x_3 ". The diagram so obtained illustrates the relation between x_2 and x_1 " other
things being equal " or, more exactly, " other relevant things being
equal ". A second diagram may be constructed comparing x_3
and $x_1 - 2x_2$ (in general, $x_1 - b_2x_2$).

Imperfect
multiple
correlation.
The same technique [1] can be usefully employed
in cases where no figures b_2, b_3, etc., can be found
which make $b_2x_2 + b_3x_3 + ...$ exactly equal to x_1,
for each time-point. This, in fact, is generally the
case as long as the number n of series considered
is smaller than the number N of time-points.[2] We must be satisfied
if certain values for b_2, b_3, ... give a fairly good fit. As in the case
of only two variates, such coefficients b_2, b_3, ... can be calculated
after choosing the way in which deviations are to be measured
and minimised. Again, b_2, b_3 are called regression coefficients, and
the expression

$$x_1^* = b_2x_2 + b_3x_3 + ...$$

is called the *regression equation* of x_1 on x_2, x_3, etc.; x_1^* is often called
the *calculated or theoretical value* of x_1. The differences $x_1 - x_1^*$
for each point of time are called *residuals*. If the line of best
fit is chosen so as to make the sum of the squares of these residuals

---

[1] An example of this technique is found in Graphs III. 9-III. 11.

[2] If n equals N, then values b_2, b_3, etc., can always be found, as the number
of unknowns b_2, b_3, etc., equals the number of relations which must be
fulfilled.

as small as possible (*i.e.*, by application of the principle of least squares to the residuals), it is called the *first elementary regression*. The corresponding values for b_2, b_3, etc., will be written as

$$b_{12}, \ b_{13}, \ \ldots$$

The deviations might, however, have been measured in other directions—*e.g.*, in that of x_2, by trying to find an expression $x_2^* = b_{21}x_1 + b_{23}x_3 + \ldots$ which shows a minimal sum of the squares of $x_2 - x_2^*$. This is the second elementary regression. Of course, there are n such elementary regressions. In the calculations discussed in later chapters, the first elementary regression will generally be used; but information as to the other regressions will also be included.

The *total correlation coefficient* R between x_1 and x_1^* can be used as a measure of the degree of accordance between x_1 and x_1^*, and therefore, to some extent, as a measure of the success obtained.

The technique of partial scatter diagrams is again helpful to show whether or not the correlation obtained is satisfactory.

Multiple curvilinear correlation. Partial scatter diagrams are especially helpful in order to test whether or not the assumption that the relation between x_1 and x_2, x_3 ... is linear, fits the facts.[1] If the partial scatters show curvilinearity, this assumption is no longer valid. Two ways are open for further attempts. First, more complicated algebraic formulæ can be tried and treated in a similar way to the linear ones; secondly, graphic methods can be used. These, however, can only start with a scatter between x_1 and one other variate (say, x_2), it being difficult to plot three or more variates in one chart. This scatter may show a tendency to a curvilinear relation, which may be drawn as a freehand curve through the cloud of dots. Let its ordinates (*cf.* Graph II. 8) be called $x_1^* = \varphi(x_2)$. Then for each point the difference between x_1 and the value x_1^* corresponding to its x_2 may be calculated, and this difference may be plotted again as x_3. If a close correlation—perhaps also curvilinear—is found, the curvilinear explanation may be more acceptable than the rectilinear one. Many alternatives are possible; to give details regarding them

---

[1] Graphs III. 9-III. 11 provide some examples.

and regarding the refinements of the method would, however, lead us too far.

Graph II. 8.

GRAPHIC ANALYSIS OF CURVILINEAR CORRELATION.

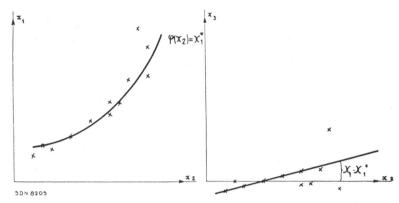

5DN 8205

As a rule, curvilinear relations are considered in the following studies only in so far as strong evidence exists. A rough way of introducing the most important features of curvilinear relations is to use changing coefficients—for instance, one system of coefficients for the description of situations not far above normal and another for the description of extremely high levels. This amounts to approximating a curve by means of two straight lines (*cf.* Graph II. 9). Another way of introducing curvilinear relations is to take squares of variates, or still other functions, among the " explanatory series ".

Lags may also be introduced in multiple correlation analysis. The best lag, however, can no longer be determined by mere examination of historical graphs, since it depends on the relative influence of the various explanatory fac-

Graph II. 9.

APPROXIMATION OF A CURVILINEAR RELATION BY TWO RECTILINEAR ONES.

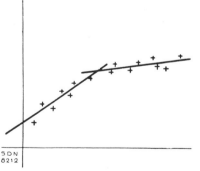

5DN 8212

tors, and this relative influence varies in turn with the lag chosen. In principle, all possible lags must be tried and the regression coefficients calculated on each assumption. In practice, simplifications of procedure are possible if, for instance, one series only is of major influence and the others are secondary.

Graphic representation chosen. As a rule, the results of multiple correlation calculations will be represented as in Graph II. 10. At the top, the actual series to be " explained " is indicated by dots, and on the same scale the theoretical values are indicated by a continuous line. Below the two lines, the various composing series b_2x_2, b_3x_3, etc., are drawn.

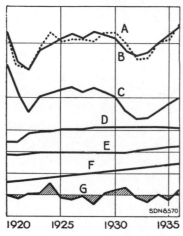

Graph II. 10.

GRAPHIC REPRESENTATION
OF A CORRELATION CALCULATION.
" EXPLANATION " OF IRON AND STEEL
CONSUMPTION.
UNITED KINGDOM 1920-1936.

A = Actual iron and steel consumption.
B = Calculated iron and steel consumption.
C = Influence of profits one year before.
D = Influence of interest rate ½-year before.
E = Influence of price of iron ½-year before.
F = Influence of time.
G = Residuals, *i.e.*, A-B.

The ordinates of these lines are proportional to—not equal to—x_2, x_3 (and even proportional only in cases of linear formulæ). They represent what have been called " the influence of x_2 ", " the influence of x_3 ", etc. The advantages of this procedure are, first, that the scale of these series is comparable with that of the first series, and secondly, that it can be seen at once which of the series are important (*a*) in general or (*b*) for the explanation of any particular feature.

Example. For example, Graph II. 10 is the result of a calculation aiming at " explaining " the fluctuations in iron and steel consumption in the United Kingdom 1920-1936; the explanatory series are profits of all industries one year before, bond yield and iron price half-a-year before, and time. The regression equation found is

$$x_1^* = 1.17x_2 - 0.08x_3 - 0.24x_4 + 2.39x_5$$

where x_1^* represents the calculated physical volume of iron and steel consumption in percentage deviations from average;

x_2, profits, all industries, percentage deviations from average;
x_3 bond yield, deviations from average in hundredths of 1%;
x_4 iron prices, percentage deviations from average;
x_5 time, years.

Obviously, this relation may be interpreted as a demand relation for iron where the series x_2, x_3 and x_5 have been taken as the other chief causes for changes in demand, and where a lag of one year for x_2 and of half-a-year for x_3 and x_4 has been assumed to exist. The movements of the three series x_2, x_3 and x_5 are responsible for the shifts in the demand curve during the period under review. The partial scatter diagram between $x_1 - 1.17x_2 + 0.08x_3 - 2.39x_5$ and x_4 would give the usual representation of the demand curve, shifts having been eliminated. As both x_1 and x_4 have been measured in percentage deviations from average, it will readily be seen that the elasticity of demand for iron would amount to $- 0.24$ for prices and quantities near to their average values. Economically, the negative signs of the coefficients of x_3 and x_4 are as they should be. In addition, it may be mentioned that the " influence " of x_3 and x_4 is only small.

§ 6.   STATISTICAL SIGNIFICANCE OF RESULTS

Reliability of results.   The reliability of results may be judged by statistical as well as economic criteria. In general, the figures used are not exact. They are often derived from samples, or otherwise more or less inadequate for the problem under consideration. In addition, a number of minor explanatory causes are omitted; this seems to be the chief reason why observed and calculated values of x_1 in general do not coincide, and this lack of coincidence is responsible for a certain ambiguity in the results obtained. The question arises whether limits may be indicated for this uncertainty. As nothing is known about the factors omitted, it can be answered only if certain additional hypotheses are made.

Various methods of statistical testing have been worked out, using different hypotheses and leading, therefore, to different results. Some account of these methods will now be given. The non-mathematical reader should be warned that their comprehension will make somewhat greater demands on his attention than has the foregoing exposition of the method of multiple correlation analysis itself; and he may perhaps prefer to take the remainder of this chapter, together with Appendix A, on trust.

The classical method. The classical method goes back to LAPLACE and GAUSS. It will be considered here in the final form that has been given to it by Professor R. A. FISHER.[1] According to this method, it is assumed that the unexplained parts—the residuals—are due to the circumstance that the " explained " variate, though essentially a linear function of the " explanatory " variates, contains an additional component representing the influence of neglected explanatory variates and may, moreover, be subject to errors of measurement. This so-called " *erratic component* " or " *disturbance* " in the explained variate not only gives rise to unexplained residuals, but also causes the regression coefficients calculated from the observations to differ from the coefficients of the true relation connecting the variates. The probable average magnitudes of these differences are derived from the assumption that the disturbances in subsequent time intervals are to be considered as " random drawings " from the " universe " of all possible values of these disturbances. In that " universe " there will be larger and smaller values of these disturbances, and these values are assumed to be normally distributed. This normal distribution means that the number of cases present in each class of magnitude will be determined by the so-called Gaussian law. In ordinary speech, small disturbances will be numerous and large disturbances will be few, their frequency obeying a simple law. The square root of the mean value of the squares of these disturbances is called their *standard deviation*, and is denoted by σ.

On certain further assumptions of a rather technical nature, it becomes possible to calculate what results with respect to the regression coefficients would have been obtained if another sample of disturbances had—by accident, so to say—been drawn. By comparing all possible results, one may say within what limits the results of the great majority of the possible cases will lie. These limits depend again on the choice one makes as to the " majority ". Often 99% or 95% is taken. If b_2 is one of the regression coefficients calculated, and σ_{b_2} the so-called standard error of b_2, about 95% of the cases lie between

[1] Cf. *Statistical Methods for Research Workers*, London and Edinburgh, 1936; " The goodness of fit of regression formulæ and the distribution of regression coefficients ", *Journ. Roy. Stat. Soc.*, **85**, 1922, p. 597; applications of " Student's " distribution, Metron, **5**, 3, 1926, p. 3.

$b_2 + 2\sigma_{b_2}$ and $b_2 - 2\sigma_{b_2}$, *i.e.*, in a range of width $4\sigma_{b_2}$ around b_2. About 99.7% lies between $b_2 \pm 3\sigma_{b_2}$.

This standard error σ_{b_2} is nothing else than the " standard deviation " of the differences between the calculated and the true regression coefficient in repeated samples. It depends—and with it the range of uncertainty in the calculated regression coefficients—on the following figures:

(1)   The number (N) of observations containing mutually independent disturbances. The larger this number, the smaller σ_{b_2}. In economic problems, however, it is not always certain how large should be the time interval to which one observation refers in order to make successive values of the disturbances virtually independent.

(2)   The number $(n - 1)$ of explanatory series. The larger this number, the larger σ_{b_2}. This will be understood if it is realised that, by $n = N$ (*i.e.*, if the number of explanatory series is one less than the number of observations), a perfect correlation can be obtained by any set of mutually independent explanatory series, even if they do not bear at all on the subject.

(3)   The total correlation coefficient (R). The nearer to 1 this number is, the smaller is σ_b; for $R = 1$, σ_b becomes zero, except when there is perfect correlation between one of the explaining variates and a group of other explanatory variates.

(4)   The correlations between two or more of the explanatory series. If at least one of these correlations is high, some of the regression coefficients show a larger σ_b (*i.e.*, are very uncertain). This, too, is easy to understand. In fact, in the extreme case, where two explanatory series were exactly parallel, it is clear that a substitution of one of them for the other would not change the correlation. The " best " fit could therefore be obtained with each of an infinite number of different combinations, in which one series would successively be substituted to a larger and larger extent for the other. The two regression coefficients of these two series would be entirely indeterminate; only some combination of them would be determinate.

Now even if the correlation between two explanatory series is not exact, small disturbances—which are always present—can change the result considerably, and therefore the various possible " samples " would show considerable differences. Hence σ_b will be large. The exact expression for σ_b and its computation are given in Appendix A, § 4.

Frisch's method.   Professor R. FRISCH,[1] in his treatment of these problems, does not use the concept of some unknown " universe " from which a " sample " is drawn. He considers *every* variate as being built up of a systematic part and a disturbance. The relations assumed between the variates are supposed to hold good exactly between the systematic parts, and the regression coefficients in these relations

---

[1] Cf. *Statistical Confluence Analysis by Means of Complete Regression Systems.* Universitetets Økonomiske Institutt, Publ. Nr. 5, Oslo, 1934.

are called the true coefficients. The calculated coefficients may again show deviations from the true, and the object is to find these deviations or a limit to them.

On the further assumptions that there is no correlation (*i.e.*, that the correlation coefficient is zero) between: (i) the disturbances of different variates; (ii) the disturbances of one and the systematic part of another variate; and (iii) the disturbances and the systematic part of the same variate; it may be shown that, at least for problems of two variates the *true regression lies between the elementary regressions*.

Bunch-map analysis. This is why Professor Frisch proposes to construct what he calls *bunch maps*. These indicate the regression slopes obtained for one pair of variates, if all possible elementary regression equations are solved. For a technical reason all variates are normalised—*i.e.*, expressed in their own standard deviation as units.

In order to explain the principle, a three-variate problem may be considered, where an endeavour is made to " explain " x_1 by x_2 and x_3. The first elementary regression equation provides an " explanation "

$$x_1' = b_{12 \cdot 3} x_2 + b_{13 \cdot 2} x_3 \qquad (1)$$

with a regression coefficient $b_{12 \cdot 3}$ for x_2 and $b_{13 \cdot 2}$ for x_3. Taking the second elementary regression, we obtain an " explanation " of x_2

$$x_2' = b_{21 \cdot 3} x_1 + b_{23 \cdot 1} x_3,$$

which may, however, be transformed into an " explanation " of x_1 by putting $x_2' = x_2$ and solving for x_1:

$$x_1'' = \frac{1}{b_{21 \cdot 3}} x_2 - \frac{b_{23 \cdot 1}}{b_{21 \cdot 3}} x_3 \qquad (2).$$

The two dashes have been added to indicate the second elementary regression as the origin of this estimate. Similarly, the third elementary regression

$$x_3' = b_{31 \cdot 2} x_1 + b_{32 \cdot 1} x_2$$

gives
$$x_1''' = - \frac{b_{32 \cdot 1}}{b_{31 \cdot 2}} x_2 + \frac{1}{b_{31 \cdot 2}} x_3 \qquad (3).$$

The equations (1), (2) and (3) are three estimates of the relation between the variates; two bunch maps are constructed to illustrate them. The first compares the three coefficients (in graphical representation, the slopes) obtained for the influence of x_2, viz. $b_{12 \cdot 3}$ from (1), $\frac{1}{b_{21 \cdot 3}}$ from (2) and $- \frac{b_{32 \cdot 1}}{b_{31 \cdot 2}}$ from (3). They are represented by three beams, numbered 1, 2 and 3 (being the numbers of the variates in whose direction the minimising has been performed). The beams 1 and 2 will be marked $\odot$, indicating that the slopes are those between 1 and 2, 1 (the lower numbered variate) being considered as the variate to be " explained ". The second bunch map compares the three coefficients obtained for the influence of x_3 upon x_1 viz., $b_{13 \cdot 2}$, $- \frac{b_{23 \cdot 1}}{b_{21 \cdot 3}}$

and $\frac{1}{b_{31\cdot 2}}$. The beams are again numbered 1, 2 and 3, but here 1 and 3 are marked $\odot$.

Similar bunch maps are made for all conceivable combinations of variates, starting with the simplest and ending with the " complete set " including all variates. The bunch maps for a two-set are of course extremely simple: they always consist of two beams only, which, by the choice of units referred to above, are necessarily situated symmetrically with respect to the two axes.

In general, each bunch map consists of a number of beams, two of which —the " leading beams "—have their ends marked $\odot$ (*cf.* Graph II. 11). The numbers at the ends of these two beams indicate the variates, the regression between which is being studied. In the cases considered in Chapters III, IV and V, the variate with the lower number will always be taken as the one " to be explained ". Every other beam bears a number, and all the numbers together represent the group of variates used. The number attached to any beam

Graph II. 11.
SPECIMEN OF BUNCH MAP.

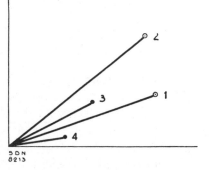

represents the variate used as the left-hand variate in the regression equation before transformation. In other words, it indicates the direction in which deviations have been minimised in constructing the regression formula studied.[1]

A case of perfect relationship without any ambiguity is provided by bunch maps where all beams coincide; for it cannot make any difference in what direction we decide to measure deviations, if there are no deviations to be measured. But if in any case one of the explaining variates has been omitted, perfect correlation cannot exist, and no perfectly closed bunches appear.

Useful, superfluous and detrimental variates. If, therefore, in a given case the bunch is not closed, the aim of further research, and in particular of including further variates in the analysis, is to close the bunch. Any economically significant variate which helps to close the bunch, or brings about a distinct change in the various slopes in the bunch without making it less closed, is called a *useful variate.*

Any new variate which only slightly changes the bunch is called *superfluous.* There is, however, a third possibility: the bunch may " explode "—*i.e.*, show a larger spread after a new variate has been introduced. This happens if there is a high correlation between the new series and one or several of the previous explanatory factors. We are then faced with a situation which is called " *multicollinearity* ". It has been shown that,

---

[1] An explanation of differences in the length of the beams would lead us into too much technical detail.

in such a case, some of the regression coefficients become very uncertain; it is therefore possible that quite different results will be obtained if the deviations are measured in different directions. The new variate, or one of the older variates, is then called *detrimental*. This should be interpreted as meaning that, if all variates are included at the same time, no trustworthy measurement can be made. This does not mean that the variate in question may not be economically significant, but only that, owing to some circumstance (fortuitous or systematic), complete measurement is impossible. A less ambitious measurement may still be possible. Because of the great importance which attaches to these cases, the following simple example may be given.

Suppose one tries to determine the demand function for butter; x_1, the quantity of butter sold, has to be explained by

x_2 the price of butter,
x_3 the price of margarine,
x_4 the income of consumers.

Now we find that butter and margarine prices (at least their annual averages) are fairly highly correlated. Hence in the proposed demand equation

$$x_1' = b_2 x_2 + b_3 x_3 + b_4 x_4, \tag{1}$$

while b_4 may perhaps be readily determined, it will be impossible to find b_2 and b_3 separately with sufficient accuracy. One expedient, however, may be adopted. If x_3 is left out, the equation

$$x_1'' = b_2' x_2 + b_4' x_4 \tag{2}$$

may be tried; it will be possible to determine b_2' and b_4' provided the correlation coefficient found is not too bad (b_4' will be approximately equal to b_4). Equation (2) may be used instead of (1) if it is kept in mind that x_2 now stands for the combined influence of x_2 and x_3; it will be found that approximately $b_2' x_2 = b_2 x_2 + b_3 x_3$. This holds good only as long as the correlation between x_2 and x_3 persists. Equation (2) may therefore be used in all problems in which this correlation does not fail. For example, if the price of butter is raised by State regulation, but the price of margarine is raised as well so as to maintain the correlation between the two prices, then the consequences of the policy on the amount sold may be calculated. If, on the contrary, the regulation does not maintain the correlation, the formula becomes useless for this purpose.

A combination of the two methods. Dr. T. KOOPMANS [1] has pointed out that the classical method and that of FRISCH are complementary rather than alternative. Each of them deals with a part of the margin of uncertainty which must be assigned to calculated regression coefficients. That part of this margin which constitutes the object of Fisher's argument could be called the *error of sampling*. According to Fisher's hypotheses, it is due to the fact that the disturbances in the explained variate may affect the calculated regression coefficients to an unpredictable

---

[1] *Linear Regression Analysis of Economic Time Series*, Haarlem, 1936.

amount, which can be dealt with only by means of laws of probability. Since FISHER does not assume disturbances in the explanatory series, he thus rules out the type of uncertainty studied by Frisch. For this additional uncertainty arises from the circumstance that we usually do not know to what extent the disturbances found to be present in the whole set of data must be ascribed to this or that variate entering into the relation; or, in more technical terms, since we do not know exactly, in calculating the regression coefficients, what relative weights should be applied to express the relative accuracy of each of the several statistical series representing the variates, we incur, by any choice of weights whatever, the risk of introducing an *error of weighting* in the calculated coefficients. On the other hand, the error of sampling is excluded from Frisch's argument by his somewhat restrictive assumptions which have been indicated above.

Koopmans therefore combines the two theories into one method which deals simultaneously with the error of sampling and the error of weighting in the calculated coefficients. His procedure is as follows: For any set of relative weights of the variates that we may choose—*i.e.*, for any numerical guess we may make about the *relative* strength of the disturbances in the several variates,— mathematical deductions lead to:

(1) A set of " best estimates " for the regression coefficients, which takes the place of the first elementary regression in the classical method;

(2) A set of " standard errors " indicating the degree to which each of these estimates may be subject to errors of sampling; these standard errors correspond to those of the classical theory;

(3) A set of estimates of the standard deviations of the disturbances in each of the statistical series employed, which estimates measure the *absolute* strengths of these disturbances.

Where normally the correct relative weights are unknown, it appears that, under certain conditions including mutual independence of disturbances in different variates, the estimates of the regression coefficients mentioned under (1) remain within certain limits for all *a priori* possible weights. These limits correspond to those found by Frisch for the case of two variates, and are given by the two ultimate beams (not always the two " leading " beams) in the bunch map for the corresponding coefficient in the complete set of variates. They constitute ultimate limits to the error of weighting.

In a number of cases, however, narrower limits can be established with the help of the estimates mentioned under (3). It is often very improbable that the disturbances in any variate are of a size comparable to that of the variate itself. If such a result were arrived at from any presumed set of relative weights, such weights could be discarded as being inacceptable. Thus, frequently, the elementary regressions corresponding to variates that exercise only a secondary influence on the explained variate are excluded by this rule. Interpreting this proposition in terms of the bunch-map analysis, it might be said that, in these cases, the beams corresponding to such series should be disregarded, or at least be assigned less importance than the others, even if they are " leading " beams.

3

CHAPTER III

FLUCTUATIONS IN INVESTMENT

§ 7. THE RELATION TESTED

Problem chosen for testing. In this and the two following chapters, a number of the results obtained in applying the method described above to one of the central relations in business-cycle theory will be discussed. The relation in question may be defined as that indicating the " proximate " objective causes of changes in investment activity, looked at from the demand side—*i.e.*, from the side of investing entrepreneurs and public authorities.

Calculations have been made for investment in general, as well as for residential building and railways as important special cases.

As emphasised in Chapter I, the principles underlying the procedure are that economic theory has to suggest the factors to be considered, while the statistical testing process shows the maximum degree of accordance obtainable and the relative strength of each factor required to obtain that degree of accordance.

For the investigation of investment in general, the choice of the relevant factors has been based on the following considerations. Total investment activity is the sum of the investment activity of those individual entrepreneurs who decide to invest at all. The larger this *number*, the greater in general will the volume of investment be. Whether or not an entrepreneur decides to invest depends first of all on whether he expects to make profits or not. Therefore, the *number* of entrepreneurs planning investment will depend on profit expectations.[1]

---

[1] It is almost a tautology to say that investment is governed by profit expectations. It is not quite a tautology, however, since with the same profit expectations there may be different volumes of investment in different conditions, some of which will be mentioned later.

Next, the *extent* of the plans of those entrepreneurs who are planning investment will depend on a number of items entering into their calculations. These calculations, of course, partly reflect the profit expectations of the entrepreneur. There are, however, in them other elements of a more technical order. How much will be invested will also depend, *e.g.*, on the existing unused capacity to produce and on new technical possibilities.

Marginal profits and total profits. One aspect of these calculations may be considered in somewhat greater detail, with the help of Graph III. 1, which represents marginal profits (K) as a function of the number (I) of capital goods units in existence at a given moment. When this number is I″ at the moment of planning, the entrepreneur

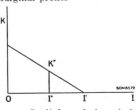

Graph III. 1.

Marginal profits

Capital goods invested

will *tend* to invest so many units that the point I′ with zero marginal profits [1] is reached. (If profits are understood to be taken before deducting interest payments, marginal profits minus interest payments are zero at point I′.) Provided that the curve K″I′, when it shifts upward and downward, does not change its slope—as is ordinarily assumed to be the case—I″K″, marginal profits, and the area OI″K″K, total profits on the existing plant, will show proportional changes. This parallelism will cease to be exact as soon as the curve K″I′ changes its slope too. Moreover, each addition to capital will, for the next time-unit, slightly change the base OI″ of the area, and so invalidate somewhat the proportionality between changes in total and changes in marginal profits in successive (instead of alternative) positions. Since, however, the effects of changes in marginal profits seem to be much greater than those due to this correction, in the statement that investment is determined by profit expectations the latter may with a fair degree of approximation be taken as expected total profits on existing plant.

---

[1] Evidently the argument of this paragraph also holds, *mutatis mutandis*, for *expected* marginal profits and *expected* total profits.

Finally, for many entrepreneurs—especially for public authorities planning to make investments—the *possibility of financing* investment activity will exert a considerable influence. From the theoretical point of view, it is perhaps superfluous to mention this aspect separately, since in profit calculations, in their widest sense, this financial possibility has somehow to be included. From the practical point of view it seems, however, useful to make the distinction, even 'if it cannot be maintained everywhere in the considerations which follow.

We shall now consider more closely the elements mentioned. Profit expectations themselves are, of course, hardly accessible to statistical measurement; but they will largely be determined by some objective criteria in the minds of most entrepreneurs. These objective criteria will in the first place be included as factors in our analysis.

Factors influencing profit expectations. The factors which as a rule exert the greatest influence on *profit expectations* are by most authors assumed to be

(1)   the magnitude of currently earned profits;
(2)   the price of capital goods; and
(3)   the rate of interest.

It might seem as if the rate of interest and the price of capital goods ought not to be included separately, since they enter through interest payments and depreciation into currently earned profits; but the interest rates and prices entering into these calculations are some sort of average over a long period and will therefore show almost no connection with the latest prices in both markets. Present investment will be governed by the rate of interest and the price of capital goods now prevailing, or at most will exhibit a fairly small and definite lag. For this reason, these factors are included separately; for most other cost items, this is not necessary.

Profit margin or total profit ? (4)   Other authors have preferred to include as chief explanatory factor profit margins instead of total profits, profit margins representing the margin between average selling price and average prime cost. The chief reason for taking this course must lie in the hypothesis that the entrepreneur who plans to invest takes for granted the amount of additional output which he will be able to sell as the result of his act of investment; in this case his expectation of profits will depend entirely on the margin between prices and prime cost. The possibility that his sales expectations will depend on the general business situation seems to have been neglected in this hypothesis. For entrepreneurs far from the margin, this may be justified to some extent; profit margins, as well as profits, have therefore been included as an explanatory variate. It may be asked whether it would not be preferable to include profit margin and volume of production separately as explanatory variates instead of total profits (which is about the same thing as the product of margin and volume of production) and profit margin. Since, however, statistics of total profits are, in general, more reliable than those of profit margins, and it may be expected that total profits as such have an important influence, it seems better to take total profits as one of the variates.

Profits and profit rates. No distinction has so far been made between amount of profits and profit rate—*i.e.*, profit as a percentage of capital. Actually, this rate is commonly considered as the factor which has to be taken for our purpose. As will be seen below, in a number of cases figures are available and have been used. In other cases, however, only the amount of profits is available. From the statistical point of view the difference is very small. Generally the two series are very highly intercorrelated, as a consequence of the smooth movements of total capital stock. The results will therefore be very nearly the same—*i.e.*, the regression coefficient found for profits may be assumed to equal that which would be found for profit rate if the latter was used as explanatory series, provided that due corrections for changes in units were made.

(5) Another factor which has been mentioned is the rate of increase in prices. The underlying idea is that rising prices stimulate and falling prices curtail investment activity. Objects bought or constructed in times of rising prices show rising values and, therefore, rising possibilities of yielding a profit when sold; the reverse is true in periods of falling prices. The argument is of course more especially true for goods that are easily marketable, but applies also to some extent to capital goods, which may, *e.g.*, be constructed in advance when prices rise.

The factors determining the financial possibilities
Financial of investment are already included in the list just
possibilities. given. They are, first of all, currently earned profits,
which are not only important for a great number of
smaller enterprises, but also for public authorities. Public budgets
will, with some lag, reflect private economic conditions and determine, in a high degree, the possibilities for public authorities to
make large investments.

Indirectly, high current profits are also important for big enterprises, in so far as the raising of money by issuing new shares will
be facilitated. The " easiness " of getting money in this way may
also be inversely indicated by the share yield, which in some sense
indicates the movements in the " interest rate " which the public
expects to receive on new shares.

In addition, ordinary interest rates will be another indication.
Long-term interest rates may play a rôle for those enterprises which
usually finance their investments by bonds or mortgages (railways,
building), or which base their calculations on those rates; short-term
rates may influence financing by bank credits.

Apart from profit expectations, some technical
Technical circumstances also influence the volume of invest-
circum- ment, as has already been observed. Apart from
stances. " autonomous " technical changes, to be discussed
later, two factors seem outstanding.

Investment activity will be lower, the lower actual production
is in proportion to existing productive capacity. As in general,
and especially in the pre-war period, total capacity is a very
smoothly moving series, the influence of that series may be neglected, since all our investigations deal only with the shorter
fluctuations. As for the actual volume of production, it is so
highly correlated with the volume of investment that it must not
be included in our analysis as a separate series. Any calculation
aiming at explaining investment activity will automatically take
account of the circumstance discussed here.[1]

---

[1] Indicating by v the volume of investment, by $u + v$ the total volume
of production, and summarising in R all other factors in the " explanation "
of investment activity, the relation to be tested will be: $v = a(u + v) + R$.
Since $u + v$ is very near to bv (b constant), it follows that the equation may

(6)   The second factor will be the rate of increase in the volume of production.[1]   The larger this rate of increase, the larger the need for new capital goods.   This is the tendency upon which the well-known " acceleration principle " is based.   This connection is only a close one if no excess capacity is available; and this will be the case for only a small proportion of enterprises.   In consequence, the strength of the force will be less than the pure theory of the simplest case would suggest.[2]   Nevertheless it may have an influence.

Here, again, a mathematical difficulty presents itself under certain conditions—namely, when, as is the case in various periods and countries,[3] investment activity and consumers' goods production (and therefore also general production) are highly correlated. The rates of increase in the general production level and in investment activity are then also highly correlated.   To include the series now proposed would therefore be almost the same as to include the rate of increase of the variate that is to be explained.   It may be proved mathematically that this means introducing a small change in lag.[4]   The new variate may therefore be given any importance (within some limits) one likes, if only the lag in the relation explaining investment activity be accordingly changed.   Only if that lag may be known *a priori* will the problem be absolutely solvable.   A further condition is, of course, that the lag, as well as the coefficient found for the rate of increase in total production, must be positive.

Series rejected.   The list of explanatory series omits two other series which have been emphasised by some authors and might possibly be considered as influencing investment fluctuations.   These series have been rejected partly for *a priori* reasons, partly as a consequence of some provisional correlation calculations.

---

also be written: $(1 - ab)$ $v = R$ or $v = cR$, meaning that $u + v$ could be left out as an explanatory variate.

[1] Not only consumers' goods production, since for the production of other goods machines, etc., are equally necessary.

[2] *Cf.* G. HABERLER, *Prosperity and Depression*, page 84.

[3] *Cf.* discussion of results in § 10.

[4] *Cf.* end of § 8, p. 48.

(1)
" *Weighted*
average of
previous
production."

Some theorists have emphasised a new " explanatory " series by paying attention to what has been called the " echo effect ". Suppose the duration of life of all capital goods were strictly equal to a given period: then production required for replacement of worn-out capital goods would be an exact repetition of total production of investment goods some time before. If, *e.g.*, that period were strictly seven years, then production in 1929 would be partly destined to replace capital goods produced in 1922, production in 1930 to replace those produced in 1923, etc. Now it is clear that (i) the life of various capital goods shows an enormous spread and (ii) even the life of, *e.g.*, one particular machine depends on business conditions in the year in which it is replaced. There will be a tendency to replace more in good than in bad years, even if the technical duration of life be the same. The first circumstance leads to the necessity of taking, for the explanation of 1929 production, not the year 1922 only, but a weighted average of a number of years which perhaps have their centre in 1922. Some experiments give the impression that the weighting flattens the curves so radically that practically no movements are left.[1] For this reason, as also on account of the uncertainty of the exact distribution of the duration of life, the variate "weighted average of previous production of capital goods " has been omitted. The second circumstance mentioned above—viz., the influence of the business position on replacement—is already taken into account by the inclusion of profits as one of the determining factors.

(2)
Autonomous
changes in
investment.

Apart from the factors discussed, a number of extra-economic or autonomous factors will influence investment activity. Important inventions may do so; or political events which suddenly change expectations. These influences are considered, in this analysis, as non-systematic disturbances which act largely accidentally, in an irregular way, like lottery drawings. In general, such influences will exist whenever many mutually independent and small forces are acting, which will be the case in

---

[1] See also: P. DE WOLFF, " The Demand for Passenger Cars in the United States ", in *Econometrica*, 6 (1938), page 113.

normal times. This is the approach to business-cycle problems which is known as the " shock theory of cycles ".[1] Some very exceptional events which do not obey these " laws " will be generally known, so that they may easily be eliminated before the analysis. This has been done, *e.g.*, with the English coalminers' strike in 1926, while for the American calculations the period since 1933 has been treated separately. With the exception of such events, the other autonomous influences are assumed to be included in the statistical residuals.

Two stages of investigation.
To sum up, there would be reason to include at least six explanatory series (indicated by the numbers 1-6), namely:

(1)   current profits;

(2)   price level of capital goods;

(3)   interest rates (long, short or both);

(4)   profit margin;

(5)   the rate of increase of prices;

(6)   the rate of increase in the volume of production.

To include this large number of series in all calculations would have meant such an amount of work that it seemed advisable to make the investigation in two consecutive stages. In the first stage, where a general orientation about the importance of each variate is the object, all series are included, but only three cases are considered (Germany and the United Kingdom before the war;

---

[1] *Cf.* R. Frisch: " Propagation Problems and Impulse Problems in Dynamic Economics " in *Economic Essays in Honour of Gustav Cassel*, London, 1933. The difference between this type of business-cycle theory and the other theories may be shortly characterised as follows: whereas most theories do not pay very much attention to external disturbances, and in most cases only start their argument with the assumption of an initial disturbance, the shock theory supposes that such disturbances work at very short intervals and are each of them of only little importance. From this simple fact, this theory concludes—by mathematical deductions—that the resulting movement may show, apart from the " endogenous " periods, apparent periods which are only the consequence of the cumulative effect of disturbances. The word " shock " has been chosen in analogy with physics, where such problems were already known.

the United States after the war), and the calculations are limited to regression formulæ and correlation coefficients. In the second stage, the calculations include the more important series only, but they are more detailed and cover six cases (adding to the above France and the United States before the war and the United Kingdom after the war). In addition, the significance of the latter calculations has been tested in various ways.

A rough and fairly easy first test of the significance of results consists in dividing up the period studied and repeating the calculations for the shorter periods. Similar results, with coefficients of the same order of magnitude, should be found: otherwise the significance of the results must be doubted. A number of calculations for the pre-war period have accordingly been repeated for two sub-periods—up to 1895 and from 1895 onwards. The year 1895 has been chosen as it is the turning-point of one of the so-called long waves.

In addition, another experiment has been made. As it has often been suggested that the " laws " governing upward phases and those governing downward phases of the cycle are different, the calculations have been repeated for (1) all years in upward phases and (2) all years in downward phases.

In addition, the more exact significance calculations mentioned in Chapter II have been made for some characteristic cases. They have not been repeated for all cases, as they are very laborious.

§ 8.   The Statistical Material

The following details of the statistical series used in the calculations may now be given.

The countries and periods studied are:

Countries and periods.

Pre-war: Germany 1871-1912 (42 years);*
United Kingdom 1871-1910 (40 years);*
United States 1877-1913 (37 years);
France 1871-1908 (38 years).

Post-war: United Kingdom 1920-1936 (17 years);
United States 1919-1933 (15 years).*

Only the cases indicated with an asterisk have been included in the first stage.

The post-war figures for Germany are too much vitiated by autonomous events to afford a good basis for research. The period after 1933 for the United States has been left out, as the policy of the Government may have changed the relations investigated; the calculations have, however, been extrapolated (*cf.* Section 11).

Series used.

I. *Total investment* has as a rule been represented (a) *Descrip-* by estimates of the consumption of iron and steel (ϱ_i). *tion of series.* Alternatively, pig-iron production has been used.

The main difference between the two series consists in exports of iron and steel (not included in consumption) and in scrap used in steel production (not included in production of pig-iron). The inclusion of exports may be interpreted as an attempt to take into consideration not only the home market, but also foreign markets. The exclusion of the second item is in most cases not serious, as there is a good parallelism between cycles in pig-iron and steel production. Only for the United Kingdom 1900-1910, where there was a marked divergency, must the consumption figures be preferred; it is interesting, however, to compare the results of the two attempts.

In the case of the United States, a more accurate estimate of the volume of investment (ϱ) is available for the post-war years in the figures calculated by Kuznets.[1] These figures, which distinguish between producers' durable goods, consumers' durable goods, and building, have also been used. Building has been excluded in all cases except one, where residential building (as estimated by Wickens and Foster)[2] has been subtracted, and non-residential building retained.

---

[1] S. Kuznets, *Gross Capital Formation*, Bulletin 52, National Bureau of Economic Research, New York, 1934.

[2] D. L. Wickens and R. R. Foster, *Non-farm Residential Construction* 1920-1936, Bulletin 65, National Bureau of Economic Research, New York, 1937.

The exact series used is indicated in each table. In general, the results obtained for the various series are not very different.

II. The explanatory series are taken from the following sources.

(1) *Profits earned* have been represented by the series indicated in the following table:

Country and period	Description of series	Source
United States, pre-war	(n) Share price index.	*Review of Economic Statistics.*
United Kingdom, pre-war	(E) Non-labour income.	BOWLEY, *Economic Journal*, 1904, completed with the help of data by STAMP, *British Incomes and Property* (based on Income Statistics).[a]
Germany, pre-war	(d) Dividends earned in % of capital.[b]	DONNER, *Die Kursbildung am Aktienmarkt, Vierteljahreshefte zur Konjunkturforschung*, Sonderheft 36.
	(n) Share price index.	Same source.
France, pre-war	(n) Share price index.	Statistique générale de la France.
United States, post-war	(Z^c) Net income of corporations.	*Statistics of Income.*
	(n) Share price index.	Standard Statistics Co.
United Kingdom, post-war	(Z^c) Net profits earned in % of capital.[b]	*Economist.*

a Some experiments with statistical methods devised to find the annual figures out of the three-year-moving averages given by Income Statistics seemed to show that the cyclical movements of the latter and those of the former do not differ very much.
b Year of earning is taken to precede year of distribution.

(2) *Price of capital goods.* — The price of pig-iron (q_i) has been taken throughout, as it represents the most fluctuating item in the cost of capital goods. The sources are indicated in the following table:

Country and period	Description of series	Source
United States, pre-war	Price of No. 1 foundry pig-iron at Philadelphia.	*U.S.A. Statistical Abstract.*

Country and period	Description of series	Source
United Kingdom, pre-war	Sauerbeck's index of price of pig-iron.	S. KUZNETS: *Secular movements in Production and Prices.*
Germany, pre-war	Average price of pig-iron produced.	*Statistisches Handbuch (1907); Statistische Jahrbücher.*
France, pre-war	Average price of pig-iron produced.	*Annuaire statistique de la France.*
United States, post-war	Price of Bessemer pig-iron at Pittsburgh.	*U.S.A. Statistical Abstract.*
United Kingdom, post-war	Price of Cleveland-Middlesbrough pig-iron.	Statist's index number of wholesale prices, *Journal of the Royal Statistical Society*, Part II.

(3) *Interest rates.* — In most cases, calculations have been made with (i) (m_s) market rate of discount or some other short-term interest rate and (ii) (m_{Lb}) bond yields.

In addition, some calculations have been made with (m_{Ls}) share yield, as representing a special category of " interest rates ", viz., the rate attributed to funds raised by share issues. The sources are summarised in the following table:

Country and period	Description of series	Source
United States, pre-war	(m_{Lb}) Long-term: 1890-1899: Yield on ten American railroad bonds.	*Review of Economic Statistics*, 1919.
	1900-1913: Yield on sixty bond issues combined.	Standard Statistics Co.
	(m_s) Short-term: market rate on 60-90 days paper.	I. FISHER, *The Theory of Interest.*
United Kingdom, pre-war	(m_{Lb}) Long-term: Yield on 2 ½% Consols.	,,
	(m_s) Short-term: market rate of discount.	,,
Germany, pre-war	(m_{Lb}) Long-term: Yield on fixed interest bearing securities.	DONNER, see under (1).
	(m_s) Short-term: market rate of discount.	
France, pre-war	$(^1/m_{Lb}$ Long-term: Index of price of 3% " rente ".	*Bulletin de la Statistique générale de la France*, 1919/20.

Country and period	Description of series	Source
United States, post-war	(m_{Lb}) Long-term: Bond yield, 60 issues combined.	Standard Statistics Co.
	(m_s) Short-term: market rate on 4-6 months commercial paper.	I. FISHER: *The Theory of Interest; League of Nations Monthly Bulletin of Statistics.*
	(m_{Ls}) Share yield: (i) Cash dividends of corporations in % of (ii) total capital stock.	(i) Statistics of Income. (ii) Statistics of Income; prior to 1925, estimates based on new security issues and index of share prices.
United Kingdom, post-war	(m_{Lb}) Long-term: Yield of $2\frac{1}{2}\%$ Consols.	Statistical Abstract of the United Kingdom; Statistical Summary of the Bank of England.

(4)   The calculation and sources of the figures for *profit margins* $(p-\frac{1}{2}\, l_w)$ are given in this table:

Country and period	Description of series	Source
United States, pre-war	Index of cost of living — $\frac{1}{2}$ index of hourly earnings.	National Industrial Conference Board.
United Kingdom, pre-war	(i) Index of prices of exported finished products — $\frac{1}{2}$ (ii) index of wage rates.	(i) Calculation L.o.N. based on trade statistics. (ii) Index of Bowley and Wood, reproduced from Layton: *Introduction to the Study of Prices.*
Germany, pre-war	(i) General index of wholesale prices — $\frac{1}{2}$ (ii) index of wages (both in % deviations from trend).	(i) JACOBS & RICHTER: Grosshandelspreise. *Vierteljahreshefte zur Konjunkturforschung,* Sonderheft No. 37. (ii) J. KUCZYNSKI: *Löhne und Ernährungskosten in Deutschland.*

(5)   The sources of the figures for (u) *production of consumers' goods* are:

Country and period	Description of series	Source
United Kingdom, pre-war	Index of production of consumers' goods.	HOFFMANN: *Weltwirtschaftliches Archiv,* vol. 40.
Germany, pre-war	Index of the Institut für Konjunkturforschung.	WAGENFÜHR, Die Industriewirtschaft. *Vierteljahreshefte zur Konjunkturforschung.* Sonderheft No. 31.

Country and period	Description of series	Source
United States, post-war	League of Nations estimates based on study by Warburton in:	*Journal of the American Statistical Association*, vol. 30.

(6) The figures for the *rate of increase in general price level* and their sources are:

Country and period	Description of series	Source
United Kingdom, pre-war	(Δq_i) Rate of increase in price of pig-iron. [a]	*Vide supra.*
Germany, pre-war	(Δq_i) *Idem.* [a]	*Idem.*
United States, post-war	(Δp) Rate of increase in cost-of-living index.[a]	National Industrial Conference Board.

[a] For pre-war times the general price level seemed to be well represented by that of investment goods.   For post-war times iron prices are no more representative.

(b) *Trends.* — As the relation studied claims to represent only the causation of short-run movements in the volume of investment, deviations from trend have been taken throughout, except when otherwise stated.   In general, trends have been calculated as nine-year moving averages for pre-war periods—which are long enough to allow of the first and last four years being omitted—and as rectilinear trends for post-war periods—which are too short to allow of omitting eight years.[1]

(c) *Other series included.*   As has already been stated (Chapter III, § 7), an attempt has been made throughout to explain production of pig-iron or consumption of iron and steel (v_i) or total physical investment (v) by some of the six explanatory series mentioned above.

---

[1] The trend chosen for the American figures (post-war period) may be somewhat biased by the fact that the period starts with a boom year and ends with a slump year.

In order to judge the importance of the trend, the first calculation of Table III.4 was made without correction for trend.   The correlation coefficient was hardly affected, nor was the regression coefficient of profits (0.33 instead of 0.29). The combined influence of price and interest must therefore have been nearly the same; of the respective influence of these two factors, nothing can be said owing to a very high intercorrelation between the two variates (*cf.* Chapter II, § 6, page 29).

In some cases it has seemed useful to include still further series, sometimes in substitution for one of those mentioned already. In the case of the United States (pre-war), in order to obtain a fairly good explanation, it seemed necessary to include building volume (v_B) as a separate variate. This may be justified by the fact that the factors affecting the building volume are rather poorly represented in the four explanatory series: *e.g.*, building profits, which might play a rôle, are not reflected immediately in share-price indices. The same applies even more to other factors. The inclusion of building volume means, of course, only a postponement of the problem; the factors affecting building itself are to be studied afterwards (Chapter IV).

Lags considered.   (i)   As a general starting-point, a lag of *half-a-year* was assumed to exist between the explaining series and investment activity.[1] In most cases, this seemed to be not far from reality.[2]

(ii)   In the second stage, various experiments were made with *other lags*. They consisted either in assuming a lag of one year for all variates, or in introducing the same variate both with a lag of one year and without any lag and comparing the regression coefficients. For example, if the best explanation turns out to be: $0.8\,z + 0.4\,z_{-1}$, where z_{-1} stands for z one year earlier, this result represents a case of so-called " distributed lag "[3] with an average lag of 1/3 year. Similarly, lags of half-a-year may be introduced by simply taking as a variate $\frac{1}{2}\,(z + z_{-1})$ instead of z.

(iii)   Here it should be remarked that an infinity of different interpretations can be given to the above formula, which, mathematically speaking, all come to the same. Instead, *e.g.*, of giving the above interpretation, one could read the formula:

$$1.2z - 0.4\,(z - z_{-1})$$

---

[1] Except for the United Kingdom, where preliminary calculations showed a lag of one year for non-labour income to be preferable.

[2] A number of estimates available for the length of the production period would seem to indicate a few months for machinery, six months for house building, and one year for shipbuilding. *Cf.* " The Length of Certain Production Processes " (Dutch), *De Nederlandsche Conjunctuur*, August 1934, page 32.

[3] This term is due to Professor Irving Fisher. Distributed lags seem to be even more probable than simple lags.

saying that there are two influences, viz.:

(a) an influence of z, without lag and with strength 1.2;
(b) an influence of the rate of increase in z, with an (average) lag of half-a-year and a strength — 0.4.

§ 9. CHIEF RESULTS

Before giving a detailed account of all the cases considered and results obtained, the conclusions drawn may be shortly summarised as follows.

(a) On the assumption that our estimate of iron and steel consumption (or the alternatives used) is a just index of investment activity, there is fairly good evidence that the fluctuations in investment activity are in the main determined by the fluctuations in profits earned in industry as a whole some months earlier.

(b) The influence of the other factors included is not considerable and is therefore, in many cases, numerically uncertain. This fact is reflected in

(i) the significance calculations in the ordinary sense, and
(ii) the fact that the "influence" of these other factors is sometimes positive and sometimes negative, and almost always small (cf. Chapter II, § 5).[1]

Nevertheless, for particular countries, fairly certain results are obtained (cf. next few sections).

(c) No systematic differences of a general character have been found to exist between upward and downward phases;

(d) As was to be expected, the difficulties arising from "multicollinearity"[2] increase with the number of variates and prevent the complete solution of a number of problems.

---

[1] The chief significance of this result is that in past cycles the rôle of interest rates and of prices of iron has been far less important than that played by profit changes. It does not follow for all cases—though it does for most of them—that interest rates might not have exerted a great influence if they had fluctuated more violently than in fact they have done.

[2] See Chapter II, § 6.

§ 10. Details of Results, First Stage.

The results of the calculations of the first stage are summarised in Tables III. 1, III. 2 and III. 3, giving the correlation and regression coefficients for the cases and variates indicated. The tables have been constructed in the following way. The chief explanatory variate, namely profits, has always been included; in the case of the United States two such variates were taken, namely profits and share yield. The selection of these variates has been based on their coefficient of simple correlation with investment activity v' and on the " influence " (*cf.* Chapter II) which they show in the more complete " explanations ".

The chief variate or the couple of chief variates has then been combined with each of the other variates, and with certain combinations of larger numbers of the latter. Variates showing regression coefficients with wrong signs have sometimes been excluded in order to reduce the number of possible combinations; *e.g.*, the variate profit margin, $(p_A - \frac{1}{2} l_w)_{-1/2}$ in the case of the United Kingdom in the four- and five-sets, and the variate rate of increase in price level (Δq) in the three-set. The same applies to variates showing a very small influence. This influence may be found by multiplying the standard deviation, given at the bottom of the tables, by the regression coefficients. In order to give an *a posteriori* test, this has been done for the highest regression coefficient in each column.

The tables have been used for three purposes. First, the increase in the correlation coefficient as the consequence of the inclusion of a new variate may be studied, and secondly, the stability of the regression obtained for one variate in various cases. Thirdly, conclusions as to the relevance of the variates may be drawn. These latter are based on:

   (i)   whether or not the variate in question increases the correlation coefficient to any considerable extent,

  (ii)   whether or not the sign of a fairly stable regression coefficient is right, and

 (iii)   whether or not the influence of that variate is perceptible.

Carrying out this programme for each of the variates, the following conclusions seem legitimate.

Table III. 1. " Explanation " of Investment Activity, First Stage.

United Kingdom, 1871-1910: Iron and Steel Consumption (v_i).

Case	Regression coefficients of: [1]							Correlation coefficients
	E_{-1}	$(q_i)_{-1/2}$	Δq_i	$(m_{Lb})_{-1/2}$	$(m_s)_{-1/2}$	Δu	$(p_A - \frac{1}{2} l_w)_{-1/2}$	R
11	1.85							0.552
21	3.20	— 0.31						0.664
22	1.92		0.17					0.649
23	1.92			— 0.366				0.643
24	2.85				— 0.051			0.611
25	1.79					0.43		0.606
26	2.65						— 0.44	0.655
31	3.29	— 0.32	0.13					0.729
32	3.16	— 0.28		— 0.330				0.726
33	3.41	— 0.26			— 0.021			0.670
34	3.16	— 0.31				0.45		0.714
35	3.16	— 0.20					— 0.24	0.680
41	3.28	— 0.30	0.15	— 0.239				0.783
51	3.45	0.27	0.15	— 0.229	— 0.016			0.786
52	3.25	— 0.31	0.13	— 0.223		0.27		0.797

Standard deviations of variates: [1]

v_i 7.48	2.23	13.25	14.90	6.74	57.87	4.38	7.26	
Maximum influence [2]	7.69	4.24	2.53	2.47	2.95	1.97	3	

[1] Units used: all series in percentage deviations from trend, except series m_{Lb} and m_s, which are in absolute deviations from trend, in units of 0.01 % and Δq_i and Δu, which are in percentages of the trend values of q_i and u respectively.

Meaning of symbols (for fuller explanation, see § 8).

v_i:	consumption of iron and steel.	m_{Lb}:	bond yield
E :	non-labour income.	m_s:	short-term interest rate.
q_i:	price of iron.	Δu:	rate of increase in consumers' goods production.
Δq_i:	rate of increase in $q_i = q_i - (q_i)_{-1}$.	$p_A - \frac{1}{2} l_w$	profit margin.

[2] Absolute value of product of largest regression coefficient with right sign and standard deviation.

[3] Wrong signs.

Table III. 2. " Explanation " of Investment Activity, First Stage.

Germany, 1871-1912: Iron and Steel Consumption (v_i).

Case	Regression coefficients of: [1]							Correlation coefficients
	$d_{-\frac{1}{2}}$	Δu	$(p-\frac{1}{2}l_w)_{-\frac{1}{2}}$	$(m_{LS})_{-\frac{1}{2}}$	$(q_i)_{-\frac{1}{2}}$	Δq_i	$(m_S)_{-\frac{1}{2}}$	R
11	5.37							0.853
21	5.37	0.23						0.857
22	5.18		0.10					0.854
23	5.63			— 0.013				0.854
24	5.39				— 0.006			0.853
25	5.51					— 0.05		0.854
26	4.96						0.027	0.865
31	4.98	0.32	0.21					0.859
32	5.70	0.25		— 0.017				0.857
33	5.19	0.28			0.038			0.857
34	5.44		0.09	— 0.013				0.854
35	5.32	0.28			— 0.101			0.856
36	5.78			— 0.015	— 0.020			0.854
41	5.80	0.36	— 0.13	— 0.024		— 0.07	0.034	0.875

Standard deviations of variates: [1]

v_i 11.09	1.76	3.52	5.25	44.80	12.85	9.42	65.88	
Maximum influence [2]	10.21	1.27	1.47	1.08	1.30	3	3	

[1] Units used: all series in percentage deviations from trend except series d, m_{LS} and m_S, which are in absolute deviations from trend, in units of 1%, 0.01% and 0.01 % respectively. For Δu and Δq_i, see table III. 1.

Meaning of symbols (for fuller explanation, see § 8).

v_i:	consumption of iron and steel.	m_{LS}:	share yield.
d:	dividends in % of capital.	q_i:	price of pig-iron.
Δu:	rate of increase in consumers' goods production.	Δq_i:	rate of increase in price of pig-iron.
$p-\frac{1}{2}l_w$:	profit margin.	m_S:	short-term interest rate.

[2] Absolute value of product of largest regression coefficient with right sign and standard deviation.

[3] Wrong signs.

Table III. 3. "Explanation" of Investment Activity, First Stage.

United States, 1919-1933: Deliveries of Producers' Durable
Commodities + Non-residential Building (v').

Case	Regression coefficients of:[1]								Correlation coefficients
	$Z^c_{-\frac{1}{2}}$	$(m_{LS})_{-\frac{1}{2}}$	$(q_i)_{-\frac{1}{2}}$	$(p-\frac{1}{2}l_w)_{-\frac{1}{2}}$	t	Δp	Δu	$(m_s)_{-\frac{1}{2}}$	R
11	0.19	—0.076							0.986
21	0.19	—0.074	—0.02						0.987
22	0 17	—0.083		0.10					0 987
23	0.18	—0.079			—0.13				0 986
24	0.20	—0.074				—0.29			0 990
25	0.19	—0.076					0.01		0.986
26	0.18	—0.078						0.004	0.986
31	0.16	—0.077	—0.01	0.27					0.989
32	0.18	—0.081	—0.07		—0.63				0.987
33	0.20	—0.071	—0.02			—0.29			0.991
34	0.17	—0.076		0.19	0.57				0.987
35	0.19	—0.076			0.02	—0.29			0.990
36	0.20	—0.072			0.10	—0.29			0.990
41	0.16	—0.075	—0.14	0.31	0.13				0.989
51	0.18	—0.071	—0.07	0.14	0.10	—0.23			0.991
52	0.16	—0.077	—0.17	0.31	—0.13		—0.06		0.989
53	0.17	—0.067	—0.18	0.24	0.27			0.012	0.990

Standard deviations of variates:[2]

v'									
19.85	96.50	154.20	25.49	17.81	4.32	7.44	7.48	130.23	

Maximum influence[3]									
19.30	12.80	4.54	5.52	2.72	[3]	0.07	[3]		

[1] Units used: All series in percentage deviations from the average, except series m_{LS} and m_s, which are in absolute deviations from average, in units of 0.01 %. For Δp and Δu, see table III. 1 (Δq_i and Δu).

Meaning of symbols (for fuller explanation see § 8).

v':   deliveries of producers' durable goods + non-residential building.
Z^c: profits of corporations.
m_{LS}:   share yield.
q_i: price of pig-iron.
$p-\frac{1}{2}l_w$:   profit margin.
t: trend.
Δp: rate of increase in cost of living.
Δu: rate of increase in consumers' goods production.
m_s: short-term interest rate.

[2] Absolute value of product of largest regression coefficient with right sign and standard deviation.

[3] Wrong signs.

The importance of profits (Z), and, in the case of the United States, of share yield (m_{Ls}), is confirmed: the increase in correlation and the influence of the variate are considerable; the signs are right.

Increase in correlation. The increase in correlation obtained by the inclusion of each variate may be taken from the following table:

Average Increase in Correlation Coefficient obtained by adding Each of the Following Variates.

Country	Profits	Share yield	Short-term interest rate	Price of iron	Rate of increase in production	Rate of increase in prices	Profit margin
United Kingdom 1871-1910	0.552	0.069 [a]	0.023	0.078	0.039	0.073	0.060 *
Germany 1871-1912	0.853	0.001	0.012 *	0.001	0.004	0.001 *	0.002
United States 1919-1933	0.795	0.191	0.001 *	0.001	0.000	0.003 *	0.001

[a] Bond yield.
* In this case the sign of the regression coefficient is wrong.

Signs. For the variates: short-term interest rate (m_s), rate of increase in price (Δq or Δp) and profit margin ($p - \frac{1}{2} l_w$), the results vary in different countries. All these variates show wrong signs in all cases for at least one country.

For the other variates and countries, the signs are right, but share-yield data for the United Kingdom are not available. The variate Δu, rate of increase in consumers' goods production, shows positive signs in at least one case for each country, but its influence is found to be small. In addition, as has been observed in the theoretical part of this chapter (§ 7), this influence may always be replaced by a shift in the lag assumed, especially in case of a high correlation between investment activity and consumers' goods production. Price of iron (q_i) shows negative signs in most cases for each country.

Influence. Taking the standard deviation of v_i equal to 100 in each country, the maximum influence found is the following:

Country	Profits	Share yield	Short-term interest rate	Price of iron	Rate of increase in:		Profit margin
					produc-tion	prices	
United Kingdom	103	33 *a*	39	57	26	34	*
Germany	92	10	*	12	11	*	13
United States	97	64	*	23	0	*	28

a Bond yield.   * Wrong signs in all cases considered.

Conclusions. From the foregoing we conclude that, as stated already, the factors short-term interest rate, price of iron, rate of increase in production and in prices, and profit margin are, in the mean, far less important than profits and share yields. In particular cases some of them seem to be important, but a general indication is lacking. The most important variates that are to be considered in the second stage are therefore profits (and for the United States, post-war, also share yield), and in addition the price of iron and interest rates, since the theoretical considerations given in § 7 require that these should be considered at the same time. A second reason for including these two factors is the great importance which many economists attach to them as causal factors of investment.

§ 11.   Details of Results, Second Stage.

A.   *Examination of Regression Equations found.*

Correlation found. The correlation coefficients found (*cf.* Tables III. 4 to III. 9) are, in general, fairly high, their median value being about 0.80; and it is satisfactory that —in view of the better statistics available for post-war years—the post-war correlations are considerably higher than the pre-war ones for the same country. Especially interesting is the improvement obtained by taking such a careful estimate ᴀs Kuznets' index of investment activity instead of pig-iron production.

"Influence"
of profits.

A feature common to all results is, as has already been observed, the important part which profits (or one of the series reflecting them) play in the " explanation ". The other factors play only a secondary part, as is easily seen from Graphs III. 2—III. 5, constructed in accordance with the rules laid down in Chapter II, § 5.

Graph III. 2.

"Explanation" of Investment Activity.
United States of America, 1919-1933.

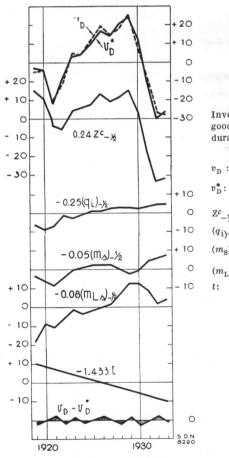

Investment = Flow of producers' durable goods to enterprises, plus flow of consumers' durable goods to enterprises and households.

v_D : investment activity, actual.

v_D^* : investment activity, as explained by:

$Z^c_{-\frac{1}{2}}$: profits

$(q_i)_{-\frac{1}{2}}$: price of iron

$(m_S)_{-\frac{1}{2}}$: short-term interest rate

$(m_{LS})_{-\frac{1}{2}}$: share yield

t : trend.

lagged ½-year.

Graph III. 3.
"Explanation" of Iron and Steel Consumption.
United Kingdom, 1920-1936.

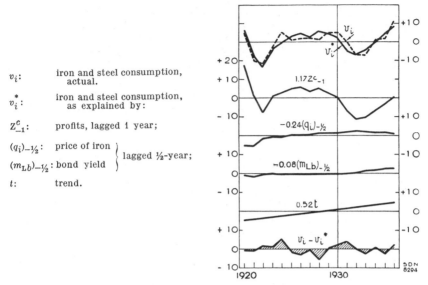

v_i: iron and steel consumption, actual.

v_i^*:   iron and steel consumption, as explained by:

z_{-1}^c: profits, lagged 1 year;

$(q_i)_{-1/2}$:   price of iron ⎫
                                    ⎬ lagged ½-year;
$(m_{Lb})_{-1/2}$: bond yield ⎭

t: trend.

Regression coefficients. The regression coefficients of profits vary according to the series taken to represent them. It is found in using such a comprehensive figure as corporation profits, for the United States, that when there is an increase in these profits of 1% of their average level, there is a corresponding increase in investment activity of 0.3% of its average level. The figure found for Germany (pre-war) is about twice as great, whereas the English figure (post-war) is nearly four times as great; but the latter is based on the *Economist* sample of profits, which seems to show relatively small percentage fluctuations.

It is natural that share prices,[1] if used as representative of profits, obtain a larger coefficient, lying between 0.6 and 1.0.[2] This means that the change in investment caused by a 1% change in share prices is also of the order of 1%.

[1] For in pre-war times share prices in general showed smaller percentage fluctuations than dividends or profits. In the United States after the war the situation was different; the share yield was at a minimum in 1929 when prices were at a maximum.

[2] As far as the figures in Table III. 4 are concerned. Some of the exceptional figures in the other tables are explained below.

Graph III. 4.

"EXPLANATION" OF IRON AND STEEL CONSUMPTION.
UNITED KINGDOM, 1871-1910.

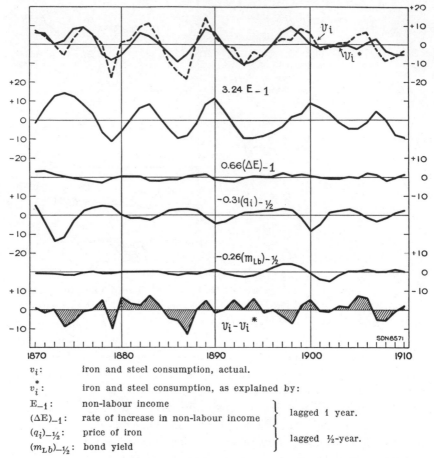

v_i:	iron and steel consumption, actual.
v_i^*:	iron and steel consumption, as explained by:
E_{-1}:	non-labour income
$(\Delta E)_{-1}$:	rate of increase in non-labour income
$(q_i)_{-1/2}$:	price of iron
$(m_{Lb})_{-1/2}$:	bond yield

E_{-1}, $(\Delta E)_{-1}$ lagged 1 year.

$(q_i)_{-1/2}$, $(m_{Lb})_{-1/2}$ lagged ½-year.

Lag.   In order to obtain an impression of the empirical evidence regarding the lag between profits and investment activity, Graph III. 6 has been constructed from all cases where a " free " lag was used in the calculations, *i.e.*, where both profits without lag and with one-year lag[1] were intro-

---

[1] Or, which comes to the same thing, profits and the rate of increase in profits. In Graphs III. 4 and III. 5, the latter's influence has been shown separately, whereas in the tables (except Table III. 10) it has been combined with the influence of profits.

Graph III. 5.

"EXPLANATION" OF IRON AND STEEL CONSUMPTION.

GERMANY, 1871-1912.

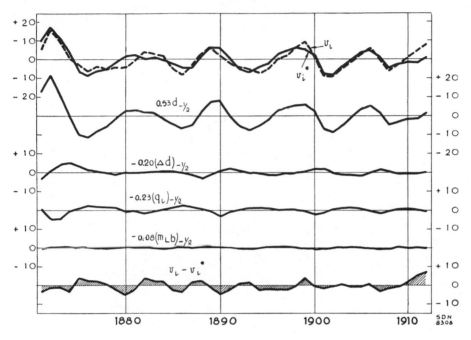

v_i:	iron and steel consumption, actual.
v_i^*:	iron and steel consumption, as explained by:
$d_{-\frac{1}{2}}$:	dividend in % of capital
$(\Delta d)_{-\frac{1}{2}}$:	rate of increase in dividend in % of capital
$(q_i)_{-\frac{1}{2}}$:	price of iron
$(m_{Lb})_{-\frac{1}{2}}$:	bond yield

lagged ½-year.

duced and the real lag was assumed to be the average of these two, weighted by the regression coefficients corresponding to each. Graph III. 6 gives the frequency distribution of the lags found, the average length of which is about eight months. This figure supports fairly well the *a priori* reasoning in § 8.

Graph III. 6.
FREQUENCY DISTRIBUTION OF LAGS.

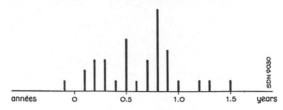

At this point, the validity of our general result, that profits have a large influence on investment activity, may be discussed in a more general framework. It is clear that, between these two variates, profits $(\bar{\bar{Z}})$ and investment activity $(\bar{\bar{v}})$, there exists another relation—viz., the definition (or, if one prefers it, the calculation) of profits. Writing

The two relations between profits and investment activity.

$\bar{\bar{u}}$ for consumption goods production

and

$\bar{\bar{z}}$ for the general profit margin,

profits will be defined (or calculated) by the equation [1]

$$\bar{\bar{Z}} = (\bar{\bar{u}} + \bar{\bar{v}})\,\bar{\bar{z}}\ .$$

Hence we would have two relations between profits and investment activity.

This fact might give rise to doubts as to the value of the preceding results in two respects:

(1) Is it not possible that only the second relation between profits and investment exists and that hitherto this has been wrongly taken as an *influence* of profits on investment ?

(2) Granted that there are two relations, is there not reason to fear that the coefficient found for the influence of profits is partly attributable to the other relation ?

It seems reasonable to answer both questions in the negative.

(1) As has been stated in the Introduction,[2] an essential element of our method is that the variates playing a rôle in each equation

---

[1] For the purpose of our argument, it is immaterial whether or not slightly different definitions (or methods of calculation) are adopted.

[2] *Cf.* p. 12.

must be known on *a priori* grounds. This also applies here. Even without any statistical evidence, few economists would deny that there is a causal influence of profits on investment.

But let us suppose, nevertheless, that evidence on this point is sought for in the statistics. A test should then be devised to prove that the apparent parallelism between profits and investment activity is not only due to the composition of profits but also to the causal connection between the two variates.

The obvious high correlation between Z and a combination of u, v and z does not imply that each of these three variates is closely correlated with Z. If the other relation between v and Z also exists, it is to be expected that the correlation between v and Z will be closer than that between u or z and Z. In most cases considered, however, u is closely correlated with v—as a consequence of what has been called the "multiplier" effect—which results in the fact that a high correlation between v and Z also causes a high correlation between u and Z and, hence, to some extent between the third variate z and Z. In these cases, therefore, the proposition cannot be tested along these lines. Only where u and v are not closely correlated will the test be possible.

Such a case is that of Germany before the war (*cf.* Graph III. 7, left-hand part). The upper pair of curves compares profits—represented here by dividends, d—with the *a priori* combination $u + v$, and z (for lack of better data, z has been approximately represented by the expression $(p — \frac{1}{2}l_w)$ where p is the general price level, l_w the wage rate, $\frac{1}{2}$ being approximately the wage quota in prices). The three other pairs of curves compare d with each of the variates u, v and z separately.

The correlation between d and the combination is close. Of the three other correlations, that between d and v is the nearest. This is demonstrated by the following correlation coefficients:

$$
\begin{aligned}
\text{Between } d \text{ and combination}: &\quad 0.80 \\
\text{,,} \quad d \text{ ,, } v_{+\frac{1}{2}} \qquad\qquad &: \quad 0.70 \\
\text{,,} \quad d \text{ ,, } u \qquad\qquad\quad &: \quad 0.44 \\
\text{,,} \quad d \text{ ,, } p — \tfrac{1}{2}\, l_w &: \quad 0.64 \\
\text{,,} \quad u \text{ ,, } v \qquad\qquad\quad &: \quad 0.26.
\end{aligned}
$$

The result is therefore favourable to our thesis, though not strikingly so.

Another clear case is that of Germany in the years around 1929. The fluctuations in profits (Z) may be accounted for by the fluctuations in the factors $u + v$, volume of production, and p/l_w, the proportion between prices and wage-rates (following Donner,[1] who prefers the proportion to the margin). It is especially noticeable that the volume of total production is not correlated with home investment (v) so closely as profits are (*cf.* Graph III. 7, right-hand part). In this particular case, this must be ascribed to the fact that 1929 already showed a decline in the internal business-cycle position, whereas exports were even higher than in 1928. The satisfactory correlation between profits and investment activity —including, as a further variate, interest rates (m_s) with a negative sign—cannot therefore be a consequence of profits' depending chiefly on the volume of production and the latter's depending chiefly on the volume of investment; for the volume of production shows a lower correlation both with profits and with investment than these two series do with each other.

In most other cases for which data are available, the correlation between u and v is much closer. The only test possible in such cases is to ascertain whether the correlation between profits (Z) and v is higher than that between Z and z. This is found to be the case for the United Kingdom before the war—where, however, the figures for z are very unreliable—and for the United States after the war.

But, it must be repeated, the greatest importance must be attributed to the *a priori* argument to include profits in the explanation of investment.

(2) The problem of the reliability of the coefficients when two equations exist between two variates arises also in the statistical determination of supply and demand curves: the variates " price " and " quantity exchanged " occur both in the demand and in the supply function. Often a doubt is expressed as to whether in

---

[1] DONNER: " Die Kursbildung am Aktienmarkt ", *Vierteljahreshefte zur Konjunkturforschung*, Sonderheft 36.

Graph III. 7.

THE TWO RELATIONS BETWEEN PROFITS AND INVESTMENT.
GERMANY 1924-1930 AND 1871-1911.

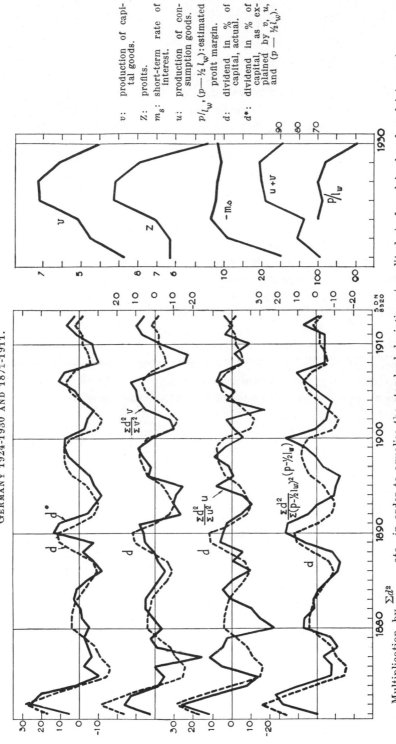

v: production of capi-
      tal goods.
Z: profits.
m_s: short-term rate of
      interest.
u: production of con-
      sumption goods.
p/l_w, $(p-\frac{1}{2} l_w)$: estimated
      profit margin.
d: dividend in % of
      capital, actual.
d*: dividend in % of
      capital, as ex-
      plained by v, u,
      and $(p-\frac{1}{2}l_w)$.

Multiplication by $\dfrac{\Sigma d^2}{\Sigma v^2} \cdots$, etc., in order to equalise the standard deviations (amplitudes) of explained and explaining series.

such a situation both relations are statistically determinable. This doubt seems to be based on what happens in a special case—viz., when both relations are supposed to contain no, or no important, other variates, or when, for lack of statistical data, these other variates are left outside the calculations. In fact, in such a case, only one statistical equation will in general be found, and it would be difficult to maintain that this represents both economic relations.

In principle, this difficulty disappears, however, when, in at least one of the relations, other important variates play a part, provided, of course, that not exactly the same set of supplementary variates occurs in both equations. As soon as different variates occur in the two relations, statistical calculations will yield different results. A special case is the one where the lags are different in both relations. In the case of demand and supply relations for one market, consumers' income, or the price of a competitive commodity will, e.g., occur as complementary variate in the demand relation, whereas, in the supply relation, cost of production or productive capacity may come in. In some special cases, these variates may be of only minor importance, but the lag between price and quantity exchanged may be different for the two relations, as was assumed to be the case for sugar in Professor Schultz's investigations.[1]

The doubt referred to above is the less justified the more important the complementary variates are. And it is interesting to note that if both relations actually contain only the two variates, without differences in lag, these variates in general will no longer be variates but constants, since, in general, two equations are sufficient to determine the value of two unknowns.

In the case of investment activity and profits, it is clear that the relation representing the calculation of profits does contain other variates—viz., those indicated above: production of consumption goods and profit margin. There is therefore no particular reason for doubt as to the significance of our coefficients.

---

[1] H. SCHULTZ: *Statistical Laws of Demand and Supply*, Chicago, 1928.

Coefficient of price of iron. The regression coefficients found for iron prices sometimes show positive signs, which contradict theoretical expectation. But these results are probably not significant, and simply illustrate the degree of indeterminateness of the figures. This makes it rather difficult to give figures for the elasticity of demand. The coefficients given in the tables are, owing to the method of measurement employed, estimates of that elasticity corresponding to trend values for the variates. None of the negative values is larger than unity; those for the three European countries are all between 0 and — 0.5, and in the case of France they are more often small positive than small negative numbers. The elasticity in those countries must have been small. The British figures are all between + 0.16 and — 0.31, and here it would appear that the elasticity is below one-half. The significance calculations (see page 80 and Table III. 10) indicate, however, that there is a wide range of uncertainty, though, even in the worst case, there is about a 95% chance that the elasticity is below 0.90. The American post-war figures are all between — 0.03 and — 0.36, which also suggests an elasticity of less than one-half; here also a rather large range of uncertainty exists.

The clearest historical example of the influence of iron prices on demand seems to be the upturn in demand in England in 1875, which took place in full depression, and followed the heaviest drop in prices among our observations. (See Graph III. 4 above.)

Coefficient of interest rates. Even greater uncertainty seems to exist concerning the coefficient of interest rates. Here again, French and German figures are centred around zero, and American figures are not very far from it (*cf.* corresponding columns in Tables III. 4—III. 9). Only the English figures (relating to the influence of long-term interest rates) show a decidedly negative tendency, again with a large spread. Their median value is — 0.31 for the pre-war calculations; the post-war figure is considerably smaller: about — 0.1. The figure — 0.31 is in itself not a small figure: it means that a reduction of 1% in the long-term interest rate would cause a 31% increase in investment activity. It should not be forgotten, however, that the largest fall per annum in the long-term interest rate

5

in any cycle before the war was 0.18% and that in most cases it was far less.

Not very different results are obtained in cases where share yield has been introduced as representing the interest rate, or where both share yield and the short-term interest rate have been used, except for the United States in the post-war period. Here share yields are found to have a considerable influence, possibly because they showed large fluctuations in a direction opposite to the usual fluctuations showed in pre-war times in Germany. This must be attributed chiefly to the exaggerated stock-exchange boom in 1928-29, which forced the yields down to very low levels, and to the confidence crisis in 1932, which resulted in very high share yields.

In addition, it must be noted that the fluctuations in share yield did not show any correlation with short-term interest rates; therefore the importance of share yield as an explanatory factor does not involve any proof of the importance of interest rates in the narrower sense.

Finally, the question may be put as to whether the influence found for a change of 1% in interest rates is the same as for a change of 1% in profit rate, (*i.e.*, profits as a percentage of capital). If it is true that the difference between these two rates is the guide for investment activity, these two influences must be about equal. Unfortunately, the question can only be answered for the cases where profit rates are known, *i.e.*, for the United Kingdom after the war and Germany before the war. Here the regression coefficients calculated on this basis compare as follows:

Influence of 1% change in	Profit rate	Long-term interest rate
United Kingdom post-war	12	— 8
Germany pre-war	6	— 8

The result is not bad: the order of magnitude is the same, a deviation in one direction being counteracted by a deviation in the opposite direction. This would, in a sense, support the results obtained. For the United Kingdom before the war the coefficient of interest rates is about 3 times as great as that found for the post-war period, but roughly the same proportion seems to apply to the coefficient for profits.

Comparison between countries. Table III. 4 (pages 68 and 69) enables us to compare the results obtained for the four countries studied. Most of the differences between these results are hardly significant, the most important being probably the difference in lags in the influence of profits. In particular, the lag of one year found for the United Kingdom (post-war) is decidedly longer than in most other cases. In addition, the influence of the price of iron and interest rates seems to be smaller in Germany and France than in England.

Comparison between production and consumption of pig-iron. Table III. 5 (pages 70 and 71) shows an interesting difference in the lag with which profits enter into the English explanations of pig-iron production and consumption. Production reacts to profits much more quickly than does consumption. It follows that consumption probably lags behind production. One has the impression that the fluctuations in foreign demand for British iron must have had a leading influence on the business position in the United Kingdom. In the case of Germany, on the other hand, the difference in lag is much smaller. Apart from this difference, no essential feature emerges from Table III. 5. As was to be expected, the influence of profits is greater on consumption than on production, the difference being greater in Germany than in England.

Comparison between periods. Table III. 6 (pages 70 and 71) shows comparable figures for three periods: (i) before 1895, the turning-point of the " long cycle ", (ii) between 1895 and the war, and (iii) after the war. If structural changes have occurred in the relation investigated, they must be reflected in changed coefficients. If, *e.g.*, it be true that investment activity at present reacts more violently to profit changes than it did before the war, this would be translated into a larger regression coefficient for profits. Unfortunately, it is almost impossible to obtain comparable figures for the pre-war and the post-war periods.

Table III. 4.

Note.— All series are in % deviations from trend, *except* series (9) and (10), indicated in brackets after each coefficient; when the lag has been determined

Country	Period	Series explained	Correlation coefficient R
(1)	(2)	(3)	(4)
United States	1919-1933	Production of pig-iron	0.94
,,	,,	Investment activity *a*	0.98
United Kingdom	1871-1910	Consumption of pig-iron	0.75
,,	1920-1936	,, ,, ,,	0.90
Germany	1871-1912	,, ,, ,,	0.87
United States	1895-1913	Production of pig-iron	0.77
Germany	1871-1912	Consumption of pig-iron	0.79
France	1871-1908	,, ,, ,,	0.81
United States	1895-1913	Production of pig-iron	0.76
Germany	1871-1912	Consumption of pig-iron	0.83

a Flow of producers' and consumers' durable commodities, building excluded.

Activity, Second Stage.

Comparison of Countries.

which are in absolute deviations from trend in units of 0.01%. The lag in years is
" freely ", the coefficient is in italics.

| Regression coefficients and lags of: | | | | | |
profits	non-labour income	share prices	price of pig-iron	short-term interest rate	long-term interest rate
(5)	(6)	(7)	(8)	(9)	(10)
† 0.29 (½)			— 0.03 (½)		† — 0.32 (½)
† 0.28 (½)			— 0.36 (½)		† — 0.05 (½)
	3.24 (0.8)		— 0.31 (½)		— 0.26 (½)
1.17 (1)			— 0.24 (½)		— 0.08 (½)
0.53 (0.9)			— 0.23 (½)		— 0.08 (½)
		0.85 (½)	— 0.51 (½)		— 0.27 (½)
		0.72 (½)	— 0.13 (½)		0.21 (½)
		0.94 (0.9)	0.10 (½)		— 0.08 (½)
		1.05 (0.4)	— 0.54 (½)	0.02 (½)	
		0.61 (0.3)	— 0.17 (½)	0.06 (½)	

† Intercorrelation between 0.75 and 0.80.

Table III. 5. Comparison of

Note. — See note to Table III. 4.

Country	Period	Series explained	Correlation coefficient R
(1)	(2)	(3)	(4)
United Kingdom	1871-1910	Production of pig-iron	0.79
,,	,,	Consumption ,, ,,	0.75
Germany	1871-1912	Production ,, ,,	0.75
,,	,,	Consumption ,, ,,	0.88
France	1871-1908	Production ,, ,,	0.69
,,	,,	Consumption ,, ,,	0.81

Table III. 6. Comparison

Note. — See note to Table III. 4.

Country	Period	Series explained	Correlation coefficient R
(1)	(2)	(3)	(4)
United States	1877-1895	Production of pig-iron	0.75
,, ,,	1895-1913	,, ,, ,,	0.68
,, ,,	1919-1924	,, ,, ,,	0.83
,, ,,	1919-1933	,, ,, ,,	0.61
United Kingdom	1871-1895	Consumption of pig-iron	0.77
,, ,	1896-1910	,, ,, ,,	0.68
,, ,,	1920-1936	,, ,, ,,	0.90
Germany	1871-1895	Consumption of pig-iron	0.90
,,	1895-1912	,, ,, ,,	0.88

† Intercorrelation between 0.75 and 0.80.
a Because of the lack of correlation. the calculation of a lag has no point in this case.

ACTIVITY, SECOND STAGE.

Pig-iron Production and Consumption.

		Regression coefficients and lags of:			
profits	non-labour income	share prices	price of pig-iron	short-term interest rate	long-term interest rate
(5)	(6)	(7)	(8)	(9)	(10)
	1.96 (0.1)		— 0.17 (½)		— 0.39 (½)
	3.24 (0.8)		— 0.31 (½)		— 0.26 (½)
0.23 (½)			0.08 (½)	— 0.01 (½)	
0.53 (0.8)			— 0.26 (½)	0.02 (½)	
		0.49 (0.1)	0.17 (½)		— 0.03 (½)
		0.94 (0.9)	0.10 (½)		— 0.08 (½)

of Various Periods.

		Regression coefficients and lag of:			
profits	non-labour income	share prices	price of pig-iron	short-term interest rate	long-term interest rate
(5)	(6)	(7)	(8)	(9)	(10)
		0.94 (0.2)			
		0.74 (0.2)			
		2.71 (0.3)			
		0.18 a			
	3.29 (0.8)		— 0.33 (½)		— 0.56 (½)
	† 1.43(lead 0.1)		† — 0.11 (½)		— 0.07 (½)
1.17 (1)			— 0.24 (½)		— 0.08 (½)
† 0.31 (½)			† 0.10 (½)	0.02 (½)	
0.90 (½)			0.13 (½)	— 0.03 (½)	

Profit figures for the United Kingdom and for the United States as used in post-war calculations are not available for pre-war years. Share prices, which in pre-war United States could probably be used as an indicator of profits, are no longer representative of profits in the entire post-war period, as they are quite out of line at the top of the 1929 boom. As a consequence, (i) the correlation obtained with share prices is no longer good and (ii) the regression coefficient obtained for the period 1919-1933 is quite different from that obtained for the period 1919-1924. The intensity with which investment activity reacts to share prices would seem to have decreased as compared with pre-war times according to the figure for the whole period, whereas it would seem to have increased very much according to the 1919-1924 figures. For the United Kingdom a post-war estimate for "non-labour income" by C. Clark,[1] which is about comparable to pre-war figures, leads to a regression coefficient considerably lower (1.36). There is therefore some evidence of a more intensive reaction after the war in the United States and a less intensive in the United Kingdom.

Comparison of the figures for the two pre-war periods shows that the coefficient for profits after 1895 is, in Germany, considerably higher than in the period before 1895, slightly lower in the United States and considerably lower in the United Kingdom. The American coefficients for the two sub-periods, as well as the 1871-1895 English coefficient, are in line with those for the entire pre-war period; the 1896-1910 English is quite out of line and, moreover, a lead instead of a lag has been found here between profits and investment. This lead may, however, be interpreted as an influence of the rate of increase in profits. In addition, the British business-cycle pattern was rather weak, partly perhaps because the Boer war counteracted the 1901 depression;[2] with less pronounced fluctuations, disturbing elements become more important and the results less reliable. Anyhow, the result for the period 1896-1910 is not satisfactory.

---

[1] *National Income and Outlay*, London, 1937, page 60.

[2] *Cf.* Graph III. 4. It shows that pig-iron consumption fell only by about 10% from 1899 to 1901, whereas it fell by some 20 to 30% in the crises preceding 1901 and by 40% in Germany, *cf.* Graph III. 5, in 1901. The employment figures also showed the smallest fall ever seen in a crisis.

Extra-polation for the United States, 1934-37.

It has already been mentioned that one of the calculations for the United States has been extra-polated in order to cover the years 1934-37. In other words, the regression coefficients for the period 1919-33 have been applied to subsequent years (*cf.* Graph III. 8).

Graph III. 8.

" EXPLANATION " OF PIG-IRON PRODUCTION.
UNITED STATES, 1919-1937.

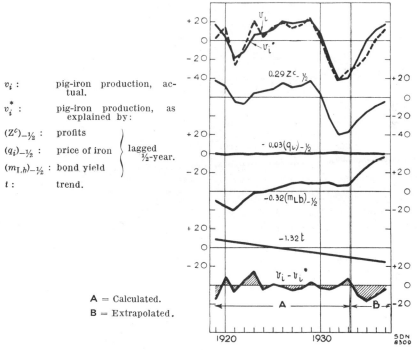

v_i : pig-iron production, actual.

v_i^* : pig-iron production, as explained by:

$(Z^c)_{-1/2}$: profits

$(q_i)_{-1/2}$: price of iron $\Big\}$ lagged ½-year.

$(m_{L,b})_{-1/2}$: bond yield

t : trend.

A = Calculated.
B = Extrapolated.

As Kuznets' estimates of investment activity are not available after 1933,[1] it was only possible to extrapolate the calculation for pig-iron production. One of the determining factors in the calculation being total profits, these had to be estimated for 1936 and 1937.

---

[1] It has not been possible to make use of the figures that have recently been published by KUZNETS in *National Income and Capital Formation in the United States, 1919-1935.*

"EXPLANATION" OF INVESTMENT

Table III. 7. Comparison of

Note. — See note to Table III. 4. — Series (11) is in absolute deviations from

Country	Period		Series explained	Correlation coefficient
(1)	(2)		(3)	(4)
United States	1877-	Upward	Production of pig-iron	0.86
	1913	Downward	,, ,, ,,	0.78
United Kingdom	1871-	Upward	Consumption of pig-iron	0.79
	1910	Upward	,, ,, ,,	0.78
		Downward	,, ,, ,,	0.59
Germany	1871-	Upward	Consumption of pig-iron	0.90
	1912	Downward	,, ,, ,,	0.89
France	1871-	Upward	Consumption of pig-iron	0.85
	1908	Downward	,, ,, ,,	0.79

† Intercorrelation between 0.75 and 0.80.   * Multiple correlation over 0.80.

Table III. 8. Comparison of

Country	Period		Series explained	Correlation coefficient
(1)	(2)		(3)	(4)
United States	1877-	Upward	Production of pig-iron	0.78
	1913	Downward	,, ,, ,,	0.60
United Kingdom	1871-	Upward	Consumption of pig-iron	0.68
	1910	Downward	,, ,, ,,	0.53
Germany	1871-	Upward	Consumption of pig-iron	0.84
	1912	Downward	,, ,, ,,	0.84
,,	1871-	Upward	,, ,, ,,	0.72
	1912	Downward	,, ,, ,,	0.85
France	1871-	Upward	Consumption of pig-iron	0.81
	1908	Downward	,, ,, ,,	0.75

Activity, Second Stage.

Upward and Downward Phases I.

trend, in units of 0.01%; series (12) is in % deviations from trend.

	Regression coefficients and lags of:					
profits *a*	share prices	price of pig-iron	short-term interest rate	long-term interest rate	share yield	building volume
(5)	(7)	(8)	(9)	(10)	(11)	(12)
	* 0.26 (0.3)	* 0.42	—0.03 (½)			*0.27 (0)
	0.69 (0.9)	0.23	0.01 (½)			0.55 (0)
2.46 (0.8)		0.16 (½)		—0.27 (½)		
2.79 (0.8)				—0.29 (½)		
1.38 (0.8)				—0.31 (½)		
	0.36 (½)		0.04 (½)		0.13 (½)	
	† 0.54 (½)		0.04 (½)		†— 0.03 (½)	
	0.88 (1.3)	0.27 (½)		—0.29 (½)		
	† 3.15 (0.7)	—0.36†(½)		0.25 (½)		

a United Kingdom: non-labour income.

Upward and Downward Phases II.

	Regression coefficients and lags of:	
profits	non-labour income	share prices
(5)	(6)	(7)
		0.73 (0.2)
		0.58 (1.2)
	2.24 (1.5)	
	1.41 (0.7)	
0.46 (½)		
0.41 (½)		
		0.57 (½)
		0.58 (½)
		1.92 (0.8)
		2.24 (0.7)

The estimate was based on two very high correlations found for the period 1919-1933, which held also for 1934 and 1935. The first " explains " profits by (1) total receipts of all corporations during the same year and (2) total receipts during the preceding year. The inclusion of lagged receipts is justified by the fact that " total deductions " (*i.e.*, the amounts to be deducted from total receipts in order to obtain profits of all corporations) are very closely correlated with receipts lagged over a few months, since they represent an " adaptation of costs to receipts " which takes some time. The second correlation is between " total receipts of all corporations " and

(1) Index of industrial production (Federal Reserve Board), multiplied by index of wholesale prices (Bureau of Labor Statistics); and

(2) Department-stores sales.

This latter correlation served to estimate total receipts for 1936 and 1937, which in turn determined the estimate of profits for 1936 and 1937. The result of the extrapolation is shown in Graph III. 8. The general direction of actual and calculated production of pig-iron is the same, but there seems to be a more or less systematic difference in level which might reflect the result of the changed structure.

Comparison between phases. Tables III. 7 and III. 8 (pages 74 and 75) give comparable results for two sets of years; those showing a lower, and those showing a higher, investment figure (measured in deviations from trend) than the preceding year. The former set of years is called " downward phases ", the latter " upward phases " of the cycle. As the calculations for upward and downward phases are chiefly intended to be an illustration of the degree of uncertainty in the general results, it did not seem worth while to construct bunch maps, etc. As in Tables III. 4 to III. 6, only cases in which the correlation coefficients between the " explanatory " series do not exceed 0.80 have been included, in order to exclude—although admittedly only in a very rough way—cases of multicollinearity. Some of the cases given in Table III. 7 are probably still unreliable, however, in that respect, and Table III. 8 has therefore been added; in this table, only the chief variate—profits—or a representative series is employed, and multicollinearity is therefore impossible.

No systematic differences can be discovered. The regression coefficients of profits in Table III. 7, although rather divergent, do not differ from those for the whole period by more than three times the standard errors of the latter (*cf.* Table III. 10) in the case of the United Kingdom and Germany. For the United States and France, the results of either the upward or the downward phases are very uncertain because of a high intercorrelation between some of the explanatory variates. In Table III. 7, downward phases show a lower coefficient for the United Kingdom and a higher for Germany and the United States. These differences disappear, however, almost entirely in Table III. 8, except for the United Kingdom. The coefficients of the secondary factors sometimes show larger relative differences, but even these are not significant, as the coefficients are rather uncertain (*cf.* standard errors, Table III. 10), the only possible exception being the influence of building in the United States. It is therefore difficult to obtain evidence regarding the necessity of explaining downward phases by other relations than upward phases.

Inclusion of more variates. Table III. 9 (pages 78 and 79) gives, for a few cases, the successive results obtained if more and more variates are included in the explanation. It is chiefly intended to show the great importance of profits as against the other variates in the " explanation ", and the relatively small improvements in correlation and the small change in regression consequent upon their inclusion. Nevertheless, these improvements will prove to be significant.

Partial scatter diagrams. Graphs III. 9 to III. 11 represent partial scatter diagrams (*cf.* Chapter II, § 5) for three cases. As has already been observed, they enable us to test whether the hypothesis of rectilinear relationship is fulfilled or not. It may be seen from the graphs that there is no wide departure from rectilinearity, but that nevertheless a tendency to curvilinearity is present in a number of cases. The graphs containing the price of iron as the independent variate represent the demand curve for iron. (This is not quite correct in the case of the United States as the investment index includes other investment goods, but, owing to the rather large parallelism between the production of the various kinds of investment goods, the error cannot be important.)

"Explanation" of Investment

Table III. 9. Influence of

Note. — See note to Table III. 4 and III. 7. Δ stands for "rate of increase in".

Country	Period	Series explained	Correlation coefficient R
(1)	(2)	(3)	(4)
United States	1919-33	Investment activity *b*	0.97
,, ,,	,,	,, ,,	0.98
,, ,,	,,	,, ,,	0.99
United Kingdom	1871-1910	Consumption of pig-iron	0.59
,, ,,	,,	,, ,, ,,	0.65
,, ,,	,,	,, ,, ,,	0.75
Germany	1871-1912	Consumption of pig-iron	0.79
,,	,,	,, ,, ,,	0.79
,,	,,	,, ,, ,,	0.83
,,	,,	,, ,, ,,	0.85

a For United Kingdom, non-labour income.
b Flow of producers' and consumers' durable commodities, building excluded.

Table III. 10. Results of Significance Calculations: Serial

Case	Correlation coefficient	Serial correlation of residuals	Regression coefficients, with		
			Profits	Δ profits	Non-labour income
(1)	(2)	(3)	(4)	(5)	(6)
I	0.99	—0.46 ± 0.27	0.24 ± 0.02 (½)		
II	0.77	0.01 ± 0.20			3.29 ± 0.84 (1)
III	0.75	0.16 ± 0.16			3.24 ± 0.58 (1)
IV	0.90	0.00 ± 0.25	1.17 ± 0.17 (1)		
V	0.87	0.43 ± 0.16	0.53 ± 0.09 (½)	—0.20 ± 0.11 (½)	

I United States, Investment activity *a*. 1919-1933.
II } United Kingdom. ⎰ 1871-1895.
III } Consumption of pig-iron. ⎱ 1871-1910.
IV ⎰ 1920-1936.
V Germany. Consumption of pig-iron, 1871-1912.

a Flow of producers' and consumers' durable commodities, building excluded.

ACTIVITY, SECOND STAGE.

Number of Variates included.

Series (13) is expressed in % of average level of price of pig-iron during period.

		Regression coefficients and lags of:				
profits a	share prices	price of pig-iron	short-term interest rate	long-term interest rate	share yield	Δ price of pig-iron
(5)	(7)	(8)	(9)	(10)	(11)	(13)
0.31 (½)						
0.28 (½)					— 0.04 (½)	
0.24 (½)		— 0.25 (½)	— 0.05 (½)		— 0.08 (½)	
1.82 (0.6)						
1.90 (0.8)				— 0.33 (½)		
3.24 (0.8)		— 0.31 (½)		— 0.26 (½)		
	0.59 (½)					
	0.59 (½)	0.00 (½)				
	0.61 (0.3)	— 0.17 (½)	0.06 (½)			
	0.56 (0.9)	— 0.15 (½)	0.03 (½)			0.35 (½)

Correlation of Residuals and Standard Errors of Regression Coefficients.

		their standard errors, and lags of:		
Δ Non-labour income	Price of pig-iron	Short-term interest rate	Long-term interest rate	Share yield
(7)	(8)	(9)	(10)	(11)
	—0.25 ±0.12(½)	—0.05 ±0.02(½)		—0.08 ±0.02(½)
0.54 ±0.54 (1)	—0.33 ±0.13(½)		—0.56 ±0.49(½)	
0.66 ±0.42 (1)	—0.31 ±0.10(½)		—0.26 ±0.14(½)	
	—0.24 ±0.14(½)		—0.08 ±0.10(½)	
	—0.23 ±0.17(½)		—0.08 ±0.14(½)	

B. *Significance calculations.*

Table III. 10 (pages 78 and 79) gives details regarding the significance calculations made. These have been restricted to five cases which seem representative and call for the following comments.

Serial correlation for residuals. First, the serial correlation for the series of the residuals has been calculated; *i.e.*, the correlation of that series with itself if lagged one year. This calculation serves to test the hypothesis at the basis of Fisher's theory—viz., that the residuals are to be considered as sample drawings from a " normally distributed universe ". At the same time, it gives information as to whether the regression chosen satisfies the scheme of the shock theory (*cf.* § 7). In order to see whether the serial correlation differs from zero to any significant extent, the serial correlation coefficient has to be compared with its standard error, which equals $\dfrac{1}{\sqrt{N-1}}$.[1]
It then appears that the greatest deviation from zero is found for Germany before the war, where the result is, however, still within a distance of three times the standard error.

Standard errors. The standard errors, calculated with Fisher's formula (*cf.* Appendix A, § 4) are such that all the regression coefficients for profits or the series replacing them are with a very high probability significantly positive: in all five cases, the regression coefficients are more than three times their standard error.

Only five out of ten coefficients tested for iron prices and interest rates are rigorously significant, *i.e.*, with a probability of over 95 %. This fact is illustrated by Graph III. 12, where for each case the ranges within once the standard error on either side of the regression coefficient (*i.e.*, $b \pm \sigma_b$) have been indicated in black, those within twice the standard error (*i.e.*, $b \pm 2\sigma_b$) by shading. It will be seen that five of the latter areas go beyond the zero point. Nevertheless, there is more probability of the regressions, being negative. Moreover, it is satisfactory to the statistician that the range of error is generally smaller for post-war than for pre-war figures.

---

[1] *Cf.* M. S. BARTLETT: " Some Aspects of the Time Correlation Problem ", *Journal of the Royal Statistical Society*, 1935 (98), page 537, quoted in T. KOOPMANS, *loc. cit.*, page 129.

Graph III. 9.
Partial scatter diagrams.
INVESTMENT ACTIVITY: UNITED STATES, 1919-1933.

	Ordinates		*Abscissæ*
I	Investment activity (flow of durable producers' goods to enterprises, plus	I	Profits $_{-1/2}$
II	flow of durable consumers' goods to	II	Price of pig-iron $_{-1/2}$
III	enterprises and households) corrected for influence of other " explanatory	III	Share yield $_{-1/2}$
IV	variates", *i.e., ceteris paribus.*	IV	Short-term interest rate $_{-1/2}$

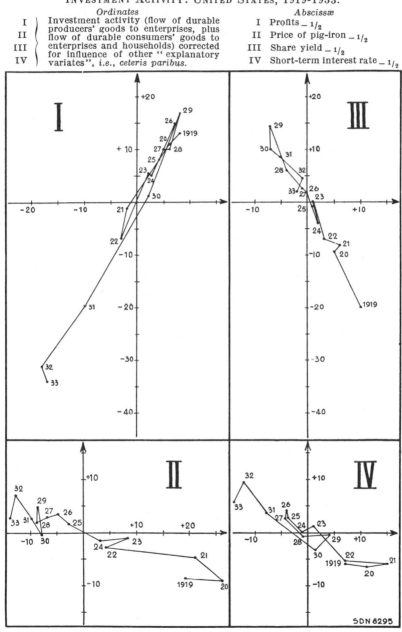

SDN 8295

6

Graph III. 10.

Partial scatter diagrams.

PRODUCTION OF PIG-IRON: UNITED KINGDOM, 1920-1936.

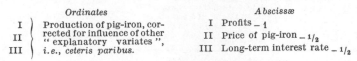

	Ordinates		*Abscissæ*
I	Production of pig-iron, cor-	I	Profits $_{-1}$
II	rected for influence of other "explanatory variates",	II	Price of pig-iron $_{-1/2}$
III	*i.e., ceteris paribus.*	III	Long-term interest rate $_{-1/2}$

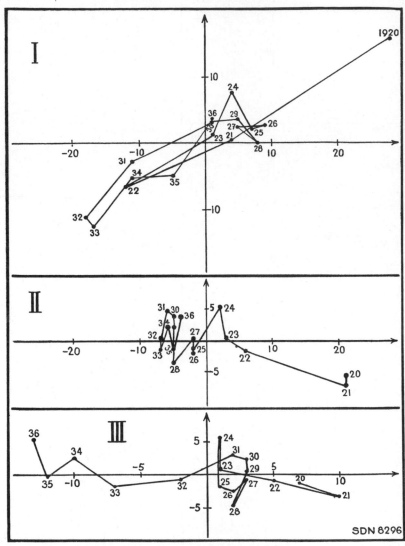

SDN 8296

Graph III. 11.

Partial scatter diagrams.

CONSUMPTION OF IRON AND STEEL: UNITED KINGDOM, 1871-1910.

	Ordinates		*Abscissæ*
I	Consumption of pig-iron,	I	Non-labour income $_{-1}$
II	corrected for influence of	II	Δ non-labour income $_{-1}$
III	other "explanatory vari-	III	Price of pig-iron $_{-1/2}$
IV	ates", *i.e., ceteris paribus.*	IV	Long-term interest rate $_{-1/2}$

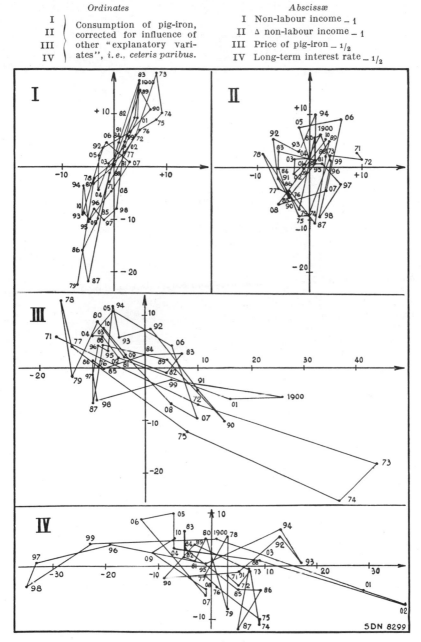

SDN 8299

Graph. III. 12.

REGRESSION COEFFICIENTS AND RANGES OF INCERTITUDE.

Regression Coefficients of Iron Price.

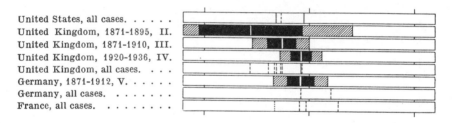

United States, 1919-1933, I. . . .
United States, all cases. . . . . .
United Kingdom, 1871-1895, II.
United Kingdom, 1871-1910, III.
United Kingdom, 1920-1936, IV.
United Kingdom, all cases. . . .
Germany, 1871-1912, V. . . . .
Germany, all cases. . . . . . .
France, all cases. . . . .

Regression Coefficients of Interest Rate.
A. Long-term, in 0.01 %.

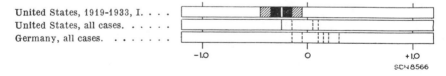

United States, all cases. . . . . .
United Kingdom, 1871-1895, II.
United Kingdom, 1871-1910, III.
United Kingdom, 1920-1936, IV.
United Kingdom, all cases. . . .
Germany, 1871-1912, V. . . . . .
Germany, all cases. . . . . . .
France, all cases. . . . .

Regression Coefficients of Interest Rate.
B. Short-term, in 0.05 %.

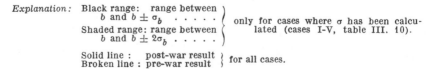

United States, 1919-1933, I. . . .
United States, all cases. . . . . .
Germany, all cases. . . . . . .

SCN 8566

Explanation: Black range: range between ⎫
b and $b \pm \sigma_b$ . . . . . ⎬ only for cases where σ has been calcu-
Shaded range: range between ⎬ lated (cases I-V, table III. 10).
b and $b \pm 2\sigma_b$ . . . . . ⎭

Solid line : post-war result ⎱ for all cases.
Broken line : pre-war result ⎰

Graph III. 13.

Bunch map.

INVESTMENT ACTIVITY: UNITED STATES 1919-1933

1 = Investment activity (flow of durable producers' goods to enterprises, plus flow of
durable consumers' goods to enterprises and households).

2 = Profits$_{-1/2}$.   3 = Price of iron$_{-1/2}$.   4 = Short-term interest rate$_{-1/2}$.

5 = Share yield$_{-1/2}$.

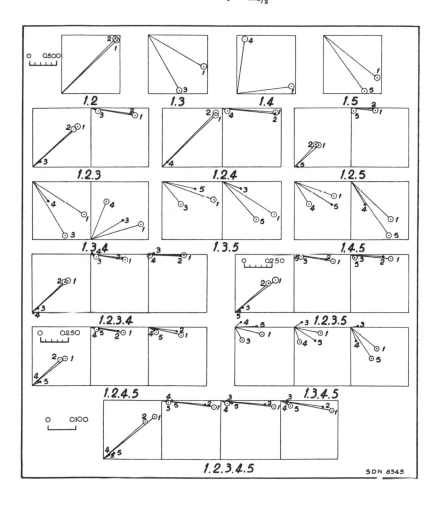

Bunch
maps.

In Graphs III. 13 to III. 16 a number of bunch maps are reproduced.

Graph III. 13 (page 85), relating to one of the United States post-war calculations, is very satisfactory, and even more so if—following Koopmans' argument—only the beams with numbers 1 and 2 are considered. In fact, in the 5-set (the case including all five variates) they coincide almost entirely, indicating a high degree of determinateness of all regression coefficients found. These findings are in close agreement with the findings on standard errors.

Graph III. 14, relating to the post-war calculation for the United Kingdom, is also very satisfactory, and the above observations apply. This case is particularly suitable for illustrating Koopmans' result regarding the minor importance of beams corresponding to variates which exercise only a secondary influence. Table III. 11 shows the coefficients of the four elementary regression equations, together with the probable limits to the true regression coefficients that take into account both the error of weighting

Graph III. 14.
Bunch map.

CONSUMPTION OF IRON AND STEEL: UNITED KINGDOM, 1920-1936.

1 = Consumption of iron and steel. 2 = Profits$_{-1}$. 3 = Price of iron$_{-\frac{1}{2}}$
4 = Long-term interest rate$_{-\frac{1}{2}}$.

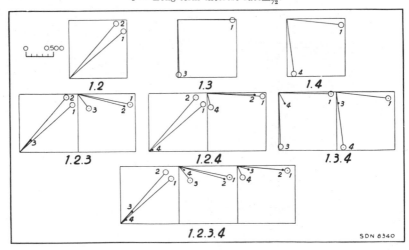

SDN 6340

and the error of sampling in these coefficients. For the calculation of these limits, see Appendix A. 5. The assumption underlying the calculation of the limits to the error of weighting is that the standard deviation of the disturbances in each of the three explaining variates is not greater than a third of the standard deviation of the corresponding variate itself. Allowance for sampling errors of regression coefficients has been made by extending the limits to both sides by twice the standard error of sampling.

Table III. 11.   Probable Limits to the True Regression Coefficients. Consumption of Iron and Steel: United Kingdom, 1920-1936. [a]

Explaining variate		2 Profits$_{-1}$	3 Price of iron$_{-\frac{1}{2}}$	4 Long-term interest rate$_{-\frac{1}{2}}$
1st	elementary regression coefficient	1.17	—.24	—.07
2nd		1.49	—.29	—.07
3rd		1.44	—1.31	—.21
4th		.11	—.07	—1.74
Limits to the error of weighting given by ultimate beams in bunch map	upper	1.49	—.07	—.07
	lower	.11	—1.31	—1.74
Maximum fraction of standard deviation admitted for disturbances		1/3	1/3	1/3
Narrower limits to the error of weighting:				
According to the rule of thumb	upper	1.34	—.07	—.07
	lower	.99	—.28	—.09
According to the strict rule	upper	1.28	—.24	—.07
	lower	1.17	—.28	—.09
Final limits including allowance for sampling errors	upper	1.62	.04	.12
	lower	.84	—.56	—.28

[a] For units, cf. Table III. 4.

Graph III. 15 concerns one of the calculations for the United Kingdom before the war.   It is certainly less good than the post-war cases: the beams spread much more widely.   Nevertheless the result indicates the significance of all coefficients found.   Here, it is interesting to see how the direction of the relation between variates 1 and 4 (consumption and price of iron) is changed by the inclusion of the other variates; even if only 2 is added (*cf.* set 124). The significance of variate 3 might be doubted, but if only the beams 1 and 2 are considered, the regression coefficient for 3 is again very well determined.

Graph III. 15.
Bunch map.

CONSUMPTION OF IRON AND STEEL: UNITED KINGDOM, 1871-1910.

1 = Consumption of iron and steel.   2 = Non-labour income$_{-1}$.
3 = Δ non-labour income$_{-1/2}$.   4 = Price of iron$_{-1}$.   5 = Bond yield$_{-1/2}$.

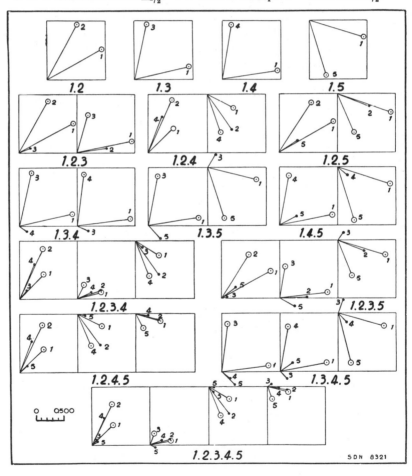

SDN 8321

Graph III. 16, concerning one of the German (pre-war) calculations, is very similar to Graph III. 15. The spread of the beams is about the same; the relation between variates 1 and 4 is also reversed by the introduction of other variates and the regression coefficients of variates 3 and 5 are well determined if only beams 1 and 2 are considered. But the bunch map for Germany is less satisfactory in that the relation between variate 1 and variate 2 (profits) is not improved by the addition of any or all of the secondary variates.

Graph III. 16. Bunch map.

CONSUMPTION OF IRON AND STEEL: GERMANY, 1871-1912.

1 = Consumption of iron and steel. 2 = Dividends$_{-1/2}$. 3 = Δ dividends$_{-1/2}$.
4 = Price of iron$_{-1/2}$. 5 = Long-term interest rate$_{-1/2}$.

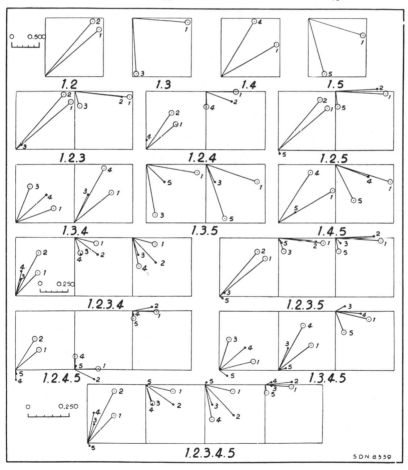

5DN 8339

CHAPTER IV

RESIDENTIAL BUILDING

—

§ 12. THE RELATION TESTED

Only private building studied. The example to be considered next relates to a special type of investment activity—namely, the construction of dwelling-houses. So far as possible, the investigation has been confined to private activity in this field, as building by public authorities and societies may be governed by different considerations.[1]

Two groups of " explanatory " variates. The " explanatory factors " included may be separated into two groups. The first group consists of some factors which roughly determine the profitability of owning houses. In a perfect market, this would be the most natural incentive to build. The second group forms, in a sense, a corrective to the first group, necessary because of the imperfection of the market.

First group of variates. The profitability of owning houses depends chiefly on:
(*a*) The rent level;
(*b*) The cost of maintenance;
(*c*) Interest payments and
(*d*) Amortisation.

The amounts of interest payments and amortisation will first of all depend on the level of building costs; amortisation may be

---

[1] In pre-war time, building of dwellings by public authorities was non-existent or insignificant. For the post-war period, no detailed figures are available for the United States, but State intervention started only in 1933 and was rather indirect. For Sweden, the data for 296 cities cover all residential building, but those for Stockholm relate to private building only.

said to be a fixed percentage of the latter—which will be not far from 1 %,[1] whereas interest will be the product of three factors, viz.:

(1) building costs;
(2) the percentage of building costs which on the average will be covered by mortgages; and
(3) the interest rate for mortgages.

It is rather difficult to get exact series on the cost of maintenance, but in general it will move about parallel to building cost, as it includes many elements also included in the latter. Its level may be roughly estimated to be about 1% of building cost per annum.

Series included.

It follows from the above that the following series should, first of all, be included in the " explanation ":

(1) The rent level;
(2) The cost of construction; and
(3) The rate of interest on mortgages.

Their relative " influence " may be deduced from the regression coefficients which will be calculated.

A priori determination of relative influence.

It may, however, also be determined by *a priori* considerations, based upon the structure of the profit account for holding houses.

Indicating the construction costs of a certain house by 100, this account will approximately show items of the following order of magnitude:

Receipts: rent 8
Deductions: amortisation and
maintenance 2
interest on mortgage . . . $0.7\overline{\overline{m}}_{Lb}$, where $\overline{\overline{m}}_{Lb}$ represents the interest rate.

If rents are measured by an index $\overline{\overline{m}}_R$, with average $\overline{m}_R = 100$, construction costs by an index $\overline{\overline{q}}_B$ with average $\overline{q}_B = 100$, and

---

[1] This figure may be somewhat too low in some cases; what matters, however, for the calculations is the total of amortisation and maintenance, which has been taken at 2% (see below).

interest rates $\overline{\overline{m}}_{Lb}$ in natural units (per cents), then profits, in per cents, from the holding of houses will be represented by

$$0.08\overline{\overline{m}}_R - 0.02\overline{\overline{q}}_B - 0.007\overline{\overline{q}}_B\overline{\overline{m}}_{Lb} = \overline{\overline{z}}$$

This expression may be also written as

$$0.08\,(\overline{m}_R + m_R) - 0.02\,(\overline{q}_B + q_B) - 0.007\,(\overline{q}_B + q_B)\,(\overline{m}_{Lb} + m_{Lb})$$

where the unbarred minuscules indicate deviations from average or from trend. These deviations will, in general, be small in comparison with the average values, and therefore their mutual products may be neglected. We then get:

$$\overline{\overline{z}} = (6 - 0.7\overline{m}_{Lb}) + 0.08m_R - (0.02 + 0.007\overline{m}_{Lb})q_B - 0.7m_{Lb}.$$

The first term in brackets is a constant, the average value of the expression: $\overline{z} = 6 - 0.7\overline{m}_{Lb}$. The deviations may as usually be indicated by z:

$$z = 0.08m_R - (0.02 + 0.007\overline{m}_{Lb})\,q_B - 0.7m_{Lb}.$$

The value of $\overline{m}_{Lb}$ will change from case to case, but usually it is of the order of magnitude of 5, which leads to

$$z = 0.08m_R - 0.055q_B - 0.7m_{Lb}.$$

Two sorts of calculation. Two sorts of calculation have been made; calculations using m_R, q_B and m_{Lb} as separate variates (Table IV. 1), and calculations using z in their place (Table IV. 2).

Second group of variates. Apart from these variates, a second group has been included. Their inclusion is due to the imperfection of some of the markets which play a rôle in our problem.

The variates of the second group are:

(4) The number of unoccupied houses (h') or the total number of houses present (h);

(5) Some income series (E).

Imperfection of market for housing services. The reason for including the number of unoccupied houses is that it may directly discourage building, even if rents, building costs and interest rates are in a favourable relation to each other. In a perfect market for housing services, such a situation would not occur: rents would fall. The stickiness of rents, closely connected with the long duration of letting contracts and further imperfections in this market, prevents such a rapid adaptation and, consequently, the number of unoccupied houses is a largely independent factor which also influences building activity.

In one of the cases where no series for empty houses was available, the total number of houses could be included, after elimination of its trend. The trend elimination, together with the inclusion of an income series, forms a rough correction for the need for dwellings in that case.[1]

Income series are also included with another intention: they represent a demand factor, in so far as a number of houses are not built for letting at all, but by their future occupants. In the United States, about 50% of all inhabitants live in owned houses; it was estimated that about 75% of the new dwellings built during the last building boom in England were not for letting. Again this may be called an imperfection of the market for housing services.

Imperfection of credit markets. In some investigations by other authors, explanatory series have been included which are connected immediately with the imperfection of credit markets. An extreme case is the one treated by Professor C. F. Roos,[2] concerning St. Louis, where, for the period studied, mortgage rates had not moved at all. Professor Roos includes instead the " foreclosure rate ", giving the number

---

[1] The number of family units is often used as an indication of the " need " for dwellings. As long, however, as family incomes are not taken into account, the number of family units reflects potential rather than actual demand; although the distribution of income over the various items of the budget is of course influenced by the number of families. For long-term investigations, it may be a useful guide; for an analysis of fluctuations it seems less important, as the number of family units usually develops smoothly. An exceptional growth of the number of family units is, however, regarded as one of the causes of the " building boom " in the United Kingdom from 1933 to 1936.

[2] *Dynamic Economics*, Bloomington, 1934, pages 69-110.

of foreclosures per 100,000 families. This rate he considers as a good inverse index of the willingness of banks to grant credits. A closer investigation shows that it is highly correlated with the number of unoccupied houses a short time before, which seems quite natural. In a sense, therefore, this factor is already included in our series h', provided we take the right lag.

A number of authors lay stress on the general state of confidence as a factor of importance, because of its close relation to the willingness to grant credits. This factor may be introduced in two different ways. As far as the fairly systematic changes in confidence during the business cycle are concerned, the income series will be a good index; and it has already been included. As far as acute and specific confidence crises occur, the years in which they have presented themselves may perhaps best be excluded. As a test, it may be investigated afterwards whether or not these years show, as compared to " calculated " building activity, an abnormally low level.

Profits of owning houses and of constructing houses. Finally, it may be stated that the selection of the explanatory series, based as it is upon the profitability of owning houses, presupposes that the market for houses so nearly approaches perfection that the builder acts in the same way as the future owner of houses would have done: *i.e.*, it is assumed that his behaviour is not deflected by imperfect foresight with regard to the possibilities of selling the houses which he builds. This assumption cannot easily be avoided, as the statistical material available for prices of houses—and it is prices, not rents, which directly influence the mind of the builder—is very scanty.

Long and short waves. Trend elimination. Several authors have pointed out the existence of a specific building cycle of fifteen to twenty years duration,[1] on which fluctuations of lesser duration would be superimposed. The present investigation has not been directed specially to the study of these long waves. For post-war years, the actual movement of building activity, without any correction for trend or long

---

[1] *Cf.*, *e.g.*, C. F. Roos, *loc. cit.*; J. R. Riggleman, "Building Cycles in the United States 1875-1932", *Journal of the American Statistical Association*, Vol. 28, pages 174-183.

cycle, has been explained. For pre-war, the secular trend has been eliminated, leaving both long and short waves to be studied. In the case of Sweden, however, satisfactory results were only obtained when the long cycle was in turn eliminated, by the use of moving averages of variable length. In this case, therefore, conclusions apply solely to short waves.

§ 13. THE STATISTICAL MATERIAL

The countries and periods studied are:

Countries and periods.

Pre-war: Germany (Hamburg) 1878-1913 (thirty-six years);
Sweden (Stockholm) 1884-1913 (thirty years).

Post-war: United Kingdom 1923-1935 (thirteen years);
United States 1915 or 1919-1935 (twenty-one or seventeen years);
Sweden 1924-1936, 1933 excluded * (twelve years).

In addition, extrapolations for 1936 and 1937 have been made for the United States and the United Kingdom.

Description of series.

The following table indicates the series which have been used to represent: (i) the volume of building and (ii) the explanatory factors mentioned above.

Volume of Building.

Country and period	Description of series	Source
Germany, pre-war	Net increase [a] in total number of " rooms " [b] in Hamburg.	HUNSCHA, *Die Dynamik des Baumarkts, Vierteljahreshefte zur Konjunkturforschung,* Sonderheft 17.
Sweden, pre-war	Total number of newly built rooms or kitchens in Stockholm.	*Statistisk Årsbok för Stockholms Stad.*

---

* The year 1933 has been excluded in all calculations owing to big strikes in the building industry.
[a] Gross increase was only available for a shorter period, and referred to the number of dwellings without regard to their size.
[b] Lokalitäten.

Country and period	Description of series	Source
United Kingdom, post-war	Number of houses built by private enterprise without State assistance.	*Statistical Abstract for the United Kingdom.*
United States, post-war	(i) Estimated total value of non-farm residential construction in 1923/25 dollars. [a]	National Bureau of Economic Research, *Bulletin* No. 65, and *Statistical Abstract.*
	(ii) Contracts awarded, residential building, floor space of building.	*Statistical Abstract* (data from Dodge Co.).
Sweden, post-war	(i) Gross increase in number of rooms or kitchens in 296 cities.	*Sveriges Statistisk Årsbok.*
	(ii) Number of dwellings built in Stockholm by private enterprise.	*Stockholm Stadskollegiets utlåtanden och memorial.* Bihang No. 10 A, 1935.

Rent.

Germany, pre-war	Average annual rent of occupied houses in Hamburg.	HUNSCHA: see under *Vol. of building.*
Sweden, pre-war	Average rent per room of houses to let in Stockholm.	MYRDAL, *The Cost of Living in Sweden.*
United Kingdom, post-war	Rent index of the Ministry of Labour cost-of-living index. [b]	*Abstract of Labour Statistics.*
United States, post-war	Rent index of the Bureau of Labor Statistics cost-of-living index.	*Statistical Abstract.*
Sweden, post-war	Rent index of the cost-of-living index.	*Sveriges Statistisk Årsbok.*

Construction Costs.

Germany, pre-war	Prices of building materials. [c]	JACOBS und RICHTER, *Grosshandelspreise, Vierteljahreshefte zur Konjunkturforschung,* Sonderheft 37.
Sweden, pre-war	Index of building costs.	MYRDAL, *loc. cit.*

[a] *I.e.,* value at current prices deflated by index of construction costs, 1923-1925 = 100.
[b] Up to 1928, the index relates to controlled rents; from 1929 onwards, to controlled and uncontrolled rents combined. No better index is available.
[c] When reckoning the " profitability " of holding houses, allowance was made for wage costs: these were supposed to have been constant throughout the period and to account for 35 % of total construction costs.

Country and period	Description of series	Source
United Kingdom, post-war	Index of building costs.	COLIN CLARK, *Investment in Fixed Capital in Great Britain*, Special Memorandum No. 38, London & Cambridge Economic Service.
United States, post-war	Index of construction costs of *Engineering News Record*.	*Statistical Abstract.*
Sweden, post-war	(i) Index of building costs.[a]	*Svenska Handelsbanken:* " Index".
	(ii) Index of building costs in Stockholm.	*Statistisk Årsbok för Stockholms Stad.*

Interest Rate.

Germany, pre-war	Average rate on mortgage banks' new issues.	HUNSCHA: see under *Volume of building.*
Sweden, pre-war	Savings banks' rate.	LINDAHL, etc.: *The National Income of Sweden.*
United Kingdom, post-war	Yield on 2½ % Consols.	*Statistical Abstract.*
United States, post-war	Yield on 60 bonds.	*Statistical Abstract* (from Standard Statistics).
Sweden, post-war	Savings banks' rate.	*Sveriges Statistisk Årsbok.*

Index of Housing Needs.[b]

Germany, pre-war	% of vacant dwellings in Hamburg.	HUNSCHA: see under *Volume of building.*
Sweden, pre-war	% of vacant dwellings in Stockholm.	*Statistisk Årsbok för Stockholms Stad.*
United States, post-war	Stock of houses,[c] deviations from trend.	*Statistical Abstract.*

Profits or Income.

Germany, pre-war	Dividends in % of capital.	DONNER, *Die Kursbildung am Aktienmarkt, Vierteljahreshefte zur Konjunkturforschung*, Sonderheft 36.
Sweden, pre-war	Total real income.[d]	*Sveriges Statistisk Årsbok.*

---

[a] The figure for 1923 was obtained by combining the index of prices of building materials *(Statistisk Årsbok)* and the index of hourly wages in building (BAGGE: *Wages in Sweden)* with the same weights as in index for subsequent years— *i.e.*, materials 60%, wages 40%.

[b] No data are shown for the United Kingdom. An attempt at computing the stock of houses, in deviations from its trend, led to unreliable results.

[c] Census data, interpolated on the basis of floor space of buildings for which contracts have been awarded.

[d] Total assessed income of following year deflated by cost-of-living index (MYRDAL: *The Cost of Living in Sweden*, 1830-1930).

7

Country and period	Description of series	Source
United Kingdom, post-war	Real income from wages and salaries. [a]	CLARK, *National Income and Outlay*.
United States, post-war	(i) Net income of corpo-rations.	*Statistical Abstract.*
	(ii) Urban non-workers' income.	Estimates based on S. KUZNETS: *National Income*.
	(iii) Capital gains.	Estimates based on WAR-BURTON: *Journal of Political Economy*, Vol. 43.
Sweden, post-war	Total real income. [b]	*Sveriges Statistisk Årsbok.*

[a] Money income deflated by cost-of-living index (Ministry of Labour).
[b] Total assessed income of following year deflated by cost-of-living index.

Lags used.   A uniform lag of one year has been assumed to exist between the series showing completed building and both the explanatory factors of the first group —rent, construction costs, interest rate—and the income series. In the case of the United States, where the series representing building is based either on contracts awarded or building per-mits delivered, the lag zero indicated in brackets after the re-gression coefficients corresponds to a real lag of probably not far from one year between the explanatory factors and the end of the building process.

As regards the total number of houses, or the number of vacancies, the lag was chosen between one-half and three and a-half years, according to the best result yielded.

§ 14.   RESULTS

Chief results.   The explanatory factors mentioned above permit, when rightly combined, of a good explanation of the movement of building activity, more especially after the war.   But for each country, the respective influence of the various factors in the best combination varies greatly, as may be seen from the accompanying graphs.   In the United States, the movement is dominated by the available stock of houses lagged over three and a-half years, while the influence both of the rate of interest and of income is almost negligible.

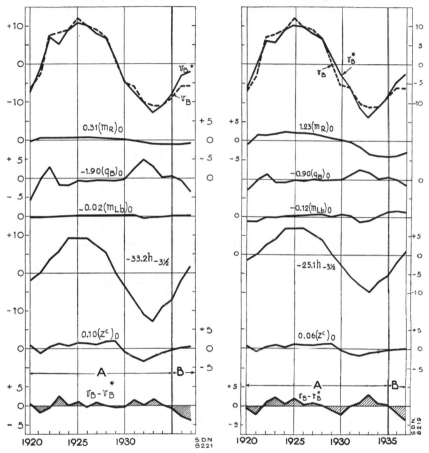

Graph IV. 1.

" EXPLANATION " OF BUILDING.
UNITED STATES 1920-1937.

(Free calculation.)

A = Calculated.
B = Extrapolated.

Graph IV. 2.

" EXPLANATION " OF BUILDING.
UNITED STATES 1920-1937.

(Rent, building costs and interest rate
combined a priori.)

A = Calculated.
B = Extrapolated.

v_B : building activity, actual.

v_B^* : building activity, as explained by :

$(m_R)_0$: rent

$(q_B)_0$: building costs } not lagged (see remark on p. 98);

$(m_{Lb})_0$: bond yield

$h_{-3\frac{1}{2}}$: number of houses (in deviation from trend), lagged 3½ years.

z_0^c : profits, not lagged.

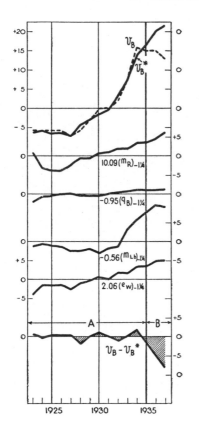

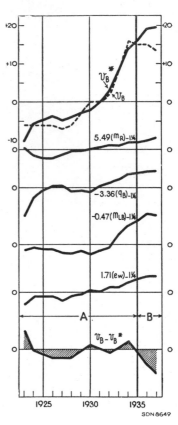

Graph IV. 3.

"EXPLANATION" OF BUILDING.
UNITED KINGDOM 1923-1937.

(Free calculation.)

Graph IV. 4.

"EXPLANATION" OF BUILDING.
UNITED KINGDOM 1923-1937.

(Rent, building costs and interest rate
combined *a priori*.)

A = Calculated.   B = Extrapolated.

SDN 8649

v_B:	building activity, actual.
v_B^*:	building activity, as explained by:
$(m_R)_{-1\frac{1}{4}}$:	rent
$(q_B)_{-1\frac{1}{4}}$:	building costs $\}$ lagged $1\frac{1}{4}$ years;
$(m_{Lb})_{-1\frac{1}{4}}$:	bond yield
$(e_w)_{-1\frac{1}{4}}$:	real labour income. lagged $1\frac{1}{4}$ years.

Graph IV. 5.

"EXPLANATION" OF BUILDING.
SWEDEN 1924-1936.

(Rent, building costs and interest rate combined *a priori*.)

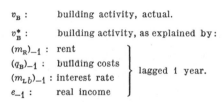

v_B :   building activity, actual.

v_B^* :   building activity, as explained by:

$(m_R)_{-1}$: rent

$(q_B)_{-1}$: building costs

$(m_{Lb})_{-1}$: interest rate

e_{-1} :   real income

} lagged 1 year.

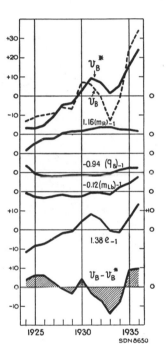

SDN 8650

In the United Kingdom and Sweden, on the other hand, the greatest importance seems to attach to the interest rate and real income.

For before the war, the results are more doubtful and will be discussed in the next section.

Graph IV. 6.

"Explanation" of Building. Germany (Hamburg) 1878-1913.
(Rent, building costs and interest rate combined *a priori*.)

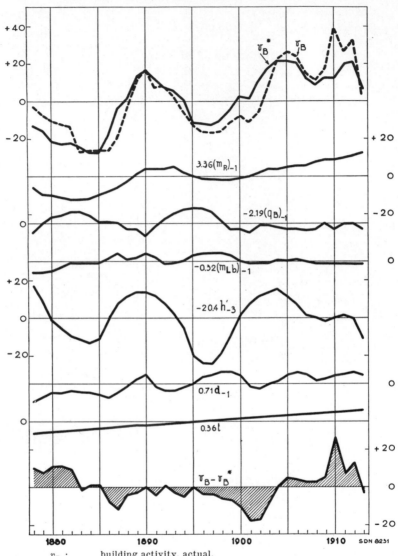

v_B :   building activity, actual.
v_B^* :   building activity, as explained by:
$(m_R)_{-1}$:   rent
$(q_B)_{-1}$:   building costs } lagged 1 year;
$(m_{Lb})_{-1}$:   interest rate
h_{-3} :   number of houses (in deviation from trend), lagged 3 years;
d_{-1} :   dividends in % of capital, lagged 1 year;
t :   trend.

The following graph affords a comparison of all the regression coefficients found in the calculations comprised in the summary Tables IV. 1 and IV. 2. While the range of variation is rather wide, there is for all variates except the number of houses a well-defined mode which coincides with the median in three cases out of four.

Graph. IV. 7.

DISTRIBUTION OF REGRESSION COEFFICIENTS.

(Tables IV. 1 and IV. 2.)

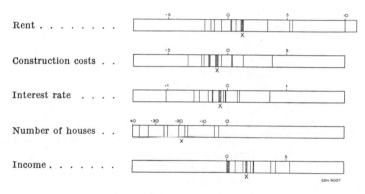

(The × indicates the median.)

The values of the medians are roughly as follows: rent + 1; construction costs — 1; interest rate — 0.1; number of houses —20; income + 1½. Owing to the choice of the units, these figures represent the various elasticities, except in the case of interest rates. In this case, the figure indicates that an increase of 0.01% in the rate of interest will produce a decrease of 0.1% in the volume of building.

Extrapolations. The equations found for the United States and the United Kingdom for the period up to 1935 have been applied to the data (or estimates) for 1936 and 1937.

For the United States, the volume of building thus calculated reflects the actual movement of building as shown by current statistics: both the free and the *a priori* calculations point

Building. Table IV. 1. Explanation

Note. — Unless otherwise stated, the units used are: for pre-war, % deviations from trend; interest rate, the deviations of which are expressed in units of 1% and 0.01% respectively. each series, see table on pages 95 *et seq.*

Country	Period	Series explained	Correlation coefficient R
Germany (Hamburg)	1878-1913	Net increase in number of rooms.	0.92
Sweden (Stockholm)	1884-1913	Number of new rooms built.	0.68
United States	1920-1935	Total volume of non-farm residential construction.	(i) 0.99 (ii) 0.99
United Kingdom	1923-1935	Number of houses built by private enterprise without State assistance.	0.99
Sweden	1924-1936*	Number of houses built in 296 cities.	(i) 0.97 (ii) 0.97
Sweden (Stockholm)	1924-1936*	Number of houses built without State assistance.	0.95

Building. Table IV. 2. Explanation of
and Interest Rate

Note. — See note to Table IV. 1.

Country	Period	Series explained	Correlation coefficient R
Germany	1878-1913	Net increase in number of rooms.	0.87
Sweden	1884-1913	Number of new rooms built.	0.59
United States	(i) 1915-1935 (ii) 1920- (iii) 1935	Floor space of contracts awarded. Volume of non-farm residential construction.	{ 0.96 0.98 0.99
United Kingdom	1923-1935	Number of houses built by private enterprise without State assistance.	0.96
Sweden	1924-1936	Number of dwellings built in 296 cities.	(i) 0.89 (ii) 0.91

a % vacant houses.
b Net income of corporations.
c Total urban non-workers' income plus capital gains.
* 1933 excluded.

of Building: Free Calculations.

for post-war, % deviations from average, except for the "profitability of building" and the
The lag, in years, is indicated in brackets after each coefficient. For a detailed description of

Regression coefficients and lags of:				
Rent	Construction costs	Interest rate	Number of houses	Income or profits earned
5.20 (1)	— 1.54 (1)	0.72 (1)	— 16.5[a] (3)	1.71 (1)
1.14 (1)	— 1.59 (1)	— 1.03 (1)	— 3.7[a] (1½)	3.75 (1)
0.31 (0)	— 1.90 (0)	— 0.02 (0)	— 33.2 (3½)	0.10[b] (0)
0.23 (0)	— 1.56 (0)	— 0.03 (0)	— 37.0 (3½)	0.16[c] (0)
10.09 (1¼)	— 0.95 (1¼)	— 0.56 (1¼)	f	2.06 (1¼)
— 1.16 (1)	0.34 (1)	— 0.24 (1)	f	2.22 (1)
— 1.43 (1)	0.39 (1)	— 0.24 (1)	f	2.25 (1)
— 0.52 (1)	3. 74 (1)	0.21 (1)	f	4.12 (1)

Building: Rent, Construction Costs
combined a priori.

Regression coefficients and lags of:					
Profitability of building				Number of houses	Income or profits earned
Total	Rent	Construction costs	Interest rate		
48.2 (1)	3.36 (1)	—2.19 (1)	—0.32 (1)	— 20.4[a] (3)	0.71 (1)
—19.0 (1)	—1.93 (1)	1.31 (1)	0.17 (1)	— 5.2[a] (1½)	5.34 (1)
13.3 (0)	1.21 (0)	—0.93 (0)	—0.12 (0)	— 17.8 (3½)	0.14[b] (0)
12.3 (0)	1.23 (0)	—0.90 (0)	—0.12 (0)	— 25.1 (3½)	0.06[b] (0)
11.9 (0)	1.19 (0)	—0.87 (0)	—0.11 (0)	— 26.5 (3½)	0.26[c] (0)
69.0 (1¼)	5.49 (1¼)	—3.36 (1¼)	—0.47 (1¼)	f	1.71 (1¼)
4.5 (1)	0.69 (1)	—0.52[d] (1)	—0.06 (1)	f	1.66 (1)
7.5 (1)	1.16 (1)	—0.94[e] (1)	—0.12 (1)	f	1.38 (1)

d Index of construction costs of Svenska Handelsbanken.
e Index of construction costs of Stockholm Statistical Office.
f Series not included.

Building.   Table IV. 3. Explanation of Building:
Combination with Rent and

Note. — See note to Table IV. 1.

Country	Period	Series explained
Germany (Hamburg)	1878-1913	Net increase in number of rooms.
Sweden (Stockholm)	1884-1913	Number of new rooms built
United States	1920-1935	Total volume of residential construction
United Kingdom	1923-1935	Number of houses built
Sweden	1924-1936*	Number of houses built in 296 cities

Building.   Table IV. 4.
Influence of Number

Note. — See note to Table IV. 1.

Country	Period	Series explained
Germany	1878-1913	Net increase in number of rooms
	,,	,, ,, ,,
	,,	,, ,, ,,
United States	1920-1935	Volume of non-farm residential building
	,,	,, ,, ,,
	,,	,, ,, ,,
	,,	,, ,, ,,
	1920-1932	,, ,, ,,
United Kingdom	1923-1935	Number of houses built without State assistance
	,,	,, ,, ,,
Sweden	1924-1936*	Number of rooms built in 296 cities
	,,	,, ,, ,,
	,,	,, ,, ,,

a Number of vacant houses, in %.
b Net income of corporations.
c Series not included.
* 1933 excluded.

**Calculations using Interest Rate in a priori.
Construction Costs, and also freely.**

Correlation coefficient R	Regression coefficients and lags of:			
	Profitability of building	Interest rate	Number of houses	Income or profits earned
0.93	76.8 (1)	1.04 (1)	— 20.1 [a] (3)	1.72 (0)
0.65	1.1 (1)	— 0.70 (1)	— 4.4 [a] (1 ½)	4.29 (1)
0.98	12.5 (0)	0.02 (0)	— 25.1 (3 ½)	0.06 [b] (0)
0.97	20.5 (1 ¼)	— 0.56 (1 ¼)	c	3.11 (1 ¼)
0.97	— 5.3 (1)	— 0.35 (1)	c	2.02 (1)

**Explanation of Building.
of Variates included.**

Correlation coefficient R	Regression coefficients and lags of:			
	Profitability of building	Number of houses	Income or profits earned	Capital gains
0.66	3.8 (1)			
0.82		— 15.5 [a] (3)		
0.87	48.2 (1)	— 20.4 [a] (3)	0.71 (0)	
0.78	33.0 (0)			
0.97		— 36.0 (3 ½)		
0.98	10.5 (0)	— 29.8 (3 ½)		
0.98	12.3 (0)	— 25.1 (3 ½)	0.06 [b] (0)	
0.99	11.6 (0)	— 22.5 (3 ½)	— 0.06 [b] (0)	0.003 (0)
0.96	88.8 (1 ¼)			
0.96	69.0 (1 ¼)		1.71 (1 ¼)	
0.82	11.9 (1)			
0.87			2.36 (1)	
0.89	4.5 (1)		1.66 (1)	

to a slackening of residential building in 1937 as compared with 1936. For the United Kingdom, on the other hand, the extra-polations of both calculations point to a continuous rise through 1936 and, in a somewhat lesser degree, 1937, which does not agree with the actual stability in 1936 and decline in 1937. The explanation of this difference seems to lie in the special fact that the building boom, which consisted largely in the construction of small houses for the upper working-class and the lower middle class, had, round about 1935, attained a limit, which could only have been surpassed by making these owner-inhabited houses accessible to the earners of smaller incomes.

Details of results. Tables IV.1-IV.4. In Tables IV. 1-IV. 4 the results of the principal calculations are set out. In Table IV. 1, all the explanatory factors enumerated above have been included separately in the correlation calculations; in Table IV. 2, the three factors of the first group have been combined *a priori* so as to reflect the profitability of building. In Table IV. 3, the interest rate has been added as a separate factor in addition to entering into the " profitability "; this is a way of introducing interest rates with a free coefficient—in order to find whether there is accordance with the *a priori* case—without increasing by two the number of variates, as is the case in Table IV. 1. Table IV. 4. shows the influence of the number of variates included.

Correlation coefficients. With the exception of the case of Sweden, pre-war, all correlation coefficients in Tables IV. 1 and IV. 2 —the most important ones—vary between 0.87 and 0.99; for post-war, the median is even as high as 0.97.

Signs of regression coefficients. All coefficients in Table IV. 1 have the right sign except the interest rate in the case of Germany, pre-war, which is positive instead of negative and all coefficients but two of the components of profitability for Sweden, post-war.

For Sweden, pre-war, the regression coefficient of profitability is negative in Table IV. 2, but it is reversed in Table IV. 3, which seems to point out that the influence of the rate of interest is much higher than assumed when calculating the " profitability ".[1]   Table IV. 3 is otherwise not very satisfactory: two of the columns contain coefficients with a wrong sign.

In Table IV. 4, on the other hand, all signs are right.

Comparison between countries.   The main divergencies between countries as regards the order of magnitude of the regression coefficients of Tables IV. 1 and IV. 2—leaving aside those with a wrong sign[2]—may be briefly summarised:

Table IV. 1: In the United States, interest rate and rent have a much smaller coefficient than the average, while in the United Kingdom the coefficient of the latter is much greater.   The coefficients of construction costs, in so far as they have the right sign, are rather close to each other; the coefficients of the number of houses, on the other hand, show a very wide spread.

In the United States, post-war, the coefficients for the income series are almost negligible.[3]

Table IV. 2: the coefficient of profitability is much larger than the average in Germany, pre-war, and the United Kingdom, post-war, and smaller in Sweden, post-war.

The coefficients for the number of houses are not very different from those in Table IV. 1.   The coefficient of profits in the United States is, again, very small.

Comparison of Tables IV. 1 and IV. 2.   A comparison of the coefficients of rent, construction costs and interest rate in Tables IV. 1 and IV. 2 should make it possible to test the assumptions made when combining these factors into an index of profitability.   To facilitate this comparison, the coefficients have been inserted in the following table.   Unfortunately, the results show a rather wide range of variation.

---

[1] This might be explained by the fact that the interest rate is, at the same time, a measure of the desirability of investing in bonds, and that this desirability influences the incentive to build.

[2] It may, in this connection, be noted that both the rent index and the construction costs index for Sweden, post-war, which obtain only wrong signs in Table IV. 1, are not very representative.

[3] These coefficients were somewhat raised when real instead of money income was used, but they still remained very low.

Graph IV. 8.

Bunch Map.

BUILDING: UNITED STATES 1915-1935.

1 = Building (contracts awarded).   2 = Profitability of building.
3 = Number of houses_ 31/2.   4 = Profits.

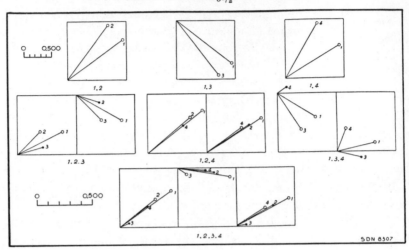

Graph IV. 9.

Bunch Map.

BUILDING: UNITED STATES 1920-1935.

1 = Building (total non-farm residential construction).   2 = Profitability of building.
3 = Number of houses_31/2.   4 = Profits.

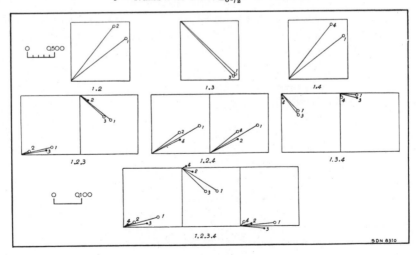

In the German pre-war case, the coefficients of rent and construction costs are not too dissimilar. For after the war, the coefficient for rent is greater and that for construction costs smaller for the United Kingdom in the free calculation; but the reverse is true for the United States.

The two factors of the second group, on the other hand, have fairly stable coefficients.

Tables IV. 1 and IV. 2 combined.[a]

A = Free calculations.   B = A priori calculations.

Country	Regression coefficients of:									
	Rent		Construction costs		Interest rate		Number of houses		Income	
	A	B	A	B	A	B	A	B	A	B
Germany 1878-1913	5.20	3.36	—1.54	—2.19	b	b	—16.5	—20.4	1.71	0.71
Sweden 1884-1913	b	b	b	b	b	b	— 3.7	— 5.2	3.75	5.34
United States 1920-1935	0.31	1.23	—1.90	—0.90	—0.02	—0.12	—33.2	—25.1	0.10	0.06
Utd. Kingdom 1923-1935	10.09	5.49	—0.95	—3.36	—0.56	—0.47	c	c	2.06	1.71
Sweden 1924-1936	b	b	b	b	—0.24	—0.06	c	c	2.22	1.66

[a] For the sake of clearness, the description of series, the indication of lags, and all footnotes have been omitted.
[b] Cases including wrong signs have not been included.
[c] Series not included.

Significance calculations.

For the United States, three bunch maps have been drawn, two representing a priori calculations. and the third the free calculation for 1920-1935.

As regards the first a priori calculation (Graph IV. 8, contracts awarded, 1915-1935), the final set (1234) is very satisfactory as to variate 2 (profitability). It is somewhat less satisfactory as to variates 3 (number of houses) and 4 (profits), the coefficients of which are not to be determined with the same degree of exactness, the angles between the beams being larger.

Bunch Map.   *Graph*

BUILDING: UNITED STATES 1920-1935.

1 = Total non-farm residential construction.   2 = Rent.   3 = Construction

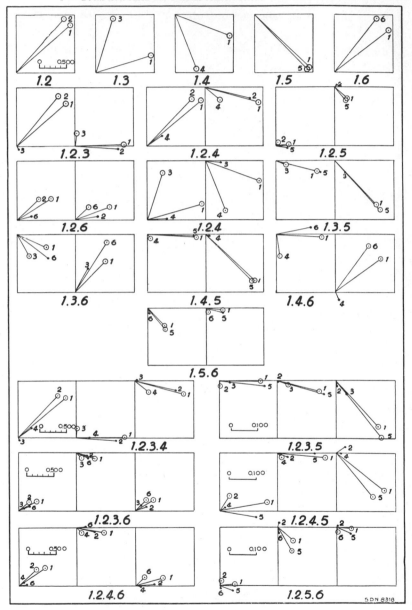

S.D.N. 8318

IV. 10.   Bunch Map.

BUILDING: UNITED STATES 1920-1935.

costs.   4 = Interest rate.   5 = Number of houses $_{-31/2}$.   6 = Profits.

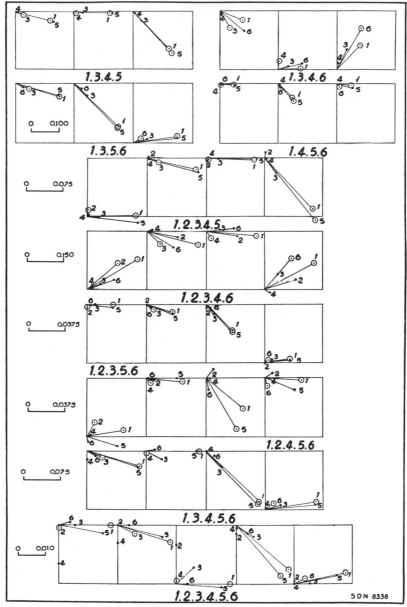

SDN 8338

8

Taking account of the fact that, in this case, variates 2 and 4 appear to be the more important ones, one may, however, disregard beam 3 in the middle and right-hand parts of set 1234; the regression coefficients for 3 and 4 then become more certain, though that of 3 is small (small inclination of beams).

For the other *a priori* calculation (total non-farm residential construction, 1920-1935), the bunch map (Graph IV. 9) is less good; here the regression coefficient of 3 (the number of houses) is found to be both important and well determined if the two other variates, the coefficients of which are found to be small, are disregarded.

The bunch map (Graph IV. 10) for the free calculation over this period shows, in its final set (123456), a tendency to explosion, but nevertheless the variates 3 (construction cost), 5 (number of houses) and 6 (profits) are found to have well defined and important influences, especially 5. From the " best " sub-sets (" best " from the point of view of determinateness of regression coefficients)—viz., (135), (145), (1345), (12345)—similar conclusions are to be drawn.

CHAPTER V

NET INVESTMENT IN RAILWAY ROLLING-STOCK

---

§ 15. The Relation tested

Acceleration principle and profit principle.

In § 9, the result was obtained that, in the case of general investment activity, the acceleration principle yields an explanatory factor of only minor importance as compared with profits. For railways, it is possible to take a slightly different view. The two facts, (*a*) that railways usually are not permitted to refuse passengers or freight offered for transport and (*b*) that, generally, they are public enterprises or under some sort of control of public authority, both tend to replace pure profit considerations by more technical considerations as far as new investment is concerned. There is some reason to assume that profit considerations are in this case wholly or partially replaced by the considerations at the basis of the acceleration principle. For this reason, three types of calculation have been made. An attempt has been made to explain the net investment in railway rolling-stock v_R by the following primary factors:

(1) The rate of increase in traffic Δu_R only (" acceleration principle ");
(2) The profit rate Z_R only (" profit principle ");
(3) Both Δu_R and Z_R (" mixed principle ").

Secondary factors; lags.

As secondary factors the same factors have been chosen as in Chapter III, viz.,

The price of iron q_i ;

The long term rate of interest m_{Lb}.

About the probable lag, some information is available in the lags between orders of locomotives and of cars and the rate of increase in total stock of locomotives and of cars with the American railways. These data show a lag of about 1 year for cars and of about 1½ years for locomotives. As the lag between any incentive to invest and the actual increase in rolling-stock may be larger than the purely technical lag between orders and increase, it seemed a fair estimate to take 1½ years for all rolling-stock. To begin with, calculations with this lag were made. Inspection of the graphs showed that the lag seemed to be somewhat shorter for the United States, especially in the case of the profit principle; perhaps somewhat longer for France, and decidedly longer (2½ years) for Germany, if for these two countries the acceleration principle was accepted as the explanatory principle. Therefore, a lag of 2½ years for Germany has been taken, whereas for the other countries the lag of 1½ years was retained, with the exception of the profit principle for the United States, where a lag of 1 year was also considered. These lags may roughly be considered as the lags giving the highest correlation.

For the profit principle, somewhat more complicated calculations (indicated as calculations 2′) were made in addition: viz., calculations in which profits with two different lags are introduced as variates. This may give somewhat more accurate indications about lags, which will be discussed together with the results.

Significance calculations. Significance calculations have been made only for some of the most typical cases. As railway rolling-stock plays a decreasing rôle in total investment, it did not seem necessary for the ultimate objects of this enquiry to go into very much detail, the more so because the results were only moderately good.

§ 16. The Statistical Material

The countries and periods studied are:

Countries and periods.
France, 1876-1908 (thirty-three years).
Germany, 1874-1908 (thirty-five years).
United Kingdom ,1873-1911 (thirty-nine years)
United States, 1896-1913 (eighteen years).

All necessary data on railways are taken from the Statistical

Year-books of these countries. For the secondary factors, the data referred to in Chapter III are taken.

Computation of indices. Some preliminary work was involved in calculating the necessary indices.

Investment index. An index ν_R of net investment was calculated as a weighted arithmetic average of the percentage rates of increase in locomotives, freight cars and passenger cars. As weights, there were taken the products of the number of each type of rolling-stock present at the end of 1895 (for the United States 1905) by a weight factor which was taken as

20 for locomotives,
10 for passenger cars, and
1 for freight cars.

For the United Kingdom, where no separate data for both types of car were available, one weight factor 2 was used for all cars. The influence of the weights on the shape of the investment index is not large, as the rate of increase in locomotives and cars is usually highly correlated.

Profit series. As profit series (Z_R), the following have been used:
United States: " Net operating income " as a percentage of " investment " (*i.e.*, capital invested);
United Kingdom: Ratio of net receipts to paid-up capital;
Germany: Profits as percentage of invested capital;
France: Net income per kilometre divided by cost of construction of one km.

Rate of increase in traffic. An index for the rate of increase in traffic was calculated as a weighted arithmetic average of the percentage rates of increase in passenger traffic and freight traffic. The weights chosen are numbers roughly proportional to the total receipts for passenger traffic and freight traffic at about the middle of the period studied. They are indicated in the table below, together with the exact description of the traffic series used.

Traffic series and weights used.

Country	Passenger traffic		Freight traffic	
	Series used	Weight	Series used	Weight
United States	Passengers carried 1 mile	1	Freight carried 1 mile	3
United Kingdom	Total ordinary passenger journeys	4	Total tonnage of goods conveyed	5
Germany	Passengers carried 1 kilometre	1	Freight carried 1 kilometre (tons)	2
France	Passengers carried 1 kilometre	4	Freight carried 1 kilometre (tons)	5

For pig-iron prices and long-term interest rates, the same series have been used as described in Chapter III.

Trends. In order to eliminate trends, deviations from nine-year moving averages have been taken for all series except iron prices, where percentage deviations from nine-year moving averages were taken.

§ 17. RESULTS

Details of the results obtained are presented in Tables V. 1 to V. 3 and Graphs V. 1 to V. 4. The following general features seem worth mentioning:

Results not better than for general investment activity. (i) Looking at the correlation coefficients obtained, one finds that the results are not, as might have been expected, better than those obtained for general investment activity. It therefore seems that the advantage of having more homogeneous material is counteracted by the larger influence of disturbances in a more restricted field of activity.

Lags. (ii) As has been said already, the lags chosen in the case of the acceleration principle are roughly those which give the best fit. They are $1\frac{1}{2}$ years for the United States, the United Kingdom and France, and $2\frac{1}{2}$ years for Germany. For the profit principle, these lags were tested by the calculations summarised in columns (7) to (9), Table V. 1. In the case of the United Kingdom and France, the regression coefficients obtained for profits with 2½ years lag are small in comparison to those obtained for profits with 1½ years lag. This means that the optimum lags are near to 1½ years—somewhat more in France,

Graph V. 1.

" EXPLANATION " OF INVESTMENT IN RAILWAY ROLLING-STOCK.
UNITED STATES 1896-1913.

Left-hand side: " Mixed principle " — Right-hand side: " Profit principle ".

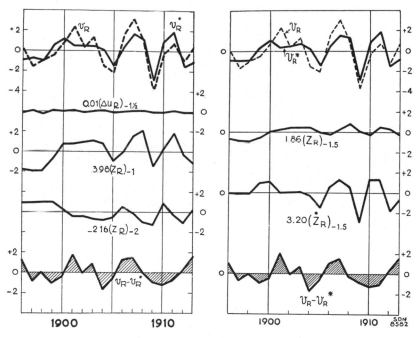

v_R :	investment in railway rolling-stock, actual.
v_R^* :	investment in railway rolling-stock, as explained by:
$(\Delta u_R)_{-1\frac{1}{2}}$:	increase in traffic, lagged 1 ½ years;
$(Z_R)_{-1}$:	profits, lagged 1 year;
$(Z_R)_{-2}$:	profits, lagged 2 years;
$(Z_R)_{-1\frac{1}{2}}$:	profits
$(\dot{Z}_R)_{-1\frac{1}{2}}$:	rate of increase in profits

} lagged 1½ years.

somewhat less in the United Kingdom. For Germany, both coefficients are equally important, pointing to an optimum lag of 2 years.

The regression coefficients obtained in the case of the United
States indicate that a considerably smaller lag than even 1 year
would be the optimum lag if profits were to be the only explanatory variate. This is, however, inacceptable, as delivery of rolling-

Graph V. 2.

" EXPLANATION " OF INVESTMENT IN RAILWAY ROLLING-STOCK.
UNITED KINGDOM 1873-1911.

" Mixed principle ".

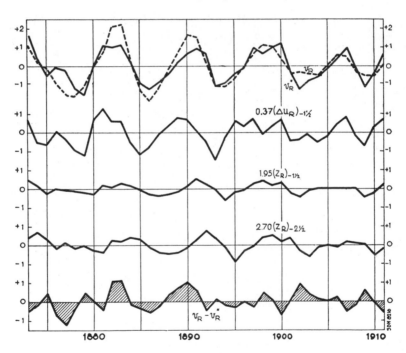

v_R :	Investment in railway rolling-stock, actual.
v_R^* :	investment in railway rolling-stock, as explained by:
$(\Delta u_R)_{-1\frac{1}{2}}$:	rate of increase in traffic, lagged $1\frac{1}{2}$ years;
$(Z_R)_{-1\frac{1}{2}}$:	profit rate, lagged $1\frac{1}{2}$ years;
$(Z_R)_{-2\frac{1}{2}}$:	profit rate, lagged $2\frac{1}{2}$ years.

stock requires at least one year (see above). The profit principle in its simplest form—viz., that the amount of profits determines the volume of investment—is therefore inapplicable here; the regression equation yielded by this calculation could, however, be written in the form:

$$v_R = 0.93\,[(Z_R)_{-1} + (Z_R)_{-2}] + 3.20\,[(Z_R)_{-1} - (Z_R)_{-2}]$$

Graph V. 3.

"EXPLANATION" OF INVESTMENT IN RAILWAY ROLLING-STOCK.
GERMANY 1874-1908.

"Mixed principle".

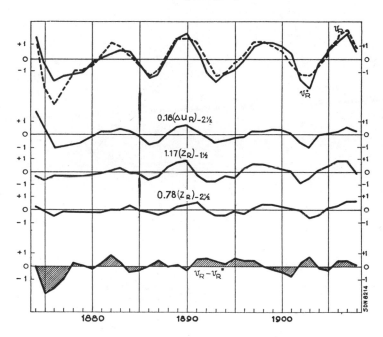

v_R : investment in railway rolling-stock, actual.

v_R^* : investment in railway rolling-stock, as explained by:

$(\Delta u_R)_{-2\frac{1}{2}}$: rate of increase in traffic, lagged $1\frac{1}{2}$ years;

$(Z_R)_{-1\frac{1}{2}}$: profit rate, lagged $1\frac{1}{2}$ years;

$(Z_R)_{-2\frac{1}{2}}$: profit rate, lagged $2\frac{1}{2}$ years.

where the first expression in brackets is very near to twice profits with a lag of $1\frac{1}{2}$ years and the second expression in brackets is the rate of increase in profits with a lag of $1\frac{1}{2}$ years. Thus the rate of increase of profits, as well as profits themselves, is represented as exercising an influence on investment. Briefly, and very approximately, we get

$$v_R = 1.86\,(Z_R)_{-1.5} + 3.20\,(\dot{Z}_R)_{-1.5} \quad (cf.\ \text{Graph V. 1}).$$

Graph V. 4.

"EXPLANATION" OF INVESTMENT IN RAILWAY ROLLING-STOCK.
FRANCE 1876-1908.

"Mixed principle".

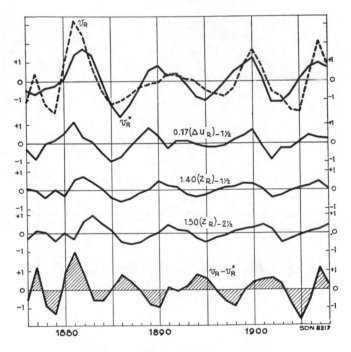

v_R :	investment in railway rolling-stock, actual.
$v_R{}^*$:	investment in railway rolling-stock, as explained by:
$(\Delta u_R)_{-1\frac{1}{2}}$:	rate of increase in traffic, lagged $1\frac{1}{2}$ years;
$(Z_R)_{-1\frac{1}{2}}$:	profit rate, lagged $1\frac{1}{2}$ years;
$(Z_R)_{-2\frac{1}{2}}$:	profit rate, lagged $2\frac{1}{2}$ years.

(iii) The correlation coefficients obtained with the *Acceleration* calculations (1) and (2) mentioned above (§ 15) are *principle and* not, on the average, very different (Table V. 1, *profit* columns (3) and (5)). So far as the differences are *principle.* significant, it is remarkable that the acceleration principle gives a lower correlation than the profit principle for the United States and France, and about the same correlation as the profit principle for Germany and *Mixed* England. Calculations (3) (Table V. 1, columns (10) *principle.* to (13)), using both principles, show practically no influence of the rate of increase in traffic in the case of the United States; and the regression coefficients for profits are quite near to those found in columns (8) and (9).

To sum up, for the United Kingdom the correlation is considerably improved if the principles are combined; for France and Germany there is also some improvement, whereas for the United States the improvement is almost nil.

Calculations including "secondary factors" (*cf*. Tables *Calculations* V. 2 and V. 3) show considerable improvements in cor- *using* relation if based upon the acceleration principle, and *secondary* less improvement if based on the profit principle. The *factors.* results obtained with the acceleration principle in table V. 2, with the exception of those for the United States, become somewhat better than those obtained with the profit principle, notwithstanding that the number of variates included is one less.

The regression coefficient obtained in case (1)— *Regression* whether or not secondary factors are included makes no *coefficient* difference—is far lower than the acceleration principle *for* in its simplest form [1] would suggest. In fact, it is *acceleration* often suggested that a given percentage increase in *principle.* traffic would lead to an equal percentage increase in rolling-stock. Instead of unity, the coefficient found in Table V. 1, column (4), is, however, only one-sixth to one-third, or if the ratio between the standard deviations is taken, about

---

[1] As given by HABERLER: *Prosperity and Depression*, pages 84 and 85.

Table V. 1. " Explanation " of Investment

Units: Investment: Percentage increase in rolling-stock, deviations from 9 years moving average.
Δ Traffic: Percentage increase in traffic, deviations from 9 years moving average.
Profits: Percentage profits,[1] deviations from 9 years moving average.

Country	Period	(1) Acceleration principle		(2) Profit principle	
		Correlation coefficient	Regression coefficient and lag of Δ traffic	Correlation coefficient	Regression coefficient and lag of profits
(1)	(2)	(3)	(4)	(5)	(6)
United States	1896-1913	0.54	0.15 (1½)	0.63	3.20 (1)
United Kingdom	1873-1911	0.63	0.34 (1½)	0.66	4.80 (1½)
Germany	1874-1908	0.79	0.34 (2½)	0.74	2.41 (2½)
France	1876-1908	0.57	0.24 (1½)	0.67	3.42 (1½)

[1] Or the best approximation to it available.

Table V. 2. " Explanation " of Investment

Introduction of iron prices and long-term interest rates as

Country	Period	1. Acceleration principle			
		Correlation coefficient	Regression coefficients and lags of:		
			traffic	iron price	interest rate
(1)	(2)	(3)	(4)	(5)	(6)
United States	1896-1913	0.78	0.04 (1½)	— 0.04 (1½)	— 0.09 (1½)
United Kingdom	1873-1911	0.75	0.27 (1½)	0.02 (1½)	— 0.04 (1½)
Germany	1874-1908	0.88	0.40 (2½)	— 0.04 (2½)	0.01 (2½)
France	1876-1908	0.83	0.19 (1½)	0.06 (1½)	— 0.05 (1½)

in Railway Rolling-stock.

Interest rates: deviations from 9 years moving average, in 0.01 %.
Iron prices: percentage deviations from 9 years moving average.
Lags: years.

(2′) Profit principle (distr. lag)			(3) Mixed principle			
Correlation coefficient	Regression coefficients and lags of profits		Correlation	Regression coefficients and lags of:		
				Δ traffic	profits	
(7)	(8)	(9)	(10)	(11)	(12)	(13)
0.77	4.13 (1)	— 2.27 (2)	0.77	0.01 (1½)	3.98 (1)	— 2.16 (2)
0.66	5.10 (1½)	— 0.55 (2½)	0.84	0.37 (1½)	1.95 (1½)	2.70 (2½)
0.83	1.52 (1½)	1.53 (2½)	0.88	0.18 (2½)	1.17 (1½)	0.78 (2½)
0.68	3.00 (1½)	0.71 (2½)	0.75	0.17 (1½)	1.40 (1½)	1.50 (2½)

in Railway Rolling-stock (continued).

supplementary explanatory factors.   Units: see Table V. 1.

2′. Profit principle				
Correlation coefficient	Regression coefficients and lags of:			
	profits		iron price	interest rate
(7)	(8)	(9)	(10)	(11)
0.87	2.55 (1)	— 1.80 (2)	— 0.02 (1½)	— 0.07 (1½)
0.70	3.80 (1½)	— 1.35 (2½)	0.02 (1½)	— 0.03 (1½)
0.84	2.14 (1½)	1.58 (2½)	0.01 (2½)	0.04 (2½)
0.86	1.89 (1½)	0.81 (2½)	0.03 (1½)	— 0.01 (1½)
0.79	2.15 (1½)	— 0.35 (1½)	0.04 (1½)	— 0.05 (1½)

Table V. 3. " Explanation " of Investment

Calculations using only interest rates

Country	Period	1. Acceleration principle		
		Correlation coefficient	Regression coefficient and lags of:	
			Δ traffic	interest rate
(1)	(2)	(3)	(4)	(5)
United States	1896-1913	*0.69*	0.09 (1 ½)	— 0.07 (1 ½)
United Kingdom	1873-1911	*0.67*	0.29 (1 ½)	— 0.03 (1 ½)
Germany	1874-1908	*0.79*	0.34 (2 ½)	0.00 (2 ½)
France	1876-1908	*0.69*	0.19 (1 ½)	— 0.06 (1 ½)

one-half,[1] which means a considerably smaller sensitivity of investment. After the introduction of the " secondary factors " and of the
mixed principle, these coefficients grow less uniform, but in general
still smaller, especially in the case of the United States. Nevertheless, the more general significance of the acceleration principle—viz.,
that percentage fluctuations in capital goods industries are larger
than percentage fluctuations in consumers' goods industries—is not
invalidated by these figures. The relatively low influence of the
principle may be attributed to the fact that the technical necessity
for its operation in its simplest form exists only if capacity is
already being fully used. In all other circumstances, changes in
capacity may be less than in proportion to changes in production.[2]

Influence
of iron
prices.
Not very much evidence is found of any influence
of iron prices in the European countries. The regression coefficients found (Table V. 2, columns (5)
and (10)) are positive and in general unimportant.
Only in the United States do they seem to be clearly
negative; the elasticity of demand at the point of the demand curve
corresponding to trend values of prices and quantities (which, by

---

[1] This figure is obtained by dividing column (4) by column (3), and is
therefore:

U.S.A.	U.K.	Germany	France
0.28	0.54	0.43	0.42

[2] In the case of the mixed principle for the U.K. and Germany, the correlation would improve if a continuous fall in the regression coefficients were
assumed to exist (*cf.* Graph V. 2 and V. 3).

in Railway Rolling-stock (continued).
as supplementary factors.   Units: see Table V. 1.

Correlation coefficient	2′. Profit principle		
	Regression coefficient and lags of:		
	profits		interest rate
(6)	(7)	(8)	(9)
0.85	2.68 (1)	— 2.65 (2)	— 0.07 (1 $\frac{1}{2}$)
0.67	4.62 (1 $\frac{1}{2}$)	— 0.56 (2 $\frac{1}{2}$)	— 0.02 (1 $\frac{1}{2}$)
0.84	1.76 (1 $\frac{1}{2}$)	1.71 (2 $\frac{1}{2}$)	0.03 (2 $\frac{1}{2}$)
0.83	1.37 (1 $\frac{1}{2}$)	1.59 (2 $\frac{1}{2}$)	— 0.01 (1 $\frac{1}{2}$)
0.76	2.27 (1 $\frac{1}{2}$)	0.87 (2 $\frac{1}{2}$)	— 0.05 (1 $\frac{1}{2}$)

the choice of units, is indicated by 30 × the regression coefficient) would be about unity.

Influence of interest rates.   On the other hand, the influence of interest rates seems to be quite clear (Table V. 2, columns (6) and (11), and Table V. 3, columns (5) and (9)). Here, as in other cases, the United States and Germany seem to represent two extremes between which France and the United Kingdom are situated, the influence of interest rates being largest in the United States. Owing to our figures, a fall of 0.1% (being ten times the unit used) in bond yields would, in the United States, lead to an increase in rolling-stock by 0.7 to 0.9% (ten times the regression coefficient found) more than normal, whereas the corresponding figures are 0.2, 0.3 and 0.4 for the United Kingdom, 0.5 and 0.6 for France, and 0.1 to —0.4 for Germany.

The decided importance of interest rates for investment activity in the field studied may find part of its explanation in the considerable length of life of railway rolling-stock and in the large part of this investment which, in the end, is financed through the capital market in the proper sense of that word. At the same time, the fact that in Chapter III, dealing with investment in general, a larger influence of interest rates on investment activity was found for pre-war times than for post-war times may now be explained, for investment in railway rolling-stock probably plays at present a less important rôle than it did before the war.

In addition to the information given in Tables V. 1
Significance to V. 3, bunch maps have been calculated for four
calculations. cases—viz., two for Germany and two for the United
States—exhibiting the " mixed principle " without
secondary factors and the acceleration principle with interest
rates as a supplementary factor (*cf.* Graphs V. 5 to V. 8). These bunch

Graph V. 5.

Bunch Map.

RAILWAYS: GERMANY 1874-1908.

1 = Investment index. 2 = Δ traffic index$_{-2\frac{1}{2}}$. 3 = Profits$_{-1\frac{1}{2}}$. 4 = Profits$_{-2\frac{1}{2}}$.

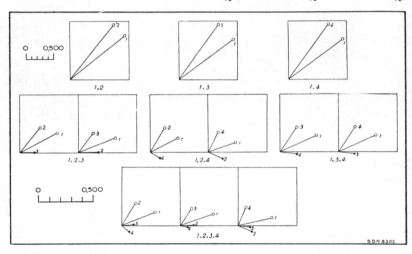

Graph V. 6.

Bunch Map.

RAILWAYS: GERMANY 1874-1908.

1 = Investment index. 2 = Δ traffic index$_{-2\frac{1}{2}}$. 3 = Interest rate$_{-2\frac{1}{2}}$.

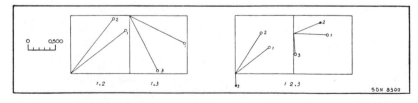

maps all seem to show that the figures obtained are very uncertain. Thus, Graph V. 6 gives a very wide spread for the beams in the right-hand part of set 123 which relates to the regression coefficient for 3 (interest rates). As 2 appears to be the most important explanatory variate in this set, beams 1 and 2 are the most important ones, which still supports our conclusion about a small

Graph V. 7.

Bunch Map.
RAILWAYS: UNITED STATES 1896-1913.

1 = Investment index.   2 = Δ traffic index$_{-1}$.   3 = Profits$_{-1}$.   4 = Profits$_{-2}$.

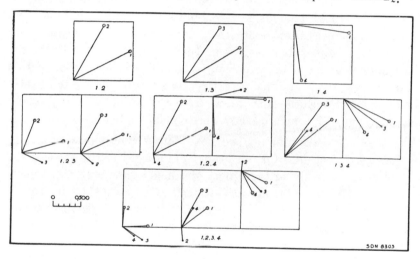

Graph V. 8.

Bunch Map.
RAILWAYS: UNITED STATES 1896-1913.

1 = Investment index.   2 = Δ traffic index$_{-1}$.   3 = Interest rate$_{-1}$.

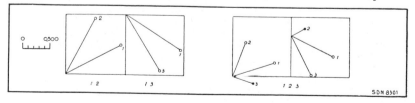

influence of interest rates in Germany. In the case of the United States (Graph V. 8), beam 3 is, however, more important, supporting the view that a high influence of interest rates is present. Only if there are strong reasons for preferring the first elementary regression (which has been used in tables V. 1 to V. 3, as usually), can confidence be placed in the regression coefficients.

In this connection, it is of some interest that, among all the elementary regressions, only number 1 yields correct signs for all regression coefficients.

Explanation Most of the differences found to exist between the *of differences* countries studied seem to point in the same direction. *between* Investment in the United States reacts more quickly, *countries.* and depends more on profits, interest rates and iron prices, and less on the purely technical acceleration principle, than it does in Europe, especially in Germany. This may be understood by realising that railways were, in the period investigated, more like free private enterprises in the United States and less so in the European countries; least of all in Germany, where already from 1878 onwards they were chiefly State enterprises.

Summary To sum up, we have found that the correlations *of findings.* obtained for this branch of industry are on the average not higher than those obtained for general investment. The influence of interest rates seems to be rather high, except in Germany. The acceleration principle gives a somewhat better explanation than the profit principle, but the regression coefficients found are far below the theoretical values. Certain differences between the four countries included could be explained.

CHAPTER VI

APPLICATION OF RESULTS: FURTHER INVESTIGATIONS

The direct use of the results obtained is restricted. They indicate the relative strength of the various causes of fluctuations in investment activity discussed in Chapters III to V. In addition, something can be deduced about the chief proximate causes of turning-points in investment activity. Thus, the crisis of 1883 and the revival in 1887 in the United Kingdom may be ascribed to changes in profits (*cf.* graph III. 4), while the revival of 1875 would seem to be primarily explained by the fall in iron prices. To give another example, the proximate causes of the well-known building boom after 1933 in the United Kingdom would appear to be the fall in interest rates and building costs and the rise in real income (*cf.* graph IV. 4). In some cases, conclusions about policy may be drawn. The reduction of long-term interest rate necessary to raise the volume of investment by a given percentage may be estimated in a few of our cases with some certainty. Thus, it would seem that for the United States in the period 1919-1932 a reduction of this rate by 1% might have led, after about half a year or so, to an increase in investment activity of about 5% of the average level.

Many questions, however, still remain unanswered. This is partly due to the degree of uncertainty in a number of results found, which can be reduced only if better statistics and more precise theories are available.

But more important is the fact that, in this pamphlet—which is primarily intended to demonstrate a method—the argument ends with the influence of profits, interest rates, etc., on the volume of investment.

The economist and the statesman may be anxious to know what in turn influences profits, and how these influences have been changed, or could be changed, by policy. This problem can also be studied by means of the method described here, if that method is applied to a larger number of inter-relations between economic variates.

In addition to the equation explaining investment fluctuations, others explaining profits, prices of investment goods, interest rates and so on, will then have to be established. The total number of such equations should be equal to the number of variates necessary to describe adequately the business-cycle mechanism. The sum total of these relations may be called a complete system. Such a complete system is required to draw conclusions of the nature indicated above.

A first attempt in this direction, covering the United States after the war, will be published shortly as the second volume of this series. An explanation will there be given of profits as the difference between (*i*) total receipts of all enterprises, public authorities, etc., included, and (*ii*) total costs.

Taking the country as a whole, and regarding it as a " closed economy''", all costs that consist in payments from one enterprise to another cancel out. Total receipts may thus be taken as the total value of consumers' goods and services produced (U), plus the total value of investment goods and services sold by their producers (V); the cost items to be deducted are:

Wages L_w and salaries L_s ;
Corporation managers' salaries L_c ;
Rent payments K_r ;
Interest payments K_i ;
Depreciation allowances N.

Calling the amount of profits Z, we therefore get:

$$Z = U + V - (L_w + L_s + L_c + K_r + K_i + N),$$

and we may test this equation from the facts. On the basis of this relation, an observed fall in profits may now be found to be due to, *e.g.*, a fall in U, total consumption. The causation of the fall in this variate must then, in turn, be investigated, and so on.

It follows that full use of any relation can only be made after a complete system has been established. Some of the most important applications of the results of the present study can therefore only be stated when the work for the next volume has been completed.

APPENDIX A

DETAILS OF CALCULATIONS

1. *Trend Calculation.*

For pre-war periods, nine-year moving averages have been taken. In a few cases where seven-year moving averages were already available, the latter were used, as the differences were small. For post-war periods, which are shorter, rectilinear trends have been calculated. For short periods, the arbitrariness of this type of trend is less than for long periods, as the difference between a rectilinear trend and a moving average is in this case generally small. In addition, the rectilinear trend has the great advantage that no years need be left out of account, whereas, in the case of nine-year moving averages, four years are lost at each end of the series.

Let any series be represented by X_t, where t indicates the year (or any other unit period used) and assumes all values from 1 to N, N being the total number of years in the period considered. Let its rectilinear trend be $X_t^{(T)}$. The latter is then of the form

$$X_t^{(T)} = a + bt \tag{1}$$

where a and b are constants, which should be chosen so as to obtain the " best " fit between X_t and $X_t^{(T)}$. This is usually done by applying the method of least squares, which prescribes that the expression

$$(X_1 - X_1^{(T)})^2 + (X_2 - X_2^{(T)})^2 + (X_3 - X_3^{(T)})^2 + \ldots$$
$$\ldots + (X_N - X_N^{(T)})^2 \quad \text{or} \quad \sum_1^N t(X_t - X_t^{(T)})^2 \tag{2}$$

be made as small as possible by a suitable choice of a and b. This problem can be solved most simply if t, X_t and $X_t^{(T)}$ are measured as deviations from their mean values. If the mean values be indicated by $\overline{t}$, $\overline{X}$ and $\overline{X}^{(T)}$ respectively, and the deviations by t', x_t and $x_t^{(T)}$, we have:

$$\overline{t} = \frac{1}{N}\sum_1^N t\,t \;;\quad \overline{X} = \frac{1}{N}\sum_1^N t\,X_t \;;\quad \overline{X}^{(T)} = \frac{1}{N}\sum_1^N t\,X_t^{(T)} \qquad (3)$$

and

$$t' = t - \overline{t} \;;\quad x_t = X_t - \overline{X} \;;\quad x_t^{(T)} = X_t^{(T)} - \overline{X}^{(T)} \qquad (4).$$

It follows immediately that:

$$\Sigma t' = 0 \;;\quad \Sigma x_t = 0 \;;\quad \Sigma x_t^{(T)} = 0 \qquad (5).$$

Assuming now that the trend equation takes the form

$$x_t^{(T)} = a' + b't' \qquad (1')$$

the method of least squares requires by analogy with (2):

$$\sum_1^N t\,(x_t - x_t^{(T)})^2 \quad \text{minimum} \qquad (2').$$

Replacing $x_t^{(T)}$ by its value (1'), this becomes:

$$\sum_1^N t\,(x_t - a' - b't')^2 \quad \text{minimum.}$$

This expression depends on a' and b', since all other variates are given numbers drawn from observation. It is therefore a function $F(a', b')$ of a' and b', and its minimum value must, according to a well-known statement in differential calculus, obey the two relations:

$$\frac{\partial F(a', b')}{\partial a'} = 0 \qquad \frac{\partial F(a', b')}{\partial b'} = 0 \; [1] \qquad (6).$$

---

[1] It can be proved that these equations yield, in this case, a minimum and not a maximum value of F.

These relations come to: [1]

$$\Sigma x_t - Na' - b' \Sigma t' = 0 \qquad\qquad \Sigma x_t t' - a' \Sigma t' - b' \Sigma t'^2 = 0.$$

Applying relation (5), they are much simplified and become:

$$a' = 0 \qquad \Sigma x_t t' = b' \Sigma t'^2 \quad \text{or} \quad b' = \frac{\Sigma x_t t'}{\Sigma t'^2} \qquad (7).$$

The trend, if measured in deviations from its mean value, is therefore of the simple shape:

$$x_t^{(\mathrm{T})} = t' \frac{\Sigma x_t t'}{\Sigma t'^2} \qquad (8).$$

To obtain its actual level, the easiest way is to introduce t' into equation (1), as follows:

$$X_t^{(\mathrm{T})} = a + b(t' + \overline{t}) = a + \overline{bt} + bt' \qquad (9).$$

As the average of $bt' = \dfrac{1}{N} \Sigma b t' = \dfrac{b}{N} \Sigma t' = 0$, it follows that $a + \overline{bt} = \overline{X}^{(\mathrm{T})}$.

On the other hand, it may be deduced directly from (2), by applying the principle of least squares, that $\overline{X}^{(\mathrm{T})} = \overline{X}$ (this, in fact, is self-evident).

Finally, from (4) and (8), it will be seen that $b = b'$: hence the trend equation in natural units will be:

$$X_t^{(\mathrm{T})} = \overline{X} + t' \frac{\Sigma x_t t'}{\Sigma t'^2} \qquad (10).$$

2. *Multiple Correlation; Calculation of Regression and Correlation Coefficients.*

The technique used in this case is much the same as that used in the trend calculations just described. The problem is to find coefficients b_1, b_{12}, b_{13}, etc., which give the best fit between any

---

[1] For simplicity, the suffixes to the sign Σ will in future be omitted.

given series X_{1t} and a linear function X'_{1t} of a number of " explanatory " series X_{2t}, X_{3t}, etc. [1]

$$X'_{1t} = b_1 + b_{12} X_{2t} + b_{13} X_{3t} + b_{14} X_{4t} \ldots \qquad (11).$$

All series may again be measured in deviations from their averages. (The suffix t will in future be omitted in the formulæ, as no ambiguities can arise.) The deviations will be denoted by x_1, x'_1, x_2, etc., and, as before, it follows from their definitions that

$$\Sigma x_1 = \Sigma x'_1 = \Sigma x_2 = \Sigma x_3 = \ldots \Sigma x_n = 0 \qquad (12).$$

By this choice, b_1 will become zero.

The problem is to find for b_{12}, b_{13} etc., values which make the expression

$$\Sigma x^2_{1.23\ldots n} = \Sigma (x_1 - x'_1)^2 = \Sigma (x_1 - b_{12} x_2 - b_{13} x_3 \ldots)^2 \quad (13)$$

a minimum. The quantities $x_{1.23\ldots n}$ will be called the residuals.

They have to fulfil the following conditions known as " normal equations " and perfectly analogous to equations (6):

$$\begin{aligned}
\Sigma x_2 (x_1 - b_{12} x_2 - b_{13} x_3 \ldots) &= 0 \quad \text{or} \quad \Sigma x_2 x_{1.2\ldots n} = 0 \\
\Sigma x_3 (x_1 - b_{12} x_2 - b_{13} x_3 \ldots) &= 0 \quad \text{or} \quad \Sigma x_3 x_{1.2\ldots n} = 0
\end{aligned} \Bigg\} \ (14)$$

. . . .

These may be written:

$$\left.\begin{aligned}
b_{12} \Sigma x^2_2 + b_{13} \Sigma x_2 x_3 + \ldots + b_{1n} \Sigma x_2 x_n &= \Sigma x_1 x_2 \\
b_{12} \Sigma x_2 x_3 + b_{13} \Sigma x^2_3 + \ldots + b_{1n} \Sigma x_3 x_n &= \Sigma x_1 x_3 \\
\text{. . . . .} & \\
b_{12} \Sigma x_2 x_n + b_{13} \Sigma x_3 x_n + \ldots + b_{1n} \Sigma x^2_n &= \Sigma x_1 x_n
\end{aligned}\right\} \ (15)$$

where $n - 1$ is the number of "explanatory series". Equations (15) are usually the most convenient to use in numerical calculations.

---

[1] In Chapters III-V, where only the first regression has been considered, X' and x' have been replaced by X^* and x^*.

All the "sum-expressions" Σx_2^2, $\Sigma x_2 x_3$, etc.... are known from observation.

A general definition of the correlation coefficient between two series is given by the formula:

$$r_{12} = \frac{\Sigma x_1 x_2}{\sqrt{\Sigma x_1^2 \, \Sigma x_2^2}} \qquad (16).$$

This definition may also be applied to the series x and x_1', and then provides the "total correlation coefficient" $R_{1.23\ldots n}$. The result can be put in the form:

$$R_{1.23\ldots n} = \sqrt{\frac{b_{12} \Sigma x_1 x_2 + b_{13} \Sigma x_1 x_3 + \ldots + b_{1n} \Sigma x_1 x_n}{\Sigma x_1^2}}$$

which is convenient for numerical calculations.

If all series are measured in so-called normalised units—*i.e.*, in such units that their standard deviations become 1, then the normal equations may be given the form:

$$b_{12} + b_{13} r_{23} + \ldots + b_{1n} r_{2n} = r_{12}$$
$$b_{12} r_{23} + b_{13} + \ldots + b_{1n} r_{3n} = r_{13}$$
$$\cdot \quad \cdot \quad \cdot \quad \cdot \quad \cdot \quad \cdot \quad \cdot \quad \cdot \quad \cdot \quad \cdot \quad \cdot \quad \cdot$$
$$b_{12} r_{2n} + b_{13} r_{3n} + \ldots + b_{1n} = r_{1n}$$

$$(17)$$

from which it will be seen that the regression coefficients in normalised units depend only on the system of correlation coefficients between all variates.

The coefficients b_{12}, b_{13}, etc., to be found from the normal equations (15) are the regression coefficients for the first elementary regression. If, for example, the second elementary regression is to be determined, the rôle of suffixes 1 and 2 should be interchanged and the coefficients in that regression —

$$x_2' = b_{21} x_1 + b_{23} x_3 + b_{24} x_4 + \ldots b_{2n} x_n \qquad (18)$$

— have to be calculated from:

$$
\left.
\begin{aligned}
b_{21}\,\Sigma x_1^2 + b_{23}\,\Sigma x_1 x_3 + \ldots b_{2n}\,\Sigma x_1 x_n &= \Sigma x_2 x_1 \\
b_{21}\,\Sigma x_1 x_3 + b_{23}\,\Sigma x_3^2 + \ldots b_{2n}\,\Sigma x_3 x_n &= \Sigma x_2 x_3 \\
\cdot\;\;\cdot\;\;\cdot\;\;\cdot\;\;\cdot\;\;\cdot\;\;\cdot\;\;\cdot\;\;\cdot\;\;\cdot\;\;\cdot\;\;\cdot\;\;\cdot\;\;\cdot\;\;\cdot & \\
b_{21}\,\Sigma x_1 x_n + b_{23}\,\Sigma x_3 x_n + \ldots b_{2n}\,\Sigma x_n^2 &= \Sigma x_2 x_n
\end{aligned}
\right\}
\qquad (19).
$$

Equation (18) should be transformed into:

$$
x_1^{''} = \frac{1}{b_{21}}(x_2 - b_{23} x_3 - b_{24} x_4 - \ldots - b_{2n} x_n) \qquad (20)
$$

by writing x_2 instead of x_2', and x_1'' instead of x_1 if it is to be used as a second estimate for the " explanatory equation " for x_1 (Frisch's method).

The regression used in this publication is the first elementary regression; for the most important cases, however, bunch maps (*cf.* 3 below) have been added.

3. *Construction of Bunch Maps.*

Here the technique outlined by Professor Frisch, who proposed the method, in his " Statistical Confluence Analysis by Means of Complete Regression Systems " [1] has been almost exactly followed. As has been pointed out in § 2, the regression coefficients in normalised units can be determined from the system of all correlation coefficients between the variates considered. Starting with these correlation coefficients, it is conceivable that every possible regression formula is calculated in the way indicated *sub* 2. Frisch's method is, however, far more efficient, as any repetition of operations is avoided. The general idea is that all symmetrical minors

---

[1] Publication No. 5 of the Economic Institute of the University of Oslo (Universitetets Økonomiske Institutt), Oslo, 1934.

of the determinant of the correlation coefficients:

$$\Delta_{12\ldots n} = \begin{vmatrix} r_{11} r_{12} \cdots r_{1n} \\ r_{21} r_{22} \cdots r_{2n} \\ \vdots \\ r_{n1} r_{n2} \cdots r_{nn} \end{vmatrix} \tag{21}$$

should be calculated, and this is done in a systematic way.

As any minor of a two-rowed determinant is itself again an element of that determinant, no calculations are needed for such cases. We begin, therefore, with the minors of three-rowed determinants. Take, as an example, the determinant

$$\Delta_{123} = \begin{vmatrix} r_{11} & r_{12} & r_{13} \\ r_{21} & r_{22} & r_{23} \\ r_{31} & r_{32} & r_{33} \end{vmatrix} \tag{22}.$$

The minor $\hat{r}_{11}$ (this notation being provisional only) corresponding with the element r_{11} is found from $\hat{r}_{11} = r_{22}r_{33} - r_{23}r_{32} = 1 - r_{23}^2$. Similarly, $\hat{r}_{22} = 1 - r_{13}^2$ and $\hat{r}_{33} = 1 - r_{12}^2$. The minor $\hat{r}_{12}$ corresponding with r_{12} equals

$$- r_{21}r_{33} + r_{23}r_{31} = - r_{12} + r_{13}r_{23} .$$

Similarly,

$$\hat{r}_{13} = - r_{13} + r_{12}r_{23}$$
$$\hat{r}_{23} = - r_{23} + r_{12}r_{13} .$$

The figures for r_{ik} and for $\hat{r}_{ik}$ are written in a table showing them in the following way:

r_{ik}	1	2	3
1	r_{11}	r_{12}	r_{13}
2		r_{22}	r_{23}
3			r_{33}

$\hat{r}_{ik}$	1	2	3
1	$\hat{r}_{11}$	$\hat{r}_{12}$	$\hat{r}_{13}$
2	$\hat{r}_{12}$	$\hat{r}_{22}$	$\hat{r}_{23}$
3	$\hat{r}_{13}$	$\hat{r}_{23}$	$\hat{r}_{33}$

Because of the symmetry, the figures below the diagonal may be left out, as has been done in the left-hand table. The figures $\hat{r}_{ik}$ can now be easily checked, as there are three ways of calculating the value of Δ_{123}:

$$\Delta_{123} = r_{11}\hat{r}_{11} + r_{12}\hat{r}_{12} + r_{13}\hat{r}_{13}$$
$$= r_{12}\hat{r}_{12} + r_{22}\hat{r}_{22} + r_{23}\hat{r}_{23}$$
$$= r_{13}\hat{r}_{13} + r_{23}\hat{r}_{23} + r_{33}\hat{r}_{33} ,$$

a well-known identity. This means simply that corresponding figures in the two above tables have to be multiplied and the results belonging to one and the same column to be added up. The same result must then be obtained, whatever column be taken.

The desired information concerning all possible regression coefficients is now obtainable from table $\hat{r}_{ik}$. The regression coefficient of variate 2 in the "explanation" of variate 1 is equal to $-\dfrac{\hat{r}_{12}}{\hat{r}_{11}}$ if the direction of minimising is that of variate 1 ; $-\dfrac{\hat{r}_{22}}{\hat{r}_{12}}$ if the direction of minimising is that of variate 2 ; and $-\dfrac{\hat{r}_{23}}{\hat{r}_{13}}$ if the direction of minimising is that of variate 3. Similarly, the regression coefficients of variate 3 in the explanation of variate 1 are respectively $-\dfrac{\hat{r}_{13}}{\hat{r}_{11}}$, $-\dfrac{\hat{r}_{23}}{\hat{r}_{12}}$ or $-\dfrac{\hat{r}_{33}}{\hat{r}_{13}}$ in the three cases mentioned. Each group of three coefficients supplies the material for the construction of one bunch map. Taking the first group, the number $-\dfrac{\hat{r}_{12}}{\hat{r}_{11}}$ indicates the slope of the beam to be indicated with $\odot$ 1, $-\dfrac{\hat{r}_{22}}{\hat{r}_{12}}$ that of beam $\odot$ 2 and $-\dfrac{\hat{r}_{23}}{\hat{r}_{13}}$ that of beam · 3; the symbol $\odot$ being used for the "leading beams"—i.e., for cases where minimising has taken place either in the direction of the variate to be "explained" or in that of the "explanatory" variate.

By the same technique, all "three-sets"—i.e., groups of three variates—can be analysed.

Here it must be emphasised that the symbols used above, $\hat{r}_{13}$, etc., are, stricty speaking, incomplete and should be written $\hat{r}_{13(123)}$, indicating that it is the minor within Δ_{123} corresponding with the element r_{13}. Otherwise there would be no possibility of distinguishing it from, e.g., $\hat{r}_{13(134)}$.

In order to make bunch maps for the next higher stage—i.e., " four-sets "—the minors $\hat{r}_{12(1234)}$, etc., have to be calculated. Those relating to elements on the diagonal—viz., $\hat{r}_{11(1234)}$, $\hat{r}_{22(1234)}$, etc.—are, owing to their definition, simply equal to Δ_{234}, Δ_{134}, etc. Those not relating to an element on the diagonal have to be calculated with the formula:

$$\hat{r}_{ij(\alpha, \beta \ldots \gamma)} = - \Sigma_{k = \alpha, \beta \ldots \gamma) j (\ldots \gamma} \hat{r}_{ik(\alpha, \beta \ldots) j (\ldots \gamma)} r_{kj}$$

$$(i \neq j) .$$

The meaning of the suffixes is the following:

α, β ... γ indicate the set studied.
i indicates the row, and
j the column of the element under consideration.
k is a " current suffix "—i.e., it assumes all values indicated under the sum-sign.
$)j($ means that k must not assume the value j, whereas the $\hat{r}_{ik}$'s have to be taken as corresponding to the set without j.

As an example, $\hat{r}_{12(1234)}$ may be taken. Here $i = 1$, $j = 2$, α, β ... γ = 1, 2, 3, 4, and k evidently has to assume the values 1, 3, 4. We find:

$$\hat{r}_{12(1234)} = - \hat{r}_{11(134)} r_{12} - \hat{r}_{13(134)} r_{32} - \hat{r}_{14(134)} r_{42} .$$

No further new elements have to be introduced in the calculations.

4. *Calculation of Standard Error of Regression Coefficients* (Classical method).

Under the hypotheses formulated in Chapter II, the standard error $\sigma_{b_{1k}}$ for any regression coefficient b_{1k} must be calculated by means of the formula:

$$\sigma^2_{b_{1k}} = \frac{N}{N-n}\sigma^2_{1.23\ldots n}\frac{M_{11.kk}}{M_{11}} \tag{23}$$

in which the symbols have the following meaning:

(a) $\sqrt{\dfrac{N}{N-n}}\,\sigma_{1.23\ldots n}$ is the standard deviation of the residuals $x_{1.23\ldots n}$, corrected for the number of coefficients in the regression formula (11) and therefore equal to:

$$\sqrt{\frac{1}{N-n}\,\Sigma x^2_{1.23\ldots n}} = \sqrt{\frac{1}{N-n}\,\Sigma(x'_1 - x_1)^2} \tag{24}.$$

The easiest way of calculating this standard deviation is given by:

$$\sigma^2_{1.23\ldots n} = \sigma^2_1(1 - R^2_{1.23\ldots n})$$

where σ_1 is the standard deviation of x_1.

(b) M_{11} is the determinant:

$$\begin{vmatrix} \Sigma x^2_2 & \Sigma x_2 x_3 & \Sigma x_2 x_4 \ldots \Sigma x_2 x_n \\ \Sigma x_2 x_3 & \Sigma x^2_3 & \vdots \\ \vdots & & \vdots \\ \vdots & & \vdots \\ \Sigma x_2 x_n & \ldots\ldots\ldots\ldots\ldots & \Sigma x^2_n \end{vmatrix}$$

i.e., the determinant formed by all moments of the " explanatory " series. In those cases in which calculations for bunch maps are already available, it can very easily be obtained from:

$$M_{11} = N^{n-1}\sigma^2_2\sigma^2_3 \ldots\ldots \sigma^2_n \begin{vmatrix} 1 & r_{23} & r_{24} & \ldots\ldots & r_{2n} \\ r_{23} & 1 & \ldots\ldots\ldots & \vdots \\ \vdots & \vdots & & \vdots \\ \vdots & \vdots & & \vdots \\ r_{2n} & \ldots\ldots\ldots\ldots & 1 \end{vmatrix}$$

$$= N^{n-1}\sigma^2_2\sigma^2_3 \ldots \sigma^2_n\Delta_{23\ldots n}$$

where $\sigma_2 \ldots \sigma_n$ are the standard deviations of $x_2 \ldots x_n$, N is the number of observations, and Δ is the symbol introduced in Appendix A, 3.

(c) M_{11kk} is the determinant remaining if the kth column and the kth row in M_{11} are dropped; e.g.:

$$M_{1133} = \begin{vmatrix} \Sigma x_2^2 & \Sigma x_2 x_4 \ldots \Sigma x_2 x_n \\ \Sigma x_2 x_4 & \Sigma x_4^2 & \Sigma x_4 x_n \\ \vdots & & \\ \Sigma x_2 x_n \ldots \ldots \Sigma x_n^2 \end{vmatrix}$$

This, again, can be calculated by:

$$M_{1133} = N^{n-2} \sigma_2^2 \sigma_4^2 \ldots \sigma_n^2 \begin{vmatrix} 1 & r_{24} & \ldots & r_{2n} \\ r_{24} & 1 & \ldots & \vdots \\ \vdots & & & \vdots \\ \vdots & & & \vdots \\ r_{2n} & & \ldots & 1 \end{vmatrix}$$

$$= N^{n-2} \sigma_2^2 \sigma_4^2 \ldots \sigma_n^2 \Delta_{24\ldots n}$$

5. *Calculation of Limits to the Error of Weighting in Regression Coefficients.*

The formulæ devised by Koopmans for computing limits to the error of weighting apply only when the signs of corresponding coefficients in all of the elementary regression equations are the same (after solving for the explained variate x_1). In terms of the bunch map, this means that in each of the maps referring to the complete set of variates, all beams should lie in one of the four right-angles formed by the axes.

If a possible regression equation is denoted by

$$x_1^* = b_{12} x_2 + b_{13} x_3 + b_{14} x_4$$

for the case of three explaining variates, where the variates are expressed in normalised units, a first set of limits to each of the b's is formed by the two ultimate beams in the corresponding bunch map involving the complete set of variates. Thus, b_{12} must lie between the largest and smallest of the four coefficients

$$b_{12}^{(1)} = -\frac{\hat{r}_{12}}{\hat{r}_{11}}, \quad b_{12}^{(2)} = -\frac{\hat{r}_{22}}{\hat{r}_{21}}, \quad b_{12}^{(3)} = -\frac{\hat{r}_{32}}{\hat{r}_{31}}, \quad b_{12}^{(4)} = -\frac{\hat{r}_{42}}{\hat{r}_{41}}$$

$$(25).$$

Additional limits to the error of weighting in b_{12}, etc., can often be imposed from the following considerations. To the first elementary regression corresponds the assumption that disturbances occur only in the first variate. In this case, the standard deviation of these disturbances is estimated, according to (24), as

$$\sqrt{\frac{N}{N-n}}\,\sigma_{1.234} = \sqrt{\frac{N}{N-n}\,(1 - R_{1.234}^2)} \qquad (26),$$

the standard deviation σ of the variate x_1 itself being equal to unity. Similarly, if only the second variate is subject to disturbances, their standard deviation is estimated by

$$\sqrt{\frac{N}{N-n}}\,\sigma_{2.134} = \sqrt{\frac{N}{N-n}\,(1 - R_{2.134}^2)} \qquad (27),$$

and so on. The expressions containing the four multiple correlation coefficients R are easily computed from

$$1 - R_{1.234}^2 = \frac{\Delta_{1234}}{\Delta_{234}}, \quad 1 - R_{2.134}^2 = \frac{\Delta_{1234}}{\Delta_{134}}, \quad \text{etc.}$$

If any one of the standard deviations (26), (27), etc., of disturbances seems too large to be accepted, *a priori* considerations may lead one to adopt limits, say,

$$\rho_1', \quad \rho_2', \quad \rho_3', \quad \rho_4', \qquad (28)$$

that should not be exceeded by the estimated standard deviations of the disturbances in the corresponding variate.

Somewhat complicated calculations or diagrams are required to find exactly which values of b_{12}, etc., are still admitted by these limitations. For practical purposes, the uncertainty concerning the error of weighting may, however, already be considerably reduced, in a number of cases, by the following thumb rule,[1] which excludes a considerable part of those values of b_{12}, etc., that are incompatible with the limitations (28), but not always all of them. This rule imposes two additional limits to each of the regression coefficients b_{12} ..., the interval between these limits partly overlapping, or falling entirely within, the interval defined by the figures (25). Only values of b_{12} ... common to both intervals, then, have to be admitted.

The additional limits for b_{12} according to this rule are the largest and smallest of the quantities

$$j_{12}^{(1)} = -\frac{\hat{n}_{12}}{\hat{n}_{11}}, \quad j_{12}^{(2)} = -\frac{\hat{n}_{22}}{\hat{n}_{21}}, \quad j_{12}^{(3)} = -\frac{\hat{n}_{32}}{\hat{n}_{31}}, \quad j_{12}^{(4)} = -\frac{\hat{n}_{42}}{\hat{n}_{41}} \quad (29).$$

Here, $\hat{n}_{12}$, etc., are the minors of the elements n_{12}, etc., in a determinant, obtained from the determinant Δ of the correlation coefficients by replacing the diagonal delements r_{11}, r_{22}, etc. (which equal unity), by

$$n_{11} = r_{11} - \rho_1, \quad n_{22} = r_{22} - \rho_2, \quad \text{etc.},$$

where

$$\rho_1 = \frac{N-n}{N} \rho_1', \quad \rho_2 = \frac{N-n}{N} \rho_2', \quad \text{etc.}$$

Mutatis mutandis, similar limits for b_{13} and b_{14} are found, which may then be converted from normalised units to the units in which the variates were originally expressed.

---

[1] This thumb rule, which has not yet been published, has been communicated to the author by Dr. KOOPMANS.

If greater precision is required, it may be useful to determine the full consequences of the limitations (28) on the coefficients b_{12}.... These can best be formulated in geometrical terms. A set of coefficients, b_{12}, b_{13}, b_{14}, may be represented by a point C in three-dimensional space having these coefficients as its rectangular co-ordinates. Then, instead of the simple limits (25) for b_{12}, and similar limits for b_{13} and b_{14}, the more restrictive proposition holds that the point C is confined to the tetrahedron formed by the four points $(b_{12}^{(1)},\ b_{13}^{(1)},\ b_{14}^{(1)})$, $(b_{12}^{(2)},\ b_{13}^{(2)},\ b_{14}^{(2)})$, etc. Further, as a consequence of the limitations (28), the point C must in addition be confined to the tetrahedron formed by the four points $(j_{12}^{(1)},\ j_{13}^{(1)},\ j_{14}^{(1)})$, $(j_{12}^{(2)},\ j_{13}^{(2)},\ j_{14}^{(2)})$, etc. Thus, the point C is confined to the common part of the two tetrahedra. In the case of four (or less) variates, the extension of this common part is most easily read from a geometrical figure, if necessary, using orthogonal projections.

In devising the maximum amounts ρ_1', ρ_2', etc., admitted for the standard deviations of the disturbances in each variate, it should be borne in mind that the disturbances in the dependent variate x_1 are also due to the omission of explaining variates of minor importance. The safest procedure, therefore, is to choose ρ_1' equal to, or at a round figure somewhat exceeding, the amount represented by (26). In this case, the limit ρ_1' does not contribute to a restriction of the possibilities left to the regression coefficients b_{12}, etc., by the remaining limitations, but only serves as an aid in computing the effect of the choice of ρ_2', ρ_3', ρ_4'.

For the computation of the errors of sampling corresponding to any of the regressions admitted by the limits to the error of weighting, reference may be made to the original publication.

APPENDIX B

———

STATISTICAL TABLES

———————

Description of series	Pig-iron production	Consumption of iron and steel	Price of pig-iron	Production of consumers' goods	Profit margin
		PIG-IRON			
Units	000's tons	000's tons	1782 = 100	1913 = 100	1907 = 100
(1)	(2)	(3)	(4)	(5)	(6)
1870	5,964	2,736	44	53.5	168
1	6,627	3,372	47	58.3	164
2	6,742	3,441	74	57.9	188
3	6,566	3,396	85	61.0	190
4	5,991	3,274	66	62.7	170
5	6,365	3,680	52	60.9	156
6	6,556	3,969	46	60.5	136
7	6,608	3,927	42	61.5	136
8	6,381	3,812	36	58.3	134
9	5,995	3,224	37	54.5	122
80	7,749	4,020	42	64.6	130
1	8,144	4,057	37	62.9	118
2	8,586	4,281	39	66.7	120
3	8,529	4,339	37	68.0	112
4	7,812	4,131	32	69.0	104
5	7,415	3,782	31	64.6	94
6	7,009	3,614	30	65.2	86
7	7,559	3,486	31	67.8	82
8	7,999	4,415	31	71.6	84
9	8,323	5,064	38	74.9	84
90	7,904	4,829	39	75.4	92
1	7,406	4,772	36	78.2	90
2	6,709	5,014	33	73.0	82
3	6,977	4,766	32	72.3	80
4	7,427	5,356	32	75.3	72
5	7,703	5,458	32	79.5	66
6	8,660	6,151	34	81.5	68
7	8,796	6,619	34	79.1	66
8	8,610	6,889	36	83.6	64
9	9,421	7,574	47	86.0	78
1900	8,960	7,693	55	84.2	100
1	7,929	7,231	41	83.7	90
2	8,680	7,491	40	84.1	82
3	8,935	7,765	40	82.2	84
4	8,694	7,739	39	80.8	86
5	9,608	8,019	42	85.7	84
6	10,184	8,247	46	87.4	92
7	10,114	7,608	48	91.4	100
8	9,057	7,133	43	90.1	96
9	9,532	7,477	42	88.7	88
10	10,012	7,860	42	89.3	94
1	9,526	8,207	41	92.8	98
2	8,751	8,055	48	98.8	100
3	10,260	9,540	50	100.0	104

Notes and Sources.

(2) Production of pig-iron and ferro-alloys. British Iron and Steel Federation: *Statistics of the Iron and Steel Industries.*
(3) Home consumption of iron and steel. Unpublished estimate by Mr. A. CAIRNCROSS, Glasgow.
(4) Sauerbeck's price index. S. KUZNETS: *Secular Movements in Production and Prices.*
(5) Index of production of consumers' goods. HOFFMANN: *Weltwirtschaftliches Archiv*, Vol. 40.
(6) Profit margin = index of prices of exported finished products (Calculation L.o.N., based on trade statistics) — ½ index of wage rates (Index of BOWLEY and WOOD, taken from LAYTON: *Introduction to the Study of Prices*).

PRE-WAR

	RAILWAYS			FINANCE		
Railway investment index	Index of increase in traffic	Profit rate	Non-labour income	Long-term interest rate	Short-term interest rate	Description of series
%	%	%	million £	%	%	Units
(7)	(8)	(9)	(10)	(11)	(12)	(1)
			460	3.24	3.1	1870
8.51		4.69	490	3.23	2.7	1
5.33	9.06	4.78	525	3.24	3.8	2
6.49	7.19	4.62	545	3.24	4.5	3
4.70	1.56	4.40	555	3.24	3.5	4
3.82	6.16	4.47	560	3.20	3.0	5
2.99	4.41	4.36	560	3.16	2.2	6
1.21	2.58	4.33	555	3.15	2.3	7
1.20	− 0.13	4.24	540	3.15	3.5	8
0.77	1.41	4.18	545	3.08	1.8	9
2.49	9.45	4.41	560	3.05	2.2	80
2.89	3.75	4.33	575	3.00	2.9	1
3.74	4.78	4.36	590	2.98	3.4	2
5.55	4.18	4.32	585	2.97	3.0	3
4.17	− 0.72	4.19	580	2.97	2.6	4
2.07	− 0.25	4.04	580	3.02	2.0	5
1.10	1.32	4.01	580	2.98	2.1	6
1.26	3.60	4.02	595	2.95	2.4	7
2.15	3.20	4.08	615	3.02	2.4	8
3.12	5.01	4.23	640	2.87	2.7	9
3.85	3.52	4.41	640	2.85	3.7	90
4.70	2.82	4.31	635	2.87	2.5	1
3.62	0.89	4.17	625	2.85	1.5	2
2.16	− 2.72	3.91	630	2.79	2.1	3
1.66	8.06	4.11	645	2.72	1.0	4
1.69	2.51	4.17	660	2.59	0.8	5
2.16	6.23	4.34	680	2.48	1.4	6
2.46	5.14	4.35	715	2.45	1.8	7
3.51	2.02	4.25	735	2.48	2.6	8
3.23	7.04	4.31	765	2.58	3.3	9
3.14	3.00	4.06	790	2.76	3.7	1900
1.36	0.05	3.89	800	2.92	3.2	1
1.29	3.34	4.06	805	2.91	3.0	2
1.01	1.13	4.07	810	2.83	3.4	3
0.55	0.89	4.02	825	2.83	2.7	4
0.25	1.42	4.05	835	2.78	2.6	5
0.57	4.92	4.09	875	2.83	4.0	6
1.59	3.77	4.10	905	2.97	4.5	7
0.37	− 1.94	3.92	895	2.90	2.3	8
0.04	0.45	4.05	910	2.97	2.3	9
0.02	3.05	4.24	940	3.08	3.2	10
0.08	1.67	4.34	985	3.15	2.9	1
1.28	− 1.40	4.18		3.28	3.6	2
				3.40	4.4	3

(7) % increase in number of locomotives and of carriages, wagons and trucks, weighted by 1 and 4 respectively. Original data from C. D. CAMPBELL: " Cyclical fluctuations in the Railway Industry " in the *Transactions* of the Manchester Statistical Society, 1929/30 session.
(8) % increase in ordinary passenger journeys and in tonnage of goods conveyed, weighted by 4 and 5 respectively. Original data from C. D. CAMPBELL, *loc. cit.*
(9) Ratio of net receipts to paid-up capital. C. D. CAMPBELL, *loc. cit.*
(10) BOWLEY: *Economic Journal,* Vol. XIV, and J. STAMP: " British Incomes and Property ". Years ending June.
(11) Yield on British Consols. I. FISHER: *The Theory of Interest.*
(12) Market rate of discount. I. FISHER: *loc. cit.*

Description of series	PIG-IRON					FINANCE				
	Pig-iron production	Consumption of iron and steel	Index of production of consumers' goods	Price of pig-iron	Profit margin	Dividends	Index of share prices	Long-term interest rate	Short-term interest rate	Share yield
Units {	10^6 metric tons	10^6 metric tons	1913 = 100	Marks per ton	%	%	Nominal value = 100	%	%	%
(1)	(2)	(3)	(4)	(5)	(6)	(7)	(8)	(9)	(10)	(11)
1870	1.39	1.40	29.3	72.8	− 7.4	9.46	126.2	4.61	4.49	7.50
1	1.56	1.78	34.7	74.7	− 0.1	12.88	147.6	4.44	3.75	8.73
2	1.99	2.32	38.0	108.6	10.8	15.13	196.7	4.26	3.95	7.69
3	2.24	2.69	36.4	107.7	12.8	12.04	185.0	4.30	4.46	6.51
4	1.91	2.04	34.5	81.1	5.3	8.56	138.1	4.24	3.23	6.20
5	2.03	2.07	34.3	68.9	− 4.6	5.22	106.2	4.25	3.70	4.92
6	1.85	1.86	37.7	58.9	− 4.3	4.18	86.6	4.22	3.04	4.83
7	1.93	1.83	38.6	55.2	− 2.0	4.33	79.7	4.23	3.17	5.43
8	2.15	1.88	37.8	52.1	− 6.3	4.37	83.7	4.25	3.07	5.22
9	2.23	1.85	38.3	49.4	− 4.4	5.47	100.6	4.18	2.60	5.24
80	2.73	1.97	34.8	58.5	4.5	6.45	129.0	4.05	3.04	5.00
1	2.91	2.04	36.9	55.3	4.2	6.64	134.9	3.97	3.50	4.92
2	3.38	2.55	38.2	57.0	0.9	6.67	133.9	3.95	3.89	4.98
3	3.47	2.63	41.8	52.5	1.0	6.63	134.8	3.93	3.08	4.92
4	3.60	2.80	44.0	47.1	− 0.6	6.26	129.5	3.88	2.90	4.83
5	3.69	2.84	45.0	42.7	− 3.4	5.73	124.9	3.81	2.85	4.59
6	3.53	2.44	45.1	39.5	− 6.6	5.49	125.9	3.73	2.16	4.36
7	4.02	2.83	49.3	40.7	− 6.8	6.18	129.1	3.70	2.30	4.79
8	4.34	3.38	49.9	43.5	− 5.1	8.05	147.1	3.64	2.11	5.47
9	4.52	3.80	54.2	47.5	4.0	9.62	178.4	3.61	2.63	5.39
90	4.66	4.01	56.1	57.0	9.8	10.22	173.2	3.67	3.78	5.90
1	4.64	3.62	58.0	49.5	9.0	8.14	148.5	3.71	3.02	5.48
2	4.94	3.89	57.7	46.0	2.4	7.00	142.9	3.67	1.80	4.90
3	4.99	3.82	58.3	43.0	− 0.6	6.80	143.6	3.66	3.17	4 74
4	5.38	4.08	61.9	42.6	− 5.3	7.70	154.5	3.55	1.74	4.98
5	5.46	4.05	68.7	43.0	− 6.0	8.38	178.8	3.37	2.01	4.69
6	6.37	5.10	67.0	46.7	− 7.1	9.97	184.5	3.34	3.04	5.40
7	6.88	5.77	69.8	50.6	− 2.0	10.50	194.5	3.36	3.09	5.40
8	7.31	5.93	75.0	51.5	0.0	11.08	200.1	3.41	3.55	5.54
9	8.14	7.12	74.2	55.6	2.9	11.14	201.6	3.54	4.45	5.53
1900	8.52	7.60	72.2	64.3	9.8	10.23	184.5	3.68	4.41	5.54
1	7.88	5.73	75.7	62.2	0.5	7.74	163.4	3.65	3.06	4.74
2	8.53	5.25	79.3	53.2	− 2.8	7.31	164.3	3.52	2.19	4.45
3	10.02	6.45	72.8	52.1	− 3.3	8.29	170.2	3.53	3.01	4.87
4	10.06	7.22	82.2	51.6	− 4.6	9.09	182.5	3.57	3.14	4.98
5	10.88	7.47	82.3	53.0	− 0.6	10.16	199.4	3.57	2.85	5.10
6	12.29	8.76	88.0	58.2	3.8	10.90	198.5	3.63	4.04	5.49
7	12.88	9.63	89.2	64.0	6.3	10.40	182.7	3.75	5.12	5.69
8	11.81	8.03	87.0	60.6	− 2.3	8.92	178.1	3.80	3.52	5.01
9	12.64	8.40	90.6	55.7	− 2.4	9.44	189.3	3.70	2.87	4.99
10	14.79	9.88	89.1	55.7	− 2.2	10.09	200.8	3.76	3.54	5.02
1	15.57	10.13	97.1	57.4	− 2.5	10.40	201.9	3.79	3.54	5.15
2	17.85	11.82	96.3	60.6	4.1	11.06	200.9	3.91	4.22	5.51
3	19.31		100.0		− 1.0	10.47	192.9	4.09	4.98	5.43

Notes and sources:

(2) *Statistisches Handbuch für das Deutsche Reich* (1907) and British Iron and Steel Federation.

(3) Pig-iron production + net imports of iron and steel and their products + steel production − consumption of pig-iron for steel production.

(4) Institut für Konjunkturforschung, *Vierteljahreshefte zur Konjunkturforschung*, Sonderheft No. 31.

(5) Average price of pig-iron produced. *Statistisches Handbuch für das Deutsche Reich (1907); Statistisches Jahrbuch.*

(6) General index of wholesale prices — ½ index of wages, both in % deviations from trend. Institut für Konjunkturforschung, *Vierteljahreshefte zur Konjunkturforschung*, Sonderheft 37, and J. KUCZYNSKI: *Löhne und Ernährungskosten in Deutschland.*

(7) Yearly dividends in %. Institut für Konjunkturforschung, *Vierteljahreshefte zur Konjunkturforschung*, Sonderheft No. 36.

(8) Index of share prices in % of nominal value. *Ibid.*

(9) Yield on fixed interest-bearing securities. *Ibid.*

(10) Market rate of discount. *Ibid.*

(11) Dividends paid in % of share prices. *Ibid.*

(12) Net increase in number of rooms (Lokalitäten) in Hamburg. Institut für Konjunkturforschung, *Vierteljahreshefte zur Konjunkturforschung*, Sonderheft 17.

(13) Number of rooms vacant as % of total. *Ibid.*

(14) Yearly average rent per room of occupied houses. *Ibid.*

	BUILDING					RAILWAYS			
Net increase in number of rooms in Hamburg	Vacancies	Rent of occupied houses	Index of price of building materials	Rate of interest of mortgage banks	Profitability of building	Investment index	Index of increase in traffic	Profit rate	Description of series
000's	%	Marks per room	1913 = 100	%	%	%	%	%	Units
(12)	(13)	(14)	(15)	(16)	(17)	(18)	(19)	(20)	(1)
						9.30	7.93	6.16	1870
						9.05	18.99	6.94	1
						17.01	17.33	5.98	2
						15.63	19.08	5.21	3
						12.87	2.14	4.71	4
						6.43	2.71	4.68	5
						3.38	3.07	4.45	6
		612	107	4.58	1.39	1.55	1.16	4.26	7
5.00	5.78	593	96	4.57	1.57	2.40	1.36	4.25	8
4.18	6.50	585	90	4.40	1.78	1.97	4.48	4.28	9
3.59	6.85	580	86	4.28	1.93	0.83	5.99	4.44	80
3.18	7.07	572	82	4.00	2.14	1.76	5.50	4.54	1
2.89	6.92	573	82	4.00	2.16	3.13	7.44	4.80	2
0.19	4.91	575	87	4.00	2.07	3.21	4.88	4.61	3
0.35	3.46	587	93	4.00	1.99	2.46	3.07	4.60	4
0.31	2.71	596	93	3.86	1.89	2.35	0.25	4.42	5
0.28	2.50	615	97	3.50	2.22	1.41	3.81	4.66	6
2.62	2.38	632	104	3.79	1.99	1.48	7.24	5.17	7
4.88	2.82	660	103	3.68	2.38	2.78	8.37	5.40	8
7.61	3.44	677	112	3.50	2.48	3.80	8.70	5.60	9
9.02	4.64	676	100	3.73	2.63	4.73	4.65	4.86	90
6.92	5.86	681	92	4.00	2.74	4.15	4.05	4.49	1
7.08	8.38	687	85	3.99	3.03	4.25	0.57	4.56	2
6.23	9.01	664	79	3.93	3.01	2.08	5.89	5.03	3
4.57	9.00	650	77	3.63	3.13	1.83	1.23	4.98	4
3.16	7.98	643	78	3.50	3.07	2.59	7.18	5.74	5
2.41	6.37	637	81	3.50	2.91	3.14	6.88	6.15	6
2.20	4.53	637	93	3.50	2.57	3.85	7.36	6.21	7
2.42	3.51	639	102	3.58	2.28	4.90	8.10	6.06	8
3.35	2.97	643	103	3.94	2.04	4.00	6.90	6.12	9
3.93	2.51	650	107	4.00	1.94	4.24	6.13	5.91	1900
2.41	2.15	665	98	4.00	2.38	3.06	− 2.01	5.14	1
4.29	2.72	676	98	3.98	2.51	2.42	3.46	5.40	2
7.40	3.54	681	101	3.78	2.61	1.91	7.31	5.95	3
10.20	4.38	686	104	3.87	2.52	2.60	4.66	6.00	4
10.72	4.80	689	102	3.84	2.63	3.37	8.04	6.29	5
10.38	5.32	694	106	3.94	2.48	4.75	8.28	6.35	6
8.60	4.65	705	103	4.02	2.64	6.42	6.44	5.60	7
8.03	4.56	714	97	4.02	2.92	5.82	− 0.33	4.51	8
8.85	4.82	709	104	4.00	2.67	4.06	6.77	5.09	9
13.39	6.87	717	97	4.00	2.97	3.17	6.20	5.74	10
10.85	7.21	724	97	4.00	3.04	3.74	8.94	6.41	1
12.16	7.16	737	104	4.03	2.94	4.05	6.37	6.29	2
6.18	6.02	747	100	4.11	3.12	5.22	2.58	5.70	3

(15) Index of price of building materials. Institut für Konjunkturforschung, *Vierteljahreshefte zur Konjunkturforschung*, Sonderheft 37.

(16) Average interest rate on new issues of German mortgage banks. Institut für Konjunkturforschung, *Vierteljahreshefte zur Konjunkturforschung*, Sonderheft 17.

(17) Profitability $= m_R - (0.65\ q_R + 0.35)(0.007\ m_{Lb} + 0.02)$

where m_R = rent index, in %, 1913 = 8.

q_R = index of cost of building materials, 1913 = 100.

m_{Lb} = interest on mortgage banks new issues.

(18) % increase in the number of locomotives, passenger cars and freight cars, with the respective weights 1, 1, 5. Original data from *Statistisches Handbuch (1907)* and *Statistisches Jahrbuch*.

(19) % increase in number of passengers and tonnage of goods carried one mile, with the respective weights 1 and 2. Original data from *Statistisches Handbuch (1907)* and *Statistisches Jahrbuch*.

(20) Net operating income in % of capital invested. *Statistisches Handbuch (1907)* and *Statistisches Jahrbuch*.

UNITED STATES OF AMERICA — PRE-WAR

Description of series	PIG-IRON			RAILWAYS			FINANCE		
	Pig-iron production	Price of pig-iron	Building volume	Railway investment index	Index of increase in traffic	Profit rate	Stock prices	Long-term interest rate	Short-term interest rate
Units	000's tons	$ per ton	1913 = 100	%	%	%	$	%	%
(1)	(2)	(3)	(4)	(5)	(6)	(7)	(8)	(9)	(10)
1877	2,067	18.9	19				39.2		5.2
8	2,301	17.7	17				42.1		4.8
9	2,742	21.7	19				44.4		5.1
80	3,835	28.5	22				53.9		5.2
1	4,144	25.2	27				66.7		5.2
2	4,623	25.8	33				60.8		5.7
3	4,596	22.4	39				55.9		5.6
4	4,098	19.8	44				46.2		5.2
5	4,045	18.0	47				48.0		4.1
6	5,683	18.7	51				55.9		4.8
7	6,417	20.9	47				55.8		5.8
8	6,490	18.9	46				54.2		4.9
9	7,604	17.8	63				61.2		4.9
90	9,203	18.4	75			4.65	57.7	5.04	5.7
1	8,280	17.5	76		3.90	4.60	53.6	5.17	5.4
2	9,157	15.8	84		9.70	4.44	65.4	4.95	4.1
3	7,125	14.5	55		6.17	4.42	53.0	5.08	6.6
4	6,657	12.7	55		— 10.52	3.80	49.4	4.90	3.0
5	9,446	13.1	73	— 0.23	0.89	3.81	51.8	4.77	3.7
6	8,623	13.0	60	1.43	10.65	3.84	44.8	4.83	5.8
7	9,653	12.1	67	0.27	— 1.66	3.93	45.2	4.66	3.5
8	11,774	11.7	58	1.41	17.22	4.39	52.2	4.49	3.8
9	13,621	19.4	70	2.65	8.57	4.95	71.0	4.23	4.2
1900	13,789	20.0	46	4.23	13.36	5.13	61.2	4.15	4.4
1	15,878	15.9	66	6.06	4.95	5.43	69.6	4.07	4.3
2	17,821	22.2	69	4.76	8.58	5.63	65.1	4.06	4.9
3	18,009	19.9	71	6.31	9.16	5.72	55.8	4.24	5.5
4	16,497	15.6	80	3.74	1.76	5.38	54.2	4.23	4.2
5	22,992	17.9	106	2.70	7.28	5.51	79.5	4.06	4.4
6	25,307	21.0	109	6.02	13.28	5.90	93.9	4.18	5.7
7	25,781	23.9	98	7.41	9.73	5.95	76.2	4.51	6.4
8	15,936	17.7	89	4.74	— 4.55	4.91	74.7	4.55	4.3
9	25,795	17.8	125	— 0.02	0.17	5.22	92.2	4.33	4.0
10	27,304	17.4	109	3.03	15.19	5.53	84.9	4.44	5.0
1	23,650	15.7	104	3.64	0.30	4.77	82.3	4.43	4.0
2	29,727	16.6	108	1.46	2.99	4.55	88.4	4.46	4.7
3	30,966	17.1	100	3.03	11.69	4.86	79.5	4.64	5.6

Notes and Sources.

(2) Production of pig-iron and ferro-alloys. British Iron and Steel Federation: *Statistics of the Iron and Steel Industries.*
(3) Price of No. 1 foundry pig-iron at Philadelphia. *U.S.A. Statistical Abstract.*
(4) W. H. NEWMAN: *The Building Industry and Business Cycles.* Chicago, 1935.
(5) Per cent increase in the number of locomotives, passenger cars and freight cars, with the respective weights 2, 1 and 4. Original data from the *U.S.A. Statistical Abstract.*
(6) Per cent increase in number of passengers carried one mile and weight of freight carried one mile, with the respective weights 1 and 3. Original data from the *U.S.A. Statistical Abstract.*
(7) Net railway operating income in per cent of total railway investment. Original data on net traffic earnings, net revenue and income or net railway operating income and on railroad investment or capitalisation from the *U.S.A. Statistical Abstracts, 1904, 1910* and *1924.* The original series have been adjusted before being linked up.
(8) Average price of industrial stocks. *Review of Economic Statistics, 1919* and *1926.*
(9) 1890-1899: Yield on ten American Railroad bonds. *Review of Economic Statistics, 1919;* 1900-1913: Yield on sixty bond issues combined. Standard Statistics Co.
(10) Market rate on 60-90-day paper. I. FISHER: *The Theory of Interest.*

FRANCE — PRE-WAR

Description of series	PIG-IRON			RAILWAYS			FINANCE	
	Production of pig-iron	Consumption of iron and steel	Price of pig-iron	Railway investment index	Index of increase in traffic	Profit rate	Index of share prices	Index of bond prices
Units	000's tons	000's tons	francs per ton	%	%	%	1901-10 = 100	1901-10 = 100
(1)	(2)	(3)	(4)	(5)	(6)	(7)	(8)	(9)
1870	1,178	1,212	92	3.7	— 9.0	4.40	89	67
1	860	836	98	3.8	8.3	5.20	77	55
2	1,218	1,162	121	8.2	19.4	4.84	81	56
3	1,382	1,344	137	5.3	4.4	4.67	85	58
4	1,416	1,380	119	4.2	— 1.1	4.44	85	62
5	1,448	1,488	108	1.9	4.8	4.65	94	66
6	1,435	1,519	98	0.8	2.8	4.59	92	70
7	1,507	1,641	95	4.6	— 1.7	4.29	95	72
8	1,521	1,663	88	3.7	9.8	4.52	99	77
9	1,400	1,527	85	1.9	— 0.1	4.33	102	82
80	1,725	1,872	93	3.2	13.5	4.80	113	86
1	1,886	2,244	91	7.4	5.6	4.82	125	87
2	2,039	2,590	91	7.8	3.6	4.44	114	84
3	2,069	2,520	81	5.2	3.0	4.08	102	81
4	1,872	2,111	75	3.8	— 4.0	3.61	96	79
5	1,631	1,744	62	2.4	— 2.7	3 36	88	82
6	1,517	1,559	55	1.6	— 2.0	3.27	86	84
7	1,568	1,444	57	1.0	4.1	3 38	87	83
8	1,683	1,651	57	1.0	3.6	3.40	92	84
9	1,734	1,506	61	1.2	11.1	3.61	97	87
90	1,962	1,723	70	0.9	0	3.50	104	94
1	1,897	1,827	65	1.2	4.5	3.42	103	97
2	2,057	2,043	61	1.6	4.3	3.16	98	100
3	2,003	2,014	58	1.0	4.4	3.10	96	100
4	2,069	2,052	57	1.1	2.4	3.23	94	103
5	2,003	1,868	55	0.8	3.3	3.40	92	104
6	2,339	2,103	56	0.6	3.4	3.57	93	104
7	2,484	2,367	58	0.6	3.5	3.69	102	105
8	2,525	2,375	63	0.6	5.8	3.86	110	105
9	2,578	2,542	72	1.5	5.1	3.93	113	103
1900	2,714	2,908	82	3.1	9.1	3.86	109	103
1	2,389	2,362	70	3.0	— 5.1	3.52	96	102
2	2,405	2,067	68	1.1	1.2	3.67	89	103
3	2,841	2,489	64	1.0	1.8	3.82	89	100
4	2,974	2,561	65	1.1	1.1	3.93	90	99
5	3,077	2,637	68	— 0.1	5.3	4.03	101	101
6	3,314	2,983	80	0.7	4.5	4.16	105	100
7	3,590	3,075	87	3.6	5.8	3.97	105	97
8	3,401	2,925	82	4.9	4.1	3.86	102	98
9	3,574	3,152	82	1.9	2.8	3.89	108	100
10	4,038	3,715	78	1.8	3 2	3.84	116	100
1	4,470	4,278	76	3.6	5.1	3.72	121	98
2	4,939	4,649		3.6	5.3	3.82	130	94
3	5,207	4,817		4.5	5.3	3.91	127	89

Notes and Sources.

(2) *Annuaire statistique de la France.*

(3) Pig-iron production + net imports of pig-iron, iron and steel and manufactures thereof. Data from *Annuaire statistique de la France* and Institut de Recherches économiques de l'Université de Paris.

(4) Average price per ton of pig-iron produced. *Annuaire statistique de la France.*

(5) % increase in number of locomotives and of passenger and freight cars, weighted by 1 and 3 respectively. Original data from *Annuaire statistique de la France.*

(6) % increase in passengers carried one km. and goods carried one km., weighted by 4 and 5 respectively. Original data from *Annuaire statistique de la France.*

(7) Net receipts per km. of line divided by cost of construction of one km. *Annuaire statistique de la France.*

(8) Index of price of variable interest-bearing securities. *Bulletin de la Statistique générale de la France, 1919/20.*

(9) Index of price of 3 % " rente ". *Bulletin de la Statistique générale de la France 1919/20.*

SWEDEN — PRE-WAR

Description of series	Number of rooms built	Vacancies	Rent index	Cost of construction index	Long-term interest rate	Profitability of building	Total assessed income	Cost of living index	Real income earned
Units	000's	%	1861-70 = 100	1861-70 = 100	%	%	million kr.	1861-70 = 100	10⁹ kr. 1861-70
(1)	(2)	(3)	(4)	(5)	(6)	(7)	(8)	(9)	(10)
1880	5.3			107	5.8		286		
1	7.6			107	5.8		304		
2	9.4	3.0		108	5.7		318	106	.31
3	8.0	3.6	112	112	5.7	2.26	332	105	.31
4	10.5	4.2	116	112	5.7	2.58	332	101	.35
5	10.8	4.8	118	110	5.6	2.93	349	96	.36
6	6.8	5.4	112	108	5.6	2.56	345	92	.38
7	6.1	6.2	105	105	5.4	2.33	350	88	.41
8	6.3	5.1	100	109	5.1	1.92	355	91	.42
9	5.4	3.9	95	109	4.9	1.68	381	96	.43
90	7.6	6.5	95	112	4.7	1.60	411	98	.43
1	4.2	5.1	94	109	4.8	1.67	418	101	.43
2	1.7	5.0	93	107	4.9	1.62	425	99	.43
3	0.9	3.5	93	106	4.8	1.68	432	95	.47
4	2.5	1.6	95	100	4.8	2.24	448	90	.52
5	4.0	1.6	100	114	4.6	2.04	465	92	.54
6	6.3	0.8	107	117	4.5	2.54	495	91	.59
7	4.5	1.2	107	119	4.4	2.52	538	94	.64
8	6.2	0.3	120	124	4.4	3.30	601	98	.67
9	7.1	1.8	135	131	4.8	3.79	660	103	.70
1900	4.2	1.1	138	125	5.1	4.08	716	104	.73
1	4.3	1.6	138	115	5.3	4.47	764	101	.76
2	5.3	1.4	132	117	5.1	4.03	765	102	.81
3	9.9	2.8	135	136	4.9	3.46	831	104	.87
4	12.2	3.5	139	127	4.9	4.23	895	103	.91
5	8.6	2.3	141	138	4.9	3.79	944	105	.97
6	11.1	1.0	145	139	5.0	3.94	1,017	107	1.07
7	11.0	1.0	160	155	5.3	3.95	1,145	113	1.11
8	7.0	1.6	175	145	5.5	5.53	1,245	114	1.11
9	8.7	2.2	176	148	5.4	5.46	1,268	113	1.11
10	7.8	2.4	169	151	5.2	5.00	1,254	113	1.28
1	5.7	2.4	166	144	5.1	5.25	1,446	112	1.36
2	8.9	2.0	172	160	5.0	4.95	1,519	119	1.39
3	12.4	3.6	169	160	5.1	5.10	1,655	119	

Notes and Sources.

(2) Total number of newly built rooms or kitchens in Stockholm. *Statistical Abstract for Stockholm.* Since 1906, adjusted for change in scope.
(3) Number of rooms vacant on December 31st as a percentage of total. *Statistical Abstract for Stockholm;* 1883-7: estimated.
(4) and (5) MYRDAL, *The Cost of Living in Sweden 1830-1930.*
(6) Interest rate of Swedish savings banks. LINDAHL: *National Income of Sweden 1861-1930.*
(7) Profitability = $m_R - (0.007 q_B m_{Lb} + 0.02 q_R)$ where m_R = rent in % (1861-70 = 8); q_B = index of construction costs, 1861-70 = 100; m_{Lb} = long-term interest rate.

(8) Assessed income from capital and wages. *Sveriges Statistisk Årsbok.*
(9) MYRDAL: *loc. cit*
(10) Assessed income of following year, divided by cost-of-living index.

SWEDEN — POST-WAR

				BUILDING					
Description of series	Rooms built in 296 cities	Dwellings built in Stockholm	Rent index	Construction costs (i)	Construction costs (ii)	Savings banks interest rate	Profitability of building (i)	Profitability of building (ii)	Real income earned
Units {	000's	000's	1.VII. 1914 = 100	1913 = 100	1914 = 100	%	%	%	10^9 Kr. 1914
(1)	(2)	(3)	(4)	(5)	(6)	(7)	(8)	(9)	(10)
1923			169	211	210	5.2	1.6	1.7	2.65
4	40.0	2.8	180	216	230	5.5	1.8	0.9	2.78
5	42.3	4.2	186	219	235	5.6	2.0	1.0	2.82
6	43.5	6.1	188	215	235	5.5	2.4	1.2	2.96
7	43.9	6.6	196	213	232	5.4	3.3	2.3	3.07
8	46.7	6.0	199	210	232	5.5	3.6	2.4	3.10
9	46.4	5.6	200	209	232	5.5	3.7	2.5	3.34
30	59.5	8.4	204	208	232	5.2	4.5	3.3	3.48
1	59.3	7.7	206	201	232	5.2	5.2	3.5	3.36
2	52.7	6.9	206	194	228	5.3	5.4	3.4	3.12
3	40.2	3.7	203	192	221	4.7	6.2	4.6	3.10
4	51.2	3.0	202	191	217	4.4	6.6	5.2	3.39
5	76.7	5.8	199	193	217	3.9	6.7	5.7	3.70
6	86.9	6.9	197	193		(3.5)			(3.90)

Notes and sources.

(2) Gross increase in number of rooms or kitchens in 296 cities. LINDAHL: *The National Income of Sweden*, Part II—and *Sociala Meddelanden*, No. 7, 1937—Adjustments have been made because the number of cities varied slightly.
(3) Number of dwellings built by private enterprise only. *Stockholm Stadskollegiets utlåtanden och memorial*—Bihang, No. 10A, 1935. — *Sociala Meddelanden*, 1937.
(4) Index entering into the cost-of-living index. *Statistisk Årsbok för Sverige.*
(5) Index of construction costs. *Svenska Handelsbanken:* Index. See note (a) on page 97.
(6) Index of construction costs in Stockholm. *Statistisk Årsbok för Stockholms Stad.*
(7) Svenska sparbank föreningen. *Statistisk Årsbok för Sverige.*
(8) Profitability $= m_R - (0.007 \, q_B m_{Lb} + 0.02 \, q_B)$ where m_R = rent index in %, 1914 = 8; q_B = index of construction costs (i), 1913 = 100; m_{Lb} = long-term interest rate.
(9) As (8), but with index of construction costs (ii).
(10) Total assessed income of following year divided by cost-of-living index. *Statistisk Årsbok för Sverige.*

Description of series	PIG-IRON			BUILDING					
	Pig-iron production	Kuznets' investment index	Price of pig-iron	Residential construction (i)	Residential construction (ii)	Rent index	Building costs	Profitability of building	Stock of houses
Units	10^9 tons	10^9 $ 1929	$ per ton	10^6 $	10^6 sq. feet	1913 = 100	1923-25 = 100	%	000,000's
(1)	(2)	(3)	(4)	(5)	(6)	(7)	(8)	(9)	(10)
1918	39.1		36.7			104.7	89.2	− 0.15	20.5
9	31.0	12.3	31.1		288	114.2	93.5	0.08	20.7
20	36.9	12.4	44.5	1122	164	134.9	118.5	− 1.28	20.9
1	16.7	9.2	25.3	1841	244	159.0	95.1	2.46	21.2
2	27.2	10.9	27.6	3115	370	160.9	82.3	4.40	21.6
3	40.4	14.2	29.0	3980	422	163.4	100.9	3.05	22.0
4	31.4	14.1	23.3	4244	442	168.0	101.6	3.46	22.5
5	36.7	15.4	22.3	4754	560	167.4	97.5	3.84	23.1
6	39.4	16.9	21.3	4314	521	165.4	98.1	3.78	23.7
7	36.6	16.2	20.4	4064	495	162.1	97.3	3.76	24.2
8	38.2	16.7	19.2	3813	568	157.6	97.5	3.45	24.8
9	42.6	18.4	20.5	2623	388	153.7	97.6	2.96	25.2
30	31.8	15.1	20.3	1456	230	149.6	95.7	3.02	25.4
1	18.4	11.3	18.7	1005	190	142.0	85.5	3.09	25.6
2	8.8	7.9	17.1	282	74	127.8	74.0	2.11	25.7
3	13.3	7.7	18.3	204	73	108.8	80.3	0.52	25.8
4	16.1		20.5	214	64	102.1	93.4	− 0.14	25.9
5	21.4		21.0	585	135	102.1	92.0	0.38	26.0
6	30.6		22.0	1202	222	104.6	97.3		
7	36.6		25.8	1278	236	110.0	109.5		

Notes and sources.

(2) Production of pig-iron and ferro-alloys. *Statistical Abstract of the United States and Survey of Current Business*, Department of Commerce.

(3) Flow of producers' durable commodities to enterprises + flow of consumers' durable commodities to households and enterprises.

(4) Price of Bessemer pig-iron at Pittsburgh. *Statistical Abstract.*

(5) Value of total new non-farm residential building. National Bureau of Economic Research *Bulletin* No. 65. To obtain an index of volume this series has to be deflated by construction costs.

(6) Construction contracts awarded, floor space of buildings. Data from DODGE Co., in *Statistical Abstract of the United States.*

(7) Index of the Bureau of Labor statistics. Figures for June of each year.

(8) Index of construction costs of the *Engineering News Record. Statistical Abstract.*

(9) Profitability $= m_R - (0.007 q_B m_{Lb} + 0.02 q_B)$

where m_R = rent index in %, average 1901-35 = 8.

q_R = index of construction costs, 1901-35 = 100.

m_{Lb} = long-term interest rate.

(10) Estimated number of houses at end of year based on census data and yearly volume of building.

POST-WAR

	PRODUCTION, PRICES, FINANCE										
Production of consumers' goods	Index of wholesale prices	Cost-of-living index	Corporations net income	Urban non-workers' income	Capital gains	Profit margin	Index of stock prices	Long-term interest rate	Short-term interest rate	Share yield	Description of series
10^9 \$ 1929	1926 = 100	1923 = 100	10^9 \$	10^9 \$	10^9 \$	1929 = 100	1926 = 100	%	%	%	Units
(11)	(12)	(13)	(14)	(15)	(16)	(17)	(18)	(19)	(20)	(21)	(1)
53	125.0	94.2	7.67				56.6	5.43	6.0	11.9	1918
51	134.4	102.3	8.42	14.1	1.2	126.4	72.6	5.49	5.6	9.0	9
50	157.7	118.2	5.87	15.9	1.1	140.2	66.1	6.12	7.5	9.1	20
45	114.0	102.3	0.46	15.0	0.5	116.4	51.6	5.97	6.8	9.6	1
53	91.4	97.4	4.77	16.4	1.3	110.6	64.7	5.10	4.7	6.9	2
59	102.0	100.0	6.31	17.9	1.4	107.8	66.6	5.12	5.0	8.1	3
59	99.6	101.3	5.36	18.7	2.0	106.4	69.6	5.00	3.9	7.7	4
61	102.9	103.7	7.62	19.9	4.6	111.2	88.4	4.88	4.0	7.3	5
65	103.2	104.3	7.50	20.2	3.6	110.4	100.0	4.73	4.2	7.3	6
66	96.5	102.0	6.51	20.9	4.4	105.8	118.5	4.57	4.0	6.4	7
70	96.4	100.6	8.23	22.1	7.8	103.0	154.3	4.55	4.9	5.1	8
74	95.9	100.1	8.74	23.7	6.2	100.0	189.4	4.73	5.8	4.6	9
66	92.5	96.7	1.55	22.4	− 3.5	93.2	140.6	4.55	3.9	5.2	30
61	78.2	87.2	− 3.29	19.5	− 10.4	78.2	87.4	4.58	2.6	6.1	1
56	67.3	77.9	− 5.64	15.7	− 5.7	69.6	46.5	5.01	2.8	8.0	2
	61.0	74.9	− 2.55	14.8		65.6	65.7	4.49	1.7	5.1	3
	72.2	79.4					81.1	4.00	1.0		4
	78.8	82.6					90.8	3.60	0.8		5
	80.6	84.8						3.24			6
	85.9	88.5						3.28			7

(11) Estimates based on data from WARBURTON, *Journal of the American Statistical Association*. Vol. 30.

(12) Index number of the Bureau of Labor Statistics. Figures for January of each year.

(13) National Industrial Conference Board.

(14) Corporations' net income minus deficit. *Statistical Abstract and Statistics of Income.*

(15) Estimates based on data from S. KUZNETS: *National Income, 1919-1935*, National Bureau of Economic Research, Bulletin No. 66.

(16) Estimates based on data from WARBURTON, *Journal of Political Economy*, vol. 43.

(17) Index of cost of living — ½ index of hourly earnings. National Industrial Conference Board.

(18) Index of Standard Statistics Co. for industrial stocks.

(19) Yield of sixty bonds combined, *Standard Statistics*. 1936 and 1937: estimates on the basis of forty-five bonds.

(20) Market rate, 4-6 months commercial paper. I. FISHER, *The Theory of Interest* and League of Nations *Monthly Bulletin of Statistics*.

(21) Cash dividends in % of total capital stock. *Statistics of Income*. Up to 1925, capital stock has been estimated on the basis of new corporate issues and index of stock prices. But for a slight difference of trend, the movements of the series of share yield thus calculated are highly correlated with those of the series published since 1926 by the Standard Statistics Co., New York.

UNITED KINGDOM

Description of series	Pig-iron production	Pig-iron consumption	Price of pig-iron	Number of houses built	Rent index
	PIG-IRON			BUILDING	
Units	10^6 tons	10^6 tons	£ per ton	000's	VII.1914 = 100
(1)	(2)	(3)	(4)	(5)	(6)
1919	7.40	5.45	6.85		105
20	8.03	5.48	10.45		121
1	2.62	2.42	6.87		148
2	4.90	2.03	4.53		153
3	7.44	4.06	5.44	67.5	148
4	7.31	5.49	4.41	69.2	147
5	6.26	4.83	3.63	66.4	147
6	2.46	* 4.95	4.38	63.9	149
7	7.29	* 4.95	3.65	60.3	151
8	6.61	4.79	3.29	64.7	151
9	7.59	5.57	3.51	91.7	153
30	6.19	5.58	3.35	125.4	153
1	3.77	4.40	2.93	128.4	154
2	3.57	3.04	2.93	142.0	154
3	4.14	2.96	3.11	207.9	156
4	5.97	4.83	3.35	286.4	156
5	6.42	4.95	3.39	271.4	157
6	7.69	6.68	3.66	273.2	159
7				257.1	159

Notes and Sources.

(2)   British Iron and Steel Federation: *Statistics of the Iron and Steel Industries.*

(3)   Production minus net exports of iron and steel and their products. British Iron and Steel Federation and *Annual Statement of the Trade of the United Kingdom.* * Average of 1926 and 1927.

(4)   Price of Cleveland-Middlesbrough pig-iron. Yearly article by the Editor of the *Statist, Journal of the Royal Statistical Society,* Part II.

(5)   Number of houses built by private enterprise without State assistance; years ending following March; *Statistical Abstract for the United Kingdom* and *Annual Report, Ministry of Health.*

(6)   Rent index of the cost-of-living index. Up to 1928, figures relate to controlled rents; since 1929, to controlled and uncontrolled rents combined. *20th Abstract of Labour Statistics* and *Monthly Labour Gazette.*

POST-WAR

BUILDING		FINANCE			
Index of construction costs	Profitability of building	Real income from wages and salaries	Profit rate	Long-term interest rate	Description of series
1929 = 100	%	10^6 £ 1914	%	%	Units
(7)	(8)	(9)	(10)	(11)	(1)
156.9	—2.64			4.62	1919
142.5	—0.28		15.2	5.32	20
115.6	2.14		10.3	5.21	1
103.6	2.55	12.5	7.0	4.42	2
99.9	2.64	13.6	9.8	4.31	3
97.1	2.75	13.6	10.3	4.39	4
97.1	2.79	13.7	10.9	4.44	5
100.0	2.73	13.0	11.3	4.55	6
100.0	2.79	14.1	10.5	4.56	7
100.0	2.78	14.2	11.1	4.47	8
96.8	3.05	14.8	10.5	4.60	9
95.2	3.25	14.7	9.8	4.48	30
93.2	3.78	15.2	7.2	4.39	1
89.5	4.27	16.4	5.8	3.74	2
88.9	4.47	16.2	6.1	3.39	3
87.9	4.70	16.7	7.2	3.10	4
88.1	4.77	17.2	8.5	2.89	5
92.7		17.4	9.7	2.94	6
					7

(7) COLIN CLARK, *Investment in Fixed Capital in Great Britain*, Special Memorandum No. 38, London & Cambridge Economic Service. This series has been continued on figures obtained from Mr. R. STONE.

(8) Profitability $= m_R - (0.007 q_B m_{Lb} + 0.02 q_B)$ where $m_R =$ rent index, in %, 1929 = 8; $q_B =$ index of construction costs, 1929 = 100; $m_{Lb} -$ long-term interest rate.

(9) Income from wages and salaries according to C. CLARK, *National Income and Outlay*, divided by index of cost of living.

(10) Ratio of profits of a sample of industrial corporations to their preferred and ordinary capital. *The Economist.*

(11) Yield of 2½% Consols. *Statistical Abstract for the United Kingdom* and *Statistical Summary of the Bank of England.*

INDEX

STATISTICAL TESTING
OF
BUSINESS-CYCLE THEORIES

II

BUSINESS CYCLES

IN THE

UNITED STATES OF AMERICA

1919~1932

BY

J. TINBERGEN

LEAGUE OF NATIONS
Economic Intelligence Service
GENEVA
1939

Series of League of Nations Publications

II. ECONOMIC AND FINANCIAL

1939. II.A. 16.

CONTENTS

3578 — S. d. N. 1695 (F.) 2390 (A.) 8/39. Imp. Atar

PREFACE

This volume on business cycles in the United States of America is the third of a series giving the results of an enquiry into the problem of the recurrence of periods of economic depression upon which the League has been engaged for some years.

The enquiry has been divided into two stages. The first was to examine existing theories with a view to ascertaining what they had in common, the points at which differences of opinion arose and, in so far as possible, the causes of those differences; the second, to confront these theories with the historical facts — to subject them, in so far as these facts can be quantitatively expressed, to statistical analysis, and in so far as they cannot be so expressed, to compare them with the recounted records of the past.

The first stage was completed with the publication of a book, of which Professor Gottfried VON HABERLER was the author, entitled *Prosperity and Depression*, a revised and enlarged edition of which has just appeared; the second was initiated by the publication this year of an introductory volume[1] by Professor J. TINBERGEN, in which the statistical methods which it was intended to employ were explained. In the present volume, also written by Professor TINBERGEN, with the assistance of Dr. J. J. POLAK, the post-war data for the United States have been employed for the purpose of subjecting to statistical test, as originally proposed, certain of the theories summarised and expounded by Professor VON HABERLER.

---

[1] *Statistical Testing of Business-cycle Theories*, Vol. I: *A Method and its Application to Investment Activity*, League of Nations, Geneva, 1939.

The phenomena of the trade cycle are complex, various forces acting and reacting on each other and constituting in the aggregate a sort of vital organism. In order to understand the manner in which this organism functions, an elaborate system of mathematical analysis is required. The system employed is briefly described in the introduction to this volume and in somewhat greater detail in Professor TINBERGEN's earlier volume.

This is not the place to enter upon any discussion of methodological problems; but it may be well to draw attention here at the outset to one point. The system of analysis employed cannot do more than submit preconceived theories to statistical test. The economist, and not the statistician, must in the first place indicate what, in the light of logical reasoning from ascertained facts, would appear to be the probable causal relationships. The statistician can then examine, with the statistical data and the mathematical tools at his disposal, which of the possible combinations of causes indicated seems in each particular case to give the best fit. He cannot do more than that. It is, indeed, for this very reason that the enquiry has been conducted in two stages — first, an analysis of theories, and secondly, a statistical testing of those theories.

But in practice in the process of testing, in the selection of each one of the "explanatory" factors employed in the various diagrams in this volume, problems of pure economics necessarily arose for consideration before the mathematical analysis could be attempted.

Owing to the nature of this problem and the consequent complexity of the form of analysis employed, a considerable part of this book will present serious difficulties to the non-mathematical reader. His attention may therefore be directed to the introduction, to the conclusions contained in Chapter VII and to the diagrams, which, with the key contained in Appendix A, are largely self-explanatory.

The results obtained can, of course, claim no sort of finality; they relate to one country only, and to a relatively brief period of time during which the economic structure was undergoing very rapid changes. It is proposed to supplement them by a parallel study for the United Kingdom. But it is hoped that it may prove possible, while this parallel study is being conducted, to subject to closer investigation certain points in connection with the work already done, to employ in certain cases monthly or quarterly data instead of annual data and to check certain results regarding post-war events by studies of previous experience.

The manuscript of this volume has been sent to a number of statisticians and economists in different countries who have been good enough to comment on it. In addition, it has been possible to arrange for meetings of small groups of experts to discuss methods and results at various stages of the work. Thanks are due to all those who have been good enough to help by their criticism and advice.

A. LOVEDAY,
Director of the Financial Section and Economic Intelligence Service.

Geneva, July 1939.

INTRODUCTION

Multiple correlation method. If one tries to understand the causation of business-cycle phenomena, one is almost invariably led to questions of the type: why did a given economic phenomenon — say, investment activity — fluctuate as it did ? Most economists would agree that, generally, a number of "causes" are present, which may all be formulated as changes in some other phenomena. A fall in investment activity may be caused by a fall in profits, or an increase in interest rates, or a change in confidence, and so on. There is less unanimity about the relative strength of these causes in various circumstances. In attempting to find evidence on this relative strength, economic reasoning may be helped and completed by statistical analysis. The ordinary elementary methods of statistical analysis are, however, sufficient for this task only in special cases. One of these ordinary methods consists in looking for months or quarters or years in which only one of the assumed causes has shown a large change, the others remaining about constant. This is, however, a very uncommon case which seldom occurs. Another elementary method is the splitting-up of figures into partial figures — say, general investment activity into investment activity in special branches. The applicability of this method of course depends very much on the statistical material available. But, even apart from that, the splitting-up of the material, however useful, is not sufficient in a considerable number of circumstances. It very often happens that two or more causes are at work even in every subdivision of a phenomenon. In such circumstances, this method is clearly insufficient.

In addition to these elementary methods, a more advanced one — the method of multiple correlation analysis — is available which enables the investigator to find out, in a number of cases, the relative strength of various influences working on the same variable. If, for example, economic reasoning suggests that the fluctuations in variable v (investment activity) depend on fluctuations in the "explanatory" variables Z (profits), q (price of investment goods), m (interest rate) and l (wage rate), then by this method the so-called regression coefficients φ_1, φ_2, etc., can be found by which the variables Z, q, m, etc., have to be multiplied in order to get an expression $v^* = \varphi_1 Z + \varphi_2 q + \varphi_3 m + \varphi_4 l$,[1] the fluctuations of which come as near as possible to those of v. These coefficients can be determined only approximately, their accuracy or significance depending on a number of circumstances which we cannot enumerate now. The details of this method have been given in the preceding publication in this series[2] and need not be repeated here. Numerous results are discussed in the following chapters, and these will serve as examples of the method.

The following features may, however, be shortly recapitulated with a view to a proper understanding of our work.

1. A priori
considerations.
The method essentially starts with *a priori* considerations about what explanatory variables are to be included. This choice must be based on economic theory or common sense. If *a priori* knowledge regarding the lags to be taken is available, these may be specified also. In many cases, for example, reactions are so quick that only lags of zero length are acceptable. If no such *a priori* knowledge is available, lags may be tried according to the same principle as coefficients — *i.e.*, by finding what lags give the highest correlation. This may be done either by trial and error — when the number of possibilities is quite small — or systematically, by introducing lagged and unlagged explanatory variables (*e.g.*, Z_{-1} and Z) and finding the regression coefficients for these two variables. The relative magnitude of the coefficients will characterise the relative importance of lagged and unlagged influences.

---

[1] As all variables will be expressed in terms of deviations from their average value over a certain period (in our case 1919-1932), no constant term is needed.

[2] *Statistical Testing of Business-cycle Theories*, I: *A Method and its Application to Investment Activity*, League of Nations, Geneva, 1939.

It has sometimes been doubted whether short
2. Lags and lags can be determined at all from *annual figures.*
annual It is maintained that quarterly or monthly figures
figures. would be better or even indispensable. No doubt
the latter, when available, contain more information. Since, however, for the most relevant variables the more
frequent figures are far less complete than the annual ones (*e.g.,*
for profits, investment activity, consumption outlay, capital
gains, etc.), and are in addition seasonal, and since some of the
accidental movements have already been automatically smoothed
out in the annual figures, the latter have been thought preferable.
The determination of lags shorter than one year is still possible
if the chief fluctuations of the series show periods materially
longer than one year. For business cycles this is clearly the
case. Further, it must not be overlooked that most lags are
by their nature averages of distributed lags,[1] and that the use
of annual figures rightly brings in — although admittedly in
a rough way — an influence of more remote events. In any
case, the significance of the average lags found to exist may
be tested along much the same lines as that of single regression
coefficients; and in many cases they are found to be significant
within the limit of a few months. Only in the case of strongly
curvilinear relations will the procedure become inaccurate for
years of extreme values.

Except in a few cases, the equations have been
3. Constant chosen linear, with coefficients that are constant
regression in the course of time. The use of linear relations
coefficients. means much less loss of generality than is sometimes
believed. In the case of small variations in variables
(*v, Z, q, m* and *l* in our example), it can even be proved mathematically that there is no loss of generality at all.[2] In the case of
bigger variations, however, it is possible to refine the method

---

[1] A notion introduced by Professor Irving FISHER.
[2] It is a well-known mathematical proposition that almost any
function $f(Z, q, m, l)$ may be developed in a series which, for small
intervals of the variables, can be reduced to a linear expression. And if
the coefficient φ_1, with which Z acts on v, itself depends on a new variable x, then it follows that $\varphi_1(x)Z$ may, for small intervals of the
variables, also be developed into a linear expression in x and Z.

when necessary. This may be done by introducing as new variables any functions of the explanatory variables, *e.g.*, m^2 or $\dfrac{l}{m}$ or $\dfrac{Z}{m}$, according to what the economist would expect to be the relevant combination.[1] On the other hand, it is interesting to note that there are astonishing examples [2] of good fits obtained with constant coefficients and linear equations, which suggest that this type of relation is more frequent than is often believed.

It goes without saying that any regression coefficient found for a market or a group of markets represents only an average for all individuals included, and cannot be applied to problems concerning one individual.

4. Statistical significance. In order to test the accuracy of results, *statistical tests of significance* must be applied. These have been discussed in the preceding volume in this series, quoted above. The danger threatening the accuracy of our results is especially that of multicollinearity. The simplest form of multicollinearity consists of a high degree of parallelism between two of the explanatory series. In more complicated cases, it may consist of a high correlation between any one of these series and a combination of some others. If such a situation occurs, the separate regression coefficients cannot be determined, though certain combinations of coefficients will still be determinable.[3] The opinion is often expressed that

---

[1] Examples of curvilinear dependence will be found in sections 3.5, 4.4 and 4.8 of this study.

[2] *E.g.*, the relation between unemployment and marriages (1870-1913) in *Vierteljahrshefte zur Konjunkturforschung*, Sonderheft 21, Berlin, 1931 (P. LORENZ, " Der Trend "), page 18; the demand curve for beef in the Netherlands (1876-1912), in H. W. METHORST and J. TINBERGEN, " Les recherches relatives à la conjoncture au Bureau Central de Statistique des Pays-Bas ", *Revue de l'Institut international de Statistique*, 1934, I, page 37; the "explanation" of interest rates in the United States before the war in Warren M. PERSONS, " Cyclical Fluctuations of the Ratio of Bank Loans to Deposits ", *Review of Economic Statistics* 1924 (VI), page 260; the "explanation" of world shipping freight rates from 1880 to 1911 in J. TINBERGEN, " Scheepsruimte en vrachten ", *De Nederlandsche Conjunctuur*, March 1934, page 23.

[3] *Cf.* equation (2.1). It may be noted that the knowledge of such combinations is helpful only in so far as periods are analysed in which these intercorrelations are present (*cf.* Vol. I, page 32).

these cases must be frequent in business-cycle research, since all relevant variables show more or less parallel cycles.[1] In the United States, in the period studied here, this was not the case. Some of the reasons for this lack of parallelism are:

(a) Interest rates and some other monetary series are much influenced by gold stock fluctuations which are not at all parallel to the general cycle;

(b) Commodity prices seem to have come into the region of inelastic supply much more in 1920 than in 1929; they showed very high peaks in 1920, but not in 1929;

(c) Share prices showed the reverse behaviour: they were very high in 1929, but not in 1920.

It goes without saying that if some explanatory factor has not changed at all in the period studied, its influence cannot be determined. If it changed only slightly, its regression co-efficient may be uncertain. Extrapolation of such results for large variations in the factors concerned is therefore not permitted. For problems of stabilisation, where the aim is to obtain smaller fluctuations, this does not seem to be a serious restriction.

5. Economic significance. Apart from the purely statistical tests, there are *economic tests* of the significance of the coefficients. The most important one is that of their algebraic sign, which in most cases the economist knows on *a priori* grounds. Sometimes further tests are available concerning the absolute magnitude of one coefficient or the relative magnitudes of several coefficients, occasionally even of different equations. Examples will be found in sections (2.1), (3.3). (3.4), (3.5), (4.3), (4.6).

6. Direct relations. The word "cause" has been used in the preceding paragraphs to indicate proximate causes only. This means that the economic considerations upon which the relation tested is based must be directed towards finding, as far as possible, "*direct causal relationships*". The variables in the relation must be directly connected either in the

---

[1] The author is indebted to Professor R. FRISCH of Oslo University for a number of important remarks on this matter, some of which have been used in what follows.

minds of some persons (*e.g.*, through the reaction of the consumer to a given income and price) or by some definition (*e.g.*, value of sales equals volume times price). This is not always possible if the strictest sense of "direct" is kept to. Investment activity may be linked up directly with profit expectations, and these are hardly measurable. The next step connecting profit expectations with actual profits and some other variables may then also be included, and investment activity may be "explained" both by actual profits and by some other variables. The more, however, such combinations of successive steps can be avoided in the formulation of relations, the better. This combination may always be undertaken afterwards — in fact, it forms the very important next step in our work — but the more explicitly it is done, the better. By keeping to this principle, one obtains relations with what Professor FRISCH calls [1] the maximum degree of "*autonomy*" — *i.e.*, relations which are as little as possible affected by structural changes in departments of economic life other than the one they belong to. It is clearly the task of economic analysis to indicate the nature of those direct causal relationships.

Complete system of equations. Returning to the example chosen as our starting-point, it will be clear that, in order to understand the mechanism of business cycles, further steps are necessary. Suppose, for example, that a successful application of multiple correlation analysis shows that the main cause of a given decrease in investment activity was a decrease of 20% in profits, we shall then want to know what caused this decrease in profits. We shall want to find an indirect, a "deeper", cause of the fall in investment activity, which at the same time is a proximate cause of profit fluctuations. This could be done by applying the same method to profits (Z) as to investment activity (*v*). Still further steps may be necessary: Z may depend partly on the value of total consumption (U), and U must therefore be investigated. If the method can be applied in all cases in which we are interested,

---

[1] In private correspondence with the author.

we get an increasing number of relations, representing the
network of causal connections forming the business-cycle
mechanism, with an increasing number of variables (*i.e.*, time
series representing economic phenomena). If we are to understand the mechanism as a whole, we must continue this
procedure until the number of relations obtained equals the
number of phenomena the course of which we want to explain.
We should not be able to calculate, say, n variables if we had
only $n-2$ or $n-1$ relations; we need exactly n. Such a
system of as many relations as there are variables to be explained may be called a *complete system.* The equations
composing it may be called the *elementary equations.* The word
"complete" need not be interpreted in the sense that every
detail in the complicated economic organism is described. This
would be an impossible task which, moreover, no business-cycle
theorist has ever considered as necessary. By increasing or
decreasing the number of phenomena, a more refined or a rougher
picture or "model" of reality may be obtained; in this respect,
the economist is at liberty to exercise his judgment. A conclusion
about the character of cyclic movements is, however, possible
only if the number of relations equals the number of phenomena
(variables) included. (The remark may be made here that
there is no separate or special variable representing "the cycle"
which has to be included in the elementary relations. It is
by the mechanism itself that all variables included are com-
pelled to perform cyclic changes.)

An example.   It is perhaps useful at this point to add a
few remarks on the nature of a complete system
of relations which has to explain business cycles.
These remarks can best be made in connection with the concrete
example of a very simple system.

Suppose, first, that the value, V_t, of investment goods
produced during the period t depends in a linear way on profits
one time period (of four months) earlier, Z_{t-1}:

$$V_t = \beta Z_{t-1} \qquad (0.1).$$

Both variables are measured as deviations from some "normal",
and β is a constant.

Suppose, further, that consumption outlay U_t is the total of:

(i) total wages L_t;

(ii) a term $\varepsilon_1 Z_{t-1}$, indicating that profits Z_t are only partly consumed, the marginal propensity to consume ε_1 being a constant, while there is a lag of four months;

(iii) a term $\dot{\varepsilon}_2 (Z_{t-1} - Z_{t-2})$, indicating that speculative gains also influence consumption outlay. Speculative gains are supposed to be proportional to the rate of increase $Z_{t-1} - Z_{t-2}$, since share prices are assumed to be a linear function of Z_t and since a lag is again assumed to exist.[1]

We therefore get a second equation:

$$U_t = L_t + \varepsilon_1 Z_{t-1} + \varepsilon_2 (Z_{t-1} - Z_{t-2}) \qquad (0.2).$$

Finally, there is an equation telling how profits Z_t are calculated:

$$Z_t = U_t + V_t - L_t \qquad (0.3).$$

Dynamic features.   Now the system of the three equations (0.1), (0.2) and (0.3) is a "dynamic" system in FRISCH's sense, since, in some of the relations ((0.1) and (0.2)), variables appear relating to different time periods. If this were not so — *i.e.*, if all lags were zero and the "speculative" term in (0.2) did not exist — no endogenous cycles could occur. In fact, in such circumstances, the system would be:

$$V_t = \beta Z_t \qquad (0.1').$$
$$U_t = L_t + \varepsilon_1 Z_t \qquad (0.2').$$
$$Z_t = U_t + V_t - L_t, \qquad (0.3').$$

which, after substitution of (0.1') and (0.2') in (0.3), gives the equation:

$$Z_t = (L_t + \varepsilon_1 Z_t) + \beta Z_t - L_t$$

or:

$$Z_t (1 - \varepsilon_1 - \beta) = 0 \qquad (0.4').$$

---

[1] Since it is only an example we are giving here, details need not be discussed. By comparison with our results in the following chapters, it will be found, however, that in many respects our assumptions are near to reality.

Since ε_1 and β are constants and $\varepsilon_1 + \beta \neq 1$, the only solution is $Z_t = 0$, meaning that the system always shows the same value of profits (Z_t being the deviation of profits from some "normal") and, through (0.1') and (0.2'), of V_t and $U_t - L_t$ also. No cycles would occur unless the extra-economic "data" determining the "normal" levels showed cycles.

It is quite different, however, in the case of the "dynamic" system (0.1), (0.2), (0.3). The simple structure of the equations still easily permits a substitution of (0.1) and (0.2) in (0.3), leading to a final equation:

$$Z_t = (\beta + \varepsilon_1) Z_{t-1} + \varepsilon_2 (Z_{t-1} - Z_{t-2}),$$

which may be written:

$$Z_t = (\beta + \varepsilon_1 + \varepsilon_2) Z_{t-1} - \varepsilon_2 Z_{t-2}.$$

Realistic values for β, ε_1 and ε_2 being 0.2, 0.4 and 1, respectively, we get:

$$Z_t = 1.6 Z_{t-1} - Z_{t-2} \tag{0.4}.$$

Determinants of the movements. This equation is of quite a different type from (0.4'). It enables us to calculate Z_t once we are given the values for Z_{t-1} and Z_{t-2}. But then, knowing Z_t and Z_{t-1}, we are again able to calculate Z_{t+1}, and so on. The following table is an example, where Z_0 and Z_1 have been chosen as 0 and $+5$ respectively:

$t =$	0	1	2	3	4	5	6	7	8	9	10
$Z_t =$	0	$+5$	$+8$	$+7.8$	$+4.5$	-0.6	-5.5	-8.2	-7.6	-4	$+1.2$

The movements we find for Z_t appear to be cyclic. It can easily be ascertained that the actual movement depends on two sorts of given numbers:

    (i) the "initial" values of Z_t, in our case Z_0 and Z_1;
    (ii) the coefficients of the final equation (0.4), in our case $(\beta + \varepsilon_1 + \varepsilon_2)$ and $-\varepsilon_2$.

The initial values more or less represent what are usually called disturbances from equilibrium; and the coefficients the

2

structure of society. A change in consumption habits would affect ε_1 and ε_2; a change in investment attitude would change β, as would changes in the relative importance of, for example, investment and consumption as a consequence of technical progress. It should be added that the coefficients may also be changed as a consequence of policy, and the problem of finding the best stabilising policy would consist in finding such values for the coefficients as would damp down the movements as much as possible. This will be attained, for example, by small values for the coefficients. *The outstanding importance of the numerical values of the coefficients may be clear from these few considerations.* In fact, it seems difficult to prove by pure reasoning alone — *i.e.*, without knowing anything about the numerical values of the coefficients — whether or not any given theory explains or does not explain cyclic movements. This may be demonstrated by two further numerical examples:

Example A: $\beta = 0.6$, $\varepsilon_1 = 0.8$, $\varepsilon_2 = 1$.
Final equation: $Z_t = 2.4 Z_{t-1} - Z_{t-2}$.

The type of movement found for any initial value of Z_0 and Z_1 is non-cyclic, with values of Z at an increasing distance from the original values.

Example B: $\beta = 0.2$, $\varepsilon_1 = 0.6$, $\varepsilon_2 = 0.1$.
Final equation: $Z_t = 0.9 Z_{t-1} - 0.1 Z_{t-2}$.

The type of movement is non-cyclic, with a tendency to return to values $Z_t = 0$ after a short time.

No theory is therefore determinate unless the values of the coefficients in a complete system of equations describing it are known, at least approximately.

Testing of theories. How, then, can business-cycle theories be tested statistically with the aid of the technique just described? The procedure consists of at least two stages: First, the explanation that a given theory provides for each of the variables of the economic system may be tested by the method of multiple correlation analysis, and secondly, it may be tested whether the system of numerical values found for the "direct causal relations" (or what comes nearest to them) really yields a cyclic movement when used in the final equation.

This may be clarified by indicating the two ways in which an unfavourable result for any theory may be found. First, it is possible that the explanation given for the fluctuations of any of the variables might prove to be poor; and, secondly, it might happen that, although these explanations were not too bad, the combination of the elementary equations would not lead to a cyclical movement.

Apart from these two ways in which a theory may fail, there is the third — already mentioned above — that the theory may prove to be incomplete — *i.e.*, that it contains less relations than variables to be explained — or indeterminate, in that it does not indicate from what other variables each variable depends and in what way.

Strictly speaking, there are very few, if any, "literary" theories that are complete and determinate in the above sense. Most of them — as will be seen from Professor HABERLER's study — emphasise some special relations, often without dealing with most of the others. Practically no single theory can therefore be used for a joint explanation of all the variables included in this statistical study. Nevertheless, many of these "literary" theories may prove highly useful in that they throw light on one detail or a number of details which are indispensable for a right understanding of the business-cycle phenomenon. They must, however, be combined, as Professor HABERLER also points out, and the most efficient way would seem to be to combine all theories open to statistical testing and to test them by means of the system of relations just described.

The present publication is one of the first attempts to construct such a complete system on a statistical basis.[1] The

---

[1] In recent times, a number of models of the sort discussed have been constructed (*e.g.*, by AMOROSO, CHAIT, FRISCH, KALECKI, LUND-BERG, Roos and others); but they have not been based on statistically tested relations, except in part. Models based on statistically determined relations are to be found in J. TINBERGEN, *An Econometric Approach to Business-cycle Problems*, Paris, 1937, and in E. A. RADICE, "A Dynamic Scheme for the British Trade Cycle, 1929-1937", *Econometrica*, January 1939.

character of the work involved is necessarily twofold. It is chiefly of a statistical nature, and to that extent consists in finding the quantitative importance of the chief factors causing fluctuations in each of the variables studied. Carrying out this task presupposes, however, that economic theory — or perhaps several competing economic theories — has indicated what the chief factors are. In this field much still remains to be done. The indispensable minimum of this work which is required in order to make the statistical part of the enquiry possible at all has also been included in this report. This may have led, at some points, to a choice which would not be approved by all economists. Clearly, this cannot be avoided, and the only excuse is that all details of the analysis have been indicated exactly.

Plan of the work. The first five chapters will contain the description and justification of the relations assumed, and tested statistically, between the phenomena considered as important. In order to treat the matter systematically, these relations are, as far as possible, subdivided into four types, well known in economic theory:

Definitional relations;
Demand equations;
Supply equations;
Income formation equations.

Some relations of another type will be added at suitable places.

Chapters VI and VII are concerned with the resolution of the complete system of equations and the conclusions which can be drawn therefrom, in respect of certain theories and of general characteristics of the business cycle.

The period studied is 1919-1932.

CHAPTER I

DESCRIPTION OF THE MODEL.
DEFINITIONAL RELATIONS

―――

(1.0) GENERAL INTRODUCTION

The construction of a model such as the one to be described here is, in many respects, a matter of trial and error. Exactly what variables are to be included and what neglected is not known beforehand; it only becomes apparent as the work progresses. Starting with some phenomenon of central importance to cyclical movements — as, for example, investment activity — it will first be asked what factors are important in the explanation of this variable; next, what variables are important in the explanation of these explanatory factors; and so on. This procedure must be continued until a number of relations is obtained equal to the number of variables which are considered to require explanation.

It would not serve much purpose to conduct the reader through all the incidental difficulties and errors, some of them at least unavoidable, which beset the course of the reasoning. It seems better to give a rounded-off picture of what has finally been arrived at as the most concise representation of the model. This picture has to start with a list of the phenomena included — a list which in some sense may seem illogical or arbitrary. The best course, therefore, seems to be to present the material in such a way that the reader can easily pick out any variable or relation in which he is specially interested, and can study in whatever order seems to him logical and useful the relations which are here formulated and tested.

The symbols introduced have as far as possible been chosen according to the following rules:

(i) All variables representing money amounts are indicated by capital letters.

(ii) Prices and physical quantities are indicated by small letters.

(iii) Coefficients — in their statistical aspect: regression coefficients; in their economic aspect: elasticity coefficients — are indicated by Greek characters.

(iv) The time period to which a variable relates is indicated by an inferior figure or index t to the right; in so far as no confusion is to be feared, inferior letters are also used for other distinctions, but not figures.

(v) Value symbols and physical symbols relating to the same sort of commodities, etc., are indicated by the same letter (*e.g.*, V and *v*).

(vi) Related variables are indicated by letters close to each other in the alphabet.

(vii) As far as possible, the same symbols are used as in some previous publications by the author.

A list of variables which may be consulted with any page of the text, will be found in Appendix A. Unbarred symbols represent deviations from the average value of the variable considered over the period 1919-1932; barred symbols represent these averages, and double-barred ones the "natural values" as found in the sources. The symbol $\int$ placed before any symbol indicates that the cumulant of that variable has to be taken. Therefore:

$$\int u_{1927} = u_{1919} + u_{1920} + u_{1921} + u \ldots + u_{1927};$$
$$\int u_{1921} = u_{1919} + u_{1920} + u_{1921}; \text{ and so on.}$$

The starting-point of the sum is indifferent, provided that it is before the beginning of the period studied ; for suppose that, instead of 1919, 1915 were taken as the starting year, this would only increase *every* value of $\int u$ by the constant amount $u_{1915} + u_{1916} + u_{1917} + u_{1918}$.

As the usefulness of the choice of the variables becomes clear only in connection with the relations chosen, the discussion of the latter may be undertaken immediately.

The relations, a summary of which is given in Appendix B, are, according to the subject of each, treated in Chapters I-V.

As the definitional relations are the least doubtful ones, they may be treated first, although they form a rather incoherent group of not very interesting relations. Not all are definitions in the true sense of the word : some are a description of the composition of some average or total; others represent the rule of computation of some variable. They could be called non-causal relations, in contrast with, for example, demand and supply relations. Some of them, with, in each case, one of the variables which they link together, have only been introduced for reasons of convenience.

The relations have, moreover, not always been given in their exact form. Sometimes they have been replaced by a linear approximation, which, for that reason, does not fit exactly; this approximation entails considerable simplification for the calculations in which the relations are ultimately used. In these cases, the "tests" therefore concern the degree of approximation obtained by these linear expressions, rather than the relations themselves, which are self-evident. The equations are given in alphabetical order of the first variable included. Their obvious nature makes a very short treatment sufficient in most cases.

———————

1.1: $A = 1.50C^i + 0.90B^i + 0.84n - 18.0m_{Lb}$

This is an approximation deduced from:

$$\overline{\overline{A}} = 0.0156\,\overline{\overline{C^i}}\,\overline{\overline{n}} + \frac{c}{\overline{\overline{m}}_{Lb}}\,\overline{\overline{B^i}},$$

where c is a constant. The total value of assets held by individuals is equal to the value of shares + the value of bonds held by them (cf. section (4.7)).

Graph 1.1.

Composition of Fluctuations in
TOTAL VALUE OF ASSETS
held by Individuals.

Graph 1.2.

"Explanation" of Fluctuations
in DIVIDENDS as a PERCENTAGE
OF CAPITAL.

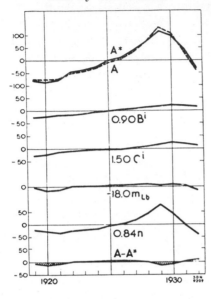

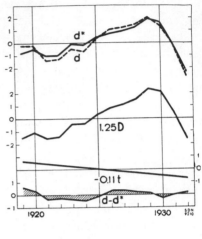

1.2: $d = 1.25D - 0.11\,t$

Here, d represents all cash dividends as a percentage of capital, and D the amount of cash dividends paid to private shareholders.

This relation has been deduced from

$$\bar{\bar{d}} = \frac{100\,\bar{\bar{D}}'}{\bar{\bar{C}}}$$

where $\bar{\bar{d}}$ is all cash dividends as a percentage of capital;

$\bar{\bar{D}}'$ is amount of all cash dividends;

$\bar{\bar{C}}$ capital, nominal value.

This relation may be written as

$$\bar{d} + d = \frac{100\,(\bar{D}' + D')}{\bar{C}\,(1 + \dfrac{C}{\bar{C}})}$$

which, by a well-known first approximation, turns into:

$$\bar{d} + d = \frac{100}{\bar{C}} (\overline{D'} + D') \left(1 - \frac{C}{\bar{C}}\right)$$

$$= \frac{100 \, \overline{D'}}{\bar{C}} + \frac{100}{\bar{C}} D' - \frac{100 \, \overline{D'}}{\bar{C}^2} C$$

where the second order term has been omitted, which for our figures is certainly admissible. The constant term $\dfrac{100 \, \overline{D'}}{\bar{C}}$ being equal to $\bar{d}$, we are left with

$$d = \frac{100}{\bar{C}} D' - \frac{100 \, \overline{D'}}{\bar{C}^2} C.$$

Here, the second term in the right-hand member is almost a trend, because C is nearly so; in addition, it is very small. Further, D' will move parallel to D; hence a regression equation between d, D and t has simply been tried, leading to formula (1.2) above.

———

1.3: $E = D + L_C + K_I + K_R + (E_E - E'_F - E''_F)$

Urban non-workers' income consists of dividends, managers' salaries, interest payments, rent incomes and entrepreneurial withdrawals without farmers' income. As the estimate for the latter may (following the National Bureau of Economic Research)[1] be taken equal to farmers' estimated consumption, it is here represented by $E'_F + E''_F$. The small amount of income from abroad has been neglected. The influence of this neglect is seen in the graph as the difference between the dotted and the full line.

———

[1] *Bulletin 59:* "Income originating in Nine Basic Industries, 1919-1934" by S. KUZNETS. New York, 1936. All farmers' savings are considered as business savings. Any net investment farmers are performing is supposed to be paid out of business savings.

Graph 1.3.

Composition of Fluctuations of
URBAN NON-WORKERS' INCOME.

Graph 1.4

"Explanation" of Fluctuations
in STOCK OF HOUSES.

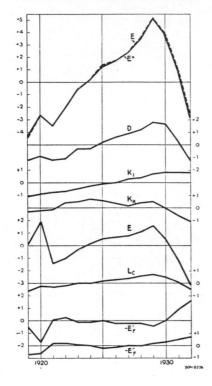

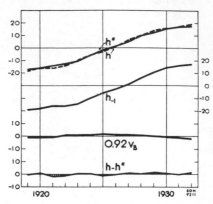

1.4: $h = h_{-1} + 0.92v_B$

The stock of houses at the end of a year is found by adding
to the stock at the end of the previous year 0.92 times the
volume of residential building during the year. The remaining
0.08 accounts for replacement (estimated according to the
figures of WICKENS and FOSTER for the relation between
replacement and total building).[1]

---

[1] " Non-Farm Residential Construction, 1920-1936 ", *Bulletin 65*,
National Bureau of Economic Research, New York, 1937, page 11.

1.5 : M = M' + M''.

Total money is equal to the sum of the amount of outside currency (M') + the amount of deposits (M'').

Graph 1.5.

Composition of Fluctuations in TOTAL MONEY.

Graph 1.6.

Fluctuations in ASSETS AND LIABILITIES OF THE BANKS.

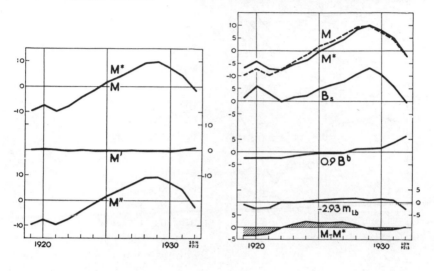

1.6 : $M = B_s + 0.9B^b - 2.93\, m_{Lb}$.

Balance equation for the banks; *cf.* section (4.5).

1.7: $m_{Ls} = 0.67d - 0.041n$

This relation is a simplified form of the definition of $\overline{\overline{m}}_{Ls}$:

$$\overline{\overline{m}}_{Ls} = \frac{100\overline{\overline{d}}}{1.56\overline{\overline{n}}}\,.$$

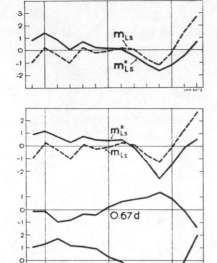

Graph 1.7.
" Explanation " of Fluctuations
in SHARE YIELD.

Upper part: $\dfrac{100\bar{\bar{d}}}{1.56\,\bar{n}}$ in deviation

from average $= m_{Ls}$

Lower part: $m_{Ls} = 0.67d - 0.041n$.

Here the factor 1.56 has been added, since in 1926, when the stock price index $\bar{n}$ was 100, the actual stock price level upon which the calculation of the share yield is based was 156.[1]

The upper part of the graph is to be considered as a test of the compatibility of the series used for m_{Ls} and d; if they were exactly compatible, no deviations should occur. The lower part shows the combined effect of the lack of compatibility and of the linear approximation. Evidently there is, in this case, a danger in using the linear approximation for extreme values like those in 1928, 1929 and 1932.

---

[1] The calculation runs as follows: $\bar{\bar{m}}_{Ls} = \bar{m}_{Ls} + m_{Ls} =$

$$= \frac{100\,(\bar{d}+d)}{1.56\bar{n}(1+\frac{n}{\bar{n}})} = \frac{100}{1.56\bar{n}}\,(\bar{d}+d)\,(1-\frac{n}{\bar{n}}) = \frac{100\,\bar{d}}{1.56\,\bar{n}} + \frac{100\,d}{1.56\,\bar{n}} - \frac{100\,\bar{d}n}{1.56\bar{n}^2},$$

neglecting the second order term.

Now $\dfrac{100\bar{d}}{1.56\bar{n}} = \bar{m}_{Ls}^{*}$; $\dfrac{100}{1.56\bar{n}} = 0.67$, and $\dfrac{100\bar{d}}{1.56\bar{n}^2} = 0.041$.

* The actual figures show a difference owing to the independence of the sources from which d, n and m_{Ls} haven been taken.

1.8: *Composition of cost of living.*

Cost of living is made up of two rather heterogeneous elements — viz., rents m_R and prices of other services and goods p', with weights of 20% and 80% respectively:

$$p = 0.80\ p' + 0.20\ m_R.$$

The "explanation" of m_R and p' is discussed in Chapter III.

<table>
<tr><td align="center">*Graph 1.8.*</td><td align="center">*Graph 1.9.*</td></tr>
<tr><td align="center">Composition of Fluctuations in
COST OF LIVING.</td><td align="center">" Explanation " of Fluctuations
in SURPLUS OF CORPORATIONS.</td></tr>
</table>

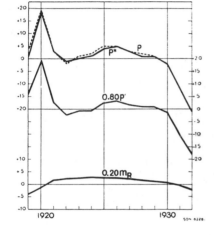
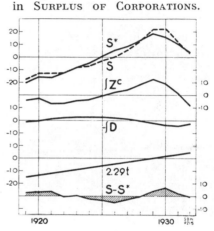

1.9: $S = \int (Z^c - D) + 2.29t$

Surplus of corporations depends on cumulated profits ($\int Z^c$) minus cumulated dividends ($\int D$). One would expect simply $S = \int Z^c - \int D$; but, it appears, additional reserves — possibly secret reserves — are constituted, so that the yearly increase in S is larger than $Z^c - D$. If we suppose these additional reserves to be constant,[1] they explain part of the trend. Another

---

[1] It was found by correlation calculus that they are not correlated with $Z^c - D$.

part, however, stands as a complement to the cumulation terms. For these being cumulations of the deviations of Z^c and D from their averages, cumulations of the constants $\overline{Z}^c$ and $\overline{D}$ have to be added, which evidently are trends. As $\overline{Z}^c - \overline{D} = 0.5$, a term of $0.5t$ corresponds to $\int(\overline{Z}^c - \overline{D})$. The rest of the trend, $1.8t$, represents the unexplained reserves mentioned above.

1.10: $U = 0.60p + 1.00u$

This relation is the simplified form of the relation

$$\overline{\overline{U}} = 0.01\overline{\overline{pu}},$$

value of production equals price times quantity, divided by 100 as the prices are measured in percentages of the level of 1929.[1]

Graph 1.10.	*Graph 1.11.*
PRODUCTION OF CONSUMPTION GOODS.	CONSUMPTION.
Relation between Fluctuations in VALUE, VOLUME and PRICE.	Relation between Fluctuations in VALUE, VOLUME and PRICE.

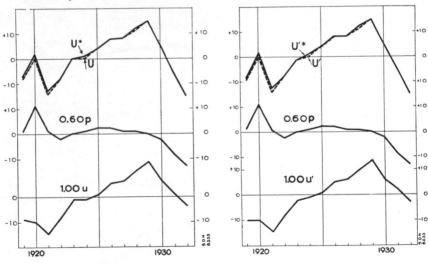

---

[1] The calculation runs: $\overline{U} = \overline{\overline{U}} + U = 0.01\,(\bar{p} + p)\,(\bar{u} + u) = 0.01\overline{pu} + 0.01\bar{p}u + 0.01\bar{u}p$, neglecting the second order term; $0.01\overline{pu} = \overline{\overline{U}}$; $0.01\bar{p} = 1.00$; $0.01\bar{u} = 0.60$.

Graph 1.12.

Relation between Fluctuations in
PRODUCTION, CONSUMPTION and
changes in STOCKS OF
CONSUMPTION GOODS.

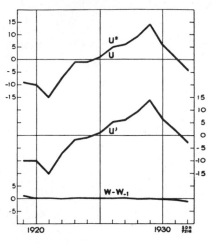

1.11: $u = u' + w - w_{-1}$

Production equals consumption + increase in stocks.

1.12: $U' = 0.60p + 1.00u'$

For explanation, see 1.10.

1.13: $V = V' + V_B$

Total value of investment goods produced consists of value of producers' durable commodities, including non-residential building, and value of residential building.

1.14: $v = v' + v_B$

Volume of investment goods produced consists of volume of producers' durable commodities, including non-residential building, and volume of residential building.

Graph 1.13.

Composition of Fluctuations
in VALUE OF PRODUCTION OF
INVESTMENT GOODS.

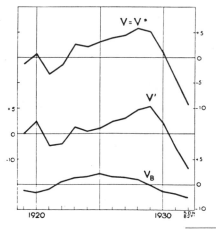

Graph 1.14.

Composition of Fluctuations
in VOLUME OF PRODUCTION OF
INVESTMENT GOODS.

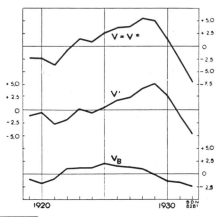

1.15: $V' = v' + 0.15q$

Same explanation as for 1.10.

1.16: $V_B = 0.98v_B + 0.028q_B$

Same explanation as for 1.10.

Graph 1.15.

PRODUCTION OF PRODUCERS'
DURABLE COMMODITIES.

Relation between Fluctuations
in VALUE, VOLUME and PRICE.

Graph 1.16.

RESIDENTIAL CONSTRUCTION.

Relation between Fluctuations
in VALUE, VOLUME and PRICE.

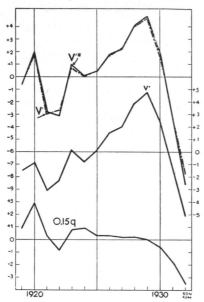

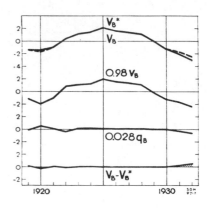

CHAPTER II

DESCRIPTION OF THE MODEL.
DEMAND EQUATIONS FOR GOODS AND SERVICES

———

(2.0) General Introduction

In this chapter, a number of relations determining the *demand for goods and services* will be discussed. The demand for holding some types of assets will be considered in Chapter IV. The goods and services expressly considered in this study are:

(i) Consumers' goods and services, excluding "housing" services;

(ii) Agricultural raw materials;

(iii) Housing services;

(iv) Houses;

(v) All other investment goods;

(vi) Labour.

The demand for these types of goods and services will not, however, be studied separately. The reasons for this treatment are mentioned below.

Groups (i) and (iii) have been combined as consumers' goods and services, including housing, since the estimates of the demand for each do not seem to be accurate enough to make a distinction possible. A separate study of the demand for housing services on the one hand, and all other consumers' goods and services on the other hand, would require the consideration of two demand functions each depending on the prices of both categories. The combined demand may — as a first approximation — be supposed to depend only on the combined item, cost of living. Moreover, a study of the combined demand is the minimum basis sufficient for any realistic model of business-cycle mechanism.

3

The demand for agricultural raw materials has not been studied separately, since it may be assumed that it shows a fairly high degree of parallelism with the demand for consumers' goods and services as a whole, given (i) the proportionality between the output of any commodity and the intake of raw materials and (ii) the tendency of consumers to divide their consumption more or less regularly between agricultural and non-agricultural products. On the other hand, there is some cause to disregard any lack of parallelism, for the simple reason that the statistics of stocks of raw materials are not very satisfactory.

Nor has the demand for labour been considered separately. The output of all final goods and services (Groups (i), (iii), (iv) and (v) above) is very exactly parallel with employment as measured by the Federal Reserve Board index of factory employment. Evidently this reflects the fact that production is a linear function of employment for short-run variations in output.

On the other hand, the demand for consumers' goods and services will be split up into four parts — viz.:

(*a*) Demand exerted by non-farmer consumers;
(*b*) Demand by farmers for farm products;
(*c*) Demand by farmers for non-farm products;
(*d*) Demand by dealers corresponding with increases or decreases in stocks.

Although in some respects arbitrary, this subdivision is useful for statistical reasons. In the first place, the factors determining one of these categories of demand will be at least partly different from those determining the others; hence a more exact determination of the coefficients will be possible if they are studied separately. In the second place, the figures for (*c*) and (*d*) have still more the character of estimates than those for (*a*) and (*b*).

In the next chapter a number of supply equations, or their equivalents, will be discussed. This means that, for some categories of goods and services, both the demand and the supply relation will be determined. The well-known question whether, and in what circumstances, a statistical determination of both relations is possible has been touched upon in the preceding volume.[1] In section (3.5), an example is elaborated.

(2.1) "Explanation" of Consumers' Outlay [2]

I. *Theoretical.*

As regards consumers' outlay — in which outlay for the purchase of new houses has not been included — it has been assumed that farmers' outlay for consumption goods is equal to their withdrawals [3] as estimated by Dr. Kuznets.

The following variables would then, by *a priori* reasoning, seem to be of importance for the explanation of the rest of consumption fluctuations:

Wages and salaries $(L_w + L_s)$;

Urban non-workers' income E;

Capital gains G;

The rate of increase in farm prices $p^f - p^f_{-1}$, or Δp^f, as an indication of speculative profits, which are not included in E but may nevertheless have influenced consumption (agricultural prices have been selected as they are especially subject to speculative influences);

Some measure of the degree of inequality of income distribution, for which Pareto's α has been taken; [4]

Cost of living p;

A trend, standing for slow changes in habits, population growth and changes in population structure.

---

[1] Vol. I, pages 62-64.

[2] *Cf.* J. J. Polak, "Fluctuations in United States Consumption, 1919-1932 ", *Review of Economic Statistics*, XXI, February 1939.

[3] All their savings being considered as business savings. *Cf.* page 25.

[4] This coefficient measures, in absolute amount, the slope of a curve representing $\log N_x$ as a function of $\log x$; where x is income and N_x the number of persons having an income above x.

It has been proved by Bortkiewicz that, in general, α is not a very accurate index for distributions deviating from the Paretian; for this reason, the values of α have been tested by comparing them to another index of in equality — viz.: the difference between the median and the average income of the $2\frac{1}{2}^0/_{00}$ of the population with the highest incomes. The correlation for this period was very high, and α showed considerable variations (the extremes being 1.39 and 2.04).

The influence of some of these variables, especially E, might be lagged. A lagged influence of G and p is somewhat less probable, as capital gains will be consumed fairly rapidly in so far as they are consumed at all; while the chief influence of cost of living will be that actual prices have to be paid which may differ from the price level upon which the consumption plans were based.

The signs of all coefficients except the trend must be positive. For E and G this will be clear at once; for p, the theoretical possibility exists of a negative influence. A negative influence would, however, mean an elasticity of total consumption which is larger than one, and this will hardly be assumed to prevail by any economist. The significance of PARETO's α being that an increase in α means a decrease in concentration, it seems logical to expect a positive influence of α on consumption.

The two income series $(L_w + L_s)$ and E show a very high intercorrelation. Hence, the coefficients to be obtained for each by including both in a correlation calculation must be expected to be rather unreliable. There are two other ways by which more reliable information might be obtained regarding the two marginal propensities to consume — viz. : (i) to have recourse to knowledge from other sources on the propensity of one of the two income classes, or (ii) to try different reasonable values for one propensity and to see whether the coefficients which result for the other are acceptable.

Some information about the relation between wages and workers' savings may be taken from family budget statistics, though these statistics give figures relating to families with

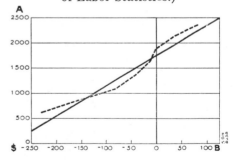

Graph 2.11.

AMOUNT SAVED AT VARIOUS INCOME-LEVELS.

(Families in New York, Portland and Atlanta, 1936; data from U.S. Bureau of Labor Statistics.)

A = Income.
B = Savings or, where negative, deficit.
- - - - Observed data.
——— Straight line general trend.

different incomes at the same moment; and it is not certain that one family, when passing (temporarily) from one income to another, will show the same change in savings. The direction of the deviation between the figures depends on whether savings are a relatively "sticky" item in the budget or not. This in turn will depend on the form of saving. If saving is effected in the form of fixed payments of insurance premia, it may be "sticky"; if small amounts are paid from time to time into savings banks, savings may be more sensitive. From a number of family budget data, represented in Graph 2.11, it would appear that the fluctuations in savings are between 0.15 and 0.20 times the fluctuations in wages.

II. *Statistical.*

In view of these results, a number of correlation calculations have been made where, in each case, the alternative of a fixed coefficient for $(L_w + L_s)$ of 1.00 and 0.80 was calculated; the

Case	Variable ex-plained	L_w+L_s*	E	G	Δp^f	α	p	E_{-1}	t	Corre-lation coeffi-cient
1 *a*		1.00	0.78	0.35					0.31	0.992
b		0.80	1.20	0.36					0.18	0.989
2 *a*		1.00	0.75	0.27	0.046				0.32	0.995
b		0.80	1.17	0.26	0.054				0.18	0.994
c		0.95	0.86	0.27	0.048				0.28	0.995
3 *a*		1.00	0.52	0.26		—6.30			0.26	0.995
b		0.80	0.93	0.26		—6.40			0.12	0.993
4 *a*	$U'—E'_F$	1.00	0.77	0.35			0.001		0.31	0.992
b		0.80	1.03	0.36			0.069		0.35	0.989
5 *a*		1.00	1.37	0.22				—0.75	0.50	0.993
b		0.80	2.01	0.17				—1.03	0.44	0.991
6 *a*		1.00	0.71	0.28	0.046		0.016		0.36	0.995
b		0.80	0.95	0.27	0.056		0.087		0.41	0.994
c		0.95	0.77	0.28	0.049		0.034		0.37	0.994

* Fixed coefficient.

two values resulting for the coefficients of the other explanatory variables suffice to calculate such values for any other coefficient for $(L_w + L_s)$ by means of a straight-line interpolation or extrapolation. The results are shown in the table on page 37.

The regression coefficient for E, which represents the "partial marginal propensity to consume (in respect to E)" is unacceptable in cases 1*b*, 2*b*, 4*b*, 5*a* and 5*b*, where it is above unity. Cases 3*b* and 6*b* are also hardly acceptable, as they represent a propensity to consume for workers which would be lower than that for the higher incomes. By interpolation, we find that the minimum coefficient for (L_w+L_s), which is higher than the corresponding coefficient for E, is as follows:

In case 1 . . . . 0.93
,,   ,,   2 . . . . 0.92
,,   ,,   3 . . . . 0.84
,,   ,,   4 . . . . 0.90
,,   ,,   5 . . . . > 1.00
,,   ,,   6 . . . . 0.87

According to the principles set out above, cases 3 and 5 are both unacceptable for the supplementary reason that they yield a negative coefficient for α and E_{-1} respectively. The remaining cases point to a coefficient for $(L_w + L_s) > 0.87$. The value 0.95 has finally been chosen for the coefficient for $L_w + L_s$.

For G and Δp^f, coefficients are obtained which are only slightly dependent on the choice of the $(L_w + L_s)$ coefficient (the spread between cases *a* and *b* is negligible). The inclusion of Δp^f increases the correlation coefficient to a not unimportant extent (case 2 as compared with case 1). The increase in the correlation by the inclusion of *p* is immaterial, but its omission is theoretically unsatisfactory. These considerations lead to the choice of an equation which includes as "explaining" variables: $L_w + L_s$, E, G, Δp^f, *p* and *t*, with a fixed coefficient for $L_w + L_s$. It has, with the standard errors [1] of the coefficients, the following form:

---

[1] *Cf.* Vol. I. For the calculation of standard errors it has been assumed throughout this publication that the random errors in all observations (to which errors the residuals are supposed to be due) are mutually independent.

$$U' - E'_F = 0.95 (L_w + L_s) + (0.77 \pm 0.32) E + (0.28 \pm 0.13) G$$
$$+ (0.05 \pm 0.02)\Delta p^f + (0.03 \pm 0.09)p + 0.37t, \qquad (2.1)$$

where the left-hand member represents urban consumption outlay.

It will be seen that even after the coefficient for $(L_w + L_s)$ has been fixed, that for E is still relatively uncertain; this is principally due to the high intercorrelation between E and p. We are bound to conclude, then, that the values of three coefficients in this equation, those for $(L_w + L_s)$, E and p, cannot be found with a high degree of precision.[1] The consequences for the system as a whole of this interchangeability of the influences of these three variables will be considered in Chapter VI.

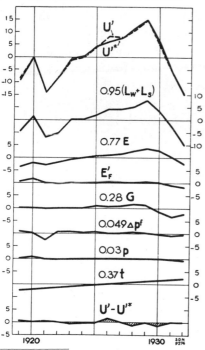

Graph 2.1.
" Explanation " of Fluctuations in CONSUMPTION OUTLAY.

The result chosen would mean that workers and lower employees have a marginal propensity to consume of 95%, urban non-workers a "partial marginal propensity to consume" of 77% in relation to " pure income " E, and a "partial marginal propensity to consume" of about 28% of realised capital gains.

This latter coefficient is, however, also rather uncertain, not on the ground of multicollinearity, but because the amplitude of the fluctuations in capital gains has been estimated very roughly.[2]

It should be borne in mind that constancy in the partial marginal propensities does not imply any constancy of the proportion of

---

[1] *Cf.* also page 42, note 2.
[2] *Cf.* also page 127.

incomes consumed, *i.e.*, of the ratio $\bar{\bar{U}}' \div (\bar{\bar{L}}_w + \bar{\bar{L}}_s + \bar{\bar{E}} + \bar{\bar{E}}'_F)$, which we may call *e*. First, when the marginal propensity to consume is smaller than the ratio of the *averages* of consumption and income, *e* will be lower in a boom than in a depression. Secondly, since capital gains will be high in the *rising* and low in the *declining* phase of the cycle, *e* has a tendency to behave accordingly. Thirdly, the trend term in the equation means that there is a slow secular increase in *e* (0.6 % per annum).

It is, of course, possible that the coefficients themselves are not constant either; but, given the nature of the statistical material, it seems almost impossible to obtain reliable information in this respect by the inclusion of more variables; the formula chosen may therefore be considered as about the best possible approximation.

III. *Durable and Non-durable Consumption Goods.*

The demand for durable goods and that for non-durable goods have not been included as separate equations in our system. This may be justified in the following way. When the demand U'_D for durable goods, apart from depending on income Y, depends on their price p_D and on the price of non-durable goods p_N:

$$U'_D = \omega_{11} Y + \omega_{12} p_D + \omega_{13} p_N,$$

and the demand U'_N for non-durable goods depends on the same factors:

$$U'_N = \omega_{21} Y + \omega_{22} p_D + \omega_{23} p_N,$$

then the equation for total demand U' may be found by adding up these two equations:

$$U' = \omega_1 Y + \omega_2 p_D + \omega_3 p_N.$$

This may be understood to mean that U' depends on income Y and some average price index for durable and non-durable goods — viz., an average with weights in the proportion of ω_2 to ω_3. It is not certain beforehand that the average price level *p* for consumers' goods will show such weights. Since, however, there will be a tendency to some parallelism between p_N and p_D — owing to the general competition on both the demand side and the supply side — there is no serious loss of generality if we replace the theoretically best average having weights ω_2 and ω_3 by our index p.

In the consumption equation (2.1), only "general variables" — *i.e.*, variables bearing on all goods, not on one category alone — occur. This implies the hypothesis that there are no factors bearing especially on durable or on non-durable goods.

Now there is one special feature in the demand for durable goods which may behave contrary to this hypothesis. Demand for durable goods consists of two parts — viz., replacement demand and so-called first purchases. The latter will, in general, depend on much the same general factors as the demand for non-durable goods — income, prices, tastes. The former will, however, depend on earlier purchases of the same goods[1] and will, in the simplest case, be equal to the quantity bought before some definite time period, representing the lifetime of the goods under consideration. (In more complicated cases — viz., where this lifetime is not a definite period, but purchases may be deferred — other determining elements may come in, such as income again. This does not, in theory, increase the difficulties.) If this echo effect proved to be of importance, it would be necessary to take it into account in the consumption equation — and it might then perhaps be useful to treat non-durable and durable goods separately. Now it appears, from a study by P. DE WOLFF on "The Demand for Passenger Cars in the United States", [2] that, at any rate for one commodity, the spread in the lifetime of the individual objects is large enough to smooth out the curve of replacement purchases to a mere trend curve. Hence, for all durable goods together, this will probably be even more so. A study of the year-to-year fluctuations in consumers' demand may for this reason neglect the echo effect.

Yet, though a separate study of the demand for durable and for non-durable goods is not essential to the present system of

---

[1] The so-called "echo effect".
[2] *Econometrica* VI (1938), page 113.

equations, this division is of such outstanding general interest that it may be worth while to digress slightly and give an "explanation" of both categories of goods. Apart from the explanatory variables used for U', it will be necessary, as mentioned above, to include in both equations p_D and p_N, the prices of durable and non-durable goods respectively. In order not to have too large a number of variables, and in view of the high intercorrelations between some of them, the income series are here combined into two groups — ordinary incomes $(L_w + L_s)$, E and E'_F and speculative incomes G and Δp^f — and in each group the series are weighted according to the coefficients they have obtained in the "explanation" of U'.[1] The results run as follows, with standard errors of the coefficients added:

Series "explained"	Coefficients and standard errors of					
	$0.95\,(L_w+L_s)$ $+$ $0.86\mathrm{E}+\mathrm{E}'_F$	$G +$ $0.16\Delta p^f$	p_D	p_N	t	R
U'_D	0.16 ± 0.05	0.03 ± 0.03	-0.028 ± 0.038	2.056 ± 0.020	-0.05	0.984
U'_N	0.73 ± 0.09	0.23 ± 0.05	-0.006 ± 0.075	0.069 ± 0.041	0.40	0.996
U' (by addition)	0.89	0.26	-0.022	0.125	0.35	
U' (case 2 c)	1.00	0.27			0.28	

The coefficient for the ordinary incomes is, for both groups together, below 1. This is due to the inclusion of p_D and p_N, which are rather highly correlated with incomes. It will be seen that in case 6c, where p is included in the explanation of U', the coefficient for E is also much lower.[2]

---

[1] Here the case with the same explanatory variables as in (2.1) except p, and a coefficient of 0.95 for L_w+L_s (case 2c) was used.

[2] The four price coefficients make it possible to check the p-coefficient in equation (2.1), if we use the approximation that p_D and p_N move parallel. The coefficient of p in the "explanation" of U' is then equal to the average of the sum of the two coefficients for p_D and the sum of the two coefficients for p_N, weighted according to the relative weights of p_D and p_N in p multiplied by their relative amplitudes. This yields 0.11, whereas we had found 0.03 ± 0.09 in the case chosen; both coefficients are, indeed, rather near to zero.

The figures point to the following elasticity of demand with respect to ordinary incomes,[1] price and the price of the competitive category of goods:

Goods	Income elasticity	Price elasticity	
		Own price	Other price
Durable	1.23 ± 0.38	$- 1.39 \pm 0.53$	0.74 ± 0.27
Non-durable	0.81 ± 0.10	$- 0.87 \pm 0.08$	0.01 ± 0.15

Somewhat higher income and price elasticities are brought out for the durable than for the non-durable group, but the significance of both differences is doubtful.

It may be interesting to apply to these data the "Slutsky condition" of the rational, consistent behaviour of consumers, the formulation of which in our symbols would be:[2]

$$\frac{\delta u'_D}{\delta p_N} - \bar{u}'_N \frac{\delta u'_D}{\delta Y} = \frac{\delta u'_N}{\delta p_D} - \bar{u}'_D \frac{\delta u'_N}{\delta Y}$$

where Y stands for $L_w + L_s + E + E'_F$.

Using the figures of the first table, this condition would be:[3]

$$5.4 - (51.8 \times 0.148) = 0.6 - (7.46 \times 0.675).$$
$$- 2.0 = - 4.5.$$

It will be seen that the coefficients, taken at their face value, do not exactly fulfil the condition. But when we take account of their standard errors,[1] the result becomes:

$$2.0 \pm 4.1 = - 4.5 \pm 7.6.$$

---

[1] There would not be much sense in calculating average income elasticities with regard to speculative incomes, since their average is, by their very nature, zero or almost zero.

To arrive at one coefficient for the three ordinary income groups, the coefficients obtained for each of them have been weighted according to their standard deviations (relative amplitudes); the weighted marginal propensity to consume for all consumption goods would be 0.924.

[2] *Cf.* H. SCHULTZ, *Theory and Measurement of Demand*, Chicago, 1938, page 621.

[3] The price coefficients are multiplied by 100 since the averages of p_D and p_N used in the transformation from U'_D to u'_D and from U'_N to u'_N are about 1, and not about 100. All coefficients, moreover, are corrected for the small deviations of $\bar{p}_D$ and $\bar{p}_N$ from 100.

It is quite possible, then, that the "true" coefficients do satisfy the condition.

(2.2, 2.3) "Explanation" of Farmers' Consumption

For this part of the investigation, rather rough assumptions have been made, as (i) the part of total income going to farmers is only about 10% and (ii) refinements would require the introduction of some new variables which would complicate the system without improving it very much.

The relative smallness of its fluctuations makes a very accurate consideration of this item unnecessary, while the rather rough estimates available do not seem to lend themselves to any detailed experiments with correlation calculus.

The prevailing factor governing gross as well as net farm incomes and the estimates of farmers' consumption is, of course, farm prices. The volume of farm production, which depends largely, in any case for the period up to 1932, on crop-yield variations, shows only irregular and not very wide fluctuations.

Farmers' consumption consists of two parts: viz., consumption of home-produced goods and of bought goods, the money values of which are indicated by E''_F and E'_F respectively. Both are supposed to depend only on farm prices p^f.

For E''_F this will be clear. For E'_F it means that the elasticity with respect to prices of non-farm products is just 1, which seems probable in view of the relatively low standard of living of the farm population. The formula found is:

$$E'_F = 0.025 \, p^f \tag{2.2}.$$

As to E''_F, the formula found, viz.:

$$E''_F = 0.015 \, p^f, \tag{2.3}$$

---

[1] Combination of standard errors according to formula:

$$\sigma^2_{(1-2)} = \sigma_1{}^2 + \sigma_2{}^2 - 2\sigma_1\sigma_2 r_{12},$$

where $r_{12} = \dfrac{M_{11}}{(M_{22} \times M_{33})^{\frac{1}{2}}}$ (cf. Vol. I, pages 142-143).

implies that the quantities of farm products retained — viz.,

$$\frac{\overline{\overline{E}}''_F}{\frac{1}{100}\overline{\overline{p}}^f} = \frac{1.7 + 0.015\ p^f}{0.97 + 0.01\ p^f} = \frac{(1.7 + 0.015\ p^f)\ (1 - 0.01\ p^f)\ [1]}{0.97}$$

$= 1.8 - 0.002\ p^f$, depend negatively on farm prices, with an average elasticity of demand of $--0.11$.

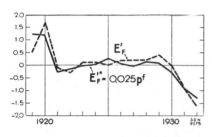

Graph 2.2.

"Explanation" of Fluctuations in FARMERS' CONSUMPTION EXPENDITURE.

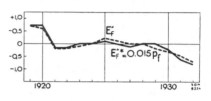

Graph 2.3.

"Explanation" of Fluctuations in FARMERS' CONSUMPTION OF HOME-PRODUCED GOODS.

(2.4, 2.5) "EXPLANATION" OF INVESTMENT ACTIVITY

Investment may take various forms, each of which is subject to its own "laws". For the purpose of this investigation, a distinction has been made between:

v' investment in durable producers' goods, including non-residential building;

v_B investment in residential building;

v_w investment in stocks of non-durable commodities (working capital).

Purchases of durable consumers' goods have simply been included in consumption.

The relations which "explain" the purchases of each type of these goods may be indicated as "demand equations for investment goods". As the first publication in this series [2]

---

[1] Owing to a well-known mathematical approximation.
[2] Vol. I, Chapters III and IV.

deals especially with these relations, they need only be mentioned briefly here.

The demand v' for *durable producers' goods and non-residential building* has been considered in combination. It has been assumed to depend on:

(i) Profits made in all industries, for which corporation profits Z^c have been taken;

(ii) Share yield m_{Ls}, as an indication of the "interest rate paid" on capital obtained by share issues;

(iii) The price of investment goods q;

(iv) The margin $p - \frac{1}{2}l$ between the price index for finished goods and the wage rate (with the weight it has in costs), as it is often held that, apart from total profits, this margin influences profit expectations.

(v) A trend, in order to account for slow changes in capital intensity of production.

For all variables a lag of half a year has been assumed.[1]

The introduction of share yield as one of the determining factors needs further elucidation. One way of looking at the matter is that, although no yield is contracted when shares are issued, the yield which satisfies investors will depend on the general situation in the share market as represented by the share yield on existing shares. It would not matter, in this train of thought, if the actual yield on new shares were systematically lower than the average yield on old shares, provided it could be maintained that there was a systematic relation in the fluctuations of both.

---

[1] Expressed somewhat more exactly, the lag is a distributed one with an average of half-a-year. In fact, by using annual data, one is only able to apply lags of 0, 1, 2 etc. years, but any combination may be taken which means a distributed lag. The average of these lags, weighted according to the regression coefficients obtained for the term corresponding to each, may be indicated shortly as "the" lag. If, *e.g.*, the following regression equation is found: $v = 0.3 Z + 0.5 Z_{-1}$, this weighted average of the lags 0 and 1 is $\dfrac{(0 \times 0.3) + (1 \times 0.5)}{0.3 + 0.5} = 0.63$.

Another way of interpreting the matter is that the " easiness " with which money is obtained by share issues could be given a numerical expression by the figure of share yields.

Still another way would be to point to the factors " behind " share yield, which fluctuates inversely to share prices and proportionately to dividends. Share prices themselves (*cf.* equation (4.82)) are influenced by both dividends and the rate of increase in share prices. Instead, therefore, of assuming investment activity to be negatively affected by share yield, one could formulate our hypothesis thus: that investment activity is favourably affected by the rate of increase in share prices, favourably affected by share prices themselves (the higher these prices, the higher the issue prices entrepreneurs are able to get), and unfavourably by dividends (which in a sense is the "payment" they are expected to make).

Graph 2.4.

"Explanation" of Fluctuations in DEMAND FOR DURABLE PRODUCERS' GOODS, including NON-RESIDENTIAL BUILDING.

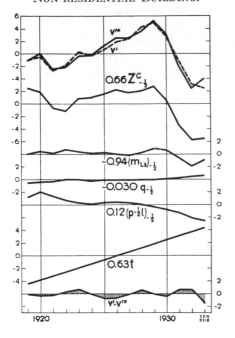

Graph 2.5.

"Explanation" of Fluctuations in RESIDENTIAL BUILDING.

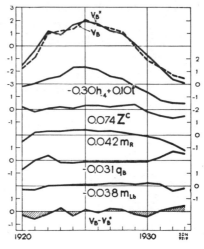

Three other variables were also tentatively included, but, as their regression coefficients were found to be exceedingly small, they have been left aside. These variables are:

(a) The rate of increase in consumers' goods' production, in order to account for a possible direct influence of the "acceleration principle";

(b) The rate of increase in prices of investment goods, in order to account for a possible speculative attitude.

(c) The interest rate for short credits (m_S).

The rejection of these variables has been considered at some length in the preceding volume in this series.[1]

The demand for new dwellings v_B has been assumed to depend on:

(i) Rent level m_R;

(ii) Cost of construction q_B;

(iii) Long-term interest rate m_{Lb};

(iv) Profits Z^c;

(v) Number of houses h;

with a lag of zero for the series (i) to (iv) and one of $3\frac{1}{2}$ years for (v). The first four series may be said to represent direct incentives which work without much lag,[2] but the last one only works slowly and indirectly. It seems to work especially through the financial condition of house-owners who let their houses. Some time after a relative scarceness or a relative abundance of houses occurs, the financial condition of owners will exhibit a reaction; and this again will only work slowly, through credit security in this branch of enterprise, upon building. This has been treated very accurately by Roos.[3]

The equations obtained for v' and v_B are, respectively:

$$v' = 0.33\,(Z^c + Z^c_{-1}) - 0.47\,[m_{Ls} + (m_{Ls})_{-1}] - 0.015\,(q + q_{-1})$$
$$+ 0.06\,[p + p_{-1} - \tfrac{1}{2}l - \tfrac{1}{2}l_{-1}] + 0.63\,t \qquad (2.4)$$

---

[1] Loc. cit.

[2] The series v_B refers to the beginning of the building process.

[3] C. F. Roos: Dynamic Economics, Bloomington, 1934, pages 69-110.

$$v_{\mathrm{B}} = -0.30h_{-4} + 0.074Z^c + 0.042m_{\mathrm{R}} - 0.031q_{\mathrm{B}} - 0.038m_{\mathrm{L}b} + 0.10t$$
$$(2.5).$$

For further details concerning these relations the reader may be referred to the first volume in this series.[1]

The way in which investment in working capital has been treated is somewhat indirect, but, in view of the rather deficient statistics, it is perhaps the best that can be adopted. It consists in regarding all enterprises as though they were integrated, without attempting to deal separately with the various vertical stages of production. This "body" of enterprises shows an output of goods and services in the final stage and an input of factors of production. If production in all stages were exactly synchronised, these factors would only be used for the production of the final goods leaving the "body". Investment in working capital means, however, that, at various places in the "body", stocks of raw materials and intermediate products accumulate — i.e., that, in some earlier stages of the process, more is produced than corresponds to final output. This will reflect itself in a greater application of factors of production, and therefore in a larger total of wages — the other factors being mainly "overhead" factors. Investment in working capital therefore finds its expression in total wages L_w and farm incomes. Because, however, of the rather short series now available for all stocks, it has not been possible to consider separately what factors seem to be important in an explanation of working capital as a whole.

Only investment in stocks of finished consumers' goods may be treated more completely.

(2.6) "Explanation" of Commodity Stocks (Consumers' Goods)

This is one of the least satisfactory parts of the present study, chiefly because of lack of adequate data. It has only been possible to consider the most important causes of changes

---

[1] *Loc. cit.*

in stocks. After inspection of the curves, these seemed to be purely technical; they may be formulated as follows:

(i) There is a tendency to hold stocks which are proportional to sales; and

(ii) This tendency is counteracted by unforeseen changes in sales, of which production cannot immediately take account.

The first tendency points to considering as the first determining factor of stocks w the amount of sales u'; the second to including as a second factor the change in sales as compared with those of the previous year; this latter with a negative sign as an increase in sales will, *ceteris paribus*, lead to low stocks. This leads to the formula:

$$w = \Omega u' - \Omega' (u' - u'_{-1})$$
$$= \Omega_1 u' + \Omega_2 u'_{-1}; \; (\Omega_1 = \Omega - \Omega'; \Omega_2 = \Omega') \qquad (2.61).$$

Further, the interest rate and price changes would seem to influence the holding of stocks of finished consumers' goods.

For the series of department-store stocks, a slight influence of the former factor [1] was found; but price changes did not seem to have a marked influence either on this series or on that of stocks of manufactured goods. A final judgment on this question will be possible, however, only when more abundant material is available. After a number of years, the statistics of corporations will certainly yield a very useful contribution; the series of data now available is, however, too short.

The relation (2.61) was tested for department-store stocks, for which it was found to fit very well. The same type of formula was therefore used for the "explanation" of w, for which the relation

$$w = 0.105u' + 0.047u'_{-1} - 0.187(m_S)_{+\frac{1}{2}} - 0.307t$$
$$(2.6)$$

was found. The trend was introduced to represent secular

---

[1] Represented in equation (2.6) by $(m_S)_{+\frac{1}{2}}$, since w represents stocks at the end of the year and m_S is an average over the year.

changes in the habits of holding stocks. It is equivalent to a decrease in stocks of some 4% per annum, which does not seem unreasonable.

Graph 2.6.
"Explanation" of Fluctuations in
STOCKS OF CONSUMERS' GOODS.

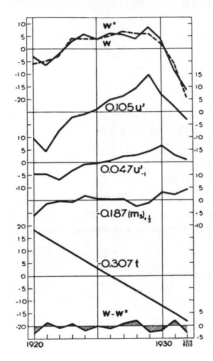

CHAPTER III

DESCRIPTION OF THE MODEL. SUPPLY OR
PRICE EQUATIONS FOR GOODS AND SERVICES

(3.0) GENERAL INTRODUCTION

Using the language of static economic theory, the relations to be considered here may be of either of two types. In the first place, they may be *supply relations* which connect up price, quantity sold and certain "supply factors" of which the characteristic is that they act only on the supply side, all "demand factors" being excluded. Let p be the price, u_S the quantity supplied, F_S a supply factor — *e.g.*, unit cost — then a supply relation will be of the form: $u_S = f_1 (p, F_S)$. A linear approximation will be of the form:

$$u_S = \omega_{1p} p + \omega_{1S} F_S \qquad (3.01).$$

The relations to be considered here, however, may also result from the combination *of a demand and a supply relation*, which is obtained by putting equal to each other the quantity demanded and the quantity supplied, and then eliminating this quantity.

Calling F_D any demand factor — *e.g.*, income — the demand relation will be of the form: $u_D = f_2 (p, F_D)$; with a linear approximation:

$$u_D = \omega_{2p} p + \omega_{2D} F_D \qquad (3.02).$$

To apply both relations to the price actually prevailing and the quantity u actually sold, we have to put the quantity demanded u_D equal to the quantity supplied u_S, and we get, in the case of the linear approximations:

$$\omega_{1p} p + \omega_{1S} F_S = \omega_{2p} p + \omega_{2D} F_D$$

which may be written

$$(\omega_{1p} - \omega_{2p})\, p + \omega_{1S}F_S - \omega_{2D}F_D = 0$$

or $p = \dfrac{\omega_{2D}F_D - \omega_{1S}F_S}{\omega_{1p} - \omega_{2p}}$ (supposing $\omega_{1p} \neq \omega_{2p}$).

In general:

$$p = f_3\,(F_D,\ F_S) \tag{3.03}.$$

Such a relation, which may for shortness be called a *price equation*, connects the price with supply factors and demand factors, but does not contain the quantity sold. It will be clear that a system of two relations consisting of a demand equation (3.02) and a supply equation (3.01) is equivalent to a system of two relations consisting of a price equation (3.03) and either the demand or the supply equation, since the third equation in each case may be deduced from the two others. It will therefore simply depend on the circumstances which of these three systems will be given. In general the demand equation will be given as such (*cf.* Chapter II), but either the supply or the price equation will also be given (in this chapter).

This procedure is only completely valid for some special types of market which exhibit freedom of supply and — as a necessary counterpart — absolute adaptability of prices. In many modern markets, this is no longer the case. Prices are "sticky" and supply is not entirely free. The demand relation in general remains in existence, although it, too, may, for psychological reasons, not react to prices immediately, but only with a lag. The supply relation takes rather the form of a "price fixation relation" — *i.e.*, of a relation telling on what factors producers or sellers base themselves when fixing the price. This relation contains the same variables as the old supply relation, but price is effect rather than cause and may therefore be lagged behind quantities and supply factors.

Using the symbols just introduced, it could be written in the form

$$p = f'_1 (F_S, u_S) \text{ or}$$
$$p = \pi_F F_S + \pi_u u_S \tag{3.04}$$

which replaces (3.01).

The fixing of price may also be effected by negotiations with the demand side (*e.g.*, the labour market) and thus depend also on demand factors; but in this case demand factors can always be eliminated again by using the demand equation, and therefore the price fixation equation in its first form may still be used.

Some applications of these notions are to be found in the following sections.

(3.1) "Explanation" of Wage Rate

The equation introduced here is a price fixation equation which, as has already been said, may be considered as a supply equation for labour, although serious objections can be raised against this terminology, in as much as it presupposes a free market. It has been assumed that wages, if looked at from the workers' standpoint, will depend on —

(i) employment,

(ii) cost of living,

(iii) labour productivity,

(iv) institutional factors, such as the changing strength of trade unions, legislation, etc.

Employment is, as far as its fluctuations are concerned, intimately correlated with volume of production. Therefore $u + v$ has been taken for the first series.

Cost of living p has also been included, whereas, for the period 1919-1932, the two remaining factors are considered as trend factors. (For the extrapolation through 1934, this hypothesis would no longer be valid.)

In view of the stickiness of wages, a lag has been introduced — though this procedure increases the difficulty of applying the ordinary concept of "elasticity of supply". The length of the lag is established by correlation analysis in introducing the wage rate of the following year l_{+1} as one of the "independent" variables.[1] This leads to a regression equation

$$l = 0.52(u + v) + 0.67p - 0.72l_{+1} + 0.89t,$$

which may be written in the form

$$l + 0.72l_{+1} = 0.52(u + v) + 0.67p + 0.89t,$$

or, combining the two terms in the left-hand member of the equation and dividing by 1.72:[2]

$$l_{+0.42} = 0.30\,(u+v) + 0.39p + 0.51t. \tag{3.1}$$

The lag in wages would thus be about five months. The average "elasticity of the supply of labour" (using this term with the reservations just mentioned) would be $\dfrac{1}{0.30} \times \dfrac{\bar{l}}{\bar{u} + \bar{v}}$

= about 4.0.[3]

---

[1] It may be added that almost the same result is obtained if one starts with a calculation "explaining" l_{+1} by l, $u + v$, p and t (i.e., when another elementary regression is used).

[2] The formula used is

$$\alpha_1 l + \alpha_2 l_{+1} = (\alpha_1 + \alpha_2)\, l_{+\frac{\alpha_2}{\alpha_1+\alpha_2}}$$

which is strictly valid only for a rectilinear development of l during any two consecutive years. For this rather small interval, this approximation is justified.

[3] Here it has been assumed that volume of production $u + v$ and employment vary proportionately; if account is taken of the discrepancy, one must deduct about 20% at most from the above figures.

Graph 3.1.

"Explanation" of Fluctuations
in WAGE RATE.

Graph 3.2.

"Explanation" of Fluctuations
in RENT LEVEL.

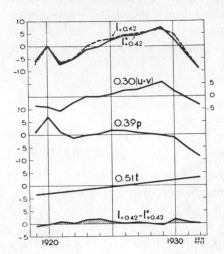

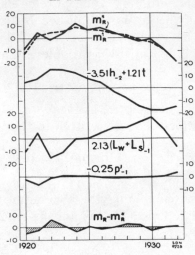

(3.2) "EXPLANATION" OF RENT LEVEL

Here a "price equation" has been chosen for the explanation. Rents have been assumed to depend on:

(i) The stock of houses h as a supply factor;

(ii) Labour income, $L_w + L_s$, being the income of the large mass of tenants, as one demand factor;

(iii) Cost of living without rent (p'), the price of the other goods and services competing for the income, as a second demand factor;

(iv) A trend, in a fixed combination with h, as an indication of the normal need for houses (*i.e.*, h is included in the calculation in deviations from its trend over the period 1910-1935, which is $2.44t$).

A lag of one year and a half for the stock of houses [1] and of one year for the other variables has been found to

---

[1] As in our system these are counted at the end of each year, we have to take h_{-2}.

give the best explanation. The following relation has been obtained:

$$m_R = -3.51 h_{-2} + 2.13 (L_w + L_s)_{-1} - 0.25 p'_{-1} + 1.21 t \quad (3.2).$$

(3.3) "EXPLANATION" OF PRICES OF CONSUMERS' GOODS AND SERVICES, EXCLUDING RENT (p')

Here a price fixation equation has been chosen. The variables included are:

(i) Farm prices, as a cost element of special behaviour to be explained afterwards;

(ii) Wages, as a direct cost element;[1]

(iii) A trend representing changes in labour productivity, which are largely secular.

There might have been reason to include a fourth variable — viz., quantity produced u. This was in fact tried in several ways (with and without a lag), but the results were not significantly different from those without u. As an extremely small influence of u was found in similar researches made for Holland[2] and for the United Kingdom (pre-war period), u was left out entirely, and the fit was still good. This would mean that, in the period considered, the elasticity of supply of manufactured consumers' goods and of consumers' services was infinite. This does not seem unrealistic in view of (a) the overcapacity which

---

[1] Assumed to reflect also mineral raw-material cost. In fact, there is a very close correlation between non-farm raw-material prices and wage rates with a trend (for changing productivity). The chief reason why these other raw materials are not treated separately is that their prices show almost no autonomous fluctuations, as is the case for agricultural products. The general laws of price formation adhered to in this study are also applicable to them.

In addition, their importance to the total cost of living is only very small; food, clothing and services, which account for about 75% of non-rent expenditure, being practically independent of non-agricultural raw materials.

[2] Cf. J. TINBERGEN: *An Econometric Approach to Business Cycle Problems*, Paris, 1938.

seemed to exist [1] and (*b*) the tendency to fixed prices (trade marks, etc.).

The relation found with the variables left is:

$$p'_{+\,0.21} = 0.47l + 0.25p^f - 1.04t \qquad (3.3).$$

The lag was determined in the same way as for wage rates (*cf.* section (3.1)).

The coefficients obtained for l and p^f are very satisfactory; they correspond fairly exactly to the proportion of direct labour cost and of agricultural raw-material cost in consumers' goods prices. The coefficient for t would seem rather low, corresponding to an annual increase in efficiency of about 1 %, but it is quite possible that other elements work in the opposite direction (such as increasing capital costs, which, in the long run, are reflected in the price).

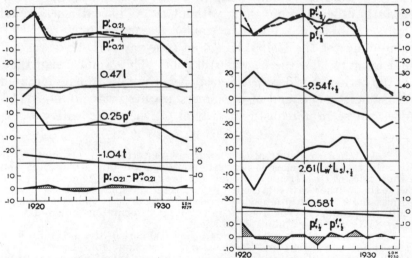

Graph 3.3.
"Explanation" of Fluctuations
in COST OF LIVING,
excluding Rent.

Graph 3.4.
"Explanation" of Fluctuations
in FARM PRICES.

---

[1] *Cf. America's Capacity to Produce*, Brookings Institution, Washington, 1935.

(3.4) "EXPLANATION" OF FARM PRICES

For the explanation of farm prices, a price equation (*cf.* general introduction to this chapter) has been used. The following elements were included:

(i) *f*, the volume of agricultural supply available for the United States market[1], *i.e.*, crops + carry-over — exports.[2] No account has been taken if the world supply of agricultural products, since the greater part of United States farm products are not subjected to competition in the world market; as regards cotton, an important exception, the share of the United States in the world supply is very large.

(ii) Total wages bill $(L_w + L_s)$ as a demand factor.

(iii) A trend, representing the rationalisation in farm production (and other possible trend influences).

No factor was included for direct costs, which are very low in agriculture.

The following regression equation was obtained for the period 1920-1932:[3]

$$p^f = -4.77f + 2.66 (L_w + L_s) - 2.23t \qquad (3.41).$$

As however, f is highly correlated with t, the coefficients for both factors are very uncertain, as is shown by their standard errors:

$$p^f = -(4.77 \pm 3.67) f + (2.66 \pm 0.27)(L_w + L_s) - (2.23 \pm 1.37) t.$$

---

[1] To be distinguished from the actual market supply, from which it differs by the amount added to stocks.

[2] Imports should not be added here, because they are of a special character and not competitive with United States production (coffee, rubber, etc.).

[3] For all series, crop year figures are used; they are therefore indicated in the graph by the suffix $+ \frac{1}{2}$. It seemed expedient not to start the calculation before the middle of 1920, as the guaranteed minimum price for wheat instituted in August 1917 was not repealed until July 1st, 1920 (*Yearbook of Agriculture*, 1921, page 141).

Hence it seems useful to consider these coefficients in the light of knowledge from other sources.[1]

As indicated under (3.0), a price equation may be considered as the result obtained by eliminating from a demand equation and a supply equation the quantity exchanged. Denoting this quantity, which is equal to the market supply, by x^f, we can write these two equations:

$$Demand: \quad x^f = -\varphi_1 p^f + \varphi_2 (L_w + L_s) \quad \Big\} \quad \text{(all } \varphi\text{'s} > 0\text{),} \quad \begin{array}{l} (3.42) \\ (3.43) \end{array}$$
$$Supply: \quad x^f = +\varphi_3 p^f + \varphi_4 f + \varphi_5 t,$$

from which we eliminate x^f:

$$p^f = \frac{-\varphi_4}{(\varphi_1 + \varphi_3)} f + \frac{\varphi_2}{(\varphi_1 + \varphi_3)} (L_w + L_s) - \frac{\varphi_5}{(\varphi_1 + \varphi_3)} t, \quad (3.44)$$

which is the general form of (3.41).

If we express all series in percentage deviations from their average, we may describe the φ's as follows:

φ_1 : price elasticity of demand;

φ_2 : income elasticity of demand;

φ_3 : elasticity of supply;

φ_4 : proportion of a positive or negative excess of available supply reflected in the actual market supply;

φ_5 : percentage cost decrease *p.a.*, divided by 100.

In order to reduce the limits of the coefficients for f and t, additional information on $(\varphi_1 + \varphi_3)$ and φ_4 *or* φ_5 is sufficient; of the latter two, φ_4 may be chosen as the coefficient on which most knowledge is available.

The fluctuations in market supply differ from those in available supply by changes in stocks. Graph 3.41 compares the latter two series for three cereals and cotton, the major United States farm products for which changes in stocks are important. It is seen that there is a rather close correlation between both

---

[1] Since $L_w + L_s$, which is the only endogenous variable in the explanation of pf, has a fairly certain coefficient, this supplementary analysis is not necessary from the point of view of the systematic cyclical forces; it is only necessary to estimate correctly the influences of changes in crops on the other variables of the system.

series for wheat (up to 1928),[1] oats and cotton, but hardly any for maize (corn). From these data it was deduced that the fluctuations in market supply constitute, on an average, the following percentages of the fluctuations in available supply:

Wheat [2] 40%
Maize 100%
Oats 33%
Cotton 0%
All other farm products . . .   100%

Graph 3.41.

Changes in Stocks of Farm Products compared with Available Supply.

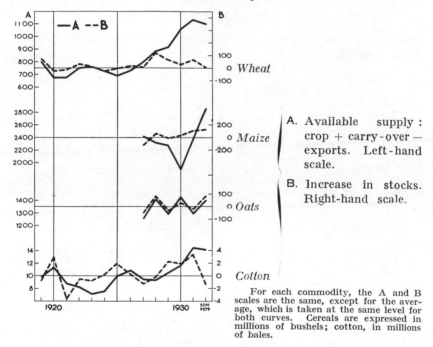

A. Available supply : crop + carry-over — exports. Left-hand scale.

B. Increase in stocks. Right-hand scale.

For each commodity, the A and B scales are the same, except for the average, which is taken at the same level for both curves. Cereals are expressed in millions of bushels; cotton, in millions of bales.

In order to obtain an average value for φ_4, these values for the individual commodities are weighted according to the relative amplitude of the available supply of each commodity

---

[1] From then on, the very large and — until 1933 — increasing stocks presumably could not react to the increased available supply in the same way as before 1929, when stocks fluctuated around a constant level.

[2] 1919-1928; *cf.* note 1.

(in values, at the price of the base year 1927).[1] This yields a value of 0.8 for φ_4.

Similarly, an average elasticity of demand has been calculated [2] on the basis of the elasticities found for twelve important agricultural commodities by Professor SCHULTZ,[3] supplemented by estimates for fruits and nuts, vegetables, poultry and eggs, and dairy products. An average of about 0.5 was found for φ_1.

The elasticity of supply (φ_3) of agricultural products must be very low in relation to the short-term reactions of suppliers that are considered here; it may be taken at 0 or, say, 0.20.

To be able to make use of these more direct estimates for φ_1, φ_3 and φ_4, we convert the coefficients of (3.41) to a basis which corresponds to the series measured in *percentage* deviations from average:

$$\begin{array}{ccc} f & L_w + L_s & t \\ -0.62 & 1.18 & -2.52 \end{array}$$

If we take, on the basis of the above:

$$\varphi_1 + \varphi_3 = 0.5 \text{ to } 0.7,$$

---

[1] Calling the base-year value of (production — export) of a commodity j, U_j; the percentage fluctuation of its production σ_j; and its coefficient for the relation between market supply and available supply φ_j, we find the average value for φ_4:

$$\varphi_4 = \frac{\Sigma_j \, U_j \, \sigma_j \, \varphi_j}{\Sigma_j \, U_j \, \sigma_j}.$$

The σ_j measure has been based on the production indices of each product or group of products, which are all on the basis 1924-1929 = 100. Calling the value of this index for a certain product in year i, u_i, σ_j is calculated with the formula:

$$\sigma_j = \overset{1932}{\underset{1920}{\Sigma_i}} |(u_i - u_{i-1})| - (u_{1932} - u_{1919})$$

where the second term represents a rough correction for the trend in u.

[2] The formula for averaging the individual elasticities η_j must take account of the degree of fluctuation of the market supply (at the base year value). It runs:

$$\varphi_1 = \frac{\Sigma_j \, U_j \, \sigma_j \, \varphi_j \, \eta_j}{\Sigma_j \, U_j \, \sigma_j \, \varphi_j}.$$

No account has been taken, in this formula, of cross elasticities (*cf.* section (2.1)). But most of Professor SCHULTZ's elasticities are also found without taking account of other prices than that of the particular commodity studied.

[3] H. SCHULTZ, *op. cit.*

we find (*cf.* (3.44)):

φ_4	φ_2 [1]	φ_5
0.31 to 0.43	0.59 to 0.83	1.26 to 1.76

It follows that the coefficient for f in (3.41) is much too low. As, however, its standard error is large, we may attribute to f in (3.41) a considerably different coefficient without really impairing the degree of correlation.[2] A value at twice the coefficient [3] found in (3.41) would be about the minimum compatible with the value of 0.8 for φ_4. The introduction into the correlation calculus of this fixed coefficient for f leaves that for $(L_w + L_s)$ practically unchanged:

$$p^f = - 9.54f + 2.61(L_w + L_s) - 0.58t, \qquad (3.4)$$

which we accept as the final formula.

Owing to the relatively small influence of f on farm prices and the small weight of exports in f, we may disregard the cyclical element which is contained in these exports, and the more since it is not very pronounced. The demand for farm products has not been considered separately, it being assumed that this demand varies parallel to the variations in demand for all consumers' goods.

(3.5) "EXPLANATION" OF FLUCTUATIONS IN PRICES OF INVESTMENT GOODS

I. *Theoretical*

Here, as in the case of section (3.3), a price fixation equation (*cf.* section (3.0)) has been chosen for the explanation.

The chief variables included are:

---

[1] On the basis of data from M. LEVEN, *c.s.*, *America's Capacity to Consume* (the Brookings Institution, Washington D.C., 1934, pages 87-88), an elasticity of the demand for food of about 0.5 could be calculated for the lower income classes (which consumed, in 1929, 84% of all food). This figure roughly tallies with the value found for φ_2, and so confirms the estimates for $(\varphi_1 + \varphi_3)$.

[2] In the case chosen, R is 0.975 as compared with 0.979 in case (3.41).

[3] Or 1.3σ above that coefficient.

(i) The variable cost per unit of product, represented by wage rate l;

(ii) The volume of production v';

(iii) A trend, representing the course of overhead cost, technical development, etc.

Since we are considering all enterprises, which are here regarded as being vertically amalgamated, practically the only element in variable cost will be variable labour cost. Its influence on price may be estimated on *a priori* grounds, which in general seem safer than any other basis. Labour cost may be estimated at about 50% of prices of investment goods. This does not correspond, however, to direct labour only, but to all labour. From the figures of the Federal Reserve Board, it may, moreover, be estimated that a 10% increase in production of durable goods is accompanied by a 7% increase in hours [1] of work. Marginal labour cost seems, therefore, to be about seven-tenths of average labour cost for average production. The price increase corresponding to a 10% increase in wages will therefore, in the short run, be equal to $5 \times 0.7\% = 3.5\%$.

The volume of production may represent, in the language of the more "practical" investigator, the strength of the seller in the market.[2] The higher the sales, the larger the addition to direct cost which the seller is able to charge. It is a well-known fact that, in times of severe depression, many enterprises in these branches are making prices only a little above variable cost, while it is only in better times that they are able to earn their overhead cost and profits. The coefficient with which volume of production enters into the equation is closely related to the elasticity of supply, which will be calculated later.

No special attention has been given to the price movements of individual metals. It is not impossible that these movements

---

[1] Hours being estimated by multiplying the employment index by the quotient, weekly wages over hourly wages (National Industrial Conference Board figures). *Cf.* J. TINBERGEN, "Profit Margin, Investments and Production" (Dutch), *De Nederlandsche Conjunctuur*, November 1935.

[2] Especially since in these markets most production is to order and over-production therefore practically impossible.

are in part also due to changes in world stocks, but since these stocks themselves depend on production with a certain lag,[1] which is already included in the explanation, it seemed advisable not to take stocks as a separate variable. Moreover, the individual fluctuations in the prices of particular metals practically disappear in a weighted average of these prices (*cf.* graph 3.51;[2] the weight chosen is the value of the world production of each metal in 1930). The average shows practically the same movements as q.

For the "explanation" of q, the period 1919-1932 cannot be considered as a whole, owing to a marked difference in market organisation between the years 1919 to about 1923 on the one hand, and the period after that year on the other. Not until about 1923 could the iron and steel industry, which had been very strongly organised many years before the war, again effectively control the price fluctuations of its products.[3] In the first five years after the war, the price formation of q may have shown other characteristics than in the more mono-polised period. The following differences might be expected:

(1) The re-monopolisation may have effected a higher general level of q;

(2) It has very probably diminished the amplitude of the cyclical fluctuations;

(3) It may, in particular, have prevented very rapid price rises when production has been very near to capacity; *i.e.*, it may have prevented bottle-necks.

On the other hand, it is reasonable to assume that the price formation of q has not changed, from the one period to the other, with regard to:

---

[1] *Cf.* L. M. LACHMANN and F. SNAPPER: "Commodity Stocks in the Trade Cycle", *Economica* V, pages 435-454, November 1938.

[2] Page 66.

[3] *Cf.* A. R. BURNS, *The Decline of Competition*, New York and London, 1936, page 211: "After the general disruption of prices owing to the war of 1914 to 1918 (*i.e.*, mainly after 1922), the prices of a number of steel products . . . again showed periods of unchanging prices for considerable periods."

(4) The reaction to changes in wages;

(5) The secular decline in prices as an effect of technical development;

(6) The lag between a change in activity (v') and a change in q. With regard to this lag, however, slightly different assumptions may easily be tried out.

For reasons mentioned under (1) to (3), the correlation calculation has been restricted to the years 1924-1932. An almost perfect correlation was obtained with the formula:

$$q = 0.35l + 0.70v' + 0.59v'_{-1} - 2.58t,$$

Graph 3.51.
PRICES OF METALS.
Indices on the base 1929 = 100.

Graph 3.52.
"Explanation" of
Fluctuations in PRICES
of INVESTMENT GOODS.

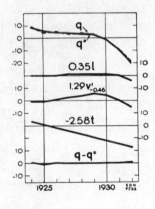

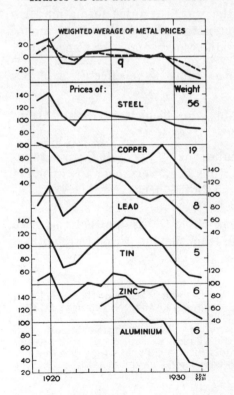

where the coefficient for l had been taken fixed. The two terms with v' may be combined in one, with an average lag of slightly under half a year:

$$q = 0.35l + 1.29\,v'_{-0.46} - 2.58t \text{ (graph 3.52)} \qquad (3.5).$$

The elasticity of supply (with the qualifications given in the general introduction to this chapter)[1] is about 5.

With the help of this formula, the possible differences between this period and the years 1919-1923 may be tested. For this purpose, we compared, in a scatter diagram (3.53)[2] $q - 0.35l + 2.58t$ with $1.29v'$, using different lags of 0.46, 0, and 1 year, in parts II, III and IV. Part I shows the points 1924-1932, which lie nearly on a straight line, at 45°.[3]

If we look at II, we see that 1919, 1921, 1922 are on a straight line with a slope of $3 \div 1$. Considering this line as the regular supply curve for this period, we may deduce that the price was three times as flexible before 1923 as after that year. A conclusion as to a possible difference in level brought about by re-monopolisation may be derived from the point of intersection of the supply line with the q-axis. In I, this point lies at about $q = 1$; in II at $q = 0.5$. This difference is too small to support the evidence that the organisation of the market has had a tendency to raise the level of q.

The points for 1920 and 1923 show a q which is definitely above the supply line. During both years there occurred, as is well-known, a bottle-neck, which was more pronounced in 1920 than in 1923. The two deviations are therefore quite acceptable. It may be seen that the price in 1920 was higher than in 1923, though production (v') was slightly lower. But certainly capacity was higher in 1923, causing bottle-necks to develop only at a

---

[1] *I.e.*, the figure is rather an inverted measure of the flexibility of prices, but it may, in the long run, be an indication of the real elasticity of supply as well.

[2] This diagram may be considered as a supply schedule, since it compares the quantity supplied (v') with the price q, corrected for other influences.

[3] The line does not pass through the origin, since the series are measured from their averages over 1919-1932.

Graph 3.53.

PARTIAL SCATTER DIAGRAM
between *q* (corrected for other influences) and *v'*.

I 1924-1932, lag 0.46 year
II ⎫
III ⎬ 1919-1923, lag ⎰ 0.46 ,,
IV ⎭   ⎱ 0 ,,
                    1 ,,

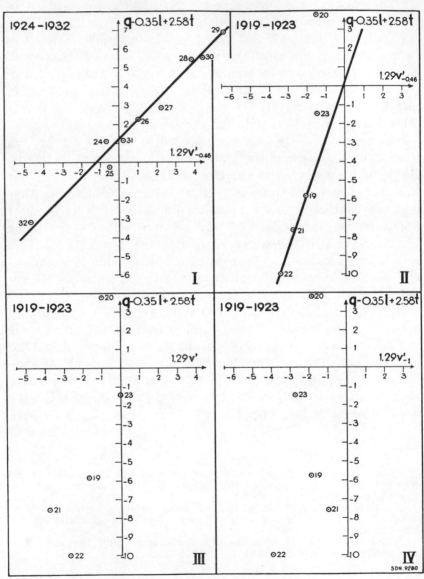

somewhat larger production. The figures do not show, of course, that these bottle-necks could have been prevented, had the industry been as strongly organised as was the case after 1923. In fact, production has probably never since been so near the limits of capacity.

The alternative cases III and IV are much less satisfactory. In neither case do the points 1919, 1921, 1922 clearly determine the supply line. In IV, moreover, the point 1923 lies to the left of those of 1919 and 1921, which would suggest a bottle-neck in the former year at both lower production and — presumably — higher capacity than the latter two. Thus, the material would seem to confirm the assumption made under (6) above.

Equation (3.5) is the "quasi supply relation" for investment goods — a price fixation equation solved for the quantity supplied, where the lag involved may be in contradiction to the Walrasian interpretation of a supply function. It may be written:

$$_{s}v' = 0.78 \, q_{+0.46} \tag{3.51}$$

where $_{s}v'$ indicates the quantity supplied, corrected for the factors making for shifts of the supply curve:

$$_{s}v'_{-0.46} = v'_{-0.46} + 0.27l - 2.00l \tag{3.52}.$$

For the years 1919-1923, the equations are:

$$_{s}v'_{-0.46} = 0.26q \tag{3.51'}$$

and

$$_{s}v'_{-0.46} = v'_{-0.46} + 0.09l - 0.67t. \tag{3.52'}.$$

It may be interesting to compare this "quasi supply equation" with the demand equation for investment goods:

$$v' = 0.66 \, Z^{c}_{-\frac{1}{2}} - 0.94 \, (m_{Ls})_{-\frac{1}{2}} - 0.03 \, q_{-\frac{1}{2}} + 0.12 \, (p - \tfrac{1}{2}l)_{-\frac{1}{2}} + 0.63t \tag{2.4}.[1]$$

---

[1] Replacing $0.33 \, (Z^{c} + Z^{c}_{-1})$ by $0.66 \, Z^{c}_{-\frac{1}{2}}$, etc.

This equation may be written in a form similar to (3.51):

$$_Dv' = -0.03q_{-\frac{1}{2}}{}^{1}\qquad(3.53)$$

where

$$_Dv' = v' - 0.66\,Z^c_{-\frac{1}{2}} + 0.94\,(m_{Ls})_{-\frac{1}{2}} - 0.12(p - \tfrac{1}{2}\,l)_{-\frac{1}{2}} - 0.63t\ (3.54).$$

Graph 3.54.

Scatter Diagram of
DEMAND AND SUPPLY RELATIONS for CAPITAL GOODS.

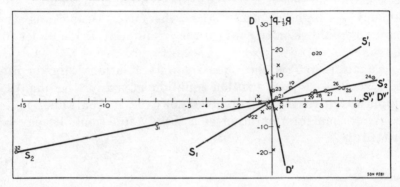

Graph (3.54) shows the supply relation (3.51) and the demand relation (3.53) in one diagram. The values for q (with the appropriate lag or lead) are measured along the vertical axis, those for $_Sv'$ and $_Dv'$ along the horizontal axis. The dots indicate the supply relation (3.51); they show — except for the bottle-neck values of 1920 and 1923 — only small deviations from the two supply curves $S_1S'_1$ for 1919-1923 and $S_2S'_2$ for 1924-1932. The demand relation (3.53) is plotted by little crosses; here the points fit the demand curve DD' less well. The scale has been chosen in such a way that the 45° lines represent an elasticity of unity.

This diagram illustrates the possibility, in this case, of deriving both the supply relation and the demand relation from one set of price and quantity data, since (i) the lag (lead) between v' and q is different in both relations; and

---

[1] It follows that the elasticity of demand is $(0.03 \times \bar{q}/\bar{v}') = 0.2$.

(ii) the other factors entering into the supply equation are different from those entering into the demand equation.[1]

The demand and supply equations for labour and consumption goods might be analysed in much the same way; the present case has been singled out only because it provides the clearest example.

(3.6) "EXPLANATION" OF BUILDING COSTS

For our purpose, it has not been necessary to give much attention to this equation. In the elimination process, the product of v_B and q_B is the only instance where q_B is used.[2] As the elasticity of demand for v_B is not far from 1,[3] this product is only slightly dependent on q_B; and as, moreover, the absolute value of building is rather small, the dependence of V_B on q_B may be neglected altogether. Hence, for the system of equations as a whole, we do not need to have an equation "explaining" q_B.

---

[1] *Cf.* Vol. I, pages 62-64.
[2] *Cf.* Appendix B, Table III, equation (5.10)′.
[3] $0.031 \times \bar{q}_B / \bar{v}_B$.

CHAPTER IV

DESCRIPTION OF THE MODEL. DEMAND AND SUPPLY
IN THE MONEY AND CAPITAL MARKETS

(4.0) INTRODUCTION

In this chapter, it is proposed to discuss the price formation
of bonds and shares, and some connected problems. This subject
belongs to the " Theory of Assets ", in which an important
development has recently taken place.[1] In this theory the
subjects considered are the various holders of assets; and the
assets considered are of various types: land, buildings, machines, commodity stocks, securities, short claims and money.
Following the principle of this study, we have, in order to make
our formulæ manageable, grouped the subjects under three
types — viz., banks, other firms, and individuals. Moreover,
as physical assets have already been treated separately,[2] we
shall be concerned here only with monetary assets.

With regard to the assets which are considered here — viz:
bonds, shares, short claims, and money[3] — the simplifying

---

[1] J. M. KEYNES, *The General Theory of Employment, Interest and
Money*, London, 1936; B. OHLIN, "Some Notes on the Stockholm
Theory of Savings and Investments", II, *Economic Journal*, 47, June
1937; J. M. FLEMING, " The Determination of the Rate of Interest ",
Economica 5, August 1938; H. MARKOWER, and J. MARSCHAK, "Assets,
Prices and Monetary Theory", *Economica* 5, August 1938; J. MAR-
SCHAK, "Money and the Theory of Assets", *Econometrica* 6, October
1938.

[2] *Cf.*, on this separation, page 74.

[3] In this chapter, the terms used for monetary assets have the
following range:

    Bonds: All private and public long-term debt + preferred stock.
    Shares: Common stock held by individuals (not by firms).
    Short claims: Loans by all banks + Bills discounted and bills
bought by the Federal Reserve Banks + Short-term Government
debt.
    Money: Time + Demand deposits of all banks + Currency held
by the public.

(The composition of the series is given in detail in appendix D.)

assumption has been made that each of the three types of subject either demands or supplies each type of asset in the way sketched in the following skeleton table:

	Type of assets			
	Bonds (B)	Shares (C^i)	Short claims (B_s)	Money (M)
Supplied by	Other firms	Other firms	Other firms Individuals	Banks
Demanded by	Individuals (B^i) Banks (B^b)	Individuals	Banks	Other firms Individuals

Banks are supposed to hold only bonds and short claims, the nominal value of which is B^b and B_s respectively; they are the only suppliers of money.

Other (*i.e.*, non-banking) firms supply bonds, shares and short claims, and demand only money; the holding of a considerable part of all shares by these firms seems to be determined rather by the desire for control than by that of earning dividends, and these shares may therefore be altogether eliminated from our collection of assets.

Lastly, individuals exert a demand for bonds and shares (nominal values B^i and C^i respectively) and money; they supply short claims for speculative purposes.

To these simplifications we may further add the assumption that the holding of money is independent of the holding of bonds or shares. The reasons for this are the following:

(1) A considerable part of total money is held by "other firms", which we assumed to hold no securities for investment purposes.

(2) A large class of individuals who hold money are not in the position to hold shares or bonds.

In all other cases where different types of assets are supplied or demanded by one group of subjects, the supply (demand) of various types has been studied jointly. Thus, the supply (demand) of each type of assets has been taken to be dependent on the total supply (total demand) and the prices of all types of assets supplied (demanded) by the group of subjects.

On the other hand, the demand and supply decisions of one group of economic subjects are considered as *independent*. Here a parallel may be drawn with the separate maximisation that is often supposed to exist for the individual's way of earning and spending income: *first* he trives to get the maximum money income, and *then* he seeks the maximum satisfaction from the given amount of money. Likewise, we may assume that firms decide *first* what is necessary for the course of production (the construction of buildings and machines, the holding of commodity stocks and the amount of debt and shares they are prepared to carry), and *afterwards* how much money they need to keep to these plans. Banks *first* decide how much money they will allow to be in existence, and *then* distribute this amount over short claims and bonds. Speculators *first* determine their holdings, and *then*, if necessary, borrow short credits.

It also follows from this division that buildings, machines and commodity stocks do not enter into consideration in this chapter. Their creation and prices have been treated separately in previous chapters.

Summarising, we may divide our task, as set out in the skeleton table on the preceding page, into five parts:

(i) The joint supply of bonds, shares and short claims by other firms and, with regard to the last item, speculating individuals (sections (4.1) to (4.3));

(ii) The supply of money by the banks (section (4.4));

(iii) The joint demand for short claims and bonds by the banks (section (4.5));

(iv) The demand for money by other firms and individuals (section (4.6)).[1]

---

[1] For reasons that will be explained in section (4.7) it is necessary to treat the demand for money before the demand for bonds and shares by individuals.

(v) The joint demand for bonds and shares by individuals (sections (4.7), (4.8), (4.9)).

(4.1) THE SUPPLY OF BONDS

The total amount of bonds outstanding at any moment (B_0) may be considered as the sum of the amounts outstanding a year before (B_{-1}) + the increase over that year (ΔB). To "explain" the supply of bonds, it seems statistically most expedient first to "explain" ΔB and then to cumulate the equation found.[1]

It may be remarked that the "explanations" given in this section and the next are rather rough because (i) the material is not good enough to allow of very much refinement and (ii), as will be shown below,[2] we shall, in any case, be obliged to approximate the "explanation" found by a mere trend term.

In view of the difference in determining factors, ΔB has been split into:

ΔB^e: bonds issued by private enterprise, States and local governments;[3]

ΔB^g: bonds issued by the Federal Government.

(4.11) ΔB^e

I. *Theoretical.*

The chief determining factors of changes in the amount of these bonds (and, equally, of shares) outstanding are assumed to be: (i) changes in the value of the stock of capital goods, and (ii) the rates of interest which determine on which market

---

[1] Issue figures could not be used instead of ΔB, since, though they are in themselves more certain than the B-figures, they represent only a part of the fluctuations in B. They have, moreover, the disadvantage that they do not cover capital reductions.

[2] *Cf.* section (4.7).

[3] The fluctuations in the increase in debt of States and local governments are too small to justify special treatment. It seemed most logical to combine this debt with that of private enterprise, with which it has in common the important factor of a limited market for its issues. Hence State and local issues fell abruptly after 1930, at the same time as the federal debt heavily increased.

the new capital goods will be financed. In greater detail, this leads to the consideration of the following series:

(1) The value of investment goods delivered (V′). It is possible that there is usually a lag between the production of investment goods and the final financing with long-term capital. Hence V'_{-1} may be included next to V′.[1]

(2) The value of depreciation, as reflected in regular repayments. These repayments have been considered as a constant.

(3) The value of writings-off, as reflected by capital reductions (this factor is probably more important for shares than for bonds). Writings-off may be considered as a readjustment of the value of the capital on a replacement basis; they may therefore be represented by the rate of change in the price of capital goods, Δq. Since writings-up are unusual, only the negative values of Δq should be taken into account; this truncated series may be represented by $(-\Delta q)''$, the sign '' indicating that only positive values of the expression between brackets are taken into account.

(4) m_{Lb} and m_{Ls}, the interest rates on the bond and the share market. In the '' explanation '' of the supply of bonds, the first series may be expected to have a negative coefficient and the second a positive; and inversely in the '' explanation '' of the supply of shares.[2]

(5) The alternative to issuing bonds or shares consists in (temporarily) financing with short-term credit. The price of

---

[1] In principle, series for stocks like B and C refer to the average of the year. Consequently, if ΔB and ΔC are to represent the increase during a calendar year, they should be calculated as the difference $B_{+\frac{1}{2}} - B_{-\frac{1}{2}}$, etc., and not as $B - B_{-1}$. For B^g and C, this has actually been done. The series B^e, however, is not accurate enough to be placed at any precise date. Hence, $B - B_{-1}$ has been taken to represent ΔB. It follows that the lag found for this series should be very carefully interpreted.

[2] A parallel may, however, be drawn here with the signs to be expected for the price coefficients of two goods on which a very large part of income is spent (*cf.* section (2.1), page 43). Hence, since a very large part of all investments is financed either by bonds or by shares, the signs for m_{Lb} and m_{Ls} may be different from those to be expected according to the general rules for commodities on which only a small part of income is spent.

this credit (m_S) has not been included in these equations, since its influence must be of minor importance as compared with that of m_{Lb} and m_{Ls} (*cf.* section (4.3)).

II. *Statistical.*

In the "explanation" of ΔB^e by the five series mentioned, a negative coefficient was found for V'_{-1}, which pointed to a lead of some months. Since this does not seem acceptable, and since a fixed combination of V' and V'_{-1}, representing a lag of half a year, gave a much worse correlation, a case without V'_{-1} was finally chosen. Here the coefficient for $(- \Delta q)''$ was so small that it was left out.

The formula finally accepted runs:

$$\Delta B^e = 0.88V' - 0.1m_{Ls} + 0.2m_{Lb}$$
$$(4.11).$$

Graph 4.11.

"Explanation" of Fluctuations in the INCREASE OF PRIVATE LONG-TERM DEBT OUTSTANDING.

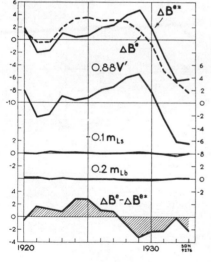

The signs for m_{Lb} and m_{Ls} are not in accordance with theoretical expectation (in its simplest form); but the coefficients do not seem to be very significant, and the influence of both series is very small (*cf.* graph 4.11).

(4.12) ΔB^g

The total increase in debt of the Federal Government, $\Delta B^g + \Delta B^g_s$,[1] is, by definition, equal to the Government's expenditure minus its revenue. Federal expenditure — in distinction to that of the lower authorities — rises in depressions, when relief payments of different kinds have to be paid, and falls in years of prosperity; revenue,

---

[1] *I.e.*, the increase in long-term and short-term Government debt.

depending on incomes, imports and similar items, tends to behave in the opposite way. As a result of both causes, the increase in debt will move counter to the cycle. On the basis of these considerations, an attempt is made to " explain " ($\Delta B^g + \Delta B_s^g$) by Z^c and Z_{-1}^c — in order to take account of possible lags — and a trend to represent a possible second-degree trend in Government debt.[1] Over the period 1920-1933, a very satisfactory fit was found with the following formula:

$$\Delta B^g + \Delta B_s^g = - 0.115Z^c - 0.155 \, Z_{-1}^c + 0.138t \qquad (4.121).$$

In order to find ΔB^g, the short-term debt may be explained separately. It stands to reason that here considerations with regard to the rate of interest are most important, in such a way that the *amount* of short-term debt outstanding (and not its *increase*) depends positively on the long-term rate of interest.[2] This hypothesis is fairly well confirmed by the facts:

$$B_s^g = 1.7 \, m_{Lb} \qquad (4.122).$$

It follows that ΔB^g depends on Z^c, Z_{-1}^c, t and the rate of increase in m_{Lb}:

$$\Delta B^g = - 0.115 \, Z^c - 0.155 \, Z_{-1}^c - \\ -1.7 \, \dot{m}_{Lb} + 0.138t \quad (4.123).$$

Graph 4.12.

" Explanation " of Fluctuations in the INCREASE OF FEDERAL GOVERNMENT DEBT.

" Explanation " of Fluctuations in SHORT-TERM FEDERAL GOVERNMENT DEBT OUTSTANDING.

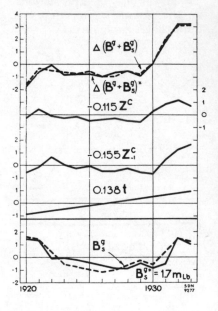

---

[1] A stable increase (linear trend) in Government debt would mean a constant Δdebt ; a linear trend in Δdebt represents a second-degree trend in debt.

[2] The short-term rate of interest, being of minor importance, has not been included.

(4.13) *Cumulation.*

The series B may be found by cumulating $\Delta B^e + \Delta B^g$:

$$B = 0.88 \int V' - 0.1 \int m_{Ls} + 0.2 \int m_{Lb} - 0.115 \int Z^c - 0.155 \int Z^c_{-1}$$
$$- 1.7 m_{Lb} + 0.07 t^2 + 4.3 t \qquad\qquad (4.131).[1]$$

Cumulations over the period covered come very near to a trend. Hence B may fairly well be approximated by a trend:[2]

$$B = 4.88 t \quad (R = 0.99) \qquad\qquad (4.1).$$

It will be taken in this form in section (4.7).

(4.2) THE SUPPLY OF SHARES

(4.21)

I. *Theoretical. Cf.* section (4.11).

II. *Statistical.*

Here, as with bonds, V' had a tendency to show a considerable lead with regard to ΔC, instead of the expected lag.[3] Hence V'_{-1} was also omitted, and so was $(-\Delta q)''$, which showed a small negative coefficient. The equation chosen runs:

$$\Delta C = 1.64 \, V' - 1.1 \, m_{Ls} + 8.8 \, m_{Lb} \qquad\qquad (4.21).$$

---

[1] The coefficient for t is equal to the average of ΔB; that for t^2 is found by integrating $0.138 t$ from (4.123).

[2] The m_{Lb}-term in (4.131), originating with that in (4.122), which is virtually not a cumulant, is small. Moreover, in all correlation calculations where t will be used as representing B, m_{Lb} will also be included as a separate variable.
The second-degree trend has a very small influence.

[3] The particular conditions of the country and period under review may perhaps explain why the figures show this lead. In the years 1927 to 1929, part of the receipts of share issues were used on the stock exchange, and were only later taken up by investment.

The signs for m_{Ls} and m_{Lb} are as expected. The coefficient for V′ is very large. Adding that for V′ in (4.11), we find that the fluctuation in the total net increase in long-term capital is about two and a half times as large as the fluctuation in investment. This does not seem reasonable; probably V′ to a certain extent takes the place of another variable not included. In view of the use that will be made of these equations, it is not at present necessary to go deeper into this question.

(4.22)   *Cumulation.*

Cumulating (4.21), we get :

$$C = 1.64 \int V' - 1.1 \int m_{Ls}$$
$$+ 8.8 \int m_{Lb} + 2.4t \qquad (4.22),$$

which is again simplified to :

$$C = 3.18\, t \quad (R = 0.95) \qquad (4.2).$$

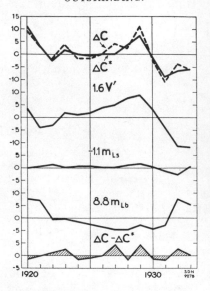

Graph. 4.21.

"Explanation" of Fluctuation in the
INCREASE OF SHARE CAPITAL
OUTSTANDING.

(4.3)   THE SUPPLY OF SHORT CLAIMS

The supply of *short-term claims* reacts, by the very nature of these claims, much more quickly to the economic situation than the supply of stocks and bonds. With only a small margin of error, it may therefore be maintained that this supply depends on the variables to be discussed, without any lag. The supply of claims being synonymous with the demand for loans, we have to consider what factors determine this demand. Three seem to be outstanding:

(i) Short-term interest rates (m_S);

(ii) Total value of all shares $0.0156\ \bar{\bar{n}}\ \bar{\bar{C}}$ (*cf.* relation 1.1) representing a demand factor for loans for speculative purposes;

(iii) Total value of production (U+V), representing a demand factor for industrial and commercial loans. This demand is composed of two parts: viz., a demand corresponding to working capital and a demand corresponding to the provisional financing of new investments, which is usually consolidated only after a certain time. The former shows fluctuations which are fairly accurately parallel to U+V, as is seen by inventory statistics, whereas the latter will be parallel to V, as only the new investment of some short period immediately before is financed in this way. Given a high parallelism between U and V and the rather subordinate rôle the present relation is found to play in the whole system, no attempt has been made to distinguish between the influence of U and that of V.

Graph 4.3.

" Explanation " of Fluctuations in SHORT CLAIMS BY SUPPLY FACTORS.

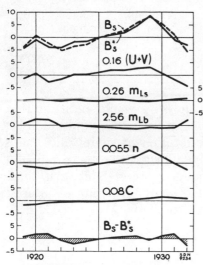

(iv) As competitive " prices ", share yield (m_{Ls}) and bond yield (m_{Lb}) may be added.

Using these explanatory variables we find the following regression equation:

$$Bs = 0.16\,(U+V) + 0.26m_{Ls} + 2.56m_{Lb} + 0.055n + 0.08C \quad (4.3).$$

6

The variable m_S has been omitted, since it obtained an insignificant positive coefficient, which is not in accordance with theoretical expectations. The value 0 which we have chosen would mean that the elasticity of this supply (which, as has been said already, is equivalent to the demand for short loans) would be *zero*. This is in harmony with our results concerning the low influence of interest rates on investment activity, as well as our hypothesis about the small influence of short-term rates on the share market.

Summary of Results of Correlation Calculations concerning the Supply of Short Claims.

Case	Regression coefficient for:					R
	U + V	C'	m_{Ls}	m_{Lb}	m_S	
1	0.11	0.04	2.27	− 3.93	1.89	0.98
2	0.18	0.05		1.40	− 0.07	0.96
3	0.19	0.05	1.22		0.67	0.98
4	0.21	0.05	0.63	1.25		0.97

The influences found for m_{Ls} and m_{Lb} would indicate that there is a considerable competition between the supply of short claims on the one hand, and the flotation of shares and bonds on the other hand. It is natural that the price to be paid for long-term credits should have much more weight with those who demand these credits than the short-term rate of interest which is to be paid only temporarily.

(4.4) THE SUPPLY OF MONEY

The supply of money may be split up into:

(4.41) the supply of currency, and
(4.42) the supply of deposits.

Indicating total money by M, currency outside banks by M′ and deposits by M″, we have

$$M = M' + M'' \qquad (4.40).$$

(4.41). The item " Money in circulation " or "Currency in circulation " of the Federal Reserve Banks balance-sheet covers not only M', but also the currency held by banks: vault cash (VC). It may be assumed that, for both items, supply follows demand automatically;[1] hence for both we have to consider demand only (cf. section (4.6)).

(4.42) In principle, the supply of deposits may be said to be regulated by acts of price fixation — i.e., fixation of the short-term interest rate m_S — by the commercial banks, on the basis of their debt position with the Federal Reserve Banks. The fact that debts (in the form of rediscounts) are permitted to be incurred only for a short period creates a tendency for the banks to fix their interest rates in such a way as to avoid such debts.[2] This means that the higher the net debt position, indicated by bills rediscounted (Bi) minus excess reserves (R^e), the higher the rate fixed.[3] This may be indicated by a relation:

$$m_S = f \, (\mathrm{B}i - \mathrm{R}^e) \qquad (4.420).$$

This relation is shown in graph 4.421. Monthly figures for Bi — R^e (abscissa) are plotted against m_S (ordinate). Where space has allowed, the different months of one year have been connected, and the first and last months indicated. Yearly figures have been plotted on 4.422, with the same scale. It will be seen that, on the right-hand part of the graph, where Bi outweighs R^e, the rate of interest rises steeply with an increase in indebtedness. More to the left, however, the reaction of the rate of interest to a position of large excess reserves becomes ever fainter; evidently m_S cannot be lower than 0, or a trifle above 0.

---

[1] Cf. L. Currie, The Supply and Control of Money in the United States, Cambridge (Mass.), 1935, Chapter X.

[2] Cf. W. W. Riefler, Money Rates and Money Markets in the United States, New York and London, 1930.

[3] One might, moreover, have expected to find an influence exercised by the gold stock — viz., a raising of discount rates when the gold cover of the liabilities of the Federal Reserve Banks becomes low. However, no evidence of such an influence is found.

The period considered in this study shows points that are nearly all on the right-hand side of the graph. For this part of the diagram, we may approximate the function of (4.420) by a straight line:

$$m_S = 4\,(Bi - R^e), \tag{4.421}$$

where the factor 4 indicates that the banks raise their rate of interest by 1% when their indebtedness with the Federal Reserve Banks increases by $250 million. It will be seen that this line very well fits the scatter in the years 1919-1932.

The original figures on indebtedness, as published by the Federal Reserve Banks, did not follow this pattern for the years 1917 to 1921 (*cf.* the black dots on graph 4.422). In these years, large amounts of United States war paper had to be absorbed by the banking system; this could only take place at the cost of increased indebtedness with the central banks. The special causes that were at work during these years made it reasonable not to include this indebtedness in Bi,[1] but rather to regard it as Federal Reserve Banks holdings of Government paper.

Accordingly, all Bi figures for 1917 to 1921 have been diminished by the amount of bills secured by Government paper each month *minus* the average amount so secured in 1922 ($230 million) — a year when normal conditions had presumably been restored.

The value of $Bi - R^e$ itself is determined by the other items occurring in the combined balance-sheets of the Federal Reserve Banks, which may be summarised as follows:

Liabilities		*Assets*	
Member bank reserve balances required	R^r	Gold stock	Au
		Bills discounted	Bi
Member bank reserve balances, excess	R^e	Bills bought, Government securities and all other items	P
Currency in circulation	$M' + VC$		

---

[1] *Cf.* RIEFLER, *loc. cit.*, page 158.

Graph 4.421.

Relation between the BANKS' INDEBTEDNESS
WITH THE FEDERAL RESERVE BANKS (Bi — Re) and the
SHORT-TERM RATE OF INTEREST (m_S).
Monthly figures, 1917-1937 (1917-1921 corrected).

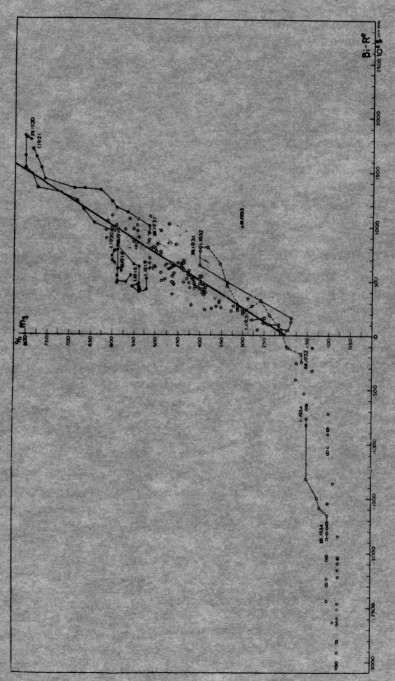

Graph XLIV.

Relation between the Banks' Indebtedness
with the Federal Reserve Banks (B₂ — B') and the
Short-term Rate of Interest (Q5A.
Monthly figures, 1917-1937 (1917-1921 corrected).

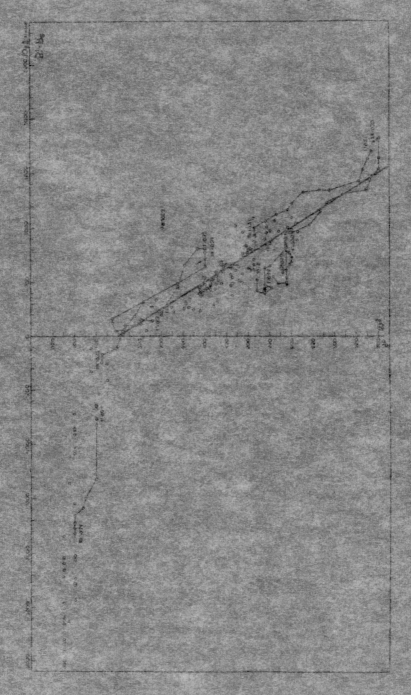

Graph 4.422.

Relation between the Banks' Indebtedness with the Federal Reserve Banks (Bi − R^e) and the Short-term Rate of Interest (m_S).

Monthly figures, 1917-1921, uncorrected (....) and yearly figures, 1919-1937 (ooooc) (1919-1921 corrected).

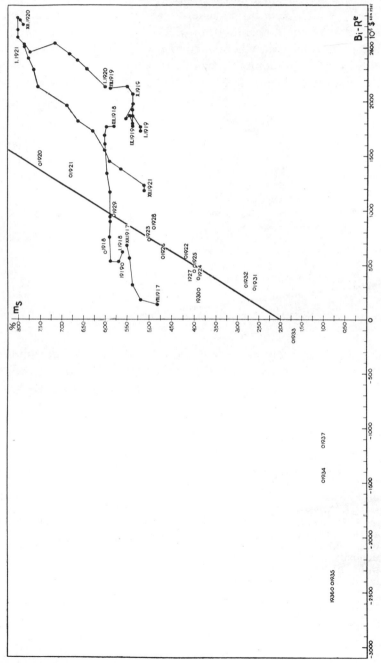

The last item includes all small assets minus all small liabilities not elsewhere mentioned;[1] its major constituents, however, are bills bought and Government securities. As these are the chief instruments of open-market policy, the item has been indicated by P, which will be considered as an autonomous (external) variable in the determination of the supply of deposits. So will the gold stock Au, whereas currency in circulation (M$'$ + VC) is determined by demand, which is also beyond the control of the banking authorities.

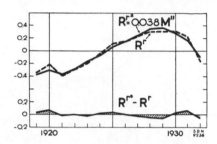

Graph 4.43.

" Explanation " of Fluctuations in Required Reserves with the Federal Reserve Banks by Total Deposits.

From the balance-sheet it follows that

$$Bi - R^e = R^r + M' + VC - (Au + P).$$

Here, R^r is technically connected with the total amount of deposits M$''$ by the reserve prescriptions. Roughly,[2] these may be assumed to be equivalent to a linear relation between R^r and M$''$:

$$R^r = \mu M''.$$

---

[1] In the years 1919-1921, P also includes the amount of rediscounts on United States Government paper, which has been subtracted from Bi (*cf. supra*).

[2] The constant relation between changes in M$''$ and changes in R^r exists only if the composition of deposits and their distribution over different types of banks change regularly with changes in all deposits. The percentage distribution of changes in all deposits over different groups, as determined from correlation calculations (taking account of trend changes) is as follows:

It follows that the price fixation equation for m_S may be written as

$$m_S = 4 \ [\mu \, M'' + M' + VC - (Au + P)] \qquad (4.422)$$

or, according to (4.40)

$$m_S = 4 \ [\mu \, M + (1 - \mu) \, M' + VC - (Au + P)] \qquad (4.423).$$

Solving (4.423) with respect to M, we find as a supply equation for money:

$$M = \frac{m_S}{4\mu} - \frac{1}{\mu} \ [(1 - \mu) \, M' + VC - (Au + P)] \qquad (4.424).$$

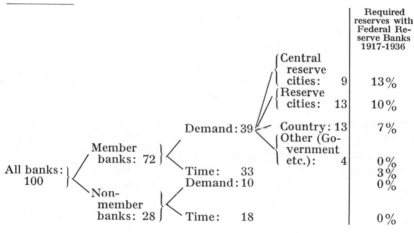

			Required reserves with Federal Reserve Banks 1917-1936
		Central reserve cities: 9	13%
		Reserve cities: 13	10%
	Demand: 39	Country: 13	7%
Member banks: 72		Other (Government etc.): 4	0%
All banks: 100	Time: 33		3%
	Demand: 10		0%
Non-member banks: 28	Time: 18		0%

If we weight the required reserve percentages, as indicated in the last column, by this distribution of the changes in deposits, we find an average "marginal reserve percentage" of 4.3 — indicating the possibility of the creation of $23 million of additional deposits on $1 million of additional reserves.

Direct correlation of R^r with M'' and a trend gives, however, a marginal percentage of 3.8 (indicating an expansion of 26 times). The difference between the two figures is probably due to the fact that, in a depression, idle money with the country banks is redeposited with city banks; which, according to the existing regulations, obliges both banks to keep reserves against them. In times of prosperity, this money is either used in the country, or directly deposited with the New York banks (1929). For this reason the ratio between reserves required and deposits in the hands of the public tends to be lower in times of prosperity, when M'' is high, and higher when M'' is low (cf. Member Bank Reserves, Report of the Committee on Bank Reserves of the Federal Reserve System (1931), pages 9-10). The coefficient found by direct correlation has been taken as μ.

As it has been found by correlation that

$$\mu = 0.038 \ (cf. \ \text{graph} \ 4.43),$$

the following equation is finally taken for the supply of M:

$$M = 6.6 \ m_S - 25 \ M' - 26 \ VC + 26 \ (Au + P) \qquad (4.4).$$

Graph 4.4 shows the fit of this relation.[1] It will be seen that M' has a large *negative* influence on M; the hoarding of some 1 or 2 milliard dollars of currency in 1931 and 1932 must, in particular, have caused 25 times as large a decrease in the supply of money.

(4.5) DEMAND BY BANKS FOR SHORT CLAIMS AND BONDS

As has already been stated, the demand by banks for short claims and for bonds is considered as joint. This means that the total amount which the banks have available to hold assets is distributed over the two categories of assets in a way depending on the price and the attractiveness of each. This amount has been derived from the combined balance-

Graph 4.4.

"Explanation" of Fluctuations in the QUANTITY OF MONEY by Supply Factors.

(In the residuals, a dotted line is drawn indicating 26 × the residuals of the yearly figures in graph 4.422.)

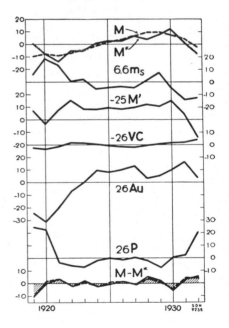

---

[1] The fit is not very good. This is due to the fact that (4.4) is found by solving (4.423) with respect to M, which plays a minor rôle in this equation. Hence the residuals have a larger relative importance. Comparison of the residuals with 26 times the residuals in (4.422) shows that the former are almost entirely due to the latter.

sheets of all banks, including the Federal Reserve Banks, which for this purpose may be summarised as follows.[1]

Liabilities		*Assets*	
Outside currency $\overline{\overline{M}}'$	$\left.\begin{array}{c} \\ \\ \end{array}\right\} \overline{\overline{M}}$	Gold stock . . .	$\overline{\overline{A}}u$
Deposits . . . . $\overline{\overline{M}}''$		Short claims . .	$\overline{\overline{B}}_s$
		Bonds	$\overline{\overline{B}}^b . \dfrac{c*}{\overline{\overline{m}}_{Lb}}$

* For explanation of this term, see below.

All other items are either almost constant or unimportant. The amount available for distribution over B_s and B_b may therefore be taken as equal to $M - Au$, or, since the fluctuations in Au are very small compared with those in M, as equal to M (*cf.* graph 1.6).[2]

The factors determining how this total holding is to be distributed over the two types of assets may be separated into two groups: their prices, and the attractiveness which each asset is expected to have for the holder. The price of short claims is taken as 1. The price of bonds is equal to $\dfrac{c}{\overline{\overline{m}}_{Lb}}$, where c is the nominal yield (averaged over all bonds in existence) and $\overline{\overline{m}}_{Lb}$ the actual yield. The variations in time of c may be disregarded; it will be taken as a constant with the value 4.5; hence bond prices may be taken to vary inversely with $\overline{\overline{m}}_{Lb}$, and, instead of prices, m_{Lb} may be taken as a variable.

The attractiveness of short claims consists in the interest income they yield; m_S must therefore be included as an " explanatory " variable. Bonds are in the first place attractive on account of the regular income in the form of interest (c) which they yield; but as c is considered as a constant, it need not be included. A second attraction of bonds may consist in

---

[1] The item " vault cash " cancels out.
[2] An attempt was made to include Au in the explanation of B_s and B^b, but no perceptible influence could be found.

expected price gains at the moment of selling; these gains are supposed to be inversely connected with the rate of increase in m_{Lb} : $\dot{m}_{Lb}$.

The banks' demand for short claims will thus be assumed to be a function $D_1(M, m_S, m_{Lb}, \dot{m}_{Lb})$ of M, m_S, m_{Lb} and $\dot{m}_{Lb}$, and their demand for bonds to be a function $D_2(M, m_S, m_{Lb}, \dot{m}_{Lb})$ of the same variables. These functions must be of such a nature that at any moment the total money value of short claims and of bonds held by the banks equals the value M.

Since the price of bonds equals $\dfrac{c}{\overline{\overline{m}}_{Lb}}$ and that of short claims is unity, the money value of assets held is $\overline{\overline{B}}_s + \overline{\overline{B}}^b \dfrac{c}{\overline{\overline{m}}_{Lb}}$, where $\overline{\overline{B}}_s$ and $\overline{\overline{B}}^b$ represent the nominal amounts held in absolute values (and not their deviations from average). This money value must be identically equal to $\overline{\overline{M}}$ — i.e., equal to $\overline{\overline{M}}$ for any values of m_S, m_{Lb} and $\dot{m}_{Lb}$:[1]

$$\overline{\overline{B}}_s + \overline{\overline{B}}^b \frac{c}{\overline{\overline{m}}_{Lb}} \equiv \overline{\overline{M}} \qquad\qquad (4.51).$$

---

[1] The treatment chosen here can perhaps best be understood by analogy with the demand for n types of consumers' goods on which together all the income of a certain group of persons is spent. (This presupposes that all consumers' goods are included and that either no saving occurs or saving is also considered as a consumers' good). Denoting the quantities demanded of the various goods by u_1, u_2, u_3, etc., their prices by p_1, p_2, p_3, etc., and total income by Y, the demand functions are:

$$u_1 (p_1, p_2, p_3 \ldots p_n, Y)$$
$$u_2 (p_1, p_2, p_3 \ldots p_n, Y), \text{ etc.}$$

They will be dependent, since they must fulfil the following relation:

$$u_1 p_1 + u_2 p_2 + \ldots u_n p_n = Y.$$

In our case, assets take the place of consumers' goods and Y is replaced by the value of all assets. In addition, the demand functions depend on other variables, since, unlike consumers' goods, these assets have changing properties which make them in a changing degree attractive to holders.

In deviations from average, this identity may be written as [1]

$$B_s + 0.9\, B^b - 2.93\, m_{Lb} \equiv M \; (cf. \text{ graph } 1.6) \qquad (4.52).$$

The identity implies that the two demand functions are not independent of each other. Assuming them to be linear, and of the form:

$$B_s = \Delta_{11}\, M + \Delta_{12}\, m_S + \Delta_{13}\, m_{Lb} + \Delta_{14}\, \dot{m}_{Lb} \qquad (4.53)$$

$$B^b = \Delta_{21}\, M + \Delta_{22}\, m_{\dot{S}} + \Delta_{23}\, m_{Lb} + \Delta_{24}\, \dot{m}_{Lb} \qquad (4.54)$$

the coefficients must fulfil certain conditions to guarantee the identity (4.52). It follows that:

$$\left. \begin{array}{ll} \Delta_{11} + 0.9\Delta_{21} & = 1 \\ \Delta_{12} + 0.9\Delta_{22} & = 0 \\ \Delta_{13} + 0.9\Delta_{23} - 2.93 & = 0 \\ \Delta_{14} + 0.9\Delta_{24} & = 0 \end{array} \right\} \qquad (4.55).$$

The correlation calculation to find these coefficients has been made in such a way that these conditions are automatically fulfilled.[2]

---

[1] The calculation runs as follows:

(1) $\overline{\overline{B_s}} = \overline{B_s} + B_s$

(2) $\overline{\overline{B^b}} = \overline{B^b} + B^b$

(3) $\overline{\overline{B^b}} \dfrac{c}{\overline{m}_{Lb}} = (\overline{B^b} + B^b)\, \dfrac{4.5}{\overline{m}_{Lb} + m_{Lb}} = (\overline{B^b} + B^b)\, \dfrac{4.5}{\overline{m}_{Lb}}\, (1 - \dfrac{m_{Lb}}{\overline{m}_{Lb}})$

(approximately) $= 0.9(\overline{B^b} + B^b - 3.26 m_{Lb})$ (neglecting a second order term and using $\overline{m}_{Lb} = 5$, $\overline{B^b} = 16.3$).

(4) $\overline{B_s} + 0.9\, \overline{B^b} = \overline{M}$.

[2] Instead of requiring separately that:

$\Sigma\, (B_s - B_s')^2$ and $\Sigma\, (B^b - B^{b\prime})^2$ be a minimum,

we require that $\Sigma\, (B_s - B_s')^2 + \Sigma\, (B^b - B^{b\prime})^2$ be a minimum.

In this function B_s' and $B^{b\prime}$ are replaced by (4.53) and (4.54), and four of the eight coefficients are eliminated with the help of (4.55). From the function so obtained, four normal equations are derived in the ordinary way. (Cf. Vol. I, pages 133-136.)

The numerical results found are

$$B_s = 0.63 \, M + 1.51 \, m_S - 1.10 \, m_{Lb} + 0.12 \, \dot{m}_{Lb} \qquad (4.56)$$

$$B^b = 0.41 \, M - 1.68 \, m_S + 4.48 \, m_{Lb} - 0.14 \, \dot{m}_{Lb} \qquad (4.57).$$

The fits are good, as is shown by graphs 4.56 and 4.57; the influence of $\dot{m}_{Lb}$ is negligible.

Graph 4.56.

"Explanation" of Fluctuations in the VALUE OF SHORT CLAIMS by Demand Factors.

Graph 4.57.

"Explanation" of Fluctuations in the NOMINAL VALUE OF BONDS HELD BY THE BANKS, by Demand Factors.

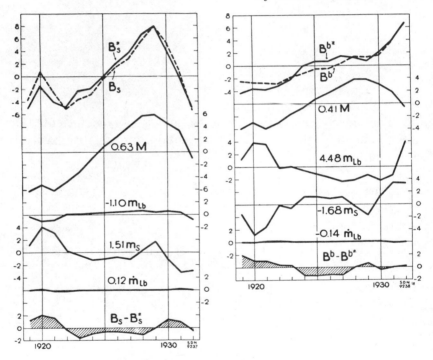

(4.6). THE DEMAND FOR MONEY

The demand for money may be split into:

(4.61) Demand for currency by the public ("outside currency");

(4.62) Demand for currency by the banks,[1]

(4.63) Demand for deposits.

(4.61). M′. The demand for " outside currency "[2] consists of two parts:

(*a*) demand for payments to and by workers and farm population, which may be taken as linearly dependent on total wages and salaries $L_w + L_s$, plus agricultural money income E'_F; and

Graph 4.611.
" Explanation " of the Fluctuations of OUTSIDE CURRENCY by Demand Factors, 1919-1929. *Extrapolation, 1930-1937.*

(*b*) demand for idle money (hoards).

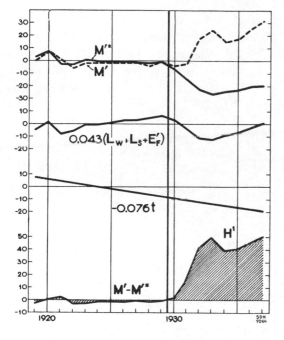

The left-hand side of graph 4.611 shows that for the years 1919-1929, when it may be taken that there was no considerable currency hoarding, the course of M′ may be very well explained by the movement of $L_w + L_s + E'_F$ and a negative trend, indicating the increasing use of cheques instead of currency. The formula runs:

$$M' = 0.043 (L_w + L_s + E'_F) - 0.076\,t \qquad (4.611).$$

---

[1] Although we do not include vault cash under the definition of money, we must nevertheless take account of it because it enters as a negative factor into the supply of deposits; *cf.* section (4.4).

[2] J. W. ANGELL, *The Behaviour of Money*, New York and London, 1936.

It has been assumed that the same relation holds good for the demand for currency for payments in the following years, and that the magnitude of the idle hoards may therefore be estimated as the residual between the actual and the calculated M'. To obtain further evidence, the calculation has been continued through 1937 (Hoarding, estimate 1). It is possible that the trend movement in favour of the cheque has not continued at the same rate after 1929 as before that year. A probably extreme alternative has therefore been calculated, where the trend term in (4.611) was supposed to be nil for the period after 1929 (Hoarding, estimate 2).

A third estimate was made according to a principle indicated by Bertrand Fox.[1] Mr. Fox assumes that hoarding started in November 1930 and that it was not effected in $1 notes or coin. So the amount of hoarding may be determined by comparing the variations in the value of outstanding notes of denominations of $5 and over, with those of the $1 notes (Hoarding, estimate 3).[2] The result of the three estimates is shown below and in graph 4.612.[3]

Hoarding	1930	1931	1932	1933	1934	1935	1936	1937
				Milliards of dollars				
Estimate 1 . . .	0.09	0.89	2.08	2.50	1.96	2.02	2.28	2.53
Estimate 2 . . .	0.02	0.74	1.85	2.20	1.58	1.57	1.76	1.93
Estimate 3 . . .	0.03	0.60	1.36	1.50	1.05	1.00	1.13	1.16

---

[1] "Seasonal Variation in Money in Circulation", *Review of Economic Statistics* XXI, February 1939, pages 21-29.

[2] The figures obtained by this procedure differ largely from those given by Mr. Fox, owing to the fact that we do not follow his assumption that hoards had been liquidated by January 1935. The argument offered in favour of this assumption — viz., that after this date " the movements of all denominations conform to the same pattern, and in turn, roughly to that of general business " (page 27) — only proves, it would seem, that there was no more *new* hoarding after that date, but not that the existing hoards had been liquidated.

[3] In an earlier publication of the League of Nations, *Commercial Banks 1925-1933* (Geneva, 1934), the amount of hoarding was estimated according to virtually the same method. The result, that "the actual amount of hoarding in June 1932 was . . . at least $1,600 million and probably more " (page 247), agrees with the present estimates.

It will be seen that the third estimate shows a good correlation with the first and the second, but with a smaller amplitude and a slight trend difference. This would suggest that there was still some hoarding of $1 notes. On the basis of the correlation between estimate 1 and estimate 3, shown in graph 4.612, lower part, the hoards of $1 notes may be estimated at about 3% of total hoarding.[1] This would not seem to be unreasonably large, and we may take our estimate 1 as final.

Graph 4.612.

Three Estimates of CURRENCY HOARDING, 1930-1937, and "Explanation" of the Fluctuations of H^1 by those of H^3 and t.

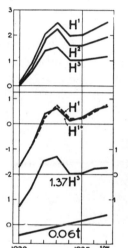

As we shall see in section (4.9), hoarding has a considerable influence on n. It is therefore of importance for the system of equations to include an "explanation" of hoarding.

This, however, raises a number of theoretical and statistical difficulties.

(i) Though there is a certain systematic, cyclical background to the phenomenon of currency hoarding, this variable, perhaps more than any other in our system, will be influenced by incidental factors. Hence we may expect large residuals in any "explanation" that is based only on endogenous factors.

(ii) The number of observations that may serve for the "explanation" is small. Hoarding started in the fourth quarter of 1930. The "explanation" by endogenous factors cannot go, it would seem, beyond the middle of 1933, when, as a consequence of the measures of bank control following the general bank holiday in March of that year, and

---

[1] In October 1930, the value of $1 notes outstanding was about one-tenth of the value of all notes. Hence $0.1 \times 0.37\ H^3$, or $0.1 \times 0.37 \times \frac{100}{137}\ H^1$, or about 3% of H^1, kept in the form of $1 notes, would be sufficient to explain the difference between the two estimates.

the somewhat improved business situation, the fear of bank failures might have ceased.[1]

The more or less stable amount of hoarding after that date should probably be ascribed to the fact that, possibly under the influence of the New Deal, a new equilibrium situation had developed, where hoards of some 2 milliard dollars were considered as normal. Our explanation must thus be restricted to the last quarter of 1930, the years 1931 and 1932, and the first two quarters of 1933. These five observations [2] clearly do not allow of a choice between different possible explanatory variables on the basis of a correlation calculus.

(iii) Different factors may have co-operated in causing the increasingly difficult position of the banks, and hence a rising distrust and an increasing tendency to hold cash rather than deposits. Apart from withdrawals of deposits by foreigners and hoarding itself, the following factors are mentioned: "the fall in commodity prices, security and real-estate values and personal incomes ".[3]

(iv) Each of these factors may have acted with an unknown but certainly not very large lag.

(v) It is not quite clear whether we must choose, of these explanatory variables, the actual value in any year, or a sum over some preceding period. It may be argued that the position of the banks becomes weaker, the longer bad trade continues — this would be a point in favour of the use of a sum; — or, on the contrary, that at any unfavourable

---

[1] Bank failures, which had involved a yearly loss of deposits of about $100 million to $300 million from 1921 to 1929, reached their peak in 1933 with a figure of $3,600 million of deposits involved. After that year, they were reduced to a negligible amount. Evidently bank failures are closely connected with hoarding, both as a cause and as an effect. But since the explanation of this phenomenon meets with the same difficulties as that of hoarding, it cannot give much help in the explanation of the latter.

[2] Nothing is gained by using eight quarterly figures for 1931 and 1932, because for almost any explanatory variable these eight values lie practically on a straight line. The heavy fluctuations in hoarding from one quarter to another are admittedly not due to the endogenous explanatory factors to be used.

[3] *Commercial Banks 1925-1933*, League of Nations, page 246.

cyclical situation, a certain number of banks fail, but that the others will be able to continue however long this situation may last. Again, hoarding may correspond to the current rate of bank suspensions, or to the cumulated total of such failures over a certain time.

Lacking both theoretical and statistical evidence, the choice may be determined by considerations of a practical nature. Only one explanatory variable will be used — viz., Z^c, corporation profits, which is a good indicator of the business situation and, at the same time, most easy to handle in the elimination process (Chapter VI). A possible small lag is neglected. On practical grounds, too, Z^c rather than $\int Z^c$ (accumulation) is chosen.[1]

Graph 4.613.

"Explanation" of Fluctuations in Currency Hoarding.

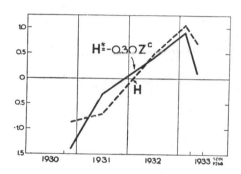

It appears from the data before 1930 that relatively small fluctuations in profits do not lead to hoarding or dishoarding. Also, the evidence since 1934 does not suggest, after a period of hoarding, a clear tendency to diminish hoards when business improves. From these facts it would follow [2] (i) that a low value of Z^c entails hoarding, but a high value no dishoarding; (ii) that the depression

---

[1] We may be pretty certain that the choice of any other possible explanatory variable — *e.g.*, (U + V) — would have given an only slightly different result.

Trials have also been made with the short-term rate of interest as the explanatory factor. The results were less convincing from a statistical point of view than those obtained with Z^c; and since there is no reason to believe that, in this particular country and period, the low rate of interest was the most important factor making for hoarding, the "explanation" by Z^c has been given preference.

[2] It must be admitted that the evidence from these last years, in which external factors may have played a large part, cannot be regarded as very conclusive.

7

must be rather serious — *i.e.*, that Z^c must have fallen a considerable amount below the preceding boom value, before hoarding starts. If we estimate this threshold value by comparing the profits in 1929 with those in the third quarter of 1930 — when hoarding had not yet appeared — we find that the minimum fall must be about 7 milliard dollars. Indicating by Z_m^c the maximum of the preceding boom, hoarding would occur when

$$Z_m^c - Z^c - 7 > 0.$$

The explanation of hoarding with Z^c over the period indicated yielded:

$$H = -0.30Z^c \quad (cf. \text{ graph } 4.613).$$

This formula may be generalised so as to cover also years with increased or slightly decreased profits, by writing

$$H = 0.30 \, (Z_m^c - Z^c - 7)'', \tag{4.612}$$

where the sign $''$ indicates that only positive values of the expression between the brackets are to be taken into account.

The general formula for outside currency now becomes:

$$M' = 0.043 \, (L_w + L_s + E'_F) - 0.076t + 0.30 \, (Z_m^c - Z^c - 7)'' \tag{4.61}$$

(4.62) Vault cash (VC) is statistically known:

(i) by weeks for reporting member banks in 101 cities;

(ii) on three or four call dates for all member banks; and

(iii) on June call dates for all banks.

As the function of vault cash is that of a small buffer stock, which is liable to relatively heavy fluctuations, not too much evidence can be gained from one, or even four, figures in a year.

Graph 4.62 shows that the figures (or estimates) [1] that may be given for the three groups, reporting member banks, other member banks and non-member banks, for June call dates (or thereabouts) and for yearly averages are not very parallel. Moreover, the graph does not suggest, as might have been expected, a correlation with deposits. This lack both of reliable data and of a pronounced movement in what material is available, suggests that the variations in VC should be disregarded, and this item should be considered as a constant. This may be done the more readily since the variation of the figures is not large in absolute terms. It is possible that cash in vault had a tendency to be somewhat larger

Graph 4.62.

"Cash in Vault" of

1. Reporting member banks.
2. Other member banks.
3. Non-member banks.

I. At June call dates.
II. Yearly average.

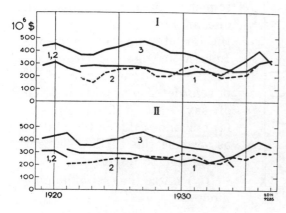

in the years 1934-1937, when the banks' excess reserves with the Federal Reserve Banks made such an increase cost very little. But the amount withheld from the reserves for this purpose was too small to have any influence on the short-term rate of interest (*cf.* section (4.42)).

---

[1] *June call dates.* All banks and member banks given in the report of the Controller of the Currency; the last week in June is taken for the reporting member banks.

Yearly averages. Reporting member banks: average of 12 monthly figures. Member banks: average of three or four call-date figures. Non-member banks: total for all banks (derived from Angell, *op. cit.,* page 178: Outside currency, and from the Federal Reserve Banks' balance-sheets: Currency in circulation) minus the figure for member banks. The figures for non-member banks are, by this procedure, also slightly influenced by the difference between Angell's and our way of estimating the yearly figures for member banks.

(4.63) M″. The following factors have been included in the "explanation" of the demand for holding deposits.

(i) (U + V), as an indication of the value of general business activity.

(ii) C′, the total market value of all shares, as an indication of the need for means of payment for speculative purposes.

(iii) t, indicating the net result of the increasing possibility to hold idle money as a consequence of increasing wealth and an increasing efficiency in the use of means of payment.[1] In a more rigorous treatment, the former trend factor might be considered as an accumulation of, say, past profits ($\int Z^c$); but for our knowledge of the system as a whole this further element would not be important.

(iv) m_S, as the cost of holding money.

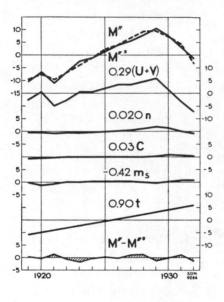

Graph 4.63.

"Explanation" of the Fluctuations in TOTAL DEPOSITS by Demand Factors.

These factors yield the following regression equation:

$$M'' = 0.29 (U + V) + 0.018C' - 0.42m_S + 0.90t,$$

or, after substitution of an expression in C and n for C′:

$$M'' = 0.29 (U + V) + 0.03C + 0.020n - 0.42m_S + 0.90t \qquad (4.63).$$

---

[1] A positive secular trend is much more characteristic of the older data available for deposits than the cyclical movements. The tremendous secular increase in deposits is shown below (ANGELL, *op. cit.*, page 175):

1890	4.0 milliard dollars	
1900	7.1 ,,	,,
1910	14.7 ,,	,,
1920	36.7 ,,	,,
1930	52.3 ,,	,,

The elasticity of demand for deposits with regard to the rate of interest turns out to be very low:

$$0.42 \times \frac{\overline{m_S}}{M''} = 0.045.$$

This is comprehensible owing to the fact that the amount of money necessary to effect payments is very inelastic in the short run.

(4.7) Demand by Individuals for Bonds and Shares

The relations determining the demand for holding bonds and shares by individuals are of the same structure as those determining the holding of assets by the banks (*cf.* section (4.5)).

The attractiveness of shares consists of two factors: the expected income (d, the rate of dividend for all companies) and the expectation as to the future course of share prices ($\dot{n}$, the rate of increase in share prices). The attractiveness of bonds consists in c (nominal rate of interest), which we have considered as a constant, and $\dot{m}_{I,b}$, which we shall disregard since we have found this factor to have a negligible influence on the banks' demand. Neither will m_S be taken into account; this implies the assumption that the influence of short-term credit conditions on the stock market is only very secondary. This has been stated by various authors — *e.g.*, OWENS and HARDY [1] and DONNER [2] — although it must be recognised that some authors — *e.g.*, Carl SNYDER [3] — seem to be of a different opinion. The latter, however, only speaks of upper turning-points, and these will be treated in a special manner in our analysis.

---

[1] OWENS and HARDY, *Interest Rates and Stock Speculation*, Washington, 1930.

[2] O. DONNER, " Die Kursbildung am Aktienmarkt", *Vierteljahreshefte zur Konjunkturforschung*, Sonderheft 36, Berlin, 1934.

[3] Carl SNYDER, " The Problem of Monetary and Economic Stability ", *Quarterly Journal of Economics*, XLIX, February 1935, page 200: " Speculation is acutely sensitive to these high rates of interest (having never survived the equivalent of a 6 per cent discount rate) . . ."

With these considerations, the demand for shares and bonds would depend on:

(i) A, the total wealth available for holding shares and bonds, which equals

$$\frac{c}{\overline{\overline{m}}_{Lb}} \; \overline{\overline{B}}^i + 0.0156\overline{\overline{n}} \; \overline{\overline{C}}^i;[1]$$

(ii) m_{Lb} and n, representing the prices of bonds and shares;

(iii) d and $\dot{n}$, representing the attractiveness of holding shares.

Thus we have the following demand equations:

$$C^i = \Gamma_1 A - \Gamma_2 m_{Lb} - \Gamma_3 n + \Gamma_4 d + \Gamma_5 \dot{n} \qquad (4.71)$$

$$B^i = B_1 A + B_2 m_{Lb} + B_3 n - B_4 d - B_5 \dot{n}, \qquad (4.72)$$

where the unknown coefficients are represented by the letters $\Gamma_1 \ldots$ and $B_1 \ldots$. These letters represent positive figures everywhere.

To these two equations the definition equation of A may be added, which, in deviations from average, runs as follows:[2]

$$A \equiv 0.90B^i + 1.50C^i - 18.0 m_{Lb} + 0.84n \qquad (4.73).$$

It may be useful, at this stage, to give some thought to (a) the purpose of the system of monetary equations [3] and (b) the way in which this purpose may be attained.

(a) The equations discussed in this chapter describe the financial sphere of the economy. The variables explained in these equations enter into the other relations of the system in a few places only: the share price index n in the explanation

---

[1] The factor 0.0156 must be included, since the absolute price level of shares in terms of nominal value was 1.56 in 1926, when the share price index stood at 100.

[2] Cf. section (4.5). The averages of B^i, C^i, m_{Lb} and n are 100, 54, 5 and 96 respectively.

[3] I.e., the equations with regard to demand and supply in the money and capital markets.

of G (5.3), the share yield m_{Ls} $(=\dfrac{d}{n})$ in the explanation of v' (2.4) and the bond yield m_{Lb} in the explanation of v_{B} (2.5); the influence of the short-term rate of interest m_{S} on stocks was not found to be appreciable (2.6). What is needed, therefore, in order to find the movements of the essential variables of our system, is the expression of n and m_{Lb} in variables not belonging to the monetary sphere. This is, in the frame of our analysis, the *raison d'être* of the present chapter.

(*b*) To find these expressions for n and m_{Lb}, the system of monetary equations must be determined — *i.e.*, must contain as many independent equations as monetary variables. To what extent, and how, is this the case ?

If we disregard, for a moment, the banks' demand for holding bonds, we shall have:

2 supply equations for B^i and C^i;

2 demand equations for B^i and C^i;

1 definition equation for A.

As the right-hand members of the two demand equations must, after multiplication by the corresponding prices, add up to the expression for A, one of the three last-mentioned equations is dependent on the two others; so we have all together four independent equations. With these, we have to determine the five unknowns A, B^i, C^i, n, m_{Lb}: our problem is undetermined. The best thing we can find with our four equations is *one* equation connecting *two* unknowns and containing further some non-monetary variables. For instance, we may find an equation expressing n in m_{Lb} and d, $\dot{n}$, etc.

On second thoughts, there is nothing peculiar in this result. If the subjects of one group hold bonds and shares, and nothing but bonds and shares, they will show a certain readiness to exchange one asset for the other (or, in other words, an indifference curve for the two assets), depending on their relative attractiveness; but there will not be a price in terms of money, since the group is supposed not to change the assets for money.

This isolation of bonds and shares from money and all other goods that are measured in terms of money will be broken if at least one of the two assets is held by at least one group of subjects that also holds money. Under our simplifications, it is the banks which establish this link.

Hence our plan becomes as follows:

(i) Determine the coefficients in one of the two interdependent equations (4.71) and (4.72);

(ii) In equation (4.71), which is then known with numerical coefficients, substitute C^i as given by its supply equation (*cf.* section (4.2));

(iii) Substitute in (4.73) the expressions given by the supply equations for bonds and shares and the definition equation:

$$B = B^i + B^b.$$

This yields, if we take the supply equations in the simplified form of trends:[1]

$$A = 8.0t - 0.9B^b - 18.0m_{Lb} + 0.84n \qquad (4.74).$$

(iv) Eliminate A from (4.71) and (4.74).

In this way we obtain a relation (4.75) between n, m_{Lb} and B^b as monetary variables on the one hand, and the non-monetary variables d, $\dot{n}$ and t on the other hand. The combination of this equation with the four demand equations for M'', M', B^b and B_s and the two supply equations of M and B_s, gives us the seven equations to determine the seven monetary variables they contain: M'', M', B^b, B_s, m_S, m_{Lb}, n.

Unfortunately, in the execution of this plan, we are repeatedly faced with serious multicollinearities which prevent us from determining some of the coefficients with any degree of precision. A way to overcome this difficulty consists in reducing,

---

[1] *Cf.* sections (4.1) and (4.2).
$$C^i = 0.755C = 0.755 \times 3.18t = 2.40t.$$

by the combination of a number of theoretical equations, the number of highly intercorrelated variables to only one, and performing the correlation calculation for the equation so found (which is the result of an elimination process) instead of for the elementary equations. We shall have recourse to this procedure every time the difficulty of multicollinearity presents itself.

Equation (4.71) is the first example. During the period studied, the movements of n were so large that they almost entirely determined the fluctuations in A. Moreover, n and a combination of d and $\dot{n}$ are very highly intercorrelated. Hence we jump (i), execute (ii), (iii) and (iv) and find (4.75) with coefficients that still contain the Γ'_s from (4.71):

$$- (\Gamma_3 - 0.84\,\Gamma_1)\,n - (18.0\,\Gamma_1 + \Gamma_2)\,m_{Lb} - 0.9\,\Gamma_1\,B^b + \Gamma_4\,d + \Gamma_5\,\dot{n}$$
$$+ (8.0\,\Gamma_1 - 2.40)\,t = 0 \qquad\qquad (4.75).$$

The six coefficients in this equation should now be found by a correlation calculation. But since in this correlation the terms with n, d and $\dot{n}$ are most important and the rôle of B^b and the trend is subordinate, and since, moreover, B^b is highly correlated with t, the determination of the coefficient for B^b is rendered illusory. Hence we provisionally [1] disregard the deviations that B^b shows from a trend, and use the purely statistical approximation:

$$B^b = 0.63t \quad (R = 0.918).$$

Further, to render the interpretation easier, we write the equation obtained by this substitution, with n explicit:

$$n = \frac{1}{\Gamma_3 - 0.84\,\Gamma_1}\,[\Gamma_4\,d + \Gamma_5\,\dot{n} - (18.0\,\Gamma_1 - \Gamma_2)\,m_{Lb} + (7.4\,\Gamma_1 - 2.40)t]$$
$$(4.76)$$

as the "explanation" of the share price.

---

[1] *Cf.* page 112 note 1.

(4.8) The Share-price Equation

The equation for n derived in the previous section may, with simplified coefficients, be written as follows:

$$n = v_1 d + v_2 m_{Lb} + v_3 \dot{n} + v_4 t \tag{4.81}$$

In this equation, the exact dependence of n on $\dot{n}$ has in particular been studied. It became evident that the fit could be improved by introducing a non-linear and even a third-degree dependence on $\dot{n}$, together with a small lag of about half a year. [1] This function — which at the same time represents the functional dependence between the demand for holding shares and $\dot{n}$ — is represented graphically in graph 4.81. It seems to show that, as long as $\dot{n}$ is not extreme, no large influence on holdings is present; but this influence becomes increasingly large, especially for positive values of $\dot{n}$. This evidently indicates what one might call "the speculative attitude " or "the boom psychology ".

The numerical expression for n is:

$$n = 19.5d - 9.1 m_{Lb} + 0.025 \, (n - n_{-1})^2 + 0.00035(n - n_{-1})^3 \\ + 0.55t \tag{4.82}$$

The linear approximation is:

$$n = 26.9d + 6.8 m_{Lb} + 0.26 \, (n - n_{-1}) + 3.88t \tag{4.83}$$

The approximation without $\dot{n}$ is:

$$n = 29.9d + 4.0 m_{Lb} + 5.7t \tag{4.84}$$

It will be seen that the coefficient for m_{Lb} gets the wrong sign in (4.83) and (4.84); but this sign is not significant, as the

---

[1] As a first approximation, this lagged value of $\dot{n}$ may be taken equal to $n - n_{-1}$. A still better approximation is of course $n_{-\frac{1}{3}} - n_{-\frac{2}{3}}$, especially as this does not contain n_0 itself, which has to be "explained". See below.

Graph 4.81.

PARTIAL SCATTER DIAGRAM BETWEEN n AND $\dot{n}_{-\frac{1}{2}}$.

× × × Actual values, corrected for influence of d, m_{Lb}, and t;
———— Third-degree curve;
- - - - - Approximation by linear parts.

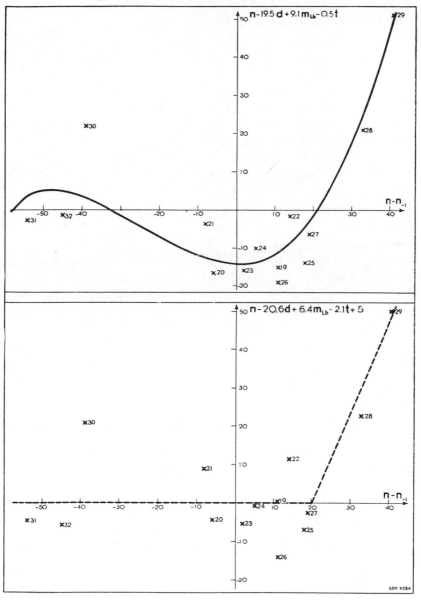

standard error of the coefficient is much larger than the coefficient itself: 12.6 in (4.83) and 12.7 in (4.84).

There is, however, a theoretical objection against the third-degree function used. If extrapolated to the right, it would rise increasingly rapidly, without limit. This does not seem to be a true picture of the attitude of the shareholder. It is more probable that, after some value of n or some level of n has been reached, the curve will rise at a decreasing rate and show a tendency to a horizontal movement. In these circumstances, it did not seem desirable to maintain the rather complicated third-degree formula, but rather to choose a simpler approximation. This may be done by distinguishing three parts of the curve separately and assuming these parts to be rectilinear. The scatter diagram between n, corrected for a provisionally determined influence of d, m_{Lb}, t and $n-n_{-1}$ suggested the following approach:

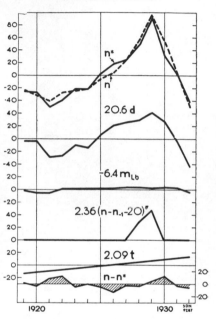

Graph 4.82.

"Explanation" of Fluctuations in SHARE PRICES.

I.   For values of $n-n_{-1} < 20$, influence on n: zero.

II. For values of $n-n_{-1} > 20$, influence on n: proportional to $n-n_{-1} - 20$.

The general formula for both parts is:

$$n = 20.6d - 6.4m_{Lb} + 2.36 (n - n_{-1} - 20)'' + 2.09t - 5 \,[1]$$

$$(4.8).$$

[1] This term must be added as a consequence of a change in averages which has to take place if the calculation is restricted to only a part of the material. For the meaning of ", *cf.* page 98.

The scatter diagram did not show very clearly on what level the third, horizontal branch should be chosen. As the maximum monthly value for n (corrected for d, m_{Lb} and t) equals about 100, it must have been at about that level or higher. This approximation of the curve by linear parts offers some convenience for the treatment of the problems considered in Chapter VI.

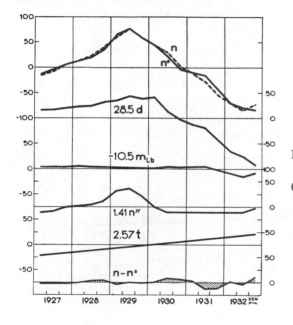

Graph 4.83.

"Explanation" of Fluctuations in SHARE PRICES, 1927-1932 (Four-monthly periods).

The dependence of n on $\dot{n}$ has been tested with shorter time units for the period where the fluctuations of n are particularly heavy: 1927-1932. By the use of time units of 4 months, $n - n_{-1}$ could be replaced by a moving average of the increases in n over these periods:

$$(n_0 - n_{-\frac{1}{3}} - 6.7)'' + (n_{-\frac{1}{3}} - n_{-\frac{2}{3}} - 6.7)'' + (n_{-\frac{2}{3}} - n_{-1} - 6.7)'' = n'',$$

assuming that the different groups of holders of shares react with lags of 2, 6 and 10 months to the increases in n that exceed 6.7 points in four months (20 points a year).

The result of an explanation with d, m_{Lb}, n'' and t over the eighteen time units considered runs as follows:

$$n = 28.5d - 10.5m_{Lb} + 1.41n'' + 2.57t \qquad (4.85).$$

The most important difference from (4.8) is the decrease in the coefficient for n'' as compared with that for $(n - n_{-1} - 20)''$. It is largely due to the fact that the fluctuations of n'' are considerably accentuated (by about 40%) in the figures for the shorter period, whereas the fluctuations of n, d and m_{Lb} are only slightly increased. The difference in the coefficients for the latter two variables between (4.8) and (4.85) does not seem to be very significant, as may be seen from the standard error of the coefficients:

Standard error of coefficients			
Equation	σ_d	$\sigma_{m_{Lb}}$	$\sigma_{(n-n_{-1}-20)''}$, $\sigma_{n''}$
(4.8)	4.3	8.8	0.63
(4.85)	2.9	5.7	0.22

(4.9) COMBINATION OF THE MONETARY EQUATIONS

Equation (4.8) gives one relation between the two monetary variables n and m_{Lb} and some non-monetary variables d, $(n - n_{-1} - 20)''$, t. Combining the other monetary equations, as planned in section (4.7), we find another equation between n and m_{Lb}, which contains in addition the variables $(U + V)$, d, Au, P, $(L_w + L_s + E'_F)$, H, t.[1] (The details of this elimination process are shown in Appendix B). These two equations serve to express both n and m_{Lb} in the non-monetary variables:

---

[1] Au and P, though monetary variables, may remain in this elimination result because they are considered as data.

H (hoarding) has not yet been reduced to its explaining variable (4.612), in order to simplify the formula; it is better to do this later.

$$n = 22.0d + 2.5(n - n_{-1} - 20)'' - 0.13(U + V)$$
$$- 0.42(L_w + L_s + E'_F) - 9.67H + 8.51(Au + P)$$
$$+ 1.86t \tag{4.91}$$

$$m_{Lb} = - 0.22d - 0.02(n - n_{-1} - 20)'' + 0.02(U + V)$$
$$+ 0.065(L_w + L_s + E'_F) + 1.51H - 1.33(Au + P)$$
$$+ 0.04t \tag{4.92}.$$

Graph 4.91.

ELIMINATION RESULT
(Monetary Equations):
n expressed in Non-monetary
Variables.

Graph 4.92.

ELIMINATION RESULT
(Monetary Equations):
m_{Lb} expressed in Non-monetary
Variables.

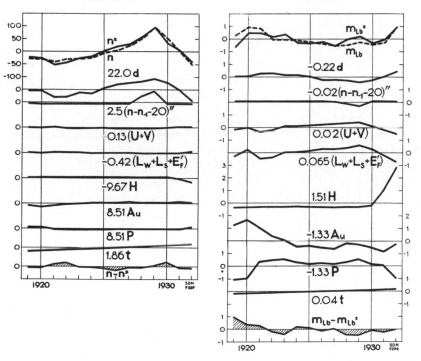

Graphs 4.91 and 4.92 show the fit of the two formulæ.
For n the result is satisfactory. For m_{Lb} it is much less good,[1]

---

[1] Owing to the fact that here the residuals in the elementary relations have been multiplied by relatively large coefficients in the course
of the elimination process.

but since m_{Lb} only enters, and with a small coefficient, into the v_B-equation, some uncertainty with regard to the m_{Lb}-equation is not a serious matter for the system.[1]

---

[1] Two alternatives may be considered.

1. $0.9\,\Gamma_1 B^b$ has been replaced by a trend (*cf.* page 105). We may now determine the possible consequences of this simplification. The numerical value of the coefficient that B^b ought to have in (4.76): $\dfrac{-0.9\,\Gamma_1}{\Gamma_3-0.84\,\Gamma_1}$ may be known within certain limits, given:

(i) the coefficient found for t in (4.8), which yields:

$$\frac{7.4\,\Gamma_1-2.4}{\Gamma_3-0.84\,\Gamma_1}=2.09;\text{ and}$$

(ii) $1.00 > \Gamma_1 > 0.35$. An increase in wealth will be distributed partly in shares, partly in bonds; hence Γ_1 cannot be > 1. When the total wealth becomes greater, there will be a tendency to increase the holding of shares by a larger percentage than that of bonds; in the average, $\overline{C}^i$ was 35% of $\overline{C}^i+\overline{B}^i$, so Γ_1 should be > 0.35.

From (i) and (ii) it follows that

$$3.5 > \frac{0.9\,\Gamma_1}{\Gamma_3-0.84\,\Gamma_1} > 0.37.$$

The extreme value of $-3.5B^b$ has been tried out as *a priori* value, and yielded

$$n+3.5B^b = 20.4d-1.9m_{Lb}+2.37\,(n-n_{-1}-20)''+4.52t \quad (4.9^*).$$

Elimination with the help of the other monetary equations in the way indicated yields variants (4.91*) and (4.92*) for n and m_{Lb} respectively.

2. The other alternative is based on the well-known view that the share price depends on the *ratio* between the rate of dividend and the long-term rate of interest: $\dfrac{\overline{\overline{d}}}{m_{Lb}}$. This variable has therefore been included instead of d and m_{Lb} separately. The resulting equation for n, after a linear approximation of the ratio $\dfrac{\overline{\overline{d}}}{m_{Lb}}$, runs:

$$n = 16.0d-18.9\,m_{Lb}+2.64\,(n-n_{-1}-20)''+1.53t \quad (4.9^{**}).$$

In combination with the other monetary equations, this gives (4.91**) and (4.92**) for n and m_{Lb}.

To facilitate the comparison of the coefficients of these alternatives with those of (4.91) and (4.92), the former are expressed as percentage deviations from the coefficients in these latter cases. Since, however, the influence (= standard deviation × coefficient) of the various explanatory variables is very unequal — as the graphs show — a like percentage deviation is not equally important for all variables. As an indication of these differences, the influence of each explaining variable in (4.91) and (4.92) is added, expressed as a percentage of the standard deviation of the "explained" series (table 4.9).

The results are satisfactory in that the series with the largest influence, both for n (d; $(n-n_{-1}-20)''$) and for m_{Lb} (Au, P; $Lw+Ls+E'_F$, H), show rather stable coefficients. Again, the results are less good for m_{Lb} than for n.

Note continued on page 113.

From the m_{Lb}-equation, the effects of open-market policy on the long-term rate of interest may be determined. The factor —1.33, which multiplies P, indicates that a $1 milliard increase of the Federal Reserve Banks' holdings of bonds or acceptances leads, *ceteris paribus*, to a fall in the long-term rate of interest of 1.33%. The two alternatives treated give coefficients for P quite near to this value: —1.37 and —1.48.

Table 4.9.

"Explained" variable	Equation	Unit	Coefficients for :					
			d	$(n - n_{-1} - 20)''$	U + V	Au+P	$(L_w+L_s+E'_F)+H$	t
n	(4.91*)	Percentage deviations from coefficients in (4.91)	+ 10	+ 9	+ 328	—125	— 69	— 6
	(4.91**)		— 10	+ 26	+ 257	+ 236	+ 234	— 83
	Influence of variables, in % of standard deviation of n							
	(4.91)	$\sigma_n = 100$	63	36	— 4	20	— 19	18
m_{Lb}	(4.92*)	Percentage deviations from coefficients in (4.92)	—632	—784	—140	+ 3	— 14	+ 725
	(4.92**)		— 8	+ 26	+ 15	+ 11	+ 11	0
	Influence of variables, in % of standard deviation of m_{Lb}							
	(4.92)	$\sigma_{m_{Lb}} = 100$	— 50	— 22	52	—258	242	32

These figures point to the conclusion that the Federal Reserve Banks are able, in view of the small year-to-year changes in m_{Lb},[1] to control to a large extent the fluctuations of the long-term rate of interest by means of not excessively large open-market purchases or sales (in a period when there are no large excess reserves).

―――――

[1] Distribution of year-to-year changes in m_{Lb}, in percentages, 1920-1937:

0 *to* $\frac{1}{4}$	$\frac{1}{4}$ *to* $\frac{1}{2}$	$\frac{1}{2}$ *to* 1	*Over* 1
11	3	3	1

CHAPTER V

DESCRIPTION OF THE MODEL.
INCOME FORMATION

(5.1) "Explanation" of Dividend Fluctuations

Dividends may be expected to be chiefly determined by profits and reserve position. Both factors may work with some lag. The relation to be tested has therefore been given the form:

$$D = \delta_0 Z^c + \delta_1 Z^c_{-1} + \delta_2 S_{-1}$$

It is not necessary to include S, as S will be dependent on S_{-1}, Z^c and D.

Graph 5.1.

"Explanation" of Fluctuations in Dividends.

Graph 5.2.

"Explanation" of Fluctuations in Entrepreneurial Withdrawals.

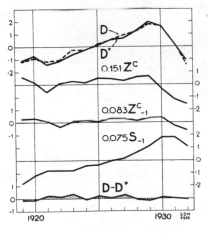

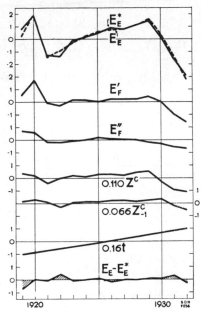

The result of the testing is given in equation (5.1) and graph 5.1. A high correlation is found, and a rather high influence of the reserve position.[1] Relation (5.1) runs:

$$D = 0.151Z^c + 0.083Z^c_{-1} + 0.075S_{-1} \qquad (5.1).$$

(5.2) "Explanation" of Entrepreneurial Withdrawals

Entrepreneurial withdrawals are only roughly estimated. Very refined experiments with these figures do not, therefore, seem possible. First, farmers' incomes (in money and in kind) were subtracted. It seemed natural to assume as the chief influencing factors for the remaining incomes:

(i) The general profit situation, which may be best characterised by corporation profits Z^c, and

(ii) A trend, representing changes in reserves.[2]

The influence of the first variable might be lagged, as corporations are probably representative of the more exposed and rapidly reacting part of business life.

A satisfactory fit was obtained with the formula:

$$E_E - E'_F - E''_F = 0.110Z^c + 0.066Z^c_{-1} + 0.16t \qquad (5.2)$$

represented graphically in graph 5.2.

(5.3) "Explanation" of Capital Gains

Capital gains will chiefly depend on the rate of increase in share prices. The only problem which arises is over what period the increase has to be taken. Judging from the distinction which is made in the statistics of income — viz., between gains on

---

[1] This influence is found to be much smaller in some European countries. *Cf. De Nederlandsche Conjunctuur*, August 1935.

[2] This factor was introduced by analogy with the case of corporation dividends where a large influence of surplus was found. Surplus shows only rather slow movements which, over the period covered, may be approximated by a trend.

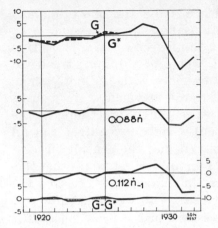

Graph 5.3.

"Explanation" of Fluctuations
in CAPITAL GAINS.

(For the years 1930 to 1932 G
has been taken equal to G* for
lack of reliable figures.)

assets held less than two years and gains on assets held two years
and more — considerable lags seem possible. Statistical investigation confirmed this view, and the best fit was obtained
by the formula :

$$G = 0.088\,\dot{n} + 0.112\,\dot{n}_{-1} \tag{5.3}$$

which means that the average period over which gains were
taken was one year.[1] This is, of course, not in contradiction
with the above, for the average will no doubt include both
longer and shorter lags, the latter originating largely from stock-
exchange speculation.

(5.4) "EXPLANATION" OF INTEREST PAYMENTS

Total interest payments are the product of "debt outstanding" and some average interest rate. This interest rate is an
average of rates for various types of long-term debt [2] — i.e., debts
carrying various degrees of risk and incurred at various dates
over a considerable period of previous time. Both factors tend
considerably to smooth out fluctuations from year to year in

---

[1] In fact, $0.088\,\dot{n} + 0.112\,\dot{n}_{-1}$ is very near to $0.20\,\dot{n}_{-0.56}$ (*cf.* page 46,
note 1), which again is almost equal to $0.20\,\dot{n}_{-0.5} = 0.20\,(n - n_{-1})$.
This expression would be obtained if all capital gains resulted from a
holding of one year.

[2] Short-term interest payments have been considered as inter-
business payments, as is done by Dr. KUZNETS, *loc. cit.*

this average interest rate. Hence only the most marked changes in business-cycle conditions find an expression in it, and even these are smoothed out and lagged. The same is true for the total of debts outstanding, where, in addition, a trend will be present. These two reasons, together with the fairly small size of the fluctuations in total interest payments, are a justification for applying only a rather rough procedure in the "explanation" of these movements. Only two rather general suppositions will be made, — viz.: (i) that the general business position, as measured by Z^c, exerts an influence, and (ii) that this influence is lagged and cumulative in character — *i.e.*, that the values of Z^c for many preceding years also exert an influence. The simplest mathematical expression which reflects both types of force is:

$$K_I = \varkappa_1 \textstyle\int Z^c_{-1} + \varkappa_2 \int Z^c_{-2} + \varkappa_3 t$$

which has therefore been chosen for testing. The best fit has been found with

$$K_I = 0.020 \left(\textstyle\int Z^c_{-1} + \int Z^c_{-2} \right) + 0.11t \qquad (5.4).$$

A trend has been added in order to account for secular changes, and for the purely mathematical reason that $\int Z^c$ is a sum of deviations, which differs from a simple sum by a trend term.

Graph 5.4.
"Explanation" of Fluctuations in INTEREST PAYMENTS.

Graph 5.5.
"Explanation" of Fluctuations in RENT PAYMENTS

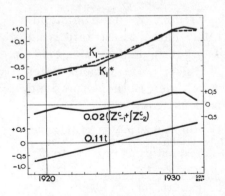
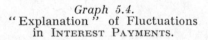
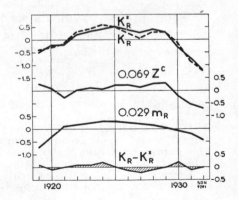

(5.5) "Explanation" of Rent Payments

Rent payments are also a minor income category, and are therefore considered only roughly. It would seem natural to assume two chief influences — viz., the general business position, most easily represented by Z^c, and the special position in the housing market, represented by m_R, rent level. The inclusion of these two factors gives a satisfactory approximation to this rather inexactly known income category. The relation found by correlation calculation is:

$$K_R = 0.069Z^c + 0.029m_R \qquad (5.5).$$

It is remarkable that no lag is found to exist in this relation.

(5.6) "Explanation" of Corporation Managers' Salaries

This category of incomes seems to depend directly on business profits, like dividends, probably with some lag. In addition, there is a structural tendency to growth in this group of incomes, which may be represented by a trend. A relation based on these assumptions was tried, and the best fit found was:

$$L_c = 0.047Z^c + 0.046Z^c_{-1} + 0.073t \qquad (5.6).$$

Graph 5.6.

"Explanation" of Fluctuations in Corporation Managers' Salaries.

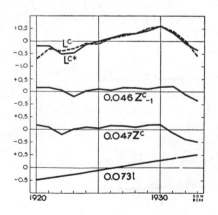

(5.7) "Explanation" of Lower Salaries

The total amount of salaries could be regarded, as will be done in the case of wages, as the product of hourly salaries and the number of hours worked by all salary-earners. A further explanation ought then to be given of the number of hours and the hourly salaries. Salary-earners' employment, however, seems to be much less directly influenced by the volume of production than workers' employment; no doubt this is largely due to the "overhead" character of their work. The level of hourly salaries will depend chiefly on the profit situation and will be slow in its adaptation. Hence, instead of "explaining" employment and hourly earnings separately by about the same factors, it seemed preferable to explain the product of the two (for which, incidentally, better statistics are available) by profits with lags of 0,1 and (tentatively) 2 years, and a trend:

$$L_s = 0.170Z^c + 0.185Z^c_{-1} + 0.225Z^c_{-2} + 0.40t, \qquad (5.7)$$
$$L_s = 0.082Z^c + 0.368Z^c_{-1} + 0.37t \qquad (5.7').$$

The fit of (5.7) (R = 0.990) is somewhat, but not very much, better than that of (5.7') (R = 0.965).

Graph 5.8.

"Explanation" of Fluctuations in WAGES.

Graph 5.7

"Explanation" of Fluctuations in LOWER SALARIES.

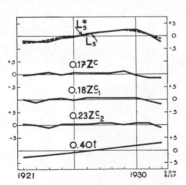

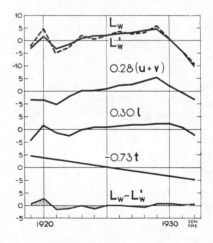

(5.8) "Explanation" of Total Wages

Total wages ($\overline{L}_w + L_w$) are the product of the wage rate ($\overline{l} + l$) by employment. Employment is closely connected with the volume of production as far as the shorter fluctuations are concerned; the long-run influence of changes in technique may be approximated by a trend. (We may disregard the dependence of this secular increase on the business cycle, which, partly because there are influences in the positive as well as in the negative direction, is only slight.)

The procedure followed consists in fitting an indirect estimate of employment $\dfrac{(\overline{\overline{L}}_w)}{\overline{\overline{l}}}$ with $(u + v)$ and a trend. The linear approximation of this result runs:[1]

$$L_w = 0.28\,(u + v) + 0.30l - 0.73t \qquad (5.8).$$

(5.9) "Explanation" of Depreciation Allowances

I. *Theoretical.*

Depreciation allowances will depend first on the value of capital goods in existence. This value is the sum of net additions during each year. Net additions will, in general, be large if gross additions are large. Gross additions being equal to V, and their sum represented by $\int$V, this last variable must be included as one of the explanatory series.

If replacement were constant through time (say $\overline{V}_r$), net investment would be equal to $\overline{V} + V - \overline{V}_r$ and total capital, to the cumulation of this value; as the cumulation of a constant is a rectilinear trend series, total capital would be equal to $\int$V + a trend. Since the average duration of life may be taken at about 24 years,[2] depreciation allowances would have to be reckoned as $0.04\int$V + a trend. If replacement moves parallel to V, the coefficient will be smaller than 0.04.

---

[1] The result is not changed appreciably if (as, strictly speaking, should be the case) $u + v$ is replaced by $u + v + u^e - u^i$, u^e and u^i representing the volume of exports and imports respectively.

[2] Calculated from data given by Fabricant, Bulletin No. 60 of the National Bureau of Economic Research.

A second influence will be that of prices of capital goods q, especially with regard to repairs which are included in N (*cf.* graph 5.9). The influence of q would be much larger if entrepreneurs based their depreciation allowances on the principle of replacement cost — but this practice seems to be rare.[1]

A third influence will be that of the actual production [2] $u + v$. In good years, more will be charged than in bad years, when no allowances at all[3] may even be made. Thus, an equation of the following type is obtained:

$$N = N_1 \int V + N_2 t + N_3 (u + v) + N_4 q.$$

II. *Statistical.*

A fairly good fit is found with the following equation:

$$N = 0.04 \int V + 0.12 t + 0.036 (u + v) + 0.037 q \qquad (5.9).$$

where the coefficient 0.04 for $\int V$ is taken *a priori*; the result of the correlation calculation was slightly, but not significantly, lower.

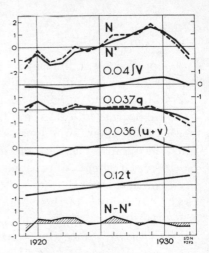

Graph 5.9.

"Explanation" of Fluctuations in DEPRECIATION ALLOWANCES.

(Dotted line in q : value of repairs included in N.)

---

[1] *Cf.* S. FABRICANT, *Capital Consumption and Adjustment*, National Bureau of Economic Research, New York 1938, page 73.

[2] As a consequence of the "service-output method", as Fabricant calls it (*op. cit.*).

[3] Writings-off of capital losses are not included in the variable N. This is correct, since Z, at least for its principal purpose of explaining investment activity, should not take account of them either. There might be some influence of these writings-off on dividends, but no indication is found of its being important.

(5.10) "Explanation" of Profit Fluctuations

Profits play a central rôle in a society which is chiefly based on free enterprise. They will in many respects influence and determine the attitude of the entrepreneurs, and hence, indirectly, business activity and many other economic phenomena. It follows that, for our purpose (the explanation of real events), the definition of profits — which from the theoretical point of view is so ambiguous — has to be adapted as much as possible to the standpoint of entrepreneurs themselves, whether or not this yields a definition which is satisfactory from any normative standpoint. The equation "explaining"[1] profits should therefore be a picture of the calculations which the representative entrepreneur makes in order to find his profits. For this purpose, all enterprises have been combined into two groups, viz.: (i) those producing durable capital goods and their raw materials and semi-finished intermediate goods, and (ii) those producing other goods and services. For both groups, profits are the difference between receipts and total deductions; total profits are the sum of the two group figures.[2]

Receipts are assumed to consist of the value of goods and services sold, since such items as inter-business payments of interest, rents and dividends cancel out for all industries together. Sales are composed of home sales and exports. For the two groups, their sum will be equal to $U + V + U^e$.[3]

Deductions are assumed to consist of :

Total wages and salaries $(L_w + L_s)$
Managers' salaries $\qquad (L_c)$

---

[1] In a sense, this equation could be called a definition equation, which would belong rather to Chapter I. But it is of course indifferent in which chapter each equation is discussed.

[2] A separate treatment for the two groups of enterprises seems hardly necessary. First, there is a striking parallelism between the two profit series, even after 1932; and, secondly, this separate treatment would be useful only if investment figures for these two groups separately were also known, which is not the case.

[3] One might perhaps have expected U' (home sales) instead of U (production for home market) in this formula. But when, *e.g.*, sales are lower than production, investment in stocks takes place, and the wages paid should therefore not be counted as costs for current sales. As we take in (5.10) all wages paid as costs, we must also take total production and not total sales.

Net rents $\qquad$ (K_R)
Net interest $\qquad$ (K_I)
Depreciation allowances $\quad$ (N)
Imports $\qquad$ (U^i)

Raw-material costs other than for imported raw materials, and home sales of unfinished goods are not to be included, as they cancel out within the national economy. On the other hand, all imports are to be considered as raw materials, since retail trade, etc., is included in our groups and virtually nothing will be imported directly by the ultimate consumer.

Thus, the following relation is found:

$$Z = U + V + U^e - U^i - (L_w + L_s + L_c + K_R + K_I + N) \qquad (5.10).$$

Graph 5.10.

"Explanation" of Fluctuations in PROFITS.

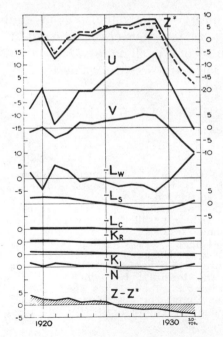

Graph 5.11.

Relation between Fluctuations in TOTAL PROFITS and in CORPORATION PROFITS.

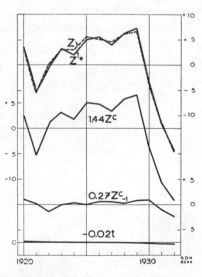

As all coefficients in this relation have values that are *a priori* equal to 1, statistical testing is extremely simple. It consists only in confronting calculated values of Z with actual ones. This has been done in graph 5.10, from which it will be seen that the chief difference is a trend difference.[1] In addition, there is a difference of nearly 5 milliard dollars in average level for which no explanation has yet been found; it must probably be ascribed to inexactitudes in average levels of other items. For the purpose of this study, this is of no importance, and the test can therefore be said to be favourable.

(5.11) " EXPLANATION " OF THE RELATION BETWEEN TOTAL
PROFITS AND CORPORATION PROFITS

The profit series used as an explanatory variable has always been corporation profits; sometimes because they actually are the influencing factor; at other times because they are more accurately known than general profits and are probably a good indication of them. This latter fact has been tested in relation (5.11) where it is actually found that the two variables move very nearly parallel, but with a difference in (absolute) [2] amplitude, a small lag of general profits behind corporation profits, and a trend difference, representing the growth of the corporation form of enterprise. The relation runs:

$$Z = 1.45\,Z^c + 0.26\,Z^c_{-1} - 0.02\,t. \qquad (5.11).$$

---

[1] The difference $U^e - U^i$, being very small, has been neglected.
[2] The percentage fluctuations of corporation profits are about twice as large as those of all profits.

CHAPTER VI

POSITIVE CONCLUSIONS ABOUT CYCLICAL
MOVEMENTS IN THE UNITED STATES, 1919-1932

_____

(6.1) CONCLUSIONS ON "DIRECT" RELATIONS

The system of relations established permits of a considerable
number of conclusions about the actual course of events in the
United States between 1919 and 1932.

A rather elementary way of reaching conclusions is simply
to consider the graphs representing the result of each correlation
calculation made. In this way it may be seen, for each year and
each variable, in what proportions the various causes of changes
— as far as they have been considered — have contributed to
these changes. Some examples may be given.

Equation (5.10) shows the relative strength of the various
components in the combined profit calculations of all entrepreneurs. Considering movements from 1928 to 1929, it
appears that the value of consumers' goods production was still
increasing, whereas that of producers' goods production was
already decreasing. In the same interval, wages were increasing,
tending to decrease profits.

Graph 1.13 shows that the decrease in value of investment
goods in those same years is wholly due to residential building
and not to other investment. Further, graph 2.5 indicates the
causes of the decline in residential building. The number of
houses some four years before was very high, and this discouraged
building in 1929.

Taking the fall in general investment from 1929 to 1930
— which contributed considerably, according to graph 5.10,
to the fall in profits in 1930 — we find from graph 2.4 that

profits one half-year before were the chief explanatory series. Here we meet a very important feature. It would seem as if this were a circular reasoning: profits fell because investment fell, and investment fell because profits fell. This is, however, an inexact statement. Profits in period t fell because investment in period t fell, but the latter fell because of a fall in profits in period $t_{-\frac{1}{2}}$; and owing to this time lag there is no danger of circular reasoning.[1] Moreover, this lag is important in that changes in it may change considerably the resulting movements of both series, as will be shown below.

Let us go back to the fall in profits in 1930 and study the influence of consumption U′as affecting production of consumers' goods U. This fell considerably, and the fall in costs which accompanied it was not able to compensate it. Relation (2.1) tells us that one of the proximate causes of the fall in consumption was a decline in wages and in other consumptive expenditure. The result of the fall in wages is, however, almost entirely counterbalanced in Z by the rôle of wages as costs. Graph 2.1 gives also the proximate causes of the fall in non-workers' consumption. Here we find that a fall in capital gains had already caused a decline in consumption out of capital gains [2] between 1928 and 1929. Consumption out of other income was still rising. Capital gains fell because the *rate of increase* in stock prices, upon which, of course, they depend, falls before stock prices themselves fall. Here, a sort of "acceleration principle", but of an economic significance quite different from the ordinary acceleration principle, has an important influence.

Taking graph 1.3, we find a remarkable divergence between the various income types; it appears that dividends D, especially, remained high in 1930, and interest income K_I remained high all through the depression. Entrepreneurial withdrawals — corresponding to profits in non-corporate enterprises — fell heavily.

---

[1] Even without lag it is possible to avoid circular reasoning, but the argument would be somewhat more complicated. Investment activity and profits would then both be determined by other variables.

[2] This is shown by figures for the sales of expensive motor-cars.

The foregoing conclusions are examples of the type of information obtainable for one special turning-point. The graphs may also be used in a slightly different way — viz., in order to obtain a number of statements valid for the period studied as a whole. This may, even more than the analysis of a single turning-point, give an impression of the forces which are most important in the business-cycle mechanism as a whole. The following is an attempt to formulate some of these statements.

The fluctuations in total value of production of both consumers' goods and investment goods have been caused much more by quantity fluctuations than by price fluctuations (*cf.* graphs 1.10, 1.15 and 1.16). The fluctuations in total profits, which are chiefly caused by fluctuations in total sales (*cf.* graph 5.10) have therefore also been chiefly governed by quantity fluctuations; only in a closer approximation are prices important. Clearly, an exception must be made for agricultural raw materials, where the reverse is true; their proportion in total production is, however, restricted to about 10%.

The influence on investment activity of what are usually considered as the most important "brakes" on an expansion — viz., interest rates and other costs — seems to have been very moderate (*cf.* graph 2.4). This is due not so much to the moderate size of fluctuations in interest rates and prices, as to the low elasticities.

Consumption outlay depends on two types of income, which are governed by rather different laws. Wages, salaries, dividends, rent and interest payments lag more or less behind general profits, whereas capital gains, by their very nature, lead (*cf.* E and G, graph 2.1).

The monetary sphere seems to be much less narrowly in contact with the physical sphere than one might expect. A superficial inspection of the graphs shows that the fluctuations in interest rates do not correlate narrowly with those in general production. The shape of the waves is clearly different for both groups. Equation (4.422) and graph 4.92 suggest that fluctuations in gold stock are a very important factor influencing interest rates; graph 4.63 suggests in addition that, the supply of money being much more elastic than the demand for it, the fluctuations in gold stock will hardly be found in total money in circulation. Apart from the influence of gold movements, there is an influence of general activity — productive as well as speculative — on interest rates. As already stated, however, the influence of interest rates on production and speculation seems to have been minimal (*cf.* sections (2.4), (2.5), (4.3) and (4.7). It must not be forgotten, of course, that these conclusions cannot be generalised for any business-cycle period in any country; to some extent they seem, on the contrary, to be very specific.

(6.2) Conclusions on Indirect Relations; the Elimination Process and the "Final Equation"

The rather elementary types of conclusion given above, which deal with one equation at a time, and hence with proximate causes only, are for that very reason somewhat superficial. The method used is not expedient, either for arriving at a picture of the course of business cycles as a whole, or for considering the consequences of economic policy. To attain the first object, starting for instance with the fall in profits after 1929, we should have to pass in endless procession from one equation to another, to find more and more remote causes. On the other hand, when studying, say, the consequence of a sudden lowering, in 1929, of wage rates by 10%, one cannot of course simply deduce that profits would have been increased by 10% of the wage sum L_w, and stop at that. A change in wage rates changes prices (3.5) and production (2.4); it changes consumption (2.1) and thereby production and. . . wage rates (3.1). Here, again, we would have to follow the effects through all equations, but now in the opposite direction.

For both purposes it is therefore necessary to have recourse to another method. The general characteristics of the business cycle may, as it is exposed in the Introduction, be found by the elimination process, which will now be taken up. Problems of policy will be dealt with in section (6.8).

9

In principle, we shall now try to eliminate all variables but one from our equations, and to obtain one equation, to be called the "final equation", in which only one of the variables — say Z^c — will appear together with a number of data. This elimination process is very laborious, and can in fact only be carried out with the help of further simplifications. According to whether more or fewer of these are adopted, we may obtain a rough first approximation or more refined second, third, etc., approximations. The latter are, of course, more exact, but far more complicated; for reasons of clearness it will therefore often be more helpful to take the less exact formulæ.

In the elimination process, all trend terms will, from the start, be disregarded. This does not involve any special simplification, but simply means that our results are obtained not for the variables as they stand, but for the deviations they show from some straight line in time (a different one for each variable).[1] This straight line will be considered as a structural development, in which we are for the moment not interested.

Further, all terms containing cumulants, like $\int Z$, will be omitted, since some calculations have shown that they have no large influence on the shape of the shorter fluctuations.[2] found for one variable may afterwards be transformed for another variable.

The exact course of the elimination process is largely dependent on the mathematician's choice. In principle, he may start where he likes and may eliminate variables in what order he likes. He may also freely choose what variable or variables he likes to keep in his final result. This does not matter very much, at least in principle, since any result found for one variable may afterwards be transformed for another variable.

---

[1] This straight line need not be the rectilinear trend of each series. It would be so if we had introduced a trend in every equation. For then, owing to a well-known theorem of multiple correlation analysis (proved by Frisch and Waugh), the regression coefficients would have been the same as if beforehand each variable had been replaced by its deviations from trend.

[2] A more exact argumentation can only be given at a further stage. *Cf.* pages 147 *sqq.*

Here, the extremely simple example of the Introduction:

$$V_t = \beta Z_{t-1} \tag{6.21}$$
$$U_t = L_t + \varepsilon_1 Z_{t-1} + \varepsilon_2 (Z_{t-1} - Z_{t-2}) \tag{6.22}$$
$$Z_t = U_t + V_t - L_t \tag{6.23}$$

may be reconsidered.

Z_t may be kept by eliminating V_t and $U_t - L_t$[1] by substituting (6.21) and (6.22) in (6.23):

$$Z_t = \beta Z_{t-1} + \varepsilon_1 Z_{t-1} + \varepsilon_2 (Z_{t-1} - Z_{t-2})$$

or:

$$Z_t - (\beta + \varepsilon_1 + \varepsilon_2) Z_{t-1} + \varepsilon_2 Z_{t-2} = 0 \tag{6.24}.$$

It is also possible to keep V_t by first solving (6.21) for Z_{t-1}:

$$Z_{t-1} = \frac{1}{\beta} V_t, \tag{6.25}$$

from which it follows that:

$$Z_{t-2} = \frac{1}{\beta} V_{t-1} \text{ and } Z_t = \frac{1}{\beta} V_{t+1} \tag{6.25'}.$$

In addition, (6.23) must be solved for $U_t - L_t$:

$$U_t - L_t = Z_t - V_t = \frac{V_{t+1}}{\beta} - V_t \tag{6.26}$$

and the result substituted in (6.22):

$$U_t - L_t = \frac{V_{t+1}}{\beta} - V_t = \varepsilon_1 Z_{t-1} + \varepsilon_2 (Z_{t-1} - Z_{t-2})$$

$$= \frac{\varepsilon_1}{\beta} V_t + \frac{\varepsilon_2}{\beta} (V_t - V_{t-1})$$

or:

$$\frac{V_{t+1}}{\beta} - \frac{\beta + \varepsilon_1 + \varepsilon_2}{\beta} V_t - \frac{\varepsilon_2}{\beta} V_{t-1} = 0 \tag{6.27}.$$

---

[1] It will be seen that $U_t - L_t$ must and can be considered as a single variable in these cases.

It will readily be seen that this equation for V is the same as (6.24) for Z; the only differences being that (6.27) has been divided by β and relates to one time unit later than (6.24).

Nevertheless, in practice it sometimes makes a good deal of difference where one starts, and the particular structure of the equations may very much facilitate some course. On closer examination of the system (*cf.* Appendix B, table I) one finds that the equations may be ranged in four groups. First there is the group of monetary equations, which may, by elimination, easily be reduced to only two equations, expressing n and $m_{L,b}$ in non-monetary variables. Secondly, there is a group of equations which may immediately be substituted in the others, each reducing thereby the number of equations and of the variables by one. Equations (1.2), (1.3), (1.7), (1.9), (1.13), (1.14), (1.15), (1.16), (2.2), (5.1), (5.2), (5.3), (5.4), (5.5), (5.6), (5.7), (5.9) and (5.11) belong to this group. After the substitution, there remains the set given in table III, which may now be subdivided in two groups:

(i) A "price" group, containing equations (1.8′), (1.10′), (1.11′), (1.12′), (3.1′) to (3.5′) and (5.8′); and

(ii) What for reasons to be mentioned later may be called the "strategic" group, containing the remaining equations (2.1′), (2.4′), (2.5′) and (1.4′), (2.6′), (4.6′), (4.91′) and (5.10′).

The structure is such that the first group consists of a number of relations "explaining" variables that play only a secondary role in the second group. The chief variables in the " strategic" group are: Z^c, corporation profits, n, share prices, v_B, residential building activity, v', other investment activity, and U′, consumption. They may be called the "strategic variables ". This grouping suggests the following treatment: the "price " variables may first be found as functions of the "strategic variables " and then be substituted in the "strategic" group of equations [1]. This has been done in tables

---

[1] The substitution must necessarily be repeated when, after further elimination, some of the strategic variables are expressed in others.

IV and V, where the whole process is given step by step. We are then left with a kernel of relations which can more easily be treated. It is, of course, not by chance that we are left with these equations and these variables. The logical structure of our system of equations, which after all is nothing but a reflection of the structure of the business-cycle mechanism, is such that they play the central rôle. This is why we call them the strategic group for the understanding of the mechanism. Their coefficients will be seen to have the largest influence on the character of business cycles.[1] In order to simplify still further, we may, within the strategic group, eliminate the variable v', which is easily expressed as a function of the other variables. For reasons to be given fully in section (6.7), we consider v_B as an external variable. Greater difficulties arise if we try also to eliminate n and Z^c; for these variables do not occur only once in these equations, but several times, with various lags. This reflects the economic fact that these variables are connected by many causal chains, working in various directions and with various lags.

The expression of n in terms of the other variables is made especially difficult by the presence of the term $2.40\,(n-n_{-1}-20)''$ and of H, which is equal to $0.3\,(Z_m^c-Z^c-7)''$. The first term intends to indicate that in a speculative boom n is much affected by its own previous rate of increase. This has the result that n moves much by its own laws, pulling with it the other variables, as we shall be able to show. The H-term means that n is depressed by currency-hoarding in a severe depression. On account of these complications, it is useful to split up our considerations into three parts relating to the three forms of the equation for n:

(i) Case I, the "normal interval", where $n-n_{-1}$ is less than 20 and has therefore no influence on n, and where Z^c either rises or does not fall so deeply that hoarding takes place;

---

[1] *Cf.* section (6.9).

(ii) Case II, the " boom interval", where $n - n_{-1} > 20$ and consequently influences n, without hoarding;

(iii) Case III, the "depression interval ", where $n - n_{-1} < 20$ and n is further kept down by the occurrence of hoarding. A fourth case, where a boom development of n would coincide with the depression phenomenon of hoarding, need not be taken into consideration.

The equation found for Z^c which still contains n-terms next to terms with Z^c and a number of variables that are taken as given for our system of equations, *e. g.*, f, runs:

$$0.770 Z^c = 0.179 Z^c_{-1} + 0.006 Z^c_{-2} - 0.015 Z^c_{-3} + 0.007 Z^c_{-4}$$
$$- 0.131 h_{-2} - 0.083 h_{-3} - 0.290 h_{-4} - 0.845 f$$
$$+ 0.335 f_{-1} + 0.081 v_{\mathrm{B}} - 0.017 (v_{\mathrm{B}})_{-1} + 0.090 n$$
$$- 0.049 n_{-1} + 0.001 n_{-2} + 0.003 n_{-3} \qquad (6.28)$$

(*cf.* Appendix B, table V, line 262 + 264).
In the next sections, we shall consider cases I, II and III for n.

Detailed Description of the Elimination Process.

The process starts in table II, where the equations of group 4 in table I are combined. Let us follow somewhat more closely the beginning of this process.

In line 1, equation (4.4) is copied, with the omission of the VC-term (the indication of the " explanatory " series is given at the top of each column to save space; for the same reason, the heading in one column is sometimes changed). In line 2, equation (4.63) is written, but transformed in an equation "explaining" M by applying equation (1.5) and adding M′ on both sides. Subtraction, in line 3, eliminates M; this equation may be written with m_S on the left-hand side (4); the factor — 0.42 has immediately been applied since it is with this coefficient that m_S occurs in M (2). (2) + (4) gives again M (5), but now without m_S. If now, in all places where M or m_S occur, we replace them by the expressions (4) and (5) so found, these variables are eliminated from the system of equations (*cf.* lines 7 and 8). The same procedure is applied to other monetary variables until, in (21) and (22), m_{Lb} and n

are expressed in non-monetary or external variables (except H, which is kept for reasons of convenience).

The eliminations in table III are of a simpler type: certain variables in some of the equations, especially of the "strategic group", are simply replaced by the expressions by which they are "explained" or defined in some other equation. Thus, in (2.1), $0.77\,E$ is first replaced by $0.77\,(D + L_c + \ldots)$ with the help of (1.3); subsequently $0.77\,D$ is replaced by $0.77\,(0.151\,Z^c + \ldots)$ equation (5.1) and finally the S_{-1}-term so introduced is reduced to 0, according to equation (1.9) in its simplified form: all cumulants and trend terms omitted. The equations used are mentioned in the column "References".

In table IV, the procedure is again of a somewhat different type. The purpose of this table is to express the prices m_R, p^f, p, l, q, and the variables $u + v$ and L_w in "strategic" variables F^1, F^2 and $U + v$, where the F's represent certain expressions in the strategic variable Z^c and the external variables h and f. In line 101, $0.80\,p'$ in (1.8') is substituted by $0.80\,(0.47\,l_{-0.21} + 0.25\,p^f_{-0.21})$. In the next line, the l-term in 101 is replaced by (3.1'). This gives an expression with p on the left-hand side and $0.147\,p_{0.63}$ on the right-hand side. In line 103, these two terms are combined to $0.853\,p_{+0.11}$, where 0.11 is the weighted lag (lead) $+ 0.11 = [(1.000 \times 0) - (0.147\times - 0.63)] \div 0.853$; then all terms of the equation are divided by 0.853 $(0.200 \div 0.853 = 0.234$, etc.) and shifted in time by $- 0.11$ year. This procedure as a whole is indicated by the reference "R". This way of elimination is continued throughout the table. Attention should be drawn to the groups of terms taken from (3.4') and (3.2') respectively which are introduced as a whole in (110) and (111). Here, as well as in the subsequent introduction of F^1 and F^2, the procedure was dictated by considerations of simplicity and the avoidance of unnecessary calculations.

In table V, the different "strategic" variables are successively eliminated. In the first place U and U' are treated. With the help of (2.1) and the results of the preceding table,[1] U' may be replaced by $U + v$, F^1, F^2, F^3, where F^3 is a new

---

[1] Cf. also note 1 on page 136.

combination, provisionally to be kept in this form. Equation (2.6′) gives another relation between U′ and U (u' and u being transformable into U and U′ via (1.12) and (1.10)). These two equations suffice to eliminate both variables, and to find U expressed in v and F's (216). It may be remarked that the same expression (206) is applied three times (in 207, 208, 209) but with different lags (0, 1 and 2 years).

In lines (217) to (224), v (or v', *cf.* (1.14)) is eliminated, and hence the result of (216) may be improved by expressing U without using v (225).

In (227) to (230), p^f is treated. The difficulty is here that F³ contains $0.049 \Delta p^f$, which causes the small p^f terms in the last column. But the latter are so small that, if they are replaced (229) by the expression for p^f in (228), the p^f terms they yield are no longer perceptible.

In (231) to (237) certain variables of tables IV and V are expressed in F¹, F², F⁴, F⁵ and v_B. Terms with lags of parts of a year are split into two terms with the same average lag.[1]

Certain combinations of these variables occur in n and Z^c (*cf.* (4.91′) and (5.10′)); their expression in F¹, etc., may now easily be found: S_n in (242) and S_z in (248).

The F's are then decomposed into terms with Z^c, n, h and f (249-252; 258-261). If we add the other terms in (4.91′) (253), we find, after a few transformations, n expressed in Z^c and external variables. We only need to substitute this expression for the n-terms in S_z to find Z^c expressed in values assumed by Z^c at moments lying 1, 2, 3 and 4 years back and in external variables (266).

(6.3) The Character of the Movements in the Absence of a Stock-exchange Boom and of Hoarding

To study case I, we omit both the term with $(n - n_{-1} - 20)''$ and that with H in line 257 (Appendix B) which explains n. We may now replace the n-terms in the Z^c-equation (*cf.* line

---

[1] The same procedure is applied to small leads, *e.g.*, $-0.022 F^1 + 0.23$ is replaced by $-0.027 F^1 + 0.005 F^1_{-1}$, with the same average lag $(-0.022 \times + 0.23 = + 0.005 \times -1)$.

262) by an expression containing only Z^c at various moments and exogenous variables. In this way we get a "final equation" for Z^c, running:

$$0.445Z^c = 0.177Z^c_{-1} - 0.098Z^c_{-2} + 0.006Z^c_{-3} + 0.012Z^c_{-4}$$
$$- 0.135h_{-2} - 0.077h_{-3} - 0.305h_{-4} + 0.74\,(Au + P)$$
$$- 0.40\,(Au + P)_{-1} - 0.822f + 0.315f_{-1} \qquad (6.30).[1]$$

In order to facilitate the understanding of this equation and its consequences, it may be written in a somewhat more condensed form:

$$Z^c_t = e_1 Z^c_{t-1} + e_2 Z^c_{t-2} + e_3 Z^c_{t-3} + e_4 Z^c_{t-4} + (AU + HO + F + R)_t$$
$$(6.31).[2]$$

Here e_1 to e_4 are numbers depending, in principle, on almost all regression coefficients in all elementary equations. They describe in an abbreviated form the structure of the economic mechanism with regard to business cycles; they will be different in other countries, or under another regime, where the economic structure of society is different.

The other four new symbols have this in common, that they may be considered as *largely independent* of the general business-cycle position. Their exact meaning may be discussed later. This co-existence in formula (6.31) of two types of terms — independent terms and terms depending on previous values of Z^c — is of importance. It represents the fact that at any moment profits Z^c (and quite similar propositions hold, as we have already indicated, for the other variables) are the product of two types of forces: forces connected with previous business-cycle situations $(e_1 Z^c_{t-1} + e_2 Z^c_{t-2} + e_3 Z^c_{t-3} + e_4 Z^c_{t-4})$, and independent forces which are often indicated as *disturbances*, since their changes cause Z^c not to follow the regular pattern of cycles. They are also indicated as *external* or *extraneous forces* (which indicates their origin; for some of them this expression is more appropriate than for others, as we shall see), or *shocks* (which of course bears

---

[1] *Cf.* Appendix B, table V, line 265.
[2] The meaning of the last four symbols will be described in the next pages.

somewhat more upon the possibility of their sudden changing and is not therefore equally applicable to all of them), or *starters* (which reminds of the possibility — especially if they come in a rather quiet period — that they may be the beginning of a new cyclic movement).[1] The causal connections which are described in equation (6.31) may be illustrated by the following diagram, where one symbol R stands instead of the sum AU + HO + F + R:

Graph 6.31.

Causal Connections between
DISTURBANCES AND PROFITS

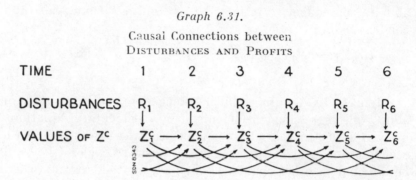

The arrows indicate causal connections. Each value of Z^c depends immediately on certain disturbances, but it depends also on the earlier ones through its connection with the Z^c-values for one, two, three and four[2] years back.

Equation (6.31) tells more than this very general statement. It tells what is the origin of the first three disturbances AU, HO and F. Going back to the equations that describe these three variables, we will even be able to determine the magnitude of the disturbances in any year.

AU represents influences coming from changes in the gold stock and in the autonomous component P in central banking policy; it is

$$AU_t = 1.66(Au + P)_t - 0.90(Au + P)_{t-1} \qquad (6.32).$$

---

[1] Dr. Johan ÅKERMAN considers as the " real causes " of the business cycle these external forces; our own preference being to indicate by that term the structure of the economy, represented by the coefficients e_1, e_2, e_3 and e_4. It is, of course, only a question of definition.

[2] In order not to overload the diagram, the arrows from Z_1^c to Z_5^c, Z_2^c to Z_6^c, etc., corresponding with the term $e_4 Z_{t-4}^c$ have not been drawn.

The isolation of these terms seems especially interesting in judging the influence of banking policy and gold movements — past as well as potential.

HO represents influences coming entirely from the housing market and, more exactly, from a development in the housing market that is largely a product of events more than three years back (and therefore, as already observed, in a very high degree independent of Z^c_{t-1}, Z^c_{t-2}, which are most important in the final equation). It is given by the formula: [1]

$$HO_t = -0.303h_{t-2} - 0.173h_{t-3} - 0.685h_{t-4} \qquad (6.33)$$

and depends on the number of houses in existence two to four years before. Through its large influence on the actual building volume, this number acts also on the present value of Z^c. The usefulness of taking it as a separate item is (i) that in no other part of the economic system were such large lags found to have a considerable influence on the cyclic movements; [2] (ii) that it shows almost autonomous cycles, to be discussed later, and (iii), that, for that reason, we are able to evaluate the influence of housing on the general business situation.

F stands for the influences, chiefly climatic, which change crops; they are generally accepted as important external forces. Again it seemed useful to isolate these terms.

$$F_t = -1.847f_t + 0.708f_{t-1} \qquad (6.34).$$

R, finally, is an agglomerate of a non-discernible multitude of disturbances which, each in itself, seem far less important than the three types mentioned, but taken together may still be important. Because of their large number and, in all probability, mutual independence, they may, however, be treated as random disturbances.

Although we have succeeded in giving separate terms for at least some of the most important external factors, there are two categories which may also be important and have not been

---

[1] *Cf.* Appendix B, table V, line 266.

[2] One could have expected that the so-called "echo principle" would also give an example of such forces, and wonder why it has no place in this system of equations. Very probably, however, these forces are of importance only for the explanation of trend movements. *Cf.* Vol. I, Chapter III, and section (2.1) of this volume.

included, viz., inventions and, in the United States especially
for the period after 1932, Government policy. The latter, if
well devised, will, however, belong rather to the class of regular
exogenous factors such as the terms HO in our example.

From the business-cycle point of view the first four terms
in equation (6.31) are the more interesting. They represent the
systematic cyclical forces. They tell us that, apart from disturbances, the situation of to-day will depend on the situations of
one, two, three and four years ago; and — if the problem is
studied more accurately — even of a number of more remote
years; the influence of the latter is, however, found to be small.

Looking for a moment at this systematic part only, we get
the relation

$$Z_t^c = e_1 Z_{t-1}^c + e_2 Z_{t-2}^c + e_3 Z_{t-3}^c + e_4 Z_{t-4}^c, \qquad (6.35)$$

which is called a "difference equation". It enables us to calculate the future movements (in the absence of new disturbances)
if there are given:

(i) four initial values, say Z_{1917}, Z_{1918}, Z_{1919} and
Z_{1920}, and

(ii) four coefficients e_1, e_2, e_3 and e_4, which depend on
the coefficients in our elementary equations and therefore
in the widest sense upon the economic structure.

In our example, the period and the damping degree of the
endogenous movements depend only on e_1 to e_4 (*i.e.*, on the
structure), whereas the amplitude depends on the initial values,
say Z_0^c, Z_1^c, Z_2^c and Z_3^c. In more complicated cases these influences
may be mixed up in various ways. If the endogenous movement
is damped, it will vanish after some time and a new movement
will develop only if fresh disturbances occur.

The numerical values for the coefficients in our case lead
to the following formula:

$$Z_t^c = 0.398Z_{t-1}^c - 0.220Z_{t-2}^c + 0.013Z_{t-3}^c + 0.027Z_{-4}^c \qquad (6.36).$$

Choosing some arbitrary initial values, *e.g.* $Z_0^c = 0$, $Z_1^c = 0$,
$Z_2^c = 0$, $Z_3^c = 3$, the further development may be calculated.
It is given in graph 6.32, and consists chiefly of a damped
cycle with a period of 4.8 years. It may be proved mathematically that this is the case independently of the initial

values of Z^c chosen;[1] this statement could be tested by some trials with other values. This cycle is somewhat longer than the well-known "short American cycle", of which the average length has been estimated at forty months. Neither of the figures should, however, be taken too literally; for, on the one hand, the average length of cycles just quoted is based upon measurements of actual cycles which are always subject to disturbances, and, on the other hand, our result too is subject to a considerable margin of error.[2] It may be shown, however, that the other conclusions — those regarding the influence of policy and of external factors — are far more certain.[3]

Graph 6.32.

ENDOGENOUS MOVEMENTS OF Z^c (within the "normal interval" for share prices and in the absence of hoarding) FOR TWO SETS OF INITIAL VALUES. Time in Years.

——— Initial values: $Z_0^c = 0$, $Z_1^c = 0$, $Z_2^c = 3$.

- - - - Initial values: $Z_0^c = -3$, $Z_1^c = 0$, $Z_2^c = 3$.

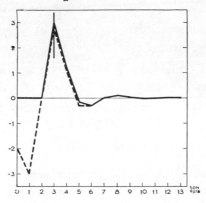

The mechanism may be made somewhat more understandable by the following analysis: Equation (6.36) shows two large forces acting on Z_t^c: first, a force in the same direction as Z_{t-1}^c;

---

[1] *Cf.* below.
[2] *Cf.* page 179.
[3] *Cf.* J. TINBERGEN: "On the Theory of Business-cycle Control", *Econometrica* VI (1938), page 22.

secondly, one in the direction opposite to Z^c_{t-2}. If now Z^c_{t-1} and Z^c_{t-2} have the same sign—*i.e.*, if the system finds itself either distinctly above normal or distinctly below normal—the positive and negative forces will counteract each other and the new Z^c will be small, *i.e.*, profits will be nearer to normal. This, in a nutshell, is the turning-point situation. If, on the other hand, Z^c_{t-1} has a sign different from that of Z^c_{t-2}, the forces will reinforce each other and the new Z^c_t will be of the same sign as Z^c_{t-1}. If the absolute value of Z^c_{t-1} is small in comparison with Z^c_{t-2} — *i.e.*, if the normal position is only just passed — Z^c_t will be larger than Z^c_{t-1}: this is the cumulative process. For a good understanding of this result, as well as of some of our further statements, it may be observed that even in the simple case with only two coefficients, $Z^c_t = e_1 Z^c_{t-1} + e_2 Z^c_{t-2}$, the connection between (i) the coefficients e_1 and e_2, and (ii) the character of the endogenous movement is not so simple as one might expect. The following types of movement are possible:

(*a*) Cyclic movements, with any period of at least two years, either
   (i) damped, or
   (ii) undamped, or
   (iii) anti-damped;

(*b*) Damped "one-sided" movements which gradually carry the system back to the "equilibrium position" $Z^c = 0$;

(*c*) "Explosive" movements which carry the system away from that position without ever returning to it;

(*d*) Several combinations of these types.

The rules indicating the connection mentioned above cannot easily be formulated in ordinary language; a mathematical formulation is the only one possible. The problem is to find a function of time,[1] say Z^c_t, which identically satisfies the equation

$$Z^c_t = e_1 Z^c_{t-1} + e_2 Z^c_{t-2} \qquad (6.371).$$

---

[1] Throughout the following pages, the variable time is supposed to assume entire values $t = \ldots 0, 1, 2 \ldots$ only, the corresponding values of Z^c_t being conceived as annual averages of profits for the year t.

The mathematician finds this function by trial, and proves afterwards that the solution found is the general one. A function [1]

$$Z_t^c \equiv Kx^t, \tag{6.372}$$

where K and x are constant, is tried. The substitution of this function in (6.371) gives

$$Kx^t = Ke_1 x^{t-1} + Ke_2 x^{t-2}.$$

From this it is clear that K may be chosen arbitrarily, since each value for K will be correct once x has been chosen so as to satisfy $x^t = e_1 x^{t-1} + e_2 x^{t-2}$, or

$$x^2 - e_1 x - e_2 = 0 \tag{6.373}.$$

This quadratic equation, formed with the coefficients of the equation (6.371), is called the characteristic equation. Its roots x_1 and x_2:

$$x_1 = \frac{1}{2}e_1 + \sqrt{\frac{1}{4}e_1^2 + e_2}, \quad x_2 = \frac{1}{2}e_1 - \sqrt{\frac{1}{4}e_1^2 + e_2}, \tag{6.374}$$

are the only values of x for which the function (6.372) satisfies (6.371). All other values of x would yield no solution at all, whatever values might be chosen for K.

As the coefficients e_1 and e_2 are real numbers, the roots x_1 and x_2 are either both real or conjugate complex. If x_1 is real and positive, but smaller than 1, the curve

$$Z_t^c = Kx_1^t \tag{6.375}$$

represents a gradual approach to an equilibrium situation ($Z^c = 0$). The deviation from equilibrium in the year $t + 1$ is found from that in the year t by dividing it by the factor

$$D = \frac{x_1^t}{x_1^{t+1}} = \frac{1}{x_1} \tag{6.376}$$

which may be called the "damping ratio" of the movement. The larger D, the faster the equilibrium is approached. If x_1

---

[1] The sign $\equiv$ indicates that the equality of Z_t^c and Kx^t is meant to be true for every value of t.

is larger than 1, however, the "damping ratio" is smaller than 1, and the movement leads farther and farther away from the equilibrium situation (upwards or downwards according to the sign of K).[1]

If both real roots x_1 and x_2 are positive, the movement

$$Z_t^c = K_1 x_1{}^t + K_2 x_2{}^t, \tag{6.377}$$

which is a combination of two solutions, each of one of the above types, also constitutes a solution. Substitution of the expression (6.377) in (6.371) shows this at once. The arbitrariness of the constants K_1 and K_2 makes it possible to choose them in such a way as to give prescribed values to Z_t^c for two points of time — e.g., $t = 0$ and $t = 1$. This only requires that K_1 and K_2 should be determined by the two equations:

$$K_1 x_1{}^0 + K_2 x_2{}^0 = Z_0^c$$
$$K_1 x_1{}^1 + K_2 x_2{}^1 = Z_1^c$$

which, since $x_1{}^0 = x_2{}^0 = 1$, reduces to:

$$\left.\begin{aligned} K_1 + K_2 &= Z_0^c \\ K_1 x_1 + K_2 x_2 &= Z_1^c, \end{aligned}\right\} \tag{6.378}$$

where Z_0^c and Z_1^c are the prescribed values of Z_t^c for $t = 0$ and $t = 1$.

Thus it will be possible to find one determinate solution for each given pair of values for Z_0^c and Z_1^c.[2]

If the roots x_1 and x_2 are conjugate complex, it may be shown that the expression (6.377) is equivalent to

$$Z_t^c = K a^t \sin \frac{2\pi}{T} (t - \tau) \tag{6.379}.$$

If the factor a^t were absent from this expression, Z^c would move in an undamped harmonic oscillation with a period of T years. The factor a^t brings about a gradual increase or decrease

---

[1] $y = Kx^t$ also represents the value in the year t of a capital K, invested in the year $t = 0$ at compound interest at the annual rate of $100 (x - 1)$ per cent.

[2] It is possible to prove that no other solutions exist.

n the amplitude of this oscillation, according as $a > 1$ or < 1. Calling, again,

$$D = 1/a$$

the damping ratio, the oscillation is damped if $D > 1$, and anti-damped if $D < 1$.

The period [1] T and damping ratio D of the solution (6.379) depend as follows on the coefficients of (6.371):

$$\tan \frac{2\pi}{T} = \frac{x_1 - x_2}{x_1 + x_2} = \sqrt{1 + 4\frac{e_2}{e_1}} \qquad (6.380)$$

$$D = \frac{1}{\sqrt{x_1 x_2}} = \frac{1}{\sqrt{e_2}} \qquad (6.381).$$

On the other hand, the initial amplitude K and phase τ of the oscillation are not prescribed by the coefficients in (6.371), but depend only on the initial values Z_0^c and Z_1^c of Z^c. They may be found in the same way as K_1 and K_2 were found in (6.378).

From (6.380) it follows that a value above two years may always be found for the period T. A limiting case is formed by a negative real root x_1, which leads to an oscillation of an exact two-year period, with a damping ratio $D = \dfrac{1}{|x_1|}$ and an initial amplitude determined by the initial values of Z^c.

In the case of the simple model quoted in the Introduction, we have (cf. equation (0.4), page 17) $e_1 = + 1.6$, $e_2 = - 1.0$, and therefore $x^2 - 1.6x + 1 = 0$; the roots x_1 and x_2 are: $0.8 \pm \sqrt{0.64 - 1}$ or $0.8 \pm 0.6i$; the corresponding movements are cyclic and undamped, and show a period of ten time units of four months. This number is found as the quotient of $360°$ (or 2π radiants) by arc $\tan \dfrac{0.6}{0.8}$.

---

[1] Though equation (6.380) admits of an infinite series of solutions T_k satisfying $\dfrac{2\pi}{T_k} = \dfrac{2\pi}{T_0} + k\pi$, $k = 0, \pm 1, \pm 2 \ldots$, with $0 < \dfrac{2\pi}{T_0} \leqq \pi$, the restriction of t to entire values (see note 1 on page 142) makes the expression (6.379) for each of these solutions mathematically equivalent to that corresponding to the value T_0.

No other types of movement than those described above occur when the final equation, unlike (6.371), contains also terms with Z^c_{t-3}, Z^c_{t-4}, etc. Every additional term, however, increases by 1 the degree of the characteristic equation, and with that the number of its roots. Thus, the general solution of a final equation containing terms up to Z^c_{t-4} is a combination of four specific movements, each of one of the above types, and each corresponding to one root of the characteristic equation. Though in general the initial relative importance of the specific movements is determined by the four initial values of Z^c, the specific movements most important for business-cycle analysis are those which have the smallest damping ratio, as such movements are most likely to persist for a longer time.

In the present case, the final equation (6.30) contains as the most important movement a cycle with a period of 4.8 years and a damping ratio of 1.89.

The period and damping ratio depend, in principle, on each coefficient in each single equation which has been used in deriving the final equation. In section (6.9), the influence of changes in some of the more important coefficients on damping and period are studied, and some indication is given of the uncertainty in the above figures ensuing from given margins of error in those coefficients. One instance, however, is sufficiently interesting to be mentioned here, as it indicates a probable bias in the above figures.

Owing to the large damping ratio, there is a tendency for damping and period to be particularly sensitive to changes in coefficients in the elementary equations that represent causal connections acting with a large time-lag. The only case of a lag above one year in the elementary equations (leaving aside the term with h_{-4} which is considered as an external variable) is in equation (5.7), and it appears that, if (5.7) is replaced by (5.7′) — see page 120 — the period works out at 5.0 years and the damping ratio at 1.59. As the fit in the explanation of L_s is nearly equally good in the two alternatives, it would seem that the choice has to depend on other considerations. Damping and period for any set of coefficients in the L_s-equation intermediate to the extreme cases (5.7) and (5.7′) may be found approximately by linear interpolation between the figures given.

For most problems to be studied in the following sections, the choice between the two possibilities is not important; to save work, only the final equation based on (5.7) has been applied in such cases. Only in the second half of section (6.9) some figures are given on the basis of both equations for L_s.

According as more terms occur in the final equation, the computation of the damping ratios and periods of its specific solutions becomes more laborious. Now that the principles have been explained for the simplified case (6.371), we shall make only two general inferences which are of great importance for business-cycle theory and business-cycle policy.

(i) The damping and period, and even the type, of the possible movements defined by the final equation depend very much on the numerical values of its coefficients.

(ii) The effect of certain measures of business-cycle policy on the stability of the economic system may be studied by means of the effect of such measures on the coefficients in the final equation. Stability will be promoted by measures that increase the damping ratio of the solutions to that equation.[1]

The omission of the cumulants in the elimination process may now be explained in somewhat more detail.

In a preliminary calculation, these terms were retained throughout the elimination process. The resulting occurrence of terms containing cumulants in the final equation influences in two ways the possible movements of the system:

(i) The period and degree of damping of the cyclical movement are to some extent affected by the presence of such terms.

(ii) Besides that, the cumulants introduce an additional root into the characteristic equation, which is real and positive, giving rise to a one-sided movement. This movement is explosive (away from the equilibrium situation) if the algebraic sum of all coefficients of cumulation terms in the final equation is positive; the movement is damped (gradual approach of the equilibrium situation) if that sum is negative.

---

[1] All this may be formulated independently of where the equilibrium lies. It is, however, quite possible that the desirability of a high equilibrium level might conflict with the requirement of a "very stable" or a "strongly damped" movement. In a private publication this problem has been studied somewhat more closely: cf. J. TINBERGEN, *Fondements mathématiques de la stabilisation des affaires* (Hermann, Paris, 1938).

The upshot of the preliminary calculations was that the $\int Z^c$-terms in the final equations, which resulted from the cumulants taken into consideration in the elementary equations, (i) had a small negative influence (about — 0.05) on the damping ratio and a small positive influence on the period of the cyclical solution (about 0.5 year); (ii) gave rise to a solution corresponding to an explosive movement (root $x_5 = 1.14$).

If such a solution really constitutes a possibility inherent to the economic system of the United States, simple calculations — for instance, numerical solutions as given in sections (6.5), (6.6) and (6.7) — show that, granted certain initial conditions, the one-sided type of movement could lead, after a few years, to values for the variables so far from the average, and, consequently, so far beyond the range in which the elementary equations have been determined, that the latter, and hence the final equation, could no longer be assumed to hold. This exponential solution, if it were kept to, would have to be interpreted as the expression of a cumulative process to which a special explanation of the turning-points, by bottle-necks and other non-linearities in the equations, would have to be added.

This last result seems unsatisfactory in two respects. First, though the conception of a cycle as consisting of two alternating cumulative processes, an upswing and a downswing, linked by two turning-points, is not uncommon in general cycle theories, [1] in few of these theories are the cumulative processes attributed to those phenomena that are represented by the $\int Z^c$-terms in the final equation — the surplus of corporations (equation (1.9)), working through its influence on dividends (equation (5.1)), the stock of capital goods through its influence on depreciation (equation (5.9)), and the amount of long-term debt outstanding, working through interest payments (equation (5.4)). An explanation of the cycle that would be largely dependent on the growth of these three assets may therefore be rejected *a priori* on theoretical grounds.

The second objection is that the cumulants in the elementary equations that have led to this explosive exponential

---

[1] *Cf.* G. HABERLER, *Prosperity and Depression.*

root are not all, and perhaps not even the most important of, the cumulants to which the economic mechanism gives rise in reality. At many places, trends have been used which properly represented cumulations of physical quantities or values. Of the cumulant, for example, of physical investment,

$$\int \bar{\bar{v}} = \int \bar{v} + \int v,$$

the first component moves very gradually, and the influence of $\int \bar{\bar{v}}$ on any other variable will be statistically distinguishable, in the sense of the correlation technique, from that of other gradually operating factors only if the oscillations in the much smaller term $\int v$ render $\int \bar{v}$ different from a smooth curve — which is not markedly the case for most cumulants (see graphs 1.9, 5.4, 5.9). Thus in a number of cases an accurate determination of the coefficients of cumulants was not possible, or not important since it was impossible in so many other cases (equations (1.2), (4.1) and (4.2), and their use in (4.82), (4.63), (5.2), and perhaps also the trends in prices: (3.3), (3.4), (3.5)).

A rough estimate of the possible effects of these " hidden " cumulants in the elementary equations showed (i) that their influence on the cyclical solution could not be very large, and would change the damping factor by a figure for which $\pm$ 0.05 could be set as an extreme limit; (ii) that the sign of the algebraic sum of the coefficients for the cumulants in the final equation, including terms resulting from the " hidden " cumulants, could not be determined without a more precise knowledge of the coefficients of these hidden cumulants than seems attainable at present. On the basis of the information available, not much more could be said than that the positive real root probably lay somewhere between 0.75 and 1.25, which leaves the possibility of either a damped or an explosive one-sided movement. The latter has to be rejected for reasons already given above; the influence of the former on the cyclical movements would be moderate and therefore in accordance with the movements observed in reality. To sum up, on the ground of their small influence under (i) and our ignorance of their effect under (ii), it seemed both advisable and justified to keep all terms containing cumulants out of the elimination process.

(6.4) An Economic Interpretation of the Final Equation in the Absence of a Stock-exchange Boom and of Hoarding

The final equation for Z^c discussed in section (6.3) may be interpreted economically. This interpretation clearly holds only for the non-speculative interval, as outside that interval the coefficient of the n-equation upsets the structure of the Z^c-equation. There are, nevertheless, two reasons for considering the Z^c-equation more closely. First, in the period up to 1927, stock-exchange speculation was in fact not very important; secondly, it seems probable that many pre-war cycles can be explained without giving so much weight to the stock exchange. Much the same factors coming into play in the Z^c-equation may have been important in that period, some of them even more important, since the explanation of undamped waves is impossible with the present coefficients.[1]

The economic explanation may be started by repeating the importance of equation (5.10) in the original system, from which the final equation has been derived. This equation states that total profits are the difference between total receipts and total costs of all enterprises. All items in receipts and costs depend, either directly or through a number of channels, on profits (for convenience, corporation profits Z^c have been taken), either at almost the same moment or some time before. The table on page 151 indicates the expression of each of these items in terms of Z^c, together with the result of adding them up or subtracting as may be necessary.[2]

The relative importance of the various components may now easily be seen. In comparing the expressions with the elementary equations, the direct influence of Z^c (which is found there) may be compared with its indirect influence. The most important terms in the table may now be considered separately. A distinction may be made between positive and negative terms, the former tending — if the totals in the columns with

---

[1] Except, of course, by the occurrence of fresh shocks (*cf.* section (6.3)).
[2] Exogenous terms are omitted.

Z^c and Z^c_{-1} are larger than 1.44 and 0.27[1] respectively — to reinforce the original deviation in Z, the latter to counteract this tendency.

	Z^c	Z^c_{-1}	Z^c_{-2}	Z^c_{-3}	Z^c_{-4}	No.
Receipts:						
U =	1.420	0.504	0.080	— 0.040	0.011	(6.41)
V =	0.467	0.529	0.109	0.046	0.006	(6.42)
Total receipts	1.887	1.033	0.189	0.006	0.017	(6.43)
Costs:						
L_w =	0.529	0.283	0.026	— 0.015	0.003	(6.44)
$L_s+L_c+K_I+K_R$ + N =	0.355	0.313	0.262	0.014		(6.45)
Total costs	0.884	0.596	0.288	— 0.001	0.003	(6.46)
Difference Z =	1.003	0.437	— 0.099	0.007	0.014	(6.47)
Also Z =	1.450	0.260				(5.11)
Therefore 0 =	— 0.447	0.177	— 0.099	0.007	0.014	(6.48)
App. B, V, 265 * 0 =	— 0.445	0.177	— 0.098	0.006	0.012	(6.49)

* Small differences between (6.48) and (6.49) are attributable to repeated omissions of small terms.

Big positive influences are those acting through U and V. They express the simple fact that high profits lead to high consumption and high investment. Profits work directly as well as indirectly: on consumption outlay as, *e.g.*, farm prices and farm consumption are high if general incomes are high; on investment outlay as high share prices facilitate high investments and are themselves — through dividends — causally correlated with high profits.

Big negative influences are, apart from the quite natural influence of higher wage totals and other incomes which are paid in times of higher employment, the following.

---

[1] These coefficients are those by which Z^c (corporation profits) and Z^c_{-1} must be multiplied in order to yield Z (total profits).

(i) The negative term in U (6.41) is partly due to the influence of commodity stocks. After a year of peak consumption, production falls somewhat more than consumption, as the readjustment of stocks to the lower level of consumption permits of a certain destocking.

(ii) The other part of the negative term in U is due to the influence of speculative gains (capital gains and gains on commodity speculation) on consumption, and thereby on production. These gains are always proportional to some rate of increase, which introduces a positive and a (necessarily somewhat more lagging) negative term, $e.g.$, $Z^c_{-1} - Z^c_{-2}$.

(iii) No negative term will be found in V (6.42); there is, of course, a negative influence of share yield (which represents a type of interest rate) due to its negative sign in (2.4) and the fact that share yield depends positively on dividends, which, in turn, depend on profits; but this negative influence is more than compensated by the direct positive influence of profits. The influences of interest rates in the narrower sense of the term, as well as of prices of investment goods, would also work negatively. These factors were, according to our calculations, almost negligible in the period studied; it is probable that they were stronger in pre-war times, and that they contributed essentially to the formation of cycles in those times.[1]

(iv) The greater incomes paid out (cf. (6.44) and (6.45)) at times of higher profits are the consequence not only of higher employment, but also of a higher rate of payment. This may also be a factor tending to reverse the movement of Z^c, especially as there is a lag in the correlation between profits and these rates. This influence is, however, weak, as 0.95 of an increase in wages and salaries is consumed and therefore reflected in U, and since the influence of a lower profit margin on investment activity is, too, not very large (cf. relation (2.4)).

----

[1] Cf. the results given for investment in the United Kingdom in Vol. I.

(6.5) Character of Movements introduced by a Stock-exchange Boom

We have now to consider the second possibility mentioned above, where the rate of increase of our index in stock prices exceeds 20 points per annum. In this case the elimination process may most easily be carried out by the following approximative method. Equation (257), table V,[1] is written in the form

$$n = 3.607Z^c + 1.941Z^c_{-1} - 0.142Z^c_{-2} + 0.012Z^c_{-3}$$
$$+ 2.40\,(\dot{n}_{-\frac{1}{2}} - 20)'' \qquad (6.51)$$

in order clearly to indicate that n is supposed to depend on a preceding rate of increase.[2] It may be combined with equation (6.28) for Z^c (omitting external terms):

$$0.770\,Z^c = 0.179\,Z^c_{-1} + 0.006\,Z^c_{-2} - 0.015\,Z^c_{-3} + 0.007\,Z^c_{-4}$$
$$+ 0.090\,n - 0.049\,n_{-1} + 0.001\,n_{-2} + 0.003\,n_{-3} \qquad (6.52).$$

The character of the movement is now considerably changed; the important fact being that the original form of the Z^c-equation matters much less to the result than the coefficients in the n-equation (6.51). The mathematical solution of equations (6.51/2) shows the movements of the system now to be unstable, *i.e.*, an initial movement in the upward direction will be reinforced in an ever-increasing degree. In order better to understand the character of the changes, we may first study the movements generated by the relation

$$n = 2.40\,(\dot{n}_{-\frac{1}{2}} - 20)'' \qquad (6.51')$$

i.e., relation (6.51) in the assumption of stable profits $Z^c = 0$. The movements may be studied for all values of $\dot{n}$ by assuming, as we did in section (4.8), that the relation between $\dot{n}_{-\frac{1}{2}}$ and n is as follows:

---

[1] External terms omitted.
[2] This, in fact, has been the sense of our equation (4.8). It is only for simplicity that until now $n - n_{-1}$ has been written. Logically, this is less correct, and for that reason it is now dropped.

I. For $\dot{n}_{-\frac{1}{2}} < 20:\quad n = 0$;

II. For $\dot{n}_{-\frac{1}{2}} > 20$, but $< 62: n = 2.40\,(\dot{n}_{-\frac{1}{2}} - 20)$; $\quad$ (6.53).

III. For $\dot{n}_{-\frac{1}{2}} > 62:\quad n = 100$;

In order to give the problem its simplest shape, we may reduce time units to one-third of their original length, *i.e.*, to four months; $\dot{n}_{-\frac{1}{2}}$ in our previous notation may then be replaced by $3\,(n_{-1} - n_{-2})$, and equation (6.51') becomes:

$$n = 7.2\,(n_{-1} - n_{-2} - 6.7)'' \qquad (6.51'')$$

which, as before, is only valid for interval II.

Table (6.53) turns into:

I. For $n_{-1} - n_{-2} < 6.7:\quad n = 0$;

II. For $n_{-1} - n_{-2} > 6.7$, but < 21 :
$$n = 7.2\,(n_{-1} - n_{-2} - 6.7);$$ $\quad$ (6.53').

III. For $n_{-1} - n_{-2} > 21:\quad n = 100$;

The movements possible under the laws contained in this table are of various types. Starting from an initial level of share prices equal to zero[1] (*i.e.*, some average level), the following possibilities exist.

If no disturbance from outside occurs, the level will remain zero; because $n_1 - n_0$ will be zero, we are in interval I, and $n_2 = 0$; again $n_2 - n_1 = 0$, therefore $n_3 = 0$, etc.

(i) If a small disturbance occurs, viz.,

$$n_1 - n_0 < 6.7,$$

then again $n_2 = 0$; therefore $n_2 - n_1 < 0$, $n_3 = 0$, etc. Share prices will immediately become stable again.

---

[1] It is of no great importance whether this level is indicated by $n = 0$ or by n equal to any other constant. It is essential, however, that the level indicated by 100 is higher.

(ii) A somewhat larger disturbance,

$$n_1 - n_0 > 6.7 \text{ but} < 8.85,$$

has similar consequences. Although n_2 will now be positive, this will not suffice to make its increase over n_1 larger than 6.7; and for $n_2 - n_1 < 6.7$, n_3 will again be zero.[1]

Graph 6.51.

MOVEMENTS OF SHARE
PRICES, WITH STABLE PROFITS.

Initial values:

(i) $n_0=0, n_1=6.$
(ii)   ,, $n_1=8.$
(iii)   ,, $n_1=9.$
(iv)   ,, $n_1=10.$

Time in years.

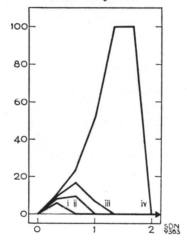

(iii) If $n_1 > 8.85$, n_2 will be at least 15.55, or 6.7 more; therefore n_3 will be positive; but it may be less than n_2; then, and even if it is less than $n_2 + 6.7$, n_4 will again be zero.

---

[1] The limiting value 8.85 for n_1 is found by asking for what value of n_1, n_2-n_1 will be > 6.7; $n_2 - n_1 = 7.2\,(n_1-n_0-6.7)-n_1 = 7.2\,(n_1-0-6.7) - n_1 = 6.2\,n_1 - 48.2.$ In order to make this > 6.7, n_1 has to be larger than $\dfrac{48.2 + 6.7}{6.2} = 8.85.$

(iv) It can be proved mathematically [1] that if n_1 surpasses 9.5, the movement will be " explosive ", *i.e.*, will not return in the way indicated under (i) to (iii). It may be more simple to give an example. Taking $n_1 = 10$, we find:

$$n_2 = 7.2 \,(10 - 0 - 6.7) = 23.8;$$
$$n_3 = 7.2 \,(23.8 - 10 - 6.7) = 51.1;$$
$$n_4 = 7.2 \,(51.1 - 23.8 - 6.7) = 148;$$
$$n_5 = 7.2 \,(148 - 51.1 - 6.7) = 649.$$

This development, however, stops as soon as the "third interval" is reached, in this case n_4; here the formula $n = 100$ is used instead of the formula $n = 7.2 \,(n_{-1} - n_{-2} - 6.7)$. The calculation would continue: $n_4 - n_3 = 100 - 51.1 = 48.9 > 21$, therefore $n_5 = 100$ again; but now $n_5 - n_4 = 0$ and we are brought back at once into interval I, yielding $n_6 = 0$. Graph 6.51 illustrates our results.

It may easily be found that any upward movement, once it passes into the "explosive" type, suddenly falls back upon the zero level in the same or a similar way.

The mechanism described by (6.53′), however simplified, seems to represent correctly the typical movements on the stock exchange; accelerated rises followed by a sudden fall. It may be changed in some respects — *e.g.*, the sudden change from interval I into II and from II into III may be smoothed out somewhat, or the coefficient 2.40 may even be lowered considerably — without changing this fundamental conclusion. The latter must certainly be completed by the remarks that (i) small external shocks may, especially at the beginning, easily interrupt the explosive development, and (ii) the top level of 100 assumed here is of course in a high degree arbitrary.

---

[1] By solving the difference equation $n_t = 7.2 \,(n_{t-1} - n_{t-2} - 6.7)$. Introducing as a new variable $n'_t = n_t + 48$, it is homogeneous: $n'_t = 8.7 \, n'_{t-1} - 8.7 \, n'_{t-2}$, and the roots of the characteristic equation are 6.0 and 1.2. This means that as soon as $\dfrac{n'_2}{n'_1} > 1.2$ or $n_2 + 48 > 1.2 \,(n_1 + 48)$, explosive movements will develop from the start. As $n_2 = 7.2 \,(n_1 - 6.7)$, this leads to the condition $n_1 > 9.5$.

But, though the details are incalculable, the main conclusion of the danger of this mechanism to the stability of the system holds. Only if the coefficient 2.40 were less than about 0.33 would the danger of explosive movements be wholly removed.[1]

A combined solution of the equations (6.51) and (6.52) for n and Z^c is very difficult. Only a numerical solution, therefore, has been given in graph 6.52.

Graph 6.52.

Movements of
CORPORATION PROFITS (Z^c) AND SHARE PRICES (n),
taking Account of the Three Intervals of Share Prices
(Time in years).

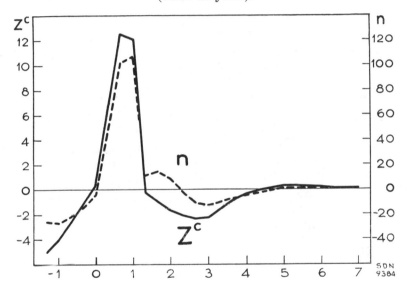

It shows one speculative boom, followed by a damped cycle like that of graph 6.32. Evidently it is largely a matter of chance whether or not another speculative boom will occur when the system recovers from the depression ensuing upon the first boom. Quite small shocks could easily lead $\dot{n}$

---

[1] Coefficients of this magnitude and lower were found for all other countries investigated in an other publication of the author: "The Dynamics of Share Price Formation". *The Review of Economic Statistics*, November 1939.

into the speculative interval again. After the boom, the asymmetry of the n-curve is somewhat less than in the case of graph 6.51, owing to the "support" given to share prices by the high profits still prevailing at the start of the crisis. The period of the Z^c equation is approximately maintained in this combined system.

In the numerical solution reproduced in graph 6.52, a reduction of the time-unit to four months is again needed to bring out adequately the short-term movements connected with a speculative boom. The speculative term in the n-equation is again given the form (6.53'), while the other terms in the right-hand members of both equations are adapted to the four-month unit by replacing Z^c_{-1} (lag one year) by

$$\frac{1}{16} Z^c_{-1} + \frac{4}{16} Z^c_{-2} + \frac{6}{16} Z^c_{-3} + \frac{4}{16} Z^c_{-4} + \frac{1}{16} Z^c_{-5}$$

(distributed lag with an average of three four-month units), etc.

(6.6) Hoarding

We shall now consider the rôle of hoarding in the cyclical mechanism. The evidence derived from one instance of hoarding over a few years clearly does not sustain a general conclusion on the cyclical importance of hoarding in the United States economy. It may be of interest, however, to study what would be the consequences if the features of hoarding observed over these few years constituted a regular system of behaviour, recurring when similar conditions recur. As described in section (4.6), we then assume hoarding to be initiated only in a deep depression where Z^c comes more than 7 milliard dollars below its previous peak value. Our form of analysis is not qualified to discover whether or when this situation will occur: the system of equations only describes, as was shown in (6.3), the *propagation* of certain shocks, and it is therefore these shocks that determine, generally, the *amplitude* of the movements, and, in particular, the occurrence of the above situation.

We can only analyse what happens to the cyclical mechanism when the situation is there, *i.e.*, when

$$Z^c_m - Z^c > 7 \tag{6.61}.$$

For that case, the following equation for H was found:

$$H = -0.3\,Z^c \qquad (6.62).$$

By the substitution of this relation for the H-terms in the final equation, we get a new final equation which describes the movements of the system in which hoarding has developed, as long as (6.61) is satisfied:

$$Z^c = 0.206\,Z^c_{-1} - 0.508\,Z^c_{-2} + 0.030\,Z^c_{-3} + 0.062\,Z^c_{-4} \qquad (6.63).$$

We may, however, take account of the fact that the coefficient for H in equation (4.91) is not very certain (*cf.* the table on page 113). For this purpose we may study the effects of varying the coefficient of Z^c in equation (6.62) which "explains" H.[1] Graph 6.61 shows the effects on the damping ratio and the period of the cyclical solution of the resulting final equation for the values of this coefficient running from 0 (the general final equation) to -0.5.[2] It is seen that the period is shortened over the whole range. Similarly, the damping ratio decreases, initially at an approximately constant rate.

At about $H = -0.4\,Z^c$, the damping ratio becomes 1; *i.e.*, at values of $H < -0.4\,Z^c$ the cycle becomes anti-damped.

It follows from these figures that the more intensively hoarding occurs, the less the cycle is damped, and it would finally

Graph 6.61.

DAMPING RATIO (D) AND PERIOD (T) as a function of the INTENSITY OF HOARDING.

$$H = \eta\,Z^c,$$
where $\eta = 0.0, -0.1 \ldots -0.5.$

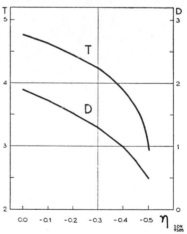

---

[1] Neglecting the relatively small changes in the other coefficients in these alternative cases.

[2] The calculations are not extended further, since it seems doubtful whether the damping ratio and the period found for $H < -0.5\,Z^c$ have any economic significance.

even become anti-damped when hoarding came to exceed a certain intensity. It should be added that, in any case, the development of Z^c would be described by the final equation (6.63) (or its variant according to other values than — 0.3 in (6.62)) for one or two years at the most: then the depression will be over (*cf.* graph 6.61) and the hoarding condition (6.61) will no longer be fulfilled.

Graph 6.62.

Movements of CORPORATION PROFITS (Z^c) and SHARE PRICES (n), under the action of a SPECULATIVE BOOM, and of HOARDING.

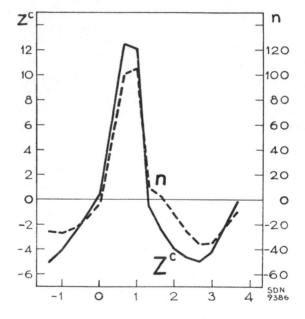

The heavy damping of the system makes it improbable — unless when very large shocks occur — that the movement of Z^c will pass from the normal interval into the hoarding interval. But it is, on the other hand, quite probable that such a heavy fall will occur after a large positive deviation from the average due to a stock-exchange boom.

The possibility of this complication has not been taken into account in section (6.5). We may do this now, and introduce into the numerical solution executed in that section the property that H is replaced by $-0.3\,Z^c$ as soon as, and as long as, $Z_m^c - Z^c > 7$. The result of this changed calculation is shown in graph 6.62.

The period is slightly shortened, to about four years. The downswing is much more rapid than in graph 6.52, and the movement is therefore not unlikely [1] to be swung back into the speculative zone. It does not, however, seem justified to continue the calculation after the depression (the fourth year). Both hoarding and speculation are phenomena in which the psychological factors may change from one cycle to another. Therefore, coefficients determined for past events cannot safely be assumed to hold with about the same values for the future.

In the interpretation of these results, it should be borne in mind that currency-hoarding only has a considerable influence on economic life when, on account of its magnitude in relation to the other items of the balance-sheet of the Federal Reserve Banks, it forces the member banks into debt with the Federal Reserve Banks (cf. section (4.4), and especially graph 4.421/2). The continuance of hoarding during the years 1933 to 1937, when it did not prevent the accumulation of excess reserves, cannot, according to the line of our deduction, be held responsible for any considerable depressive influences.[2]

The above treatment of the phenomena of hoarding and stock-exchange speculation may show to what extent the apparatus used in this study is capable, on the basis of an analysis of the elementary relations, of a gradual approach to the complicated and seemingly irregular reality of actual business cycles. In particular, it shows how an illuminating synthesis may be established between these two extreme positions with

---

[1] This conclusion must evidently be confined to the indication of certain chances. Whether the actual movement swings back to the speculative interval depends not only on the internal propagation of past shocks according to the final equation, but also on the occurrence and the direction of new shocks.

[2] In this connection, the importance for the United States of the huge gold imports becomes clear (cf. section (4.4)). Net imports of gold amounted to nearly $6 milliard between the depreciation of the dollar and the end of 1937; at that date the excess reserves figured only at $1 milliard (or, calculated according to the pre-1936 reserve percentages, $4 milliard).

regard to business cycles: the denial of any regularity in the movements on the one hand, and the assumption of cycles that are strictly regular with regard to period and damping ratio (and perhaps even amplitude) on the other hand. It is especially the rôle attributed to the shocks and the incorporation in the system of a few, but important, non-linear equations which make it possible that one cycle is completely different from another, and that it is yet, in both, one and the same mechanism that links the variables together.

(6.7) Building Activity and General Activity; the Building Cycle; a New "Multiplier" Concept

The peculiar rôle played by the housing market in the general economic system has already been mentioned (section (6.3)). Some attention may now be given to the so called "housing cycle ". The general business-cycle position, of course, influences house building to some extent, but only in a rather small degree, as a glance at graph 2.5 shows. But the chief factor for house building seems to be the relative shortage or abundance of houses some four years back (of course it is a distributed lag which must be assumed here); and as far as rents are another determinant, these themselves are also influenced to some extent by that shortage or abundance. Putting aside for a moment the smaller factors, we are left with a skeleton of relations:

$$v_B = -0.30 h_{-4} \qquad (6.71)$$
$$\Delta h = h - h_{-1} = 0.92 v_B \qquad (6.72).$$

It is easily found — as well by simply trying out with arbitrary numbers as by rigorous mathematical treatment — that this set of relations leads to cycles of a period of about sixteen years, which fits fairly well with observations even over a longer period.[1] Although this cycle existed long before

---

[1] *Cf.* Roos: *loc. cit.*; Newman: *The Building Industry and Business Cycles*, Chicago, 1935. The method of computation of the period is the one indicated in J. Tinbergen: " Ein Schiffbauzyklus ? ", *Weltwirtschaftliches Archiv* (34), 1931, II, page 151.

The explanation given by Dr. Roos, *loc. cit.*, page 78, seems to lead to the same conclusion. Dr. Roos explains residential building

the war and was remarkably unaffected by the ordinary business cycle, the exceptional reduction of the house-building level during the war accentuated the amplitude of this cycle, and must be held responsible for the exceptional high in 1925 and the exceptional low in 1933. Of course other causes existed as well for the latter low point; but it is remarkable that recovery in private building was so slow in 1934, a fact which fits perfectly well into our present representation. It is very doubtful whether such general statements as "building precedes the business cycle" and "building moves against the cycle" are justified. It all depends on the year observed; in general the direct connection is rather weak.

The fact that v_B shows largely autonomous movements has been one reason for treating it as an external variable. Another is that this procedure enables us to find out the influence of any autonomous increase in building activity on Z^c, and on any other economic variable as well. The most interesting case will be the influence on total volume of production, as this is the well-known problem of the "Multiplier".[1] In order to find the influence of a given increase in building volume v_B on total volume of production $u + v$, this latter variable has been expressed first in terms of Z^c, Z^c_{-1}, Z^c_{-2}, etc., and the external factors:[2]

$$u+v = 1.551\,Z^c + 0.417\,Z^c_{-1} - 0.153\,Z^c_{-2} - 0.097\,Z^c_{-3}$$
$$+ 0.022\,Z^c_{-4} + 1.411\,v_B - 0.257\,(v_B)_{-1} \qquad (6.73).$$

---

activity chiefly by the fluctuations in foreclosure rates two and a half years before. These foreclosure rates themselves seem, however, to be mainly dependent on the relative shortage or abundance of houses a short time before, which influences the profitability of owning houses.

[1] The multiplier concept may be applied as well to employment, income or production, but in any case it should, of course, be a comparison between two phenomena of the same sort. Since v_B has the "dimension" of a volume of production, we have here to apply it to volumes of production.

[2] The other exogenous terms are of no importance in this connection, and are therefore omitted. This is also the case for the terms with h_{-2} and h_{-3}, which relate to influence via rents. Since, in this context, v_B represents additional investment activity in general, the repercussions that are particular to investment in dwelling-houses are to be disregarded.

In this expression, Z^c may be replaced by the expression found in the final equation (6.30)[1] and so expressed in terms of Z^c_{-1}, Z^c_{-2}, etc. and $v_B{}^2$. This may be repeated. Owing to the fact that the coefficients of Z^c_{-1}, Z^c_{-2}, etc., in the final equation are smaller than that of Z^c, this procedure leads to ever-decreasing coefficients which after some time become negligible. Thus the procedure finds a natural end, leaving the following formula:

$$u + v = 4.44 v_B + 1.59 (v_B)_{-1} - 0.23 (v_B)_{-2} - 0.57 (v_B)_{-3}$$
$$- 0.02 (v_B)_{-4} + 0.15 (v_B)_{-5} + 0.04 (v_B)_{-6} - 0.03 (v_B)_{-7} + \ldots$$

From this we find that the consequences for total employ-ment of an addition of one unit to building activity in year 1 are, in consecutive years, of the following size:

Year	1	2	3	4	5	6	7	
	4.44	1.59	− 0.23	− 0.57	− 0.02	0.15	0.04	(6.74).
Year	8	9	10	11	12	13		
	− 0.03	− 0.02	0.00	0.01	0.00	0.00		

The total of this series, 5.36, is comparable with the old concept of the multiplier.[2] Yet it differs from it in many respects.

(i) The figure represents the ratio between the total effect on production and an initial increase in investment (building activity); this effect consists of u and v, and hence partly of new investment. In the theory of Mr. KEYNES,[3] on the other hand, the multiplier is defined with *total* (and not *initial*) net investment as the denominator.

(ii) The method here employed enables us to take account of a great number of repercussions, *via* many more variables

---

[1] After transformation of the term with h_{-4} to v_B and Z^c (equa-tion (2.5); the other terms in this equation may be neglected). The terms with h_{-2} and h_{-3} are disregarded (*cf.* page 163, note 2). The omittance of the q_B-term in (2.5) may be interpreted that it is cancelled out by the q_B-term in (1.16) (*cf.* section (3.6)); it follows, then, that the results found refer not to the execution of a certain *volume* of "public works", but to the spending of a certain *sum*.

[2] A calculation along the lines indicated by Mr. KEYNES would give about 6 (Method of calculation, *cf.* POLAK, *loc. cit.*, page 10).

[3] *The General Theory of Employment, Interest and Money*, London, 1936.

than can be allowed for by a procedure such as that first developed by Mr. R. F. Kahn.[1]

(iii) Previous calculations found the multiplier as the sum of the terms of a geometric series with a positive ratio; no negative terms occurred in this sum. The series (6.74), on the other hand, shows an alternation of positive and negative terms. This is due to the fact that it may be considered as the sum of:

(a) $1.411 v_B - 0.257 (v_B)_{-1}$ in (6.73);

(b) Four superposed damped cycles of the period and damping of the final equation (cf. graph 6.32), weighted with coefficients 1.551, 0.417, etc., and with a phase-difference of one year between any two cycles.

It will be clear, then, not only that part (b) contains certain negative figures, but also that its net sum over an infinitely long period of time is only positive when the cycle is damped and the sum of the weights is > 0. If the cycle had been un-damped, the sum of (b) over a certain number of years would be alternatively increasing and decreasing, passing through 0 after any 4.8 years.

(iv) It is clearly shown in this approach that the value found for the multiplier is subject to a certain restriction. We have used the final equation for Z^c based on the "normal" interval in the n-equation. Since the multiplier concept has been generally used for depression periods, this is justifiable; but it means that, if by the autonomous addition to building volume a boom develops, the formula is no longer valid. It would lead too far to go into the problems involved.[2]

Another restriction to be made is that, if the "public works" represented here by v_B were to consist in the building of residences, we should have to take account of the fact that, according to equation (2.5), to-day's building "spoils the market" for the future. This would give additional negative terms in (6.74) after the third year.

---

[1] "The Relation of Home Investment to Unemployment", *Economic Journal*, XLI (1931), page 173.
[2] *Cf.* also J. TINBERGEN: "Über die Sekundärwirkungen zusätzlicher Investitionen", *Weltwirtschaftliches Archiv* (45), 1937, I, page 39.

(6.8) The Formal Characteristics of
Business-cycle Policy

In the preceding sections, certain characteristics, in different circumstances, of the business cycle of the United States were discussed. We may now turn to the analysis of the effects on the character of this cyclic movement of measures of policy and of some much-discussed changes in the economic structure.

For a good understanding of the problems to be treated here, some methodological problems must again be touched upon.

(i) Measures of policy may, in accordance with the analysis in section (6.3), be grouped as:

(*a*) Changes in the coefficients or lags, or both, *i.e.*, changes in the economic structure of society — *e.g.*, price-stabilising measures;

(*b*) Shocks — *e.g.*, the Veterans' bonus payment in the United States in 1936;

(*c*) Changes in the average level of some variable — *e.g.*, minimum wage legislation. The effects of this last type of change are not taken into account in this study, which is concerned specially with the problem of business cycles.

The apparatus for analysing the effects of shocks has been discussed in section (6.7), where a more refined and qualified multiplier-concept has been elaborated. Nothing more need be said about these here, especially since a policy that takes the form of irregular disturbances will in general not be considered desirable, since it would increase uncertainty instead of decreasing it.

In this section we shall therefore restrict the analysis to the effects of changes in coefficients and lags.

(ii) Any measure, therefore, which is not defined in sufficient detail to be translated into a definite change in some definite coefficient cannot be discussed at all. As an example, take a proposal to make consumption less dependent on the business cycle; *e.g.*, by higher taxes during the boom, lower taxes during depression, and more stabilised ordinary expenditure by the State. Since we have seen (table, section (6.4)) that consumption outlay depends on Z^c, Z^c_{-1}, Z^c_{-2}, Z^c_{-3} and Z^c_{-4}, five coefficients might be affected by this proposal. It makes some difference which of these coefficients is changed most; measures of a given intensity but with different lags may have quite different results.[1]

(iii) In the study of the effects of a change in one coefficient, it must not be forgotten that we have not analysed why the coefficients are as large as we have found them to be; we have simply determined their magnitude by the multiple correlation technique. Hence it is not sure beforehand that a change in one coefficient will leave all other coefficients as they are: some coefficients may be linked to one another by relations into which we did not enquire: *e.g.*, a stabilisation of dividends may influence the way in which shareholders appreciate a certain value of d — *i.e.*, the coefficient ν_1 in equation (4.81). The so-called "variation problem" to be attacked now must therefore be handled with care in this respect.

(iv) The result of these variation calculations has various aspects. Any cyclic movement is characterised by period, damping degree, phase and amplitude, and each of these four may be changed. In some discussions too little care seems to have been taken to distinguish between these types of change. Such is the case in the well-known question whether the boom can be continued (once a peak level has been reached) by increased consumption or increased saving. Such a discussion generally bears upon an incidental lengthening of the boom; and such a lengthening may be the consequence of a change in phase as well as a change in period, damping degree or amplitude. The distinction between these has seldom been discussed. Nevertheless, it seems necessary to do so since, *e.g.*, changes in phase are far less important than changes in damping degree and amplitude. It is especially these latter which a systematic stabilisation tries to change. In the following pages only the

---

[1] The more important distinction, between changing the average level of consumption and changing the fluctuations in consumption, is often forgotten in more popular discussions. Here, of course, we are speaking only of the latter.

very first beginnings of the questions involved are indicated. Much more space would be required — and in fact it would involve a new subject — if these questions were to be dealt with completely.

We shall treat the variation problem in two ways. In the first place it will be assumed that for a certain variable *all* fluctuations are excluded, *i.e.*, that all coefficients in the equation "explaining" this variable are taken as zero. Secondly, the effects of relatively small changes in a number of important coefficients and lags will be taken up one by one.

It should be noted that these calculations not only give an estimate of what would be the characteristics of the American business cycle when certain changes in the equations are brought about (the problem of policy), but they also tell us to what extent our idea of the present mechanism may be falsified by the fact that some of our equations afford an inaccurate picture of reality (margins of error). The same effects on our final equation are caused by a certain coefficient's *being* in reality 5 % lower than it *seems* to be, or by its *becoming* 5 % lower than it *is*.

For reasons of exposition we start again with what has been called the "normal interval", *i.e.*, we assume the absence of a stock-exchange boom and of exceptional hoarding. Given the importance of speculation or hoarding for economic life as a whole, this point must not be neglected.

(6.9) The Effect of Some Measures of Business-cycle Policy or Changes in the Economic Structure on the Character of the Cyclic Movement

I. *All Coefficients in one Equation taken as Zero.*

First, let us consider the consequences of a complete stabilisation [1] of investment activity, *e.g.*, by compensatory public investment.

---

[1] This term must be understood not to mean that investment outlay would always have the same constant value, but that it would have some smoothly increasing ("trend") value. For some of the implications involved *cf.* J. Tinbergen: *Fondements mathématiques de la stabilisation des affaires* (Hermann, Paris, 1938).

Such a stabilisation of investment outlay assumes that all coefficients in the expression determining v are zero. As, in formula 216 (Appendix B, table V), v is still included explicitly, the corresponding final equation is easily calculated.

This final equation would run (apart from external terms):

$$0 = -0.76Z^c - 0.26Z^c_{-1} - 0.15Z^c_{-2} - 0.21Z^c_{-3} \text{ or}$$

$$Z^c = -0.34Z^c_{-1} - 0.20Z^c_{-2} - 0.03Z^c_{-3}, \tag{6.91}$$

and the corresponding cycles would be substantially more damped than the original cycles, whereas the period would be shorter (cf. table 6.91).

Table 6.91.

THE EFFECT OF SOME MEASURES OF POLICY ON THE DAMPING RATIO AND PERIOD OF THE CYCLE.

Case	Period in years	Damping ratio
No policy	4.8	1.89
Stable investment outlay . .	3.8	2.41
Stable consumption outlay .	3.2	2.62
Rigid wages	4.7	1.85
Rigid prices	4.3	1.71

Second, let us consider a stabilisation of consumption. This might be the consequence of a change in human attitude, leading to an increased rate of savings in boom periods and a decreased rate of savings in depressions. It might also be the consequence of Government policy, as has been observed already — e.g., by "compensating taxes" and a stabilisation of ordinary State expenditure. Finally, it might also partially be obtained by a less unequal distribution of incomes. The consequences can be found by much the same method as used in the case of investment stabilisation.

The final equation therefore becomes:

$$0 = -1.41Z^c - 0.17Z^c_{-1} - 0.16Z^c_{-2} - 0.03Z^c_{-3} \text{ or}$$

$$Z^c = -0.12Z^c_{-1} - 0.12Z^c_{-2} + 0.02Z^c_{-3}, \tag{6.92}$$

and the corresponding movements are even more damped than those obtained in the previous case.

In the third place, the consequences of changes in the flexibility of wages, and in the fourth place those of changes in the flexibility of prices, will be considered. Both problems have attracted a good deal of attention in economic literature. It has been held that the rigidity of wages and prices is responsible for the increased amplitude of business cycles in recent times. On the other hand, stabilisation of prices has been advocated as a means of stabilising general activity. The treatment of these problems seemed easiest when (i) wage rates l_w and (ii) all prices (p, p', p^f, q, q_B and m_r) were assumed to be absolutely rigid, and the final equations were recalculated on this basis.

They run:

Wage rigidity: $Z^c = 0.14Z^c_{-1} - 0.25Z^c_{-2} - 0.04Z^c_{-3}$ (6.93)

Price rigidity: $Z^c = -0.01Z^c_{-1} - 0.35Z^c_{-2} - 0.05Z^c_{-3}$ (6.94)

as against the normal case:

$$Z^c = 0.40Z^c_{-1} - 0.22Z^c_{-2} + 0.01Z^c_{-3} + 0.03Z^c_{-4} \qquad (6.36).$$

The case of wage rigidity hardly differs from the normal case with respect to damping ratio and period. This means that, at least in the United States, wage rigidity is not so detrimental to a stabilisation of cyclic movements as has sometimes been believed.

According to these calculations, price rigidity or price stabilisation [1] would have had a somewhat anti-damping effect. This result should, however, be accepted with some caution,

---

[1] These two words represent, of course, two very different types of policy. Price rigidity is commonly understood to be caused by monopolistic tendencies, and to be a form of policy pursued by private concerns or groups. Price stabilisation covers a far wider field; it may be used for the same private ends, but also for governmental action in which varying instruments are brought into play in order to attain a stable price level. Of this latter class, only such measures are meant here as act directly on prices themselves; *e.g.*, a policy of holding stocks of raw materials, or using raw materials as cover for note circulation,

since the coefficients for the price-variables are rather uncertain in some of the equations (*e.g.*, (2.1) and (2.4)).

Finally, it must not be overlooked that the foregoing calculations are all only valid for a period with no stock-exchange boom. Although there is no doubt that a stabilised economy would offer fewer opportunities for the development of a stock-exchange boom, it is still possible that even with a perfectly stabilised endogenous development some incidental cause may lead to a speculative boom, as described in section (6.5). Unless, therefore, the price-formation of shares is changed considerably, this part of the mechanism will continue to be a threat to stability in economic life. It follows from the above that those proposals for stabilising the so-called "general price level", in which share prices are also included, may be of still more importance than those that aim only at stabilising the prices of goods and services — provided that the method for obtaining stabilisation is indicated clearly.

II. *Changes in Coefficients.*

The most important coefficients, the effects of changes in which we wish to study particularly, occur in the equations determining

(2.1)   Consumption;
(2.4)   Investment;
(2.6)   Stocks;
(3.5)   Prices of capital goods;
(4.8)   Share prices;
(5.1)   Dividends;
(5.2)   Entrepreneurial withdrawals;
(5.3)   Capital gains;

---

or, finally, regulating prices by decree or by subsidies. Such more indirect measures of price stabilisation as act through the volume of credit, for example, are not included. They could better be designated by terms indicating what instrument is used (*e.g.*, credit rationing, discount-rate policy, etc.); and in order to discover their consequences other calculations than those made here are necessary.

which largely coincide with the equations indicated above as "strategic" equations.

We may write these equations as follows (dots indicating the terms in each equation in which no changes are made):[1]

(V2.1) $U' = (0.95 + \upsilon^L)(L_w + L_s) + (0.77 + \upsilon^E) E + E'_F$
$+ 0.28 G^2 + (0.049 + \upsilon^\Delta) \Delta p^f + (0.03 + \upsilon^p) p$

(V2.4) $v' = (0.33 + \varphi^z) Z^c + (0.33 + \varphi_1^z) Z^c_{-1} - (0.47 + \varphi^m)$
$[m_{Ls} + (m_{Ls})_{-1}] - \ldots$

(V2.6) $w = (0.105 + {}_F) u' + (0.047 + {}_{F_1}) u'_{-1}$

(V3.5) $q = 0.35 l + (1.29 + \chi) v'_{-0.46}$

(V4.8) $n = (20.6) + \nu) d - \ldots$

(V5.1) $D = (0.151 + \delta) Z^c + (0.083 + \delta_1) Z^c_{-1} + \ldots$

(V5.2) $E_E = (0.110 + \varepsilon) Z^c + (0.066 + \varepsilon_1) Z^c_{-1} + \ldots$

(V5.3) $G = (0.200 + \gamma) \dot{n}_{-\frac{1}{2}}$

The Greek letters υ^L, $\upsilon^E \ldots$, etc., represent relatively small variations in the coefficients together with which they occur. The elimination process may now be repeated with the changed coefficients, i.e., carrying on the variations to the coefficients as algebraic symbols[3] throughout the process. In this way, a final equation[4] is obtained, which contains terms with $\upsilon^L Z^c$, $\upsilon^L Z^c_{-1}, \ldots \upsilon^E Z^c, \upsilon^E Z^c_{-1} \ldots$ etc.

From this equation we may study alternatively the dependence of damping ratio and period of the resulting cyclical

---

[1] The V before the numbers indicates that the equations are obtained by *variation* of (2.1), etc.

[2] It is not necessary to treat separately the coefficient for G in this equation, since the effects of a certain change in it are equivalent to those of a change of the same relative magnitude in the coefficient γ (equation (V5.3)).

[3] As the effect of small variations only is to be studied, products or second and higher powers of variations in coefficients have been neglected.

[4] The laborious process of differentiating each intermediate coefficient in the whole elimination process with respect to these sixteen variables results in a mass of figures which it would require too much space to publish.

movement on small variations in each of the coefficients
chosen (by equating to zero all but one of the variations). The
response to a 10% change in each coefficient is given in the
following table:

Table 6.92.

EFFECT ON DAMPING RATIO AND PERIOD OF A 10% INCREASE
IN CERTAIN COEFFICIENTS.

Equa-tion	Determining	Coefficient of:	Magnitude in equation	Change in:	
				Damping ratio	Period (years)
(2.1)	U'	$(L_w + L_s)$	0.95	− 0.147	0.56
		E	0.77	− 0.033	0.18
		G	0.28	− 0.134	− 0.07
		Δp^f	0.049	− 0.039	0.09
		p	0.03*	0.072*	0.27*
(2.4)	v'	Z^c	0.33	− 0.018	0.02
		Z^c_{-1}	0.33	0.011	0.07
		Lag of Z^c	*0.50*	*0.029*	*0.05*
		$m_{Ls} + (m_{Ls})_1$	− 0.47	− 0.0004	0.02
(2.6)	w	u'	0.105	− 0.051	− 0.15
		u'_{-1}	0.047	− 0.069	0.05
		Lag of u'	*0.31*	*− 0.046*	*0.12*
(3.5)	q	$v'_{-0.46}$	1.29	− 0.010	− 0.01
(4.8)	n	d	2.06	− 0.119	0.02
(5.1)	D	Z^c	0.151	− 0.082	− 0.11
		Z^c_{-1}	0.083	− 0.082	0.13
		Lag of Z^c	*0.35*	*− 0.037*	*0.19*
(5.2)	E_E	Z^c	0.110	− 0.019	0.01
		Z^c_{-1}	0.066	0.006	0.03
		Lag of Z^c	*0.38*	*0.017*	*0.02*
(5.3)	G	$\dot{n}_{-\frac{1}{2}}$	0.200	− 0.134	− 0.07

* Since this coefficient represents a minimum, rather than an average value, the
variation has been calculated for a 100% increase.

For the treatment of this variation problem, the variant (5.7′) has been chosen for the L_s-equation (*cf.* pages 120 and 146). This choice was due to the appearance of the somewhat improbable values (due to the term with Z^c_{-2} in (5.7)), in table 6.93 which are given below as they would have been with equation (5.7) instead of (5.7′), as far as the difference is considerable ($> 10\%$ of the values of (6.92)).

Again, values corresponding to any intermediate equation for L_s, between (5.7) and (5.7′), may be approximately calculated by interpolation between the figures of tables 6.92 and 6.93.

It is, however, believed, in particular on the ground of the sign attaching to the influence of v^L on the damping ratio in table 6.93, that the figures of table 6.92 are nearer to reality.

Table 6.93.

Equation	Coefficients of:	Change in:	
		Damping ratio	Period
(2.1)	$L_w + L_s$	0.051	0.49
	p	0.105	0.11
	Δp^f	− 0.020	0.08
(2.6)	u'	− 0.063	− 0.07
	u'_{-1}	− 0.046	0.08
	Lag in u'	− 0.018	0.11

Returning to table 6.92, the general impression is that an increase in one of the coefficients in nearly all cases causes (i) a decrease in the damping ratio, and (ii) an increase in the period.

The table enables us to see what coefficients are of the greatest importance for the characteristics of the cyclical mechanism.

(2.1) Most coefficients in the consumption equation prove to be important; especially those of the series $L_w + L_s$ (with the largest standard deviation) and of G. It should be emphasised that the latter is one of the few coefficients, an increase in which causes a decrease in the period. The figures confirm the theory that lower marginal propensities to consume are an important objective for a stabilisation policy.

(2.2) Changes of the coefficients of Z^c and Z^c_{-1} in the same direction have opposite effects on the damping ratio. Hence the relative importance of a change in the lag. An increase in the lag may be represented by a decrease of the coefficient of Z^c, combined with an increase of the same magnitude in the coefficient of Z^c_{-1}; these two changes affect the damping ratio in the same direction, so as to make a larger time-lag in the investment decisions of entrepreneurs conducive to a reduction in cyclical fluctuations.

The results found with respect to this equation are, again, in harmony with what we found above — viz., that an increase in the fluctuations in investment activity intensifies the cycle.[1] The influence of changes in the m_{Ls}- coefficient is very small.

(2.6) The rôle of stocks of consumption goods proves to be rather important; if stocks were constant, and, hence, the coefficients in equation (2.6) were both zero, the damping ratio would be larger by $10 \times (0.051 + 0.069) = 1.20$.

(3.5) The coefficient of 1.29 in this equation is an inverted measure of the elasticity of supply. By varying this coefficient, we may find out how the cycle is changed by a change in the elasticity of supply of capital goods — e.g., as a consequence of a change in the organisation of the market — or when bottlenecks occur.

It was estimated in section (3.5) that, owing to the first of these two events, the coefficient for v' in the "explanation" of q had been about 3×1.29 in the years 1919, 1921 and 1922, and that it had been considerably larger in the bottle-neck years 1920 and 1923. If we take as a rough figure a 500% increase in the coefficient as representative of this latter situation, we find :

---

[1] The figures show that this statement is only true for investments that are less than about eight months lagged behind Z^c ($0.18 \div 0.29 \times$ 12 months). This would imply that public works, even if executed without a purposive policy of timing, would in fact have a certain damping effect, provided that they lagged sufficiently behind profits in private enterprise (which will often be the case). It will, of course, be clear that this effect may be greatly increased by well-balanced timing of public works.

In the case of	Coefficient increased by	Damping ratio	Period
Less monopolistic organisation .	200%	1.69	4.6
Bottle-necks	500%	1.39	4.3

It will be seen that a decrease in the elasticity of supply of capital goods diminishes the damping of the cycle; in the case of very serious bottle-necks, the cycle may even become anti-damped.

(4.8) Given the large rôle played by the share price in the system of equations, it is no surprise to find that a 10% increase in the coefficient of its most important determinant, d, has an appreciable negative influence on the damping of the system. Since, however, this coefficient is known with a considerable degree of precision (*cf*. table on page 113), there is not much danger of a serious error in the damping ratio on its account.

(5.1) The influence found for a 10% change in the dependence of dividends on profits (current and for the preceding year) is evidently still greater than that of an equally large variation in the d-coefficient in (4.8), where the effects via consumption are not included. The figures found seem especially interesting with regard to measures of policy: if the distribution of dividends could be made to be more stable, say by 25%, the damping ratio of the cycle would increase by $2.5 \times (0.082 + 0.082)$ or 0.410. The period proves to be very sensitive to changes in the lag of dividends behind profits. It may be deduced that the quick reaction of dividends to changes in profits (with an average lag of 0.35 of a year) might well be one of the main factors making for the difference in period between the European and the American cycle. If the lag of dividends behind profits were twice as large — *i.e.*, eight to nine months, or about at the magnitude it probably has in most countries in Europe — the period would be about two years longer.[1]

---

[1] To check whether the use of the figures in table 6.92 is, in this case, legitimate for so large a change in the coefficients, the elimination process has been repeated with an equation for D with a lag of nine months: $D = 0.059\,Z^c + 0.175\,Z^c_{-1}$. This calculation confirmed the prolongation of the period.

(5.2) With regard to this equation, which "explains" E_E, the influence of the lag on the characteristics of the cycle is of particular importance. According to the coefficients in equations (5.1), (5.2), (5.6), $3(E_E - E_F' - E_F'')$ is about equal to $E_E - E_F' - E_F'' + D + L_c$, the constituents of which form the most fluctuating items in E (equation (1.3)). Hence an increase of one month in the lag of entrepreneurial withdrawals behind profits is, in its effects on damping and period, equivalent to an increase in the lag of consumption due to business income $E_E - E_F' - E_F'' + D + L_c$ behind these incomes by about one third of a month. In this way, the calculated effects of the variation in the lag in equation (5.2) may serve to determine whether a possible small lag of consumption of non-workers behind their incomes, of which we found no evidence in section (2.1), might have had an appreciable effect on the damping ratio and the period. It appears that, if the incomes $E_E - E_F' - E_F'' + D + L_c$ entered in the consumption equation with a lag of three months, the damping ratio would be 0.35 higher and the period half a year longer.

(5.3) Finally, the coefficient for $\dot{n}_{-\frac{1}{2}}$ in the equation "explaining" G proves to be of very great importance. If the speculative income arising from a given rise in share prices became twice as large — or if consumption reacted with double intensity to speculative gains [1] — the cycle would become heavily anti-damped. It follows, as it does from the features of the "speculative interval" described above (6.5), that, in the period and country under review, a policy directed to diminish speculation would have a stabilising effect.

The discussion of the effects of the variation of individual coefficients on the damping ratio and the period of the cycle may also serve to determine the uncertainty of the figures found for these magnitudes (1.89 and 4.8 years). Here a possible offsetting of the effects of various coefficients in one equation must be taken into account. Let us consider the consumption-

---

[1] This comes to the same, since the only place in the equation system where G occurs is (2.1). Hence the variations with respect to (5.3) could directly be applied to the G-coefficient in (2.1).

equation (2.1). From a comparison [1] between cases 1*a* and 1*b*, and 2*a* and 2*b*, we find that a decrease in the coefficient of $L_w + L_s$ is accompanied by twice as large an increase in the coefficient of E. Accordingly, when the coefficient of $L_w + L_s$ changes by 10% (the case treated in table 6.92), that for E must change in the opposite direction, and by 25%.[2] Similarly, a comparison of cases 4*b* and 1*b*, 6*a* and 2*a* and 6*b* and 2*b* shows that, at a given coefficient for $L_w + L_s$, an increase in the coefficient for *p* is accompanied by 2.5 times as large a fall in the coefficient for E; hence a 10% decrease in the latter is to be compared with a 100% increase in the former. The effects of these *combined variations* are shown below:

Coefficient of:	Change	Effect on:	
		Damping ratio	Period
$L_w + L_s$	— 10%	0.147	— 0.56
E	+ 25%	— 0.083	0.45
Combined effect		0.064	— 0.11
E	— 10%	0.033	— 0.18
p	+ 100%	0.072	0.27
Combined effect		0.105	0.09

It will be seen that, whereas the effects of compensatory changes in the coefficients of $L_w + L_s$ and E cancel out to a great extent, this is not the case for the damping ratio when the coefficients of E and *p* (or of $L_w + L^s$ and *p*) are varied in this way.

To give an idea of the extent to which uncertainty with regard to the final equation is due to equation (2.1), the damping ratio and the period of the latter have been calculated for what would seem to be two extreme cases. The first (I) is case 2*a*,[3] the other (II) is derived from a comparison of cases 6*b* and 2*b*, but with a fixed coefficient of 0.30 for *p* (which means a price elasticity of demand for consumers' goods of $\frac{1}{2}$)[4]. The

---

[1] *Cf.* page 37. The figures in other cases are disturbed by the inclusion of other series, which lead to multicollinearity.

[2] $2 \times 10 \times 0.95 \div 0.77$. Changes in the other coefficients are for a moment left out of account.

[3] *Cf.* page 37.

[4] *Cf.* equation (1.10).

coefficients for the various variables and the corresponding damping ratio and period run as follows:

	Coefficient for:					Damping ratio	Period (years)
	$L_w + L_s$	E	G	D_p^f	p		
Case chosen . .	0.95	0.77	0.28	0.049	0.03	1.89	4.8
Extreme I . . .	1.90	0.75	0.27	0.046	—	1.82	4.7
Extreme II . . .	0.80	0.41	0.29	0.061	0.30	2.78	5.7

It follows that the errors which may be present in the consumption equation chosen would tend to cause too low a damping ratio and too short a period, rather than the opposite.

To be able to estimate the total probable error in the damping ratio and the period, we should know:

(i) The probable error in all elementary coefficients;

(ii) The degree of (positive or negative) interdependence between the probable errors of the coefficients within each equation;

(iii) The derivative of the damping ratio and the period with respect to all elementary coefficients.

Each of these three requirements is only partly fulfilled in the present investigation. Hence we cannot estimate the exact amount of the probable error in the final results. To arrive, however, at a figure from which an impression of the order of magnitude of these errors may be obtained, the error in the damping ratio and the period is calculated on these assumptions:

(i) The seventeen coefficients mentioned in table 6.92 (page 173) have each a standard error of $\pm 10\%$ of the value of the coefficient;

(ii) These standard errors are independent;

(iii) The other coefficients are free of error.

On these assumptions we find:

for the damping ratio, 1.89 ± 0.32;

for the period, 4.8 ± 0.7.

CHAPTER VII

CRITICAL CONCLUSIONS
ON SOME BUSINESS-CYCLE THEORIES

———

(7.1) INTRODUCTION; RESERVATIONS TO BE MADE

The foregoing analysis of the business-cycle mechanism makes it possible to draw a number of conclusions concerning the validity of some of the theories of the business cycle. These conclusions are subject to numerous limitations which may be shortly summarised here; further details will be found in the sections dealing with the separate relations.

(i) The period and country considered are in many respects special. It has even been said that no business cycles have occurred in the post-war period (CASSEL,[1] HAWTREY).[2] Without going so far, it may be stated that the analysis showed many abnormal features. Up to 1927, the development was fairly stable[3]; the occurrence, however, of condition favouring stock-exchange speculation — in our terms: $n - n_{-1} > 20$ — brought about a fundamental change: both the boom up to 1929 and the following depression showed rather an anti-damped character. Another exceptional feature was the absence of any considerable rise in prices in 1929.

———

[1] *The Theory of Social Economy*, Vol. II, page 538: " The economic development of post-war times has been so strikingly dominated by great monetary disturbances that trade cycles of the earlier kind are no longer applicable."
[2] *Cf.* HABERLER, *Prosperity and Depression*, revised and enlarged edition, 1939, page 14.
[3] " ... a brief examination of the period 1922-1929 shows shat the cyclical fluctuations have been notably moderate." *Recent Economic Changes*, Report of the Committee on Recent Economic Changes (New York, 1929) Vol. I, page 12.

(ii) Some important statistics used are admittedly incomplete.

(iii) Only slow changes in the coefficients have generally been assumed to take place.

(iv) Important explanatory factors for some of the variables included may have been omitted.

(v) The determination of some of the regression coefficients is interfered with by " multicollinearity ". This does not necessarily invalidate the results.

An example of a certain compensation of errors, in connection with the consumption equation, has been elaborated in the previous chapter. There are a number of similar cases in which the uncertainty of coefficients due to multicollinearity is not important for the final results. But if, for example, the series used for consumption had to be replaced by another estimate showing different fluctuations, then a revision of some results might be necessary.

(7.2) DIFFICULTIES IN THE CLASSIFICATION OF THEORIES

Let us begin with some remarks on the classification of theories. A first distinction may be made between exogenous and endogenous theories. By an exogenous theory we mean a theory explaining cyclic movements by cycles in one or several of the "data " — i.e., of the non-economic phenomena (such as crops or psychology).

Endogenous theories, on the other hand, explain the cycles without the help of cycles in data. In the Introduction and in Chapter VI, we saw that the following conditions must be fulfilled if an endogenous cyclic movement is to develop:

(i) At least one of the relations must be dynamic — i.e., must contain variables relating to different time-points (as special cases, differentials and cumulants of variables may be mentioned);

(ii) There must be an initial disturbance of the system;

(iii) The final equation must fulfil certain conditions; otherwise, either a cumulative or a one-sided damped movement only may develop. These conditions have been enumerated in detail for a second-degree characteristic equation; it would take us too far afield to give them for more complicated cases.

In the light of this knowledge, let us now consider how a logical classification of the various possible endogenous theories can be made. It is obvious that dynamic features appear in one or other of the various relations. Independently of this, the initial disturbances may occur in different parts of the system. In principle, therefore, the dynamic features in a system of variables may be present in equation 1, equation 2, equation 3, and so on, or in any pair of such equations, or in any three, etc. The same is true of the disturbances. A classification could therefore be made either according to the localisation of the dynamic features or according to the localisation of the disturbances. This, however, would lead to a very large number of possible theories, even if we considered only the most important relations, leaving out, for example, the definitional equations and those "explaining" the variables of minor importance.

Turning to the theories actually put forward by various authors, it appears that many of them are not complete in the sense of dealing with all coefficients and lags necessary to establish the equations. Some emphasise one dynamic feature (*e.g.*, AFTALION's theory; the acceleration principle); others, certain disturbances (*e.g.*, the agricultural theories). Others again do not explicitly state dynamic features, although they contain them implicitly. The over-investment and under-consumption theories are of this type. Taking the very simple case of over-production in a certain part of the system, we find on closer examination that most explanations imply either that unexpected additions to production (*i.e.*, disturbances) occur, or that production takes some time (*i.e.*, a dynamic feature), or, thirdly, that it is influenced by the rate of increase in some variable (another dynamic feature).

Finally, some of the general theories draw special attention to various sorts of "bottlenecks". The latter are not, as such, dynamic relations, but, in our language, curvilinear relations, in which each coefficient takes different values at different distances from equilibrium. For systems containing such relations, the likelihood that condition (iii) above is fulfilled is greater at least for some values of the variables. Thus, whereas curvilinear relations are not sufficient to bring about cyclic movements if dynamic features are not present in the system, they may cause a non-cyclic (cumulative) movement to become cyclic at a definite distance from equilibrium. This, by the way, is the *raison d'être* of Professor HABERLER's subdivision, in his own theory, of the cycle into four parts: two cumulative processes and two turning-points.

In conclusion, it may be stated that the points stressed as essential by various authors come under one or other of (i), (ii), or (iii) above, and this makes it difficult to give a logical classification of their theories. That is probably the reason why, in the usual classification — also followed by Professor HABERLER in his book — it is not always clear which of the above-mentioned aspects has been chosen as the principle of classification.

With these considerations in mind, let us see what is the place in our system of the relations stressed by certain prominent theories, and their relative importance for the cyclical mechanism. We shall adopt the same classification as Professor HABERLER: the rôle of monetary factors may therefore be considered first.

(7.3)   The Rôle of Monetary Factors

Professor HABERLER says:

"Money and credit occupy such a central position in our economic system that it is almost certain that they play an important rôle in bringing about the business cycle, either as an impelling force or as a conditioning factor." [1]

---

[1] HABERLER, *loc. cit.*, page 14. The reference to the "impelling force" applies more especially to the supply side of the market, and particularly to a deliberate pressure on the interest rate by the banking system.

Our study leads to the following conclusions in this respect:

(*a*) The influence of interest rates, in the restricted sense of discount rates and other short-term rates, on goods is found to have been very small (equation (2.4)).

(*b*) The influence of long-term interest rates on investment activity in durable goods is found to have been moderate, the influence of profits and, in the case of residential building, of the shortage and abundance of houses [1] being much larger (equations (2.4) and (2.5)).

(*c*) Although statistics are incomplete, it is nevertheless probable that movements in commodity stocks were dependent only in a small degree on interest rates (equation (2.6)).

(*d*) Conclusions (*a*) and (*c*) are confirmed by the results found for short-term loans, which also seem to have depended very little on the short-term rate of interest (equation (4.3)).

(*e*) The supply of short-term credits seems to have been fairly elastic (equation (4.56), in combination with equation (4.63)).

(*f*) Evidence of a change in the attitude with regard to rationing of credit, apart from the use of interest rates, is not easily found; for neither investment activity nor the demand for loans shows in 1929 any abnormalities in its dependence on its causes. In the event of deliberate rationing, we should expect actual investment activity and new loans to stand below the levels prescribed by their "demand factors" (*cf.* equations (2.4) and (4.3)).

Thus, the general impression is that the monetary system has been elastic. This means that no large influence has been exerted by monetary hindrances on the effects of other factors,

---

[1] This fact seems, even more than others, to be peculiar to the United States.

so that these other factors have been allowed to work out fairly completely. Thus the evidence does not seem to support any view according to which influences in the field of money are the chief factors in the business cycles considered.[1] Only if interest rates had showed much larger fluctuations than they actually did would their influence have been important. This does not of course imply that a direct attempt to increase the money value of total demand — e.g., by Government spending — would not be important. It did not, however, occur in a large degree in the period studied, and the cycles found must be explained otherwise.

For the period studied, only small traces are found of the tendencies emphasised by Mr. HAWTREY.[2] The proportion of wages to other incomes is only very slightly changed, and the amount of legal money in circulation did not increase in 1928 and 1929; nor were the limits of the note issue reached.

A fairly considerable influence, however, was found to be exercised by hoarding in the following years, as a consequence of the severe depression. This influence, which acted through interest rates on share prices, and from them on consumption (equations (2.1), (5.3)) and investment (equations (2.4), (1.9)), seems to be the most important from the monetary sphere.

(7.4) NON-MONETARY OVER-INVESTMENT THEORIES

We may now turn to some of the best-known *non-monetary theories* and the factors they use in the explanation of the cycle. First the question of *over-investment* may be examined.

Professor HABERLER describes over-investment as a "vertical disequilibrium or maladjustment" in the structure of production — i.e., a situation in which industries in the higher stages of production are over-developed relatively to those in the lower stages. The supporters of the over investment school maintain that such a situation arises during the upswing.

---

[1] *Cf.* HABERLER, *loc. cit.*, Chapters 2 and 3 A.
[2] *Cf.* HABERLER, *loc. cit.*, Chapter 2. It may be remembered that Mr. HAWTREY doubts whether an ordinary business cycle has shown itself in that period.

In accordance with this view, our equations show that the higher the value of Z (general profits), the higher is the ratio capital goods production bears to consumers' goods production. This fact certainly plays a rôle in the cumulative process: the greater Z is, the greater, a little later, becomes investment activity; and the greater the latter, the greater Z is at the same moment, because of the higher general activity. This process is very clearly shown in the equations, which state, on the basis of our calculations, that profits are a highly important factor for investment activity.

One special form in which the over-investment theories have sometimes — and especially in the last few years — been formulated is that of the *acceleration principle* — *i.e.*, that fluctuations in investment would be chiefly governed by the rate of increase in consumers' goods production.

> " The proposition that changes in demand for consumers' goods are transmitted with increasing intensity to the higher stages of production serves, in conjunction with other factors which have already been mentioned, as an explanation of the cumulative force and self-sustaining nature of the upward movement. . . . The matter is of the greatest practical importance for the reason that much light is shed on the fact, which in the last few years has been more and more recognised and emphasised, that it is the production of *durable* goods, of consumers' goods as well as of capital goods, which fluctuates most violently during the business cycle." [1]

This principle we have not found to be of much importance, at least so far as a *direct* influence on the *shorter* fluctuations of investment activity is concerned (equation (2.4)). It must not be overlooked, however, that there is a high intercorrelation between the production of consumers' goods and that of investment goods; but, even in countries where this parallelism was not found to exist, we found only little direct influence of the rate of increase in consumers' goods production. [2]

Over-investment is attributed by several authors to the capitalistic structure of production, and especially to the long *period required for the construction of physical capital*. [3]

---

[1] HABERLER, *loc. cit.*, pages 86-87.
[2] *Cf.* Vol. I, Chapters III and V.
[3] *Cf.* HABERLER, *loc. cit.*, pages 134-136.

In our equations, the *construction period* plays a very definite and also a rather important rôle. For houses, it is one of the causes — but here only a minor one — of the duration of the cycle. For general investment activity, the existence of a lag of about half a year has a clear influence on the damping ratio and the length of the cycles. This can be seen by changing the lag between profits and investment: this changes considerably the coefficients in the "final equation" which determine the cycles (*cf.* section (6.9)). The relation between the construction period and the period of the cycle is very complicated; at any rate, it does not follow from our calculations that cycles would be abolished, were there no lag in equation (2.4).

Before leaving these theories, a word may be said about the order of the revival in consumers' goods production and producers' goods production respectively. A good deal of attention is given to this question by SPIETHOFF,[1] CASSEL, MITCHELL, and others, and they all hold the opinion that capital goods show the cycle before consumers' goods. Statistically, no evidence of any systematic lag or lead is found, either in the United States after the war, or in a number of other countries.

(7.5) CHANGES IN COSTS

The *element of changing costs of production*, which has sometimes been stressed as a cause of crises,[2] seems to have been

---

[1] *Cf.* HABERLER, *loc. cit.*, pages 78-79:

"The phenomenon (alleged to be frequent) of consumers' goods industries feeling the setback of the depression much later than the capital-goods industry is regarded as a verification of the [over-investment] theory."

[2] *Cf.* MITCHELL, quoted in HABERLER, *loc. cit.*, pages 107-108.

"The decline in overhead cost per unit of output [which was brought about by the first increase in production after the trough of the depression] ceases when enterprises have once secured all the business they can handle with their standard equipment, and a slow increase of these costs begins when the expiration of the old contracts makes necessary renewals at the high rates of interest, rent, and salaries which prevail in prosperity. Meanwhile, the operating costs rise at a relatively rapid rate. Equipment which is antiquated and plants which are ill located or otherwise work at some dis-

of less importance. This may be supported by the following evidence.

(i) In so far as higher costs mean higher wages, they are also, if really paid, at almost the same moment, higher incomes, and in the balance of total profits they almost cancel out (relations (5.10), (2.1), (1.11)). This does not of course apply to a country with a large international trade; but the United States is to a high degree a "closed economy". Nor does it apply to those higher costs which are not paid out but which prevent production from taking place. In this connection, however, the conclusions (ii) and (iii) are of importance.

(ii) The demand for investment goods seems to be rather inelastic with regard to price; and in any case the adverse influence of a high price will as a rule, and partly as a consequence, be considerably outweighed by the favourable influence of profits occurring usually at the same time (equation (2.4)).

(iii) Consumption expenditure is also not influenced unfavourably, but rather favourably, by a rise in prices (equation (2.1)).

In short, there has been a tendency for moderate increases in costs to lift all money values to a higher level, rather than to upset the equilibrium. Equilibrium is only upset if prices go up much more than they did in 1929, as they did for instance in 1920 and in some pre-war cycles.

(7.6) OVER-INVESTMENT vs. UNDER-CONSUMPTION THEORIES

Under-consumption theories are, in a sense, the opposite of over-investment theories. Professor HABERLER summarises

---

advantage are again brought into operation. The price of labour rises, not only because the standard rates of wages go up, but also because of the prevalence of higher pay for overtime. Still more serious is the fact that the efficiency of labour declines, because overtime brings weariness, because of the employment of 'undesirables', and because crews cannot be driven at top speed when jobs are more numerous than men to fill them. The prices of raw materials continue to rise faster, on the average, than the selling prices of products. Finally, the numerous small wastes incident to the conduct of business enterprises creep up when managers are hurried by a press of orders demanding prompt delivery."

as follows their divergent conclusions:

" Is the turn from prosperity to depression brought about by a shortage of capital or by an insufficiency of the demand for consumers' goods ? Does the investment boom collapse because the supply of capital becomes too small to complete the new roundabout methods of production, or because consumers' demand is insufficient to sustain the increased productive capacity ?

. . . .

"Both theories contemplate what we have called a *vertical* maladjustment in the structure of production; but these vertical maladjustments are not of the same order. As we shall see at once, the 'top' of the structure of production according to the one theory, the 'bottom' according to the other, is over-developed in relation to the flow of money. In a sense, both theories can be described as over-investment theories. In the one case, new investments are excessive in relation to the supply of saving; in the other case, they are excessive in relation to the demand for the product. That the distinction is important may be seen from the fact that the conclusions drawn as to the appropriate policy to follow in order to avert, mitigate or postpone the breakdown are diametrically opposed. According to the one view, every measure that tends to increase consumers' demand and to reduce saving is helpful. According to the other view, exactly the opposite policy is called for." [1]

When putting the crucial question with regard to the situation that prevailed in the United States in the year 1929, one circumstance of importance stands out. The over-investment theories are based on the hypothesis of full employment of all capital goods, a situation which may have been approximately realised in some pre-war boom years. It was, however, far from existing in 1929.[2] For this reason, it is highly doubtful

---

[1] *Cf.* HABERLER, *loc. cit.*, pages 128-129.
[2] This is reflected in our equations by the absence of any bottleneck — even in capital-goods industries — in 1929 (equations (3.3) and (3.5)). The lack of capacity figures covering a representative part of industry makes it impossible to indicate how far production could still have risen in 1929 before a scarcity of capital goods would have developed.

whether the over-investment theory was applicable to that situation. There is a further reason — viz.: the elasticity of the credit system (cf. section (7.3)), even in 1929 — which makes it probable that a deficiency of savings, if it had happened, could easily have been remedied by the use of additional credits.[1] In other words, if more had been saved in 1929, it would have led to such a slight fall in interest rates that investment activity would hardly have been stimulated; and the loss of this amount of extra saving in the market for consumers' goods would probably not have been compensated.

(7.7) AGRICULTURAL THEORIES

Finally, some attention may be given to *agricultural theories*.

Professor HABERLER distinguishes between the influences exerted by agriculture — *i.e.*, by changing harvests — on general business conditions, and the influences exerted by general business conditions on agriculture.[2]

The influence of irregularities in harvests on general business conditions shows itself in the determination of farm prices (equation (3.4)) and, consequently, on general prices (equation (3.3)), as well as in the influence of farm prices on consumption (equations (2.2), (2.3) and (2.1)). Farm prices themselves are rather strongly affected by supply fluctuations (the flexibility being about 2); but it seems doubtful whether the influence of f on the system as a whole is large. This doubt

---

[1] *Cf.* G. CASSEL, reproduced in HABERLER, *loc. cit.*, page 79.

" The typical modern trade boom does not mean over-production, or an over-estimate of the demands of the consumers or the needs of the community for the services of fixed capital, but an over-estimate of the supply of capital, or of the amount of savings available for taking over the real capital produced. What is really over-estimated is the capacity of the capitalists to provide savings in sufficient quantity."

[2] *Cf.* HABERLER, *loc. cit.*, page 154.

is primarily based upon the following evidence:

(i) Farm prices fluctuate chiefly because of changes in demand; the influence of $L_w + L_s$ in equation (3.4) is much larger than that of f.

(ii) The fluctuations in farm prices are only to an extent of 20% reflected in the fluctuations of prices of finished consumers' goods and services (equations (1.8) and (3.3)).

(iii) The rôle of prices in the business cycle is restricted for reasons given above (section (7.5).

As to the influence exercised on agricultural incomes by fluctuations in industrial activity accompanied by similar fluctuations in money demand in general, Professor HABERLER remarks that "the process is tempered by two factors:

"(1) The demand for consumers' goods as a whole is more stable than the demand for all goods;

"(2) The demand for consumers' goods of agricultural origin is more stable than that for consumers' goods as a whole." [1]

The influence of general business conditions on farm prices is reflected by the term $2.61(L_w + L_s)$ in equation (3.4). This figure points to an income elasticity for expenditure on agricultural goods of about 0.5 (cf. section (3.4)), whereas we found the income elasticity for total consumption to be in the neighbourhood of 0.9; [2] these findings are in accordance with Professor HABERLER's second point. The first point is equally confirmed by our figures.

In commenting on the various "agricultural" theories, Professor HABERLER observes: [3]

"It is a more serious shortcoming of these ' agricultural ' theories that they are not agreed on the important point as to whether

---

[1] HABERLER, loc. cit., pages 165-166.
[2] A weighted average of the marginal propensities to consume with respect to urban labour and non-labour income, and farmers' income, divided by $\bar{U}'$/average income.
[3] HABERLER, loc. cit., page 154.

plentiful harvests are correlated with prosperity and poor harvests with depression, or the other way round; and their divergence in this respect is symptomatic of a fundamental disagreement as to the channels by which the influence of agricultural fluctuations is brought to bear on other departments of economic life."

In this connection, it may be pointed out that, in our final equation for Z^c, various terms occur representing the influence of autonomous changes in harvest (f), the first and largest with a negative, the second with a positive sign ($-1.847f + 0.708f_{-1}$). And it is quite probable that, in any final equation obtained for other variables, these terms will again be different from those in the equation for Z^c. All this reflects the fact that harvest fluctuations work in a complicated way, partly positively, partly negatively.

(7.8) SOME GENERAL STATEMENTS ON THE CHARACTER OF THE CYCLE

This set of observations on some of the more important business-cycle theories may be concluded by a consideration of certain very general statements made by a number of different authors on the character of cyclical movements.

1. The first is that the *depression is an inevitable consequence and a necessary readjustment of certain disproportionalities which have previously developed.*[1] Our statistical investigations show that, with the given economic structure (described by the coefficients in our elementary equations), the depression

---

[1] *Cf.* HABERLER, *loc. cit.*, pages 57-58:

"The depression was originally conceived of by the authors of the monetary over-investment school as a process of adjustment of the structure of production, and was explained in non-monetary forms. During the boom, they argued, the process of production is unduly elongated. This elongation has accordingly to be removed and the structure of production has to be shortened or, alternatively, expenditure on consumers' goods must be reduced (by retrenchment of wages and other incomes which are likely to be spent wholly or mainly on consumers' goods) sufficiently to make the new structure of production possible. This involves a lengthy and painful process of rearrangement."

is certainly a consequence of the preceding boom. It is necessary, however, only in so far as (i) the economic structure is not changed and (ii) no exogenous shocks (amongst which certain measures of policy are to be counted) occur. Several forms of policy seem to be possible which would prevent a depression from developing and yet overcome the disproportionalities.

2. A second proposition is *that there may occur an automatic revival from a depression*.[1] The mechanism found for the United States is such that an automatic revival, indeed, is to be expected for the short waves: the movements were found to be cyclical (*cf*. Chapter VI). As to movements of longer duration, we are not yet able to make a definite statement (*cf*. page 149).

3. A third statement made by a number of theorists is that *"the recovery from the depth of the depression has a wrong twist from the beginning"*. This statement must probably be understood in the sense that it is impossible to prevent a boom if once recovery has started from the bottom. In this sense it is the counterpart of the above statement 1, and seems untenable on the same grounds. This has been shown explicitly in section (6.3); and, since this demonstration is independent of any particular features of the system of equations, it may as well be formulated in this non-mathematical way: that the position in any year, though depending in part on what happened before, may be considerably influenced by fresh "shocks"; and, if such shocks are a systematic set of measures, it is certainly within the possibilities to prevent a boom from developing to dangerous heights.

---

[1] *Cf*. HABERLER, *loc. cit.*, page 391.

APPENDIX A

LIST OF VARIABLES INCLUDED IN SYSTEM

———————

(See inset at end of volume.)

APPENDIX B

TABLE I. — LIST OF EQUATIONS

1.1	$A = 1.50\,C^i + 0.90\,B^i + 0.84\,n - 18.0\,m_{Lb}$
1.2	$d = 1.25\,D - 0.11\,t$
1.3	$E = D + L_e + K_I + K_R, + (E_E - E'_F - E''_F)$
1.4	$h = h_{-1} + 0.92\,v_B$ or $v_B = 1.09\,\Delta h$
1.5	$M = M'' + M'$
1.6	$M = Bs + 0.9\,B^b - 2.93\,m_{Lb}$
1.7	$m_{Ls} = 0.67\,d - 0.041\,n$
1.8	$p = 0.80\,p' + 0.20\,m_R$
1.9	$S = \int (Z^e - D) + 2.29\,t$
1.10	$U = u + 0.60\,p$
1.11	$u = u' + w - w_{-1}$
1.12	$U' = u' + 0.60\,p$
1.13	$V = V' + V_B$
1.14	$v = v' + v_B$
1.15	$V' = v' + 0.15q$
1.16	$V_B = 0.98\,v_B + 0.028q_B$
2.1	$U' = 0.95\,(L_w + L_s) + 0.77\,E + E'_F + 0.28\,G + 0.049\,\Delta p^f + 0.03\,p + 0.37\,t$
2.2	$E'_F = 0.025\,p^f$
2.3	$E''_F = 0.015\,p^f$
2.4	$v' = 0.33\,(Z^e + Z^e_{-1}) - 0.47\,[m_{Ls} + (m_{Ls})_{-1}] - 0.015\,(q + q_{-1}) + 0.060\,[p + p_{-1} - \tfrac{1}{4}\,l - \tfrac{1}{2}\,l_{-1}] + 0.63\,t$
2.5	$v_B = -0.30\,h_{-4} + 0.074\,Z^c + 0.042\,m_R - 0.031\,q_B - 0.038\,m_{Lb} + 0.10\,t$
2.6	$w = 0.105\,u' + 0.047\,u'_{-1} - 0.187\,(m_S)_{+\frac{1}{2}} - 0.307\,t$

3.1 $l_{+0.42} = 0.30\,(u+v) + 0.39\,p + 0.51\,t$

3.2 $m_R = -3.51\,h_{-2} + 2.13\,(L_w + L_s)_{-1} - 0.25\,p'_{-1} + 1.21\,t$

3.3 $\dot{n}_{+0.21} = 0.47\,l + 0.25\,pf - 1.04\,t$

3.4 $pf = -9.54\,f + 2.61\,(L_w + L_s) - 0.58\,t$

3.5 $q = 0.35\,l + 1.29\,v'_{-0.46} - 2.58\,t$

4.1 $B = 4.88\,t$

4.2 $C = 3.18\,t$

4.3 $B_s = 0.16\,(U+V) + 0.26\,m_{Ls} + 2.56\,m_{Lb} + 0.055\,n + 0.08\,C$

4.4 $M = 6.6\,m_S - 25\,M' - 26\,VC + 26\,Au + 26\,P$

4.56 $E_s = 0.63\,M + 1.51\,m_S - 1.10\,m_{Lb} + 0.12\,\dot{m}_{Lb}$

4.57 $B^{\flat} = 0.41\,M - 1.68\,m_S + 4.48\,m_{Lb} - 0.14\,\dot{m}_{Lb}$

4.61 $M' = 0.043\,(L_w + L_s + E'_F) - 0.076\,t + H$

4.612 $H = 0.30\,(Z^c_m - Z^c - 7)''$

4.63 $M'' = 0.29\,(U+V) + 0.03\,C + 0.020\,n - 0.42\,m_S + 0.90\,t$

4.8 $n = 20.6\,d - 6.4\,m_{Lb} + 2.36\,(n - n_{-1} - 20)'' + 2.09\,t - 5$

5.1 $D = 0.151\,Z^c + 0.083\,Z^c_{-1} + 0.075\,S_{-1}$

5.2 $E_E = E'_F + E''_F + 0.110\,Z^c + 0.066\,Z^c_{-1} + 0.16\,t$

5.3 $C = 0.088\,\dot{n} + 0.112\,\dot{n}_{-1}$

5.4 $K_I = 0.02\int (Z^c_{-1} + Z^c_{-2}) + 0.11\,t$

5.5 $K_R = 0.069\,Z^c + 0.029\,m_R$

5.6 $L_c = 0.047\,Z^c + 0.046\,Z^c_{-1} + 0.073\,t$

5.7 $L_s = 0.170\,Z^c + 0.185\,Z^c_{-1} + 0.225\,Z^c_{-2} + 0.40\,t$

5.8 $L_w = 0.28\,(u+v) + 0.30\,l - 0.73\,t$

5.9 $N = 0.036\,(u+v) + 0.037\,q + 0.04\int V + 0.12\,t$

5.10 $Z = U + V - (L_w + L_s + L_c + K_R + K_I + N)$

5.11 $Z = 1.45\,Z^c + 0.26\,Z^c_{-1} - 0.02\,t$

TABLE II. — TREATMENT OF THE MONETARY GROUP

(All trend terms omitted)

No.	References	Variable "explained"	Au + P	M'	m_S	n	U + V	C	m_{Lb}	M	Omissions
1	4.4	M =	26	−25	6.6	0.020	0.29	0.03			VC [*cf.* section (4.62)]
2	4.63, 1.5	M =		1	−0.42	−0.020	−0.29	−0.03			
3	1 — 2	0 =	26	−26	7.02	−0.001	−0.02	0.03			
4	3	−0.42 m_S =	1.56	−1.56				−0.03			
5	2 + 4	M =	1.56	−0.56	1.51	0.019	0.27	0.03			
6	4.56	B_s =	0.98	−0.35		0.012	0.17	0.02	−1.10	0.63	0.12 $\dot m_{Lb}$
7	5	0.63 M =		5.61		0.004	0.06	0.01		d	
8	3	1.51 m_S =	−5.61								
9	6 + 7 + 8	B_s =	−4.63	5.26		0.016	0.23	0.03	−1.10		
10	4.3	B_s =			m_{Ls} 0.26	0.055	0.16	0.08	2.56		
11	9 — 10	0 =	−4.63	5.26	−0.26	−0.039	0.07	−0.05	−3.66	−0.17	
12	1.7, 4.2	0 =		5.26	0.26	0.011		0.05			
13	11 + 12	0 =	−4.63	5.26	$(n-n_1-20)Y$	$L_w + L_s + EF'$ −0.028	0.07		−3.66	−0.17	
14	4.8	−0.028 n =			−0.07		0.07	H	0.18	−0.58	Constant term
15	13 + 14	0 =	−4.63	5.26	−0.07		0.07		−3.48	−0.75	
16	15	m_{Lb} =	−1.33	1.51	−0.02		0.02			−0.22	
17	16	−6.4 m_{Lb} =	8.51	−9.67	0.13		−0.13			1.38	
18	4.8, 16	n =	8.51	−9.67	2.49	0.065	−0.13	1.51		22.0	Constant term
19	4.61	1.51 M' =				−0.416		−9.67			
20	4.61	−9.67 M' =									
21	16 + 19	m_{Lb} =	−1.33		−0.02	0.065	0.02	1.51	−1.10	−0.22	
22	18 + 20	n =	8.51		2.49	−0.416	−0.13	−9.67		22.0	

Explanatory variables

TABLE III. — THE PRICE GROUP AND THE STRATEGIC GROUP

(All trend and cumulants omitted)

No.	References	Equations used	Omissions
		Price group	
1.8′	1.8	$p = 0.80 \, p' + 0.20 \, m_R$	
1.10′	1.10	$U = u + 0.60 \, p$	
1.11′	1.11	$u = u' + w - w_{-1}$	
1.12′	1.12	$U' = u' + 0.60 \, p$	
3.1′	3.1	$l_{+0.42} = 0.30 \, (u + v) + 0.39 \, p$	
3.2′	3.2, 5.7	$m_R = -3.51 \, h_{-2} + 0.362 \, Z^c_{-1} + 0.394 \, Z^c_{-2} + 0.479 \, Z^c_{-3} + 2.13 \, L_{w-1}$ $- 0.25 \, p'_{-1}$	
3.3′	3.3	$p'_{+0.21} = 0.47 \, l + 0.25 \, p^f$	
3.4′	3.4, 5.7	$p^f = -9.54 \, f + 0.444 \, Z^c + 0.483 \, Z^c_{-1} + 0.587 \, Z^c_{-2} + 2.61 \, L_w$	
3.5′	3.5	$q = 0.35 \, l + 1.29 \, v'_{-0.46}$	
5.8′	5.8	$L_w = 0.28 \, (u + v) + 0.30 \, l$	

TABLE III (continued)

No.	References	Equations used	Omissions
	Strategic group		
2.1'	5.1, 2.2, 5.7, 1.3, 5.3, 5.1, 1.9, 5.6, 5.4, 5.5, 5.2	$U' = 0.452\,Z^c + 0.326\,Z^c_{-1} + 0.214\,Z^c_{-2} + 0.056\,(n - n_{-1})^*$ $+\ 0.049\,\Delta p^f + 0.95\,L_w + 0.022\,m_R + 0.025\,p^f + 0.03\,p$	
2.4'	2.4, 1.7, 1.2, 5.1, 1.9	$v' = 0.271\,Z^c + 0.237\,Z_{-1} - 0.033\,Z^c_{-2} + 0.020\,n + 0.019\,n_{-1}$ $-\ 0.030\,q_{-0.50} + 0.120\,(p - \tfrac{1}{2}l)_{-0.50}$	
2.5'	2.5	$\dagger\,v_B = -\,0.30\,h_{-4}$	$0.074\,Z^c,\ 0.042\,m_R,\ -\,0.031\,q_B,$ $-\,0.038\,m_{Lb}\ \dagger$
1.4'	1.4	$v_B = 1.09\,\Delta h$	
2.6'	2.6	$w = 0.105\,u' + 0.047\,u'_{-1}$	$-\,0.187\,(m_S)_{+\frac{1}{2}}$
4.6'	4.612	$H = 0.30\,(Z^c_m - Z^c - 7)''$	
4.91'	4.91, 1.2, 5.1, 1.9, 2.2, 5.7, 1.13, 1.14, 1.15, 1.16	$n = 4.087\,Z^c + 2.210\,Z^c_{-1} - 0.095\,Z^c_{-2} - 0.13\,(U + v) - 0.020\,q$ $-\ 0.42\,L_w - 0.011\,p^f \div 2.49\,(n - n_{-1} - 20)'' - 9.67\,H$ $+\ 8.51\,(Au + P)$	$-\,0.004\,q_B$
5.10'	5.10, 5.11, 1.13, 1.15, 1.16, 2.5, 5.4 — 5.7, 5.9	$1.45\,Z^c + 0.26\,Z^c_{-1} = U + v' - 0.29\,h_{-4} + 0.11\,q + 0.012\,m_R - L_w$ $-\ 0.036\,(u + v) - 0.213\,Z^c - 0.231\,Z^c_{-1} - 0.225\,Z^c_{-2}$	$-\,0.002\,q_B,\quad -\,0.037\,m_{Lb}$

* $0.025\,\dot{n} + 0.031\,n_{-1}$ may, with good approximation, be replaced by $0.056\,\dot{n}_{-\frac{1}{2}}$, which again may be replaced by $0.056\,(n - n_{-1})$.

† The approximating form of equation 2.5' will only be used:

(i) to study the systematic connection between 2.5 and 1.4 (section (6.6)).

(ii) in the substitution of v_B in line 265, where v_B has a very small coefficient.

In equation 5.10', however, v_B has been substituted by equation 2.5, with the omission only of the m_{Lb}-term.

TABLE IV. — TREATMENT OF THE PRICE GROUP

No.	References	Variable "explained"	Various Coeff.	Various Var.	Various Lag	m_R Coeff.	m_R Lag	p^f Coeff.	p^f Lag	$u + v$ Coeff.	$u + v$ Lag
101	1.8', 3.3'	$p =$	0.376	l	-0.21	0.200		0.200	-0.21		
102	101, 3.1'	$p =$	0.147	p	-0.63	0.200		0.200	-0.21	0.113	-0.63
103	102, R	$p =$				0.234	-0.11	0.234	-0.32	0.132	-0.74
104	103, 1.10'	$p =$	-0.079	p	-0.74	0.234	-0.11	0.234	-0.32	0.132	-0.74
105	104, R	$p =$				0.217	-0.06	0.217	-0.27	0.122	-0.69
106	1.10', 105, C, R	$(u+v) =$				-0.130	-0.06	-0.130	-0.27	0.927	$+0.05$
107	3.1', 106, 105, C	$l =$				0.046	-0.48	0.046	-0.69	0.326	-0.48
108	5.8', 106, 107, C	$L_w =$				-0.022	0.23	-0.022		0.358	-0.09
109	3.5', 107, C	$q =$	1.290	v'	-0.46	0.016	-0.48	0.016	-0.69	0.114	-0.48
110	3.4', 108, R	$p^f =$				-0.054	0.23	0.946		0.884	-0.09
111	3.2', 3.3', 107, 108, 110, C, R	$m_R =$				0.956	0.04	-0.104	-1.12	0.596	-0.99
112	110, 111, C, R	$p^f =$				-0.052	0.27	0.952		0.852	-0.07

Boxed combined expressions:

$m_R:\ -3.51\,h_{-2} + 0.362\,Z^c_{-1} + 0.394\,Z^c_{-2} + 0.479\,Z^c_{-3}$

$p^f:\ -9.54\,f + 0.444\,Z^c + 0.483\,Z^c_{-1} + 0.587\,Z^c_{-2}$

We now combine, in 111 and in 112, the first two terms and put:

$$F^1 = -3.36\,h_{-1.96} + 0.021\,Z^c + 0.299\,Z^c_{-1} + 0.330\,Z^c_{-2} + 0.373\,Z^c_{-3} + 0.992\,f - 1.12$$

$$F^2 = 0.181\,h_{-1.73} + 0.415\,Z^c + 0.441\,Z^c_{-1} + 0.536\,Z^c_{-2} - 0.015\,Z^c_{-3} - 9.084\,f - 0.01$$

[1] See note on next page.

TABLE IV (continued)

No.	References[1]	Variable "explained"	Explanatory variables								
			Various			F1		F2		U + v	
			Coeff.	Var.	Lag	Coeff.	Lag	Coeff.	Lag	Coeff.	Lag
113	111, F1	$m_R =$				1.000				0.596	−0.99
114	112, F2	$p^f =$						1.000		0.852	−0.07
115	105	$p =$				0.217	−0.06	0.217	−0.27	0.436	−0.65
116	106	$u+v =$				−0.130	−0.06	−0.130	−0.27	0.739	0.22
117	107 } 113, 114, C	$l =$				0.046	−0.48	0.046	−0.69	0.392	−0.58
118	108	$L_w =$				−0.022	0.23	−0.022		0.326	−0.06
119	109	$q =$	1.290	v'	−0.46	0.016	−0.48	0.016	−0.69	0.138	−0.59

[1] The symbols C and R are used in the column "References" to indicate:

C: a *combination* into one term of two or more terms with the same variable on the right-hand side of the equation. The coefficient of this one term is found by the addition of the coefficients of the various terms combined, and its lag is an average of the lag of the various terms weighted according to the coefficients of each of those terms:

$$\beta_1 X_{-\theta_1} + \beta_2 X_{-\theta_2} + \cdots = (\beta_1 + \beta_2 + \cdots) X_{-\frac{\beta_1\theta_1 + \beta_2\theta_2 + \cdots}{\beta_1 + \beta_2 + \cdots}}$$

R: a *rearrangement*, consisting in the combination as described above, on the left-hand side, of terms with the same variable in both members of the equation, and the subsequent application to all terms of such a factor and such a shift in time as to obtain a coefficient 1 and a lag 0 in the left-hand member.

d	5.9	−2.1	−0.2	1.3	2.0	1.4	1.2	1.0	0.3	−0.7	−0.5	−1.3	−1.4	−0.2	−0.2
l	93	−8	2	7	7	5	5	4	2	2	−1	−8	−5	4	−15
$m_L{}^b$	4.98	0.89	−0.30	−0.46	−0.28	−0.49	−0.51	−0.38	−0.26	−0.13	0.00	−0.04	0.81	0.90	0.27
$\dot{m}_L{}^b$	0.04	0.22	1.05	−0.25	−0.01	0.15	−0.15	−0.17	−0.12	−0.26	0.04	−0.51	−0.61	0.33	0.32
m_{Ls}	4.7	2.7	1.5	−0.2	−1.2	−0.7	0.1	0.2	−0.1	−0.2	0.2	−1.0	−0.3	0.2	−1.0
m_S	4.7	−1.9	−2.1	−0.8	1.1	0.2	−0.7	−0.5	−0.7	−0.8	0.3	0.0	2.1	2.8	0.9
m_R	99	−16	−7	−2	1	4	6	8	9	10	7	6	4	−11	−25
n	96	−47	−1	54	95	54	23	4	−6	−23	−27	−28	−41	−32	−25
$\dot{n}$	1	−12	−56	−57	8	40	28	12	16	14	−3	14	2	−11	7
p	100	−22	−13	−3	0	1	2	4	4	1	0	−3	2	18	2
p_D	104	−18	−14	−8	−4	−6	−7	−8	−5	−3	−1	−3	22	39	14
p_N	99	−22	−12	−2	1	2	4	6	6	2	1	−3	0	15	1
p'	99	−22	−13	−2	1	1	2	4	3	−1	−1	−3	3	25	8
p^f	97	−52	−37	−11	3	5	−2	2	10	1	0	−7	−11	48	49
q	100	−23	−12	−4	0	1	1	2	2	6	5	−5	2	19	6
q_B	98	−22	−10	0	2	2	2	3	2	6	5	−14	−1	23	−2
$f_{+\frac{1}{2}}$	11.6	1.9	2.4	1.3	1.1	0.5	0.0	−0.1	−0.8	−1.1	−1.0	−1.1	−2.3	−1.4	−1.4
h	165	15	15	14	13	11	7	3	−1	−6	−9	−13	−16	−18	−19
u	60	−4	1	6	14	9	6	5	1	−1	−1	−7	−15	−10	−9
u'	60	−3	2	6	14	9	6	5	1	−1	−2	−7	−15	−10	−10
v	18.1	−7.4	−3.1	1.2	4.7	5.0	3.4	3.0	2.2	0.5	1.1	−1.2	−4.0	−2.7	−2.6
v'	15.3	−5.1	−1.5	2.5	4.9	4.0	2.1	1.5	0.2	−0.7	0.0	−2.1	−3.0	−0.8	−1.4
v_B	2.8	−2.4	−1.7	−1.3	−0.2	1.0	1.3	1.5	2.0	1.2	1.1	0.9	−1.0	−1.9	−1.2
w	6.7	−1.9	−0.6	0.2	0.6	0.6	0.7	0.5	0.4	0.4	0.4	−0.3	−0.4	−0.6	−0.7
α	1.71	0.22	0.02	−0.08	−0.32	−0.32	−0.18	−0.12	−0.09	0.08	0.18	0.13	0.33	0.25	−0.04
t	0.0	6.5	5.5	4.5	3.5	2.5	1.5	0.5	−0.5	−1.5	−2.5	−3.5	−4.5	−5.5	−6.5

APPENDIX C *(continued)*

GRAPHS OF STATISTICAL MATERIAL USED

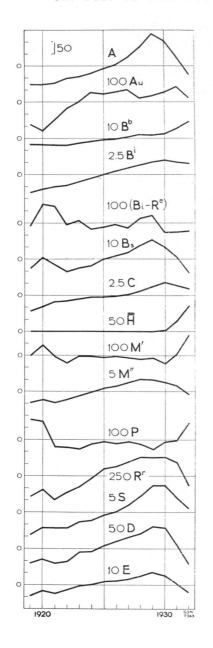

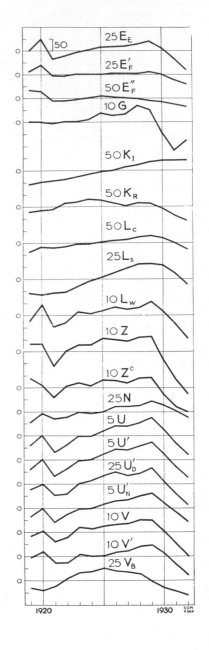

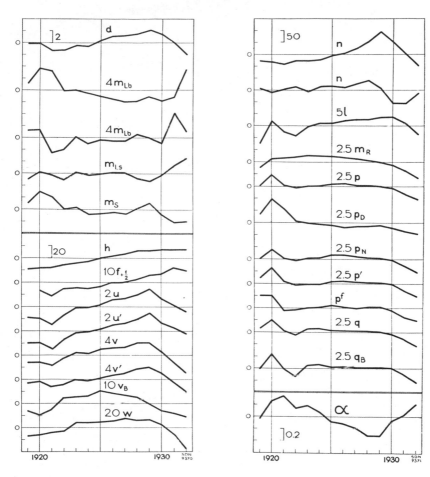

The series of figures given in the preceding table are represented graphically above. They are grouped in about the same way as in Appendix A. The unit is the same for all series in each group and the correct relative magnitude of the fluctuations of each series is obtained by multiplication by a round figure, from 2.5 up to 250.

The unit is chosen in such a way that the multiplier in the first series of each group is equal to 1.

		Unit
I.	Money Items	50×10^9 \$
II.	Interest Rates	2%
III.	Prices	50 points
IV.	Physical Quantities	20×10^9 \$ of 1929
V.	Miscellaneous: α	Pareto's unit.

14

APPENDIX D

SOURCES OF MATERIAL

Note on the System of Description.

The combination and working out of different series have been described as far as possible by formulæ rather than by words, in order to give an unambiguous and short résumé of the procedure.

I. *(1)*, *(2)* ∴ ..., *(1.1)* ..., *(1.11)* ... *(figures in italics within brackets and subdivided according to the decimal system).*[1] Each of these symbols relates to a figure, or a series of figures over time. Its meaning is explained in the section on the variable treated, either by a formula which reduces it to other symbols, or in words. The numbering of the symbols is recommenced when the next variable is discussed.

II. *(1)*$_{1929}$ ... indicates the value of series *(1)* in the year 1929. This way of writing is often used, especially when a series is brought on to another basis. The transformation of series *(1)* to the basis of series *(2)* by multiplication by a given ratio for 1929 is described as:

$$(1) \times \frac{(2)_{1929}}{(1)_{1929}}$$

III. **(1)**, **(2)** ... *(thick upright figures within thick brackets, no decimal subdivision)* refer to the list of sources used, given at the end of this appendix (page 235). For the reader's convenience, authors' names are mentioned in the text. The numbering is continuous for the whole of this appendix.

IV. **(3**$_{1928}$**)** indicates the 1928 volume of the periodical publication **(3)**. (Indication of year and pages is not given for periodicals, except when more or less special tables are used, or when the series is difficult to find.)

V. Ordinary figures are used with the same meaning as elsewhere in this publication (*cf.* Appendix C).

---

[1] In a few cases, these figures are in *thick italics* for the sake of clearness.

VI. In a few cases, upright figures in brackets are used to indicate equations; in these cases, the word " equation " is added.

VII. *(Cf.* Appendix A, *General remarks.)* Plain letters are used to indicate both deviations from average and absolute values, provided this does not lead to confusion. A single dash above a letter or a numerical symbol ($\overline{U}$ or $(\overline{1})$) indicates an average for 1919-1932.

In the description of the symbols, the wording is generally identical with that of the source from which the series is taken.
References to periods are *inclusive* of the last year mentioned.

The series are described in the order of Appendix A.

A. ASSETS HELD BY INDIVIDUALS, VALUE

$$\overline{\overline{A}} = \frac{\overline{\overline{B^i}}}{\overline{\overline{m}}_{Lb}} + 0.0156 \ \overline{\overline{nC}}^i$$

0.0156: *cf.* page 33.

Au. MONETARY GOLD STOCK

Monetary gold stock of the Federal Reserve Banks; annual average of daily figures. **(8)**

B. LONG-TERM DEBT

B $=$ **(1)** $+$ **(2)** $+$ **(3)**.

(1) *Total Private Long-term Debt.* KUVIN **(10)**, page 36.

(2) *Preferred Stocks of All Corporations, Nominal Value, Average during Year.*

$(2) =$ average of two consecutive $\left\{ \begin{array}{l} 1919\text{-}1926: \ (2.1) \\ 1926\text{-}1932: \ (2.6) \end{array} \right.$
figures of

$$(2.1) = (2.2) \times \frac{(2.6)_{1926}}{(2.2)_{1926}}$$

$$(2.2) \begin{cases} 1919\text{-}1925: \ (2.21) \times \dfrac{(2.22)}{(2.23)} \\[2mm] 1926 \qquad : \ (2.5) \end{cases}$$

$$(2.21) \begin{cases} 1919\text{-}1922: \ (2.3) \\ 1923\text{-}1925: \ (2.4) \end{cases}$$

$$(2.4) \ = \ (2.3) \ + \ \frac{(2.41)}{(2.42)}$$

$$(2.5) \ = \ (2.2)_{1925} + \frac{(2.2)_{1925} - (2.2)_{1919}}{6}$$

(2.22) Gross dividends preferred stock, all industries. KING **(9)**, page 182.

(2.23) Ditto, industries covered by *(2.3)*.

(2.3) Par value preferred stock, 7 industries 1919-1922, 6 industries afterwards. *Ibid.*, page 200.

(2.41) Gross dividends preferred stock, electric light and power industry. *Ibid.*, page 182.

(2.42) Ratio gross dividend over capital, preferred stock, same industry, in 1922. *Ibid.*, p. 203.

(2.6) Preferred stock of all corporations, corrected for corporations not submitting balance-sheets (*cf.* C). STATISTICS OF INCOME **(24)**.

(3) *Public Long-term Debt.*

$$(3) \ = \ (3.1) \ - \ B_s^g \ + \ (3.2)$$

(3.1) Public debt of the United States, June 30th **(23)**.

(3.2) Total outstanding issues of tax-exempt securities of States, countries, cities, etc. **(23**$_{1936}$**)**, page 204.

B^b. LONG-TERM DEBT, HELD BY BANKS (NOMINAL VALUE)

$$B^b \ = \ 100 \ \frac{(1) + (2)}{(4.1)} \ + \ 100 \ \frac{(3)}{(4.2)}$$

$$(2) \ = \ (2.1) \ \frac{(2.2)}{(2.3)}$$

$$(3) \ = \ (2.1) - (2)$$

(1) U.S. Government securities held by F.R. Banks; average of daily figures **(8)**.

(2.1) Total investments, all banks, average of figures of three or four call dates.[1] **(8)**

(2.2) U.S. Government obligations, member banks on Dec. 31st *(ibid.)*.

(2.3) Total investments, member banks *(ibid.)*.

(4.1) Average price of U.S. Government bonds, U.S. TREASURY DEPT. **(23)**

(4.2) Corporate bond price index (40 bonds). **(22)** page B 101.

B^e. LONG-TERM DEBT OF PRIVATE ENTERPRISE AND STATE AND LOCAL GOVERNMENTS

$$\Delta B^e = (1) - (1)_{-1} + (2)_{+\frac{1}{2}} - (2)_{-\frac{1}{2}} + (3.2) - (3.2)_{-1}$$

(1) etc.: See B.

$B^g + B^g_s$. TOTAL DEBT OF FEDERAL GOVERNMENT

$\Delta B^g + \Delta B^g_s$: Increase in total interest-bearing debt of the United States Government, Dec. 31st to Dec. 31st **(27)**.

B^i. BONDS HELD BY INDIVIDUALS

$$B^i = B - B^b$$

$Bi - R^e$. INDEBTEDNESS OF THE FEDERAL RESERVE MEMBER BANKS WITH THE FEDERAL RESERVE BANKS

Monthly and annual figures.

$$Bi - R = \begin{cases} 1918\text{-}1921: & (1) - (2) \\ 1922\text{-}1930: & (1) \\ 1931\text{-}1937: & (1) - (3) \end{cases}$$

$$(2) = (2.1) - (2.1)_{1922}$$

$$(3) = (3.1) - (3.1)_{1929}$$

---

[1] Interpolation of certain figures for 1919 and 1920: *cf.* M″.

(1) Bi. Bills discounted by the F.R.B.

(2.1) Part of *(1)* secured by Government war obligations; end-of-month figures, and average thereof. **(8)**$_{1924}$, page 43, and previous issues.

(3.1) Excess reserves, all member banks. *(3.1)*$_{1929}$ = 0.043: taken as normal excess reserves for previous years.

(1) and *(3.1)*: average of daily figures. **(8)**

B$_s$. SHORT CLAIMS

B$_s$ = *(1)* + *(2)* + B$_s^g$

(1) Total loans, all banks; average of figures for three or four call dates.[1] **(8)**

(2) Bills discounted + bills bought by the F.R.B.; average of daily figures. **(8)**

B$_s^g$. SHORT-TERM DEBT OF FEDERAL GOVERNMENT

Treasury bills + Certificates of indebtedness, June 30th (includes Treasury (= war) savings securities up to 1929). **(23)**

C. STOCK OF COMMON CAPITAL OF ALL CORPORATIONS, PAR VALUE (Middle of Year)

S. SURPLUS OF ALL CORPORATIONS (End of Year)

I. *Determination of Stock of Common + Preferred Capital (C″) and of S at End of Year.*

I*a*. 1926-1932.

$(C'') = (C''1) + (C''2)$

$(C''1) = (C''1.1) \times \left\{ 1 + (5.1) \right\}$

$(C''2) = (C''2.1) \times \left\{ 1 + (5.2) \right\}$ 　S treated as C″

$$(5.1) = \frac{\Sigma i \ (5.14)_i \ (5.13)_i}{\Sigma i \ (5.13)_i}$$

---

[1] Interpolation of certain figures for 1919 and 1920: *cf.* M″.

$$(5.14)_i = \frac{(5.11)_i}{(5.12)_i}$$

$$(5.2) \quad \begin{cases} 1928 - 1932: & (5.25) \\ 1926, 1927: & (5.27) \end{cases}$$

$$(5.25) = \frac{\Sigma_i \; (5.24)_i \; (5.23)_i}{\Sigma_i \; (5.23)_i}$$

$$(5.27) = (5.26) \; \frac{(5.25)_{1928}}{(5.26)_{1928}}$$

$$(5.26) = \frac{\Sigma_i \; (5.21)_i}{\Sigma_i \; (5.22)_i}$$

SOURCE: **(24)**

$(C''1.1) = C''$ of all corporations submitting balance-sheets showing net income.

$(C''2.1) = C''$ of all corporations submitting balance-sheets showing no net income.

$(5.11)_i = $ Number of corporations with net income, not submitting balance-sheets in income class i.

$(5.12)_i = $ Total number of corporations with net income in income class i.

$(5.13)_i = $ Total income in income class i.

$(5.21)_i$, $(5.22)_i$, $(5.23)_i$, $(5.24)_i$: as $(5.11)_i$, etc., but with *deficit* instead of net income.

I*b*. 1919-1925.

$$C'' + S = (3) \times \frac{(C'' + S)_{1926}}{(3)_{1926}}$$

$$(4.1) = \frac{S}{C'' + S}$$

$$(4.2) = (4.1)_0 - (4.1)_{-1}$$

(4.2) is correlated with Z^c, 1927-1932, and then extrapolated, 1919-1926, on the basis of this relation.

(4.1) extrapolated by using (4.2).

$$S = (4.1) \times (C'' + S)$$
$$C'' = \{1 - (4.1)\} \times (C'' + S)*$$

---

* The resultant percentage trend in C'' is about equal to that in preferred stocks, which fits in with the fact that there is no apparent trend difference between dividends paid on both kinds of stocks (*cf.* KING **(9)**, pages 189-191).

(3) = Total capitalisation (capital stock + surplus) of 3,144 large corporations, which made 43% of all corporations' profits in 1926. EPSTEIN **(6)**, page 613.

II.

6.1 = C'' — preferred stocks at end of year (*cf.* B, page 211).

$$C = \tfrac{1}{2} \left\{ (6.1) + (6.1)_{-1} \right\} *$$

$$\Delta C = C_{+\frac{1}{2}} - C_{-\frac{1}{2}}$$

C^i. SHARES HELD BY INDIVIDUALS

$$C^i = 0.755\ C$$

$$0.755 = \frac{\overset{1932}{\underset{1922}{\Sigma}} D}{\overset{1932}{\underset{1922}{\Sigma}} D'}$$

D': *cf.* page 24.

H. CALCULATED HOARDING (H^1)

Residuals (since 1930) of the correlation calculation :

$$M' = 0.043\ (L_w + L_s + E'_F) - 0.076\ t$$

M. TOTAL MONEY

$$M = M' + M''$$

M'. OUTSIDE CURRENCY

1919-1934: *(1)*

1934-1937: *(2) — (3)*

(1) Outside currency, average of 12 end-of-month figures. ANGELL **(2)**, pages 178-179.

(2) Money in circulation, June call date. **(8)**

(3) Vault cash, all banks. **(3)**$_{1935}$, page 101, etc.

-----

* It has been assumed that $(6.1)_{1918} = (6.1)_{1919}$.

M″. TOTAL DEPOSITS

Average of figures for three or four call dates.

June call date: *(1)*.

Other call dates: *(2)* × *(3)*

$$(2) \begin{cases} 1924\text{-}1932: \ (2.1) \\ 1919\text{-}1923: \ (2.2) \ \times \ (2.3) \end{cases}$$

(1) Total deposits. ANGELL **(2)**, page 175.

(2.1) Total other than inter-bank deposits, all banks in the United States. **(8)**

(2.2) *Ditto*, all member banks. *Ibid.*

(2.3) Average of $\dfrac{(2.1)}{(2.2)}$ at preceding and following June call date.

(3) Average of $\dfrac{(1)}{(2)}$ at preceding and following June call date, weighted according to relative distance of time.

———————

P. FEDERAL RESERVE BANKS' HOLDING OF GOVERNMENT SECURITIES, ETC.

$\Gamma = (1) + (2) + (3) - (4) - (5) - (6) - (7) + (8) + (9)$

(1) Bills bought.

(2) U.S. Government securities.

(3) Other Reserve Bank credit.

(4) Treasury cash holdings.

(5) Treasury deposits with F.R. banks.

(6) Non-member deposits.

(7) Other Federal Reserve accounts.

(8) Treasury currency outstanding.

(9) Correction on $Bi - R^e$ (rediscounts secured by Govt. war obligations, see $Bi - R^e$).

All series: **(8)**, yearly average of daily figures.

———————

R^r. MEMBER BANKS' REQUIRED RESERVES

Yearly average daily figures. Since 1929: $+ 0.043$ (*cf.* B $i - $ R^e). **(8)**

S. SURPLUS OF CORPORATIONS

See under C.

Z. NET INCOME OF ALL ENTERPRISES
AND GOVERNMENT

$$Z = Z^c - (1) + E_E - E_F'' + (2) + (3)$$

(1) Gains and losses on sale of capital assets, corporations (included in Z^c). 1929-1932: KUZNETS **(12)**, page 8, *n.* 7; extrapolated by means of a correlation calculus with Z^c covering 1929-1935.

(2) Non-corporate business savings: Net business savings or losses of agriculture and trade. *Ibid.*, pages 22-3.

(3) Net savings of Government. *Ibid.*, page 8.

Z^c. CORPORATION PROFITS

Statutory net income less statutory deficit.
STATISTICS OF INCOME **(24)**.

N. DEPRECIATION ALLOWANCES

$$N = (1) + (2)$$

$$(2) = (2.11) + (2.12) + (2.2) + (2.3)$$

(1) Depreciation and depletion; Repairs, renewals and maintenance, Development expenses and fire losses. FABRICANT **(7)**, page 3.

(2.11) Residences, rented, non-farm: depreciation $+$ major repairs and alterations.

(2.12) Residences, rented, farm: depreciation.

(2.2)   „   , owner-occupied, farm: depreciation.

(2.3)   „   , unallocated: fire losses.

Source of *(2)*: *ibid.*, page 15.

U. VALUE OF PRODUCTION OF CONSUMPTION GOODS AND SERVICES

May be derived from U', w and p with the help of the equations (1.10), (1.11), (1.12).

U'. CONSUMPTION EXPENDITURE

A.   1919-1929.

U' = *(3)* *All Food, Wearing Apparel and Personal Care* (consisting of *(1)* *Non-Manufactured Food* + *(2)* *Manufactured Food, Wearing Apparel and Personal Care*) + *(4)* *Shelter and Home Maintenance* + *(5)* *Other Goods and Services*; *(6)* *Corrections.*

(1) *Non-manufactured Food.*
    (1.3) = *(1.1)* + *(1.2)*
    (1)   = *(1.3)* × *(1.4)*

(1.1) Gross farm income, live-stock and live-stock products **(1)**.

(1.2) Gross farm income, crops, fruits and nuts, and vegetables, 1919 (**1**$_{1922}$) and 1924-1932 (**1**$_{1931, 1938}$); interpolated for 1920-1923 on *(1.21)* gross farm income, fruits and vegetables (**1**$_{1928}$) multiplied by $\dfrac{(1.2)_{1924}}{(1.21)_{1924}}$

(1.4) $\dfrac{11.74}{8.35}$; 8.35 = *(1.3)*$_{1929}$, 11.74 = the 1929 value of the consumption of meat, dairy products, vegetables, fruits and nuts.* WARBURTON **(28)**, page 178.

(2) *Manufactured Food, Wearing Apparel, and Personal Care.*
    (2.3) = *(2.1)* × *(2.2)*
    (2)   = *(2.3)* × *(2.4)*

(2.1) Index of production of consumption goods (exclusive of automobiles). LEONG **(18)**, page 371.

---

* This would point to a distribution margin of 40%.

(2.2) Special index of retail prices, consisting of

> *(2.21)* Cost-of-living index, National Industrial Conference Board **(25)**, Clothing, weight 12 (as in the Board's index).

> *(2.22)* Same index, Food, weight 13.2 (in the Board's index: 33, but 60% — in 1929 — of total food expenditure, according to WARBURTON, has been taken into account under *(1)*).

$$(2.4) = \frac{22.2}{(2.3)_{1929}} \; ; \quad 22.2 = 33.96 - 11.74. \quad 33.96 = (3)_{1929} \text{ according}$$

to WARBURTON, before applying the corrections for *(6.1)* and *(6.5)* mentioned below; 11.74: *cf. (1.4)*.

(3) *All Food, Wearing Apparel and Personal Care.*

> *(3.1)* = *(1)* + *(2)*

$$(3) = \begin{cases} \text{Odd years } (3.2) \\ \text{Even years } (3.1) + \frac{1}{2} \end{cases} \begin{cases} (3.2)_{+1} - (3.1)_{+1} + (3.2)_{-1} \\ -(3.1)_{-1} \end{cases}$$

(3.2) WARBURTON's estimate for *(3)*, equally uncorrected for *(6.1)* and *(6.5)*.

(4) *Shelter and Home Maintenance.*

> *(4)* = *(4.1)* + *(4.2)* + *(4.3)*

> *(4.1)* = *(4.11)* + *(4.12)*

(4.11) Rentals paid for leased non-farm homes. LOUGH **(20)**, page 243.

(4.12) Rental values of homes on leased farms (Odd years: *ibid.*; other years: straight line interpolation).

(4.2) Home equipment and decoration. Odd years: WARBURTON; even years interpolated * on Output of consumers' durable finished goods, destined for domestic consumption:

> *(4.21)* Household furniture. KUZNETS **(16)**, page 38 *sqq* +

> *(4.22)* House furnishings. *Ibid.* +

> *(4.23)* Household machinery. *Ibid.*

(4.3) Household supplies and operation. Odd years: as *(4.2)*; even years interpolated * on Output of Fuel and Lighting, Gasoline and Lubricating Oils (to household consumers only). *Ibid.*, page 18.

---

* *Cf.* formula used for *(3)*.

(5) *Other Goods and Services.*

Odd years: WARBURTON; even years interpolated* on Total Consumer Expenditure on Transportation, Personal, Recreation, Health, Education and Social. DOANE **(4)**, page 67.

(6) *Corrections.*

(6.1) Increases in stocks of consumers' goods, viz. $(w - w_{-1}) \dfrac{p}{100}$, are subtracted.

(6.2) Changes in trade margins.

$$(6.2) \;=\; \begin{cases} \text{Odd years: } (6.21) \\ \text{Even years: } (6.21) \text{ interpolated}^* \text{ on } (6.24) \end{cases}$$

$$(6.22) \;=\; \frac{(6.221)}{(6.222)}$$

$$(6.23) \;=\; (6.22) \;-\; (6.22)_{1929}$$

$$(6.24) \;=\; (6.23) \;\times\; \frac{(6.21)_{1919}}{(6.23)_{1919}}$$

(6.21) WARBURTON's series for *(6.2)*.

(6.221) Index of wholesale prices, food **(23)**.

(6.222) Index of retail prices, food **(23)**.

(6.3) The value of Government services paid out of the receipts from *indirect taxes* is subtracted.†

$$(6.3) \;=\; (6.31) \;+\; (6.32) \;-\; (6.33)$$

(6.31) Revenue from Customs **(23)**.

(6.32) Miscellaneous internal revenue **(23)**.

(6.33) Revenue from legacy and inheritance duties, included in *(6.32)* **(23)**.

(6.4) E_F'' is subtracted.

(6.5) An amount of 0.2 has been subtracted in every year on account of industrial use and preparation of meals (*cf.* WARBURTON).

(6.6) An amount of 0.2 has been subtracted in every year on account of income from urban cows, chickens and garden plots. LEVEN *c.s.*, **(19)**, page 162.

---

* *Cf.* formula used for *(3)*.
† *Cf.* WARBURTON **(28)**, page 175. (The correction could only be applied for federal taxes.)

(No correction has been made for the value of imported and exported finished consumption goods; these items could not easily be segregated from Customs statistics, nor can their difference have been of great importance.)

B. 1930-1932.

Following a suggestion kindly made to the author by Mr. H. BARGER, of the National Bureau of Economic Research, the following extrapolation has been carried out.

(7) *1930 and 1931.*

$$(7.1) = (7.2) - (7.3)$$
$$(7) = (7.1) \times 0.993$$
$$0.993 = \frac{U'_{1929}}{(7.1)_{1929}}$$

(7.2) Total consumption as estimated by LOUGH **(20)**, page 28 (Commodities + Intangibles).

(7.3) Net rental values (imputed), *ibid.*, page 243; straight line interpolation for 1930.

(8) *1932.*

$$(8) = (8.1) \times 1.011$$
$$1.011 = \frac{U'_{1929}}{(8.1)_{1929}}$$

(8.1) Consumers' outlay. KUZNETS **(17)**, page 85.

U'_D. CONSUMPTION EXPENDITURE ON DURABLE GOODS

Flow of consumers' durable commodities to households and enterprises.

KUZNETS **(11)**, page 6.

U'_N. CONSUMPTION EXPENDITURE ON NON-DURABLE GOODS, AND SERVICES

$$U'_N = U' - U'_D.$$

V. VALUE OF PRODUCTION OF INVESTMENT GOODS

(1) Flow of producers' durable commodities to enterprises +

(2) Volume of total construction.

KUZNETS **(11)**, page 96.

V'. VALUE OF PRODUCTION OF PRODUCERS' DURABLE GOODS + NON-RESIDENTIAL CONSTRUCTION

$V' = V - V_B$.

V_B. VALUE OF RESIDENTIAL BUILDING

1920-1932: Value of all residential construction. Extrapolated for 1919 on $v_B \times q_B$.

WICKENS AND FOSTER **(30)**, page 2.

---

d. DIVIDENDS AS A PERCENTAGE OF CAPITAL

$$d = \frac{(1)}{(2)} \times 100$$

(1) $\begin{cases} 1922\text{-}1932: & (1.1) \\ 1919\text{-}1921: & (1.2) \end{cases}$

$$(1.2) = D \times \frac{(1.1)_{1922\text{-}1924}}{D_{1922\text{-}1924}}$$

(1.1) All cash dividends paid out **(24)**.

(2) C + Preferred stock (*cf.* B).

---

l. WAGE RATE

$$l = \left\{ \begin{array}{l} 1921, \; 1923\text{-}1932: \; (1) \\ 1919, \; 1920, \; 1922: \; (2) \end{array} \right.$$

$$(1) \; = \; (1.1) \; \times \; \frac{100}{(1.1)_{1929}}$$

$$(2) \; = \; (2.1) \; \times \; \frac{(1)_{1924}}{(2.1)_{1924}}$$

(1.1) Index of hourly earnings in 25 manufacturing industries, all wage-earners **(23)**.

(2.1) Hourly earnings in industry as a whole. DOUGLAS **(5)**, page 205.

---

m_{Lb}. BOND YIELD

Yield in percentage, 60 issues combined. **(23)**.

---

m_{Ls}. SHARE YIELD

$$m_{Ls} = \left\{ \begin{array}{l} 1926\text{-}1932: \; (1) \\ 1919\text{-}1925: \; (2) \end{array} \right.$$

(2) = Extrapolation on correlation calculus between *(1)*, $\dfrac{d}{n'}$ and t, 1926-1932.

(1) Share yield of 90 shares. STANDARD STATISTICS Co. **(22)**.

n' Index of the price of 90 shares **(22)**, used in the calculation of *(1)*.

---

m_S. SHORT-TERM INTEREST RATE

Annual average rate on prime commercial paper (4-6 months) in New York. TINBERGEN **(26)**, page 157.

---

m_R. HOUSE RENT

Housing item in Bureau of Labor Statistics cost-of-living index, figures of June (1921: May) **(23)**, brought on to basis 1929 = 100.

D. CASH DIVIDENDS PAID OUT TO INDIVIDUALS

Dividends. KUZNETS **(12)**, page 8.

E. URBAN NON-LABOUR INCOME

$$E = D + L_c + K_I + K_R + (E_E - E_F' - E_F'') + E_A.$$

E_A. NET BALANCE OF INTERNATIONAL PAYMENTS

$E_A = (1) - (2) - (3).$

(1) Property income payments.
(2) Dividends.
(3) Interest.

KUZNETS **(12)**, page 8.

E_E. ENTREPRENEURIAL WITHDRAWALS

$E_E = (1) + (2).$

$$(2) = (2.1) \times \frac{5.1}{(2.1)_{1929}}$$

(1) Withdrawals by entrepreneurs. KUZNETS **(12)**, page 8.

(2.1) Aggregate income payments to individuals, Service + Miscellaneous industries. *Ibid.*, page 6.

5.1: Estimated total entrepreneurial withdrawals, in $\$10^9$, in these two industries. *Ibid.*, page 9.

15

E'_F. FARMERS' CONSUMPTION EXPENDITURE

$E'_F = (1) - E''$

(1) Withdrawals by farm operators. KUZNETS **(13)**, page 22.

E''_F. FARMERS' CONSUMPTION OF HOME-PRODUCED GOODS

E''_F $\begin{cases} 1924\text{-}1932\text{: } (1) - (2) \\ 1919\text{-}1923\text{: extrapolated on the basis of a correlation} \end{cases}$
calculus between E''_F and p^f over 1924-1936.

(1) Gross income from agricultural production **(23)**.

(2) Cash   „   „   „   „   **(23)**.

G. CAPITAL GAINS REALISED

G $\begin{cases} 1919\text{-}1929\text{: WARBURTON } \textbf{(29)}\text{, page 86.} \\ 1930\text{-}1932\text{: Extrapolated on equation (5.3).*} \end{cases}$

K_I. INTEREST PAID OUT TO INDIVIDUALS BY OTHERS THAN INDIVIDUALS

$K_I = (1) - (2)$

(2) $\begin{cases} (2.1)\text{: } 1929\text{-}1932 \\ (2.2)\text{: } 1919\text{-}1928 \end{cases}$

$(2.2) = (2.21) \times \dfrac{(2.1)_{1929}}{(2.21)_{1929}}$

---

* There is reason to assume that capital losses reported for these years seriously underestimated the losses really suffered as the statistics show losses only in cases where there is other income from which to deduct them.

(1) Interest. Kuznets **(12)**, page 8.

(2.1) Interest on individuals' mortgages. Kuznets **(15)**, page 184.

(2.21) Non-business interest. Leven **(19)**, page 153.

K_R. RENTS PAID OUT TO INDIVIDUALS

$$K_R = (1) - (2)$$

$$(2) \begin{cases} (2.1) : 1919\text{-}1927 \\ (2.2) : 1928 \\ (2.3) : 1929 \\ (2.4) : 1930\text{-}1932 \end{cases}$$

$$(2.2) = (2.21) \times \frac{(2.1)_{1927}}{(2.21)_{1927}}$$

$$(2.3) = (2.31) \times \frac{(2.1)_{1927}}{(2.31)_{1927}}$$

$$(2.4) = (2.41) \times \frac{(2.3)_{1929}}{(2.41)_{1929}}$$

(1) Rents. Kuznets **(12)**, page 8.

(2) Imputed rents.

(2.1) Imputed income from owned non-farm homes. Leven **(19)**, page 153.

(2.21) Gross income real estate and holding companies **(24)**$_{1927}$, page 331, *etc.*

(2.31) Rentals. Warburton **(28)**, page 178.

(2.41) Net rents and royalties. Kuznets **(14)**, page 5.

L_c. CORPORATION MANAGERS' SALARIES

Total compensation of corporate officers **(24)**.

L_s. LOWER SALARIES

$L_s = (1) - L_c$

$$(1) \begin{cases} 1919\text{-}1925: (1.1) \\ 1926\text{-}1929: (1.2) \\ 1930\text{-}1932: (1.3) \end{cases}$$

$$(1.3) = (2) \times \frac{(3)_{1929}}{(2)_{1929}} \times L_c + (4)$$

$$(2) = \frac{(2.1)}{(2.2)}$$

$$(3) = \frac{(1) - (4)}{L_c}$$

(1.1) Total salaries drawn by employees from all industries. KING **(9)**, page 138.

(1.2) Compensation of employees, salaries. LEVEN **(19)**, page 155.

(2.1) Total salaries in selected industries: mining, manufacturing, construction and transportation. KUZNETS **(15)**, page 47.

(2.2) Total compensation of corporate officers in same industries. *Ibid.*, page 50.

(4) Compensation of employees, Government service. *Ibid.*, page 192.

L_w. WAGES

$L_w = (1) - (2) - L_s - L_c$

(1) Employees' compensation. KUZNETS **(12)**, page 8.

(2) = Series *(2)* in the description of E_E.

---

n. SHARE PRICE

Annual average prices of 419 common stocks. 1926 = 100. STANDARD STATISTICS Co. (23).

$$\dot{n} = n_{+\frac{1}{2}} - n_{-\frac{1}{2}}$$

$n_{+\frac{1}{2}}, n_{-\frac{1}{2}}$: Average of monthly figures of n from July to June of next year.

---

p. COST OF LIVING

NATIONAL INDUSTRIAL CONFERENCE BOARD, annual average. (25). Brought on to basis 1929 = 100.

---

p_D. PRICE OF DURABLE CONSUMPTION GOODS

Relation ($\times 100$) between *(1)* flow of consumers' durable commodities to households and enterprises, *current prices*, and *(2) idem, 1929 prices*. KUZNETS (11), page 6.

---

p_N. PRICE OF NON-DURABLE CONSUMPTION GOODS, AND SERVICES

$$p_N = \frac{p - 0.1265\, p_D}{0.8735}$$

$$0.1265 = \frac{\overline{U'_D}}{\overline{U'}} \; ; \; 0.8735 = \frac{\overline{U'_N}}{\overline{U'}}$$

It makes only a negligible difference if a smaller weight, more in accordance with the composition of the cost-of-living index used, is taken for U'_D.

---

p'. COST OF LIVING, EXCLUDING RENT

$$p' = \frac{p - 0.20\, m_R}{0.80}$$

0.20 = weight of m_R in p, index used.

---

p^f. INDEX OF FARM PRICES

DEPARTMENT OF AGRICULTURE series. Calendar year. Brought on to basis 1929 = 100. **(1)**.

Further Data relating to Section (3.4):

Commodity *(j)*	U_j Millions of dollars	φ_j	σ_j	η_j
Wheat	815	0.40		0.08*
Maize (" Corn ")	2212	1.00		0.48*
Oats	510	0.33	100	0.57*
Barley	138			0.47*
Rye	20	0.33[1]		2.31*
Buckwheat	11			1.10*
Cotton	487	0	202	0.11*
Fruits & nuts	576			0.33††
Vegetables	614	1.00	168	
Potatoes	401			0.31*
Poultry & eggs	1101	1.00	22	0.80††
Dairy products	1894	1.00	2	
Cattle, sheep and lambs	1156	1.00	36	0.49†
Hogs	1329			0.81†
Hay	1040	1.00	132	0.55*

SOURCES:

U_j: **(1)**
φ_j: *cf.* section (3.4)
σ_j: **(1)**

η_j:
* SCHULTZ **(21)**, page 548, etc. Approximate median of 6 observations, post-war data.
† *Ibid.*, page 583.
†† Estimates.

---

q. PRICES OF CAPITAL GOODS

$$q = \frac{(1)}{(2)} \times 100$$

(1)   Total Flow of Finished Durable Commodities at current prices KUZNETS **(11)**, page 6.

(2)   *Ditto* at 1929 prices.

---

[1] Taken as for oats.

q_B. CONSTRUCTION COSTS

ENGINEERING NEWS-RECORD, annual average **(23)** brought on to basis 1929 = 100.

$f_{+\frac{1}{2}}$. AGRICULTURAL SUPPLY AVAILABLE FOR THE UNITED STATES MARKET (Crop years)

$$f_{+\frac{1}{2}} = \{(1) + (2) - (3)\} \times \frac{12.69}{\{(1) + (2) - (3)\}_{1929}}$$

$$\left.\begin{array}{l} (1)\ \text{Production} \\ (2)\ \text{Stocks} \\ (3)\ \text{Exports} \end{array}\right\}\ \text{of agricultural products}$$

12.69 = value ($\$10^9$), in 1929, of $(1) + (2) - (3)$.

(1) *Index of Farm Production*, 1924-1929 = 100.

(2)

$$(2) = (2.1) \times \frac{1.116}{(2.6)} \times \frac{(1)_{1923/5}}{(2.1)_{1923/5}}$$

$$(2.1) = \frac{(2.11) \times (2.21) + (2.12) \times (2.22)}{(2.21) + (2.22)}$$

$$1.116 = (2.3) \times \frac{(2.21) + (2.22)}{(2.22) \times \dfrac{(2.4)}{(2.4) + (2.5)}}$$

$$(2.3) = (2.31) \times (2.32)$$

$$(2.5) = (2.51) \times (2.52)$$

(2.11) Index stocks of raw materials, foodstuffs (Yearly average, 1923-1925 = 100), July (DEPT. OF COMMERCE) **(25** $_{1928, 1932, 1936}$**)**.

(2.12) *Ditto*, textile materials.

(2.21), *(2.22)* Weights of *(2.11)* and *(2.12)* in the index of commodity stocks **(25** $_{1928}$**)**, August, page 20.

(2.31) American cotton carry-over.

(2.32) Season average prices of cotton, received by farmers.

(2.4) Farm value of gross production of cotton.

(2.51) Silk imports, quantity.

(2.52) Silk price. **(25)**

(2.6) Gross income from farm production.

(2.31), *(2.32)*, *(2.4)*, *(2.51)*, *(2.52)*, *(2.6)* represent the average of the series mentioned over the years 1923-1925.

(3)
$$(3) = (3.1) \times \frac{100}{(3.1)_{1924/9}} \times \frac{(3.2)}{(3.3)}$$

(3.1) Index agricultural exports, 1910/11 to 1913/14 = 100.

(3.2) Value agricultural exports.

(3.3) Gross income from farm production.

(3.2) and *(3.3)* represent the average of the series mentioned over the years 1924-1929.

Source, except where mentioned otherwise: **(1)**

---

h. STOCK OF DWELLING-HOUSES (in 10^9 of 1929)

$$h = \frac{(1)}{0.142}$$

$$0.142 = \frac{(2)}{0.92 \left(\sum_{1920}^{1929} v_{\mathbf{B}} + \tfrac{1}{4}(v_{\mathbf{B}})_{1930} \right)}$$

0.92: *cf.* text, page 26.

(1) Number of houses, in millions. Tinbergen **(26)**, page 156.

(2) Increase in number of houses (in millions), between the censuses of 1920 (January 1st) and 1930 (April 1st). **(23)**

---

u. QUANTITY OF CONSUMPTION GOODS AND SERVICES PRODUCED

$$u = | \frac{U}{p}.$$

---

u'. QUANTITY OF CONSUMPTION GOODS AND SERVICES SOLD TO FINAL CONSUMERS

$$u' = \frac{U'}{p}.$$

---

v. QUANTITY OF INVESTMENT GOODS PRODUCED

Source as for V, but " at 1929 prices ".

---

v'. QUANTITY OF PRODUCERS' DURABLE GOODS + NON-RESIDENTIAL CONSTRUCTION PRODUCED

$$v' = v - v_{\mathrm{B}}.$$

---

v_{B}. VOLUME OF RESIDENTIAL BUILDING

1920-1932 : $v_{\mathrm{B}} = \dfrac{V_{\mathrm{B}}}{q_{\mathrm{B}}}$

1919 : Extrapolated on construction contracts awarded, floor space of buildings, residential. DODGE **(23)**.

---

w. STOCK OF CONSUMERS' GOODS, QUANTITY AT END OF YEAR

$$w = \frac{W}{p}.$$

$$W = (1) \times \frac{(2)_{1929}}{(1)_{1929}}$$

$$(1) = \left\{ (1.1) - (\overline{1.1}) \right\} \times \frac{\left\{ (2)_{1929} - (2)_{1933} \right\} : (2)_{1929}}{\left\{ (1.1)_{1929} - (1.1)_{1933} \right\} : (1)_{1929}} + (\overline{1.1})$$

(1.1) Index department store stocks **(25)**.

 (2) Value of all retail stocks. CENSUS **(23)**.

All figures, also for p, at end of year or last month of year.

α. DISTRIBUTION OF INCOME

According to Pareto's law:

$$N_x = A x^{-\alpha}$$

where N = number of persons with income $> x$,

  x = income (as shown by tax returns);

A and α are constants for any given moment.

Since this formula is supposed to hold good for any value of x (within a certain range):

$$N_{r} = A x_1^{-\alpha}$$
$$N_{x_2} = A x_2^{-\alpha}$$

and, by division:

$$N_{x_1}/N_{x_2} = (x_1/x_2)^{-\alpha}$$

$$-\alpha = \frac{\log N_{x_1} - \log N_{x_2}}{\log x_1 - \log x_2}.$$

$$x_1 = \$25,000; \quad x_2 = \$100,000.$$

SOURCE: **(23)**.

PUBLICATIONS REFERRED TO IN APPENDIX D

(1) *Agriculture, Year-Book of*   United States, Department of Agriculture.

Agricultural Statistics (since 1936)   United States, Department of Agriculture.

(2) ANGELL, J. W.   *The Behaviour of Money*, New York and London, 1936.

(3) COMPTROLLER OF THE CURRENCY, Annual Report of the

(4) DOANE, R. R.   *The Measurement of American Wealth*, New York and London, 1933.

(5) DOUGLAS, P. H.   *Real Wages in the United States, 1890-1926*, Boston and New York, 1930.

(6) EPSTEIN, R. C.   *Industrial Profits in the United States*, N.B.E.R.,[1] 1934.

(7) FABRICANT, S.   *Measures of Capital Consumption, 1919-1933*, Bulletin 60, N.B.E.R., 1936.

(8) FEDERAL RESERVE SYSTEM, Annual Report of the Board of Governors of the

(9) KING, W. I.   *The National Income and its Purchasing Power*, N.B.E.R, No. 15, New York, 1930.

(10) KUVIN, L.   *Private Long-term Debt and Interest in the United States*, National Industrial Conference Board, New York, 1936.

---

[1] N.B.E.R.: National Bureau of Economic Research, New York.

(11) KUZNETS, S. — Gross Capital Formation, 1919-1933, Bulletin 52, N.B.E.R., 1934.

(12) „ — National Income, 1919-1935, Bulletin 66, N.B.E.R., 1937.

(13) „ — Income Originating in Nine Basic Industries, 1919-1934, Bulletin 59, N.B.E.R., 1936.

(14) „ — National Income in the United States, 1929-1932, Bulletin 49, N.B.E.R., 1934.

(15) „ (U.S. Department of Commerce) — National Income in the United States, 1929-1935, Washington, 1936.

(16) KUZNETS, S. — Durable Goods and Capital Formation in the United States, 1919-1933. Part II, N.B.E.R., 1934 (mimeographed).

(17) „ — National Income and Capital Formation, 1919-1935. A Preliminary Report, N.B.E.R., 1937.

(18) LEONG, Y. S. — "Indices of the Physical Volume Production of Producers' Goods, Consumers' Goods, Durable Goods and Transient Goods". Journal of the American Statistical Association, Vol. XXX (June 1935), pages 361-376.

(19) LEVEN, M.; MOULTON, H. G.; WARBURTON, C. — America's Capacity to Consume, Brookings Institution, Washington, 1936.

(20) LOUGH, W. H. — High-level Consumption, New York and London, 1935.

(21) SCHULTZ, H. — The Theory and Measurement of Demand, Chicago, 1938.

(22) *Standard Trade and Securities* by the Standard Statistics Company, Inc., New York, N.Y.

(23) *Statistical Abstract of the United States* U.S. Department of Commerce, Bureau of Foreign and Domestic Commerce.

(24) *Statistics of Income* U.S. Treasury Department, Bureau of Internal Revenue.

(25) *Survey of Current Business* U.S. Department of Commerce, Bureau of Foreign and Domestic Commerce.

(26) TINBERGEN, J. *Statistical Testing of Business-cycle Theories — I. A Method and its Application to Investment Activity*, League of Nations, Geneva, 1939.

(27) TREASURY, Annual Report of the Secretary of the

(28) WARBURTON, C. "How the National Income was spent, 1919-1929", *Journal of the American Statistical Association*, Vol. XXX (March 1935), pages 175-182.

(29) „ "The Trend of Savings, 1900-1929", *Journal of Political Economy*, Vol. XLIII (February 1935), pages 84-101.

(30) WICKENS, D. L., and FOSTER, R. R. *Non-farm Residential Construction, 1920-1936*, Bulletin 65, N.B.E.R., 1937.

NAME INDEX

SUBJECT INDEX

APPENDIX A

LIST OF VARIABLES INCLUDED IN SYSTEM

I. MONEY ITEMS

(i) Capital Items.

More information: Section	Page		
(4.7)	101	A	= Assets held by individuals, value.
(4.4)	82	Au	= Gold stock.
(4.1)	75	B	= Total long-term debt.
(4.5)	88	B^b	= Bonds held by banks, nominal value.
(4.1)	75	B^e	= Bonds issued by private enterprise, and local and State governments.
(4.1)	77	B^g	= Bonds issued by United States Federal Government.
(4.7)	101	B^i	= Bonds held by individuals, nominal value.
(4.4)	82	$(Bi\text{-}Re)$	= Indebtedness of banks to Federal Reserve Banks.
(4.3)	81	B_s	= Short claims.
(4.1)	77	B_s^g	= Short claims issued by United States Federal Government.
(4.2)	79	C	= Capital stock of corporations, nominal value.
(4.7)	101	C^i	= Shares held by individuals, nominal value.
(4.6)	93	H	= Hoarding.
(4.4)	82	M	= Total money.
(4.6)	92	M'	= Outside currency.
(4.6)	100	M''	= Deposits.
(4.4)	82	P	= Federal Reserve Banks' holding of securities, etc.
(4.4)	82	R^r	= Member Banks required reserves.
(1.9)	29	S	= Surplus of corporations.
(4.6)	98	VC	= Vault cash.

(ii) Incomes.

(5.1)	115	D	= Dividends.
(1.3)	25	E	= Income of urban non-workers.
(1.3)	25	E_A	= Net income from abroad.
(5.2)	116	E_E	= Entrepreneurial withdrawals.
(2.2)	44	E_F'	= Farmers' consumption expenditure.
(2.3)	44	E_F''	= Farmers' consumption of home-produced goods.
(5.3)	116	G	= Capital gains realised.
(5.4)	117	K_I	= Interest payments.
(5.5)	119	K_R	= Rent payments.

(iii) *Other flows.*

II. PRICES

III. PHYSICAL QUANTITIES

u = Quantity of consumption goods and services produced.

u^e = Exports, quantity.

u^i = Imports, quantity.

u' = Quantity of consumption goods and services sold to final consumers.

v = Volume of production of investment goods.

v' = Volume of production of producers' durable goods + non-residential construction.

v_B = Volume of residential building.

w = Stocks of finished consumption goods, volume.

IV. Miscellaneous

α = Distribution of income.

t = Time.

General Remarks.

Time unit is 1 year (except where stated otherwise).

A · over a variable indicates the derivative in respect to time: $\dot{n} = \dfrac{dn}{dt}$.

A Δ before a variable indicates the increase over the preceding unit of time: $\Delta B = B - B_{-1}$.

A $\int$ before a variable indicates its cumulation over time: $\int Z_t = Z_{1919} + Z_{1920} + \dots Z^t$.

The absolute magnitude of a variable is indicated by $^=$: $\overline{\overline{Z}}$.

The average magnitude of a variable is indicated by $^-$: $\overline{Z}$.

The deviation from average of a variable is indicated by a plain letter: Z.